How did a state as small and backward as Prussia in 1700 transform itself to compete successfully in war against states with far greater human and financial resources? Richard Gawthrop finds the answer to this perennial question in the creation of a unique political culture, in which service to the Prussian state took precedence over all other relationships and commitments.

This characteristically Prussian ethos first crystallized and gained widespread acceptance during the reign of Frederick William I (1713–1740). The implications of this revolutionary cultural change were far broader, moreover, than simply an immediate increase in state power. The intensive use of every available socializing institution to inculcate this state-service ideology had a profound social and cultural impact that laid the basis for the subsequent influence of "Prussianism" on the development of modern Germany.

This ideological campaign can best be understood in terms of the history of German ascetic Protestantism, especially the Lutheran Pietist movement. Strongly influenced by English Puritanism, the spirituality of Pietism emphasized a "born-again" conversion, followed by a highly disciplined life centered around "doing good for others." How the Prussian state came to embody the values of this activist form of Christianity is the subject of this book.

PIETISM AND THE MAKING OF EIGHTEENTH-CENTURY PRUSSIA

PIETISM AND THE MAKING OF EIGHTEENTH-CENTURY PRUSSIA

RICHARD L. GAWTHROP

Assistant Professor of History, Franklin College

CAMBRIDGE
UNIVERSITY PRESS

Published by the Press Syndicate of the University of Cambridge
The Pitt Building, Trumpington Street, Cambridge CB2 1RP
40 West 20th Street, New York, NY 10011–4211, USA
10 Stamford Road, Oakleigh, Victoria 3166, Australia

First published 1993

Printed in Great Britain at the University Press, Cambridge

A catalogue record for this book is available from the British Library

Library of Congress cataloguing in publication data

Gawthrop, Richard L.
Pietism and the making of eighteenth-century Prussia/Richard L. Gawthrop.
p. cm.
Includes bibliographical references.
ISBN 0 521 43183 2 (hc)
1. Prussia (Germany) – History – 1640–1740. 2. Prussia (Germany) – History – 1740–1789. 3. Pietism – Germany – Prussia – History – 18th century. 4. Prussia (Germany) – Church history. I Title.
DD397.G39 1993
943 – dc20 92–33296 CIP

ISBN 0 521 43183 2 hardback

CE

This book is dedicated to my family

Contents

Contents

Preface

This book is intended to provide both an explanation for the rapid increase of Prussian power in the early eighteenth century and an analysis of the formation of the Prussian political culture. Accounting for Prussia's ability by 1740 to compete militarily against states with far greater human and financial resources has long been considered one of the classic problems in European historiography. Perhaps an equally compelling justification for writing such a book at this time is, however, the need for a more adequate conceptualization of the broader significance of Frederician Prussia. Prussia's historical connections with the pre-eighteenth-century German past, with the particular path of development pursued in the "West," with the "German catastrophe," and with modernity in general – all seem to require further consideration.

The approach taken in this study is to reexamine the origins of the characteristically Prussian institutions and corporate spirit in such a way as to illuminate the nature of precisely these relationships. I shall do so by synthesizing the often told tale of Prussian state building with the story of Lutheran Pietism, a German form of ascetic Protestantism. The resulting stress on the importance of Pietism is not meant, any more than was the case with the Weber thesis, to validate some form of idealist reductionism. The intent is, rather, to bring to the fore a hitherto underestimated cultural factor, without which the Hohenzollerns' administrative initiatives could never have achieved such startling results. Once the causal role played by Pietist norms in the creation of eighteenth-century Prussia has been established, moreover, the possibilities for viewing the Prussian legacy from a larger perspective are greatly enhanced. For Pietism was intimately related to a number of early modern Protestant and Catholic movements, all of which had a significant impact on the transition to modernity in their respective societies.

This book, therefore, is based on the assumption that the context within which the Prussian political culture took shape was the common effort on the part of all the post-Reformation Christian confessions to inculcate discipline, morality, and knowledge of the faith into the population at large. While normally campaigns of this nature were limited in their immediate effects by the resistance of the traditional society, including the monarchical power, such was not the case in early eighteenth-century Prussia. As a result of the far from inevitable series of events described below, the accession of Frederick William I to the Prussian throne in 1713 initiated something in the Hohenzollern lands that would occur elsewhere only at a later time and under different ideological auspices. This momentous development was the emergence of the Prussian state as *itself* the vehicle through which the imperatives generated by an activist, ascetic Christianity could be put into operation.

Although I use the term "cultural revolution" to describe this change, I do not mean to evoke thereby the image of an ideological tide that swept all before it. For despite a yet to be determined degree of social transformation, eighteenth-century Prussian society remained permeated by attitudes, customs, and institutions handed down from preceding centuries. Nor is my purpose one of emphasizing the modernity of Frederician Prussia in order to defend the cause of the old Prussian "virtues." By focusing on the elements of discontinuity introduced during the reign of Frederick William I, I am simply seeking to convey the sense in which eighteenth-century Prussia constituted the principal bridge from the essentially traditional German world of the seventeenth century to the power-oriented nation of modern times.

I would like to acknowledge here the assistance I have received toward the completion of this project. Early financial support came from the Council of European Studies and from the Institute of German Studies at Indiana University. In its characteristically generous fashion, the German Academic Exchange Service (DAAD) sponsored a year of research in Göttingen and Berlin, while a summer grant from the University of South Carolina enabled me to do additional work in the British Library. A research grant from the American Philosophical Society for work at the Herzog August Bibliothek in Wolfenbüttel assisted me in the final stage of manuscript preparation.

I would also like to express my gratitude to a number of colleagues and friends. Through his advice, his substantive criticisms, and his stylistic suggestions, Gerald Strauss has contributed greatly to this project in all its phases. I have likewise received valuable assistance from James Diehl, J. Samuel Preus, and James Riley. In addition, I would like to thank George Elison for giving me excellent advice on how to turn the original thesis into a publishable manuscript. For their encouragement and support I am also especially grateful to Margrit and Wolfgang Fulda, Martin Jay, and Deborah Robinson.

My greatest debt is to my wife, Jane, who assisted with the editing but who, more importantly, gave so much of herself to this book and inspired whatever is best about it. Finally, I would like to give thanks for our daughter, Elisabeth, who has given a new meaning to the precept that "a little child shall lead them."

Introduction

Prussia was in many ways an anomaly among eighteenth-century European states. Though in 1740 it ranked only tenth in land area and thirteenth in population, its army was the fourth largest in Europe and was qualitatively the best. The Prussian state's ability to assemble, drill, and maintain this disproportionately large force was all the more remarkable in view of the backwardness of the economy compared to those of most of its political rivals. Prussia's surprising military prowess was, moreover, only the most obvious manifestation of its unusually effective state institutions. No other polity of the *ancien régime* had the internal cohesion needed to survive the type of ordeal that Prussia endured during the Seven Years' War (1756–63), when it withstood assaults from the Austrian, French, and Russian armies. This feat shows the extraordinary strength of the Prussian state with particular clarity, since the combined populations of the coalition members fighting Prussia in that war outnumbered the Prussian total by more than fifteen to one.

As Frederick the Great (1740–86) himself observed, during the reign of his father Frederick William I (1713–40) Prussia "became the Sparta [of the North] ... our customs no longer resembled those of our ancestors or our neighbors."[1] Specifically, what gave the Prussian state its special character was the primacy of utilitarian considerations and the unparalleled emphasis on the conscientious fulfillment of official duties. Whereas in other European capitals monarchs reigned over court establishments characterized by ostentatious luxury, the Prussian kings wore military uniforms and promoted an official ethic of parsimony and frugality.[2] While most

[1] Frederick II of Prussia, *Oeuvres complètes*, ed. J. D. E. Preuss, vol. 1 (Berlin, 1846), 234.

[2] For examples and further implications of this ethic, see C. B. A. Behrens, *Society, Government and the Enlightenment: The Experiences of Eighteenth-Century France and Prussia* (New York, 1985), 80f. The principle of parsimony extended into the management of Prussian state

eighteenth-century aristocrats had come to view a commission in the armed forces as a sinecure or as a stepping stone to a position at court, the Prussian landowning nobility, the Junkers, demonstrated a deep, collective loyalty to the ethos of military service.[3] The Prussian bureaucracy was likewise committed to much higher standards of honesty and efficiency than its European counterparts. Its effectiveness was responsible not only for Prussia's ability to mobilize its resources for military enterprises but also for the state's ability to respond to emergencies in civilian society. In the European-wide subsistence crisis of 1739–42, for example, the Prussian state distributed grain through its magazine system with so much success that the Prussian mortality rate was significantly lower than that of any other areas of Europe affected by the famine.[4]

The distinctiveness of the Prussian state institutions was widely recognized – and often applauded – by contemporaries. The state's commitment to improving the material lives of its subjects, as well as a policy of religious toleration unusually broad for that time, gained for the Prussian regime the approval of many German intellectuals, who proclaimed Prussia as the prototypical "Enlightened despotism."[5] King Frederick's connections with the leading French *philosophes* gave this image European-wide currency. Nor did the admiration for eighteenth-century Prussia die with the Enlightenment; a body of opinion in revolutionary France regarded the Prussian polity as so "progressive" that it had no need for the type of revolution that had overthrown the *ancien régime* in France and other parts of Western Europe.[6]

Accounting for the quality, and strength, of eighteenth-century Prussia's state institutions has challenged historians ever since. This

finances as Prussia, until the 1790s, was the only major European state to carry no long-term debt. See James C. Riley, *International Government Finance and the Amsterdam Capital Market, 1740–1815* (Cambridge, 1980), 101, 109.

3 Even an important Marxist historian acknowledges that they were "perhaps the most devoted and disciplined aristocracy in Europe." Perry Anderson, *Lineages of the Absolutist State* (London, 1974), 225.

4 John D. Post, "Climatic Variability and the European Mortality Wave of the Early 1740s," *Journal of Interdisciplinary History*, 15 (1984): 19–20. According to Behrens, the Prussian state's performance in the famine of the early 1770s was similarly exceptional. See Behrens, *Society, Government and the Enlightenment*, 182.

5 For an account of the broad, though not entirely uncritical, support Frederick enjoyed among the German intelligentsia, see Behrens, *Society, Government and the Enlightenment*, 176–85.

6 Jacques Droz, "Diskussionsbeitrag," in Otto Büsch, ed., *Das Preussenbild in der Geschichte: Protokoll eines Symposiums* (Berlin and New York, 1981), 98.

historical problem has been a particularly significant one for our own century, when the German state directly descendent from Frederician Prussia twice nearly achieved hegemony in Europe. A number of explanations for the initial "rise of Prussia" have been proposed. Perry Anderson, for example, sees the Junkers' post-1713 accomplishments as Prussian officers and bureaucrats as resulting from entrepreneurial abilities developed through managing estates and exporting grain to Western European markets.[7] Another aspect of the situation, the Prussian state's ability to dominate society and enforce its commands, is often interpreted as being a replication, on a "higher" level, of the authoritarian lord–serf relationship characteristic of East Elbian society.[8] The motivation behind the aggressive state-building program has most frequently been attributed to the extremely competitive international political environment of seventeenth- and eighteenth-century Europe in combination with the Hohenzollerns' need to defend non-contiguous territories extending over seven hundred miles from the Rhine River to the Lithuanian frontier.[9] That the Prussian state did indeed become powerful enough to carry out this mission was, according to the most widely held view of the matter, the result of uncommonly effective leadership by a series of Hohenzollern electors/kings who together reigned for a period extending for almost one hundred and fifty years.

A critical examination of these proposed explanations shows, however, that some other factor must be considered in order to account for the transformation of Prussia, in the early to mid-eighteenth century, from a princedom comparable in rank to Saxony or Bavaria to a state able to compete within the circle of great European powers. Granted that the Junkers possessed managerial acumen,[10] it is by no means self-evident why a sig-

7 Anderson, *Lineages of the Absolutist State*, 263.

8 As, for example, in Otto Büsch, *Militärsystem und Sozialleben im alten Preussen, 1713–1807: Die Anfänge der sozialen Militärisierung der preussisch-deutschen Gesellschaft* (Berlin and New York, 1962), 72.

9 This view has long been a central tenet of nationalist German historiography, summarized by the formulaic phrase *Primat der Aussenpolitik*. But the critical importance of the competitive European state system for the internal "modernizing" transformations of European societies is now widely recognized by proponents of a wide range of theoretical perspectives. Thus Perry Anderson emphasizes the role of seventeenth-century Swedish expansion in the development of what he calls the "Eastern variant" of European absolutism. Anderson, *Lineages of the Absolutist State*, 198–202.

10 This may be a generous assumption as I am aware of no studies that have empirically established this finding.

nificant portion of that group, in an action without parallel among the other comparable elite nobilities of East Central Europe at that time, suddenly opted for careers in the public sector. Nor can one take for granted a simple continuity between the characteristically Prussian ethos of blind obedience and a supposedly preexisting tradition in Prussian society of subordination and deference; for recent research is finding that early modern German peasants, even East Elbian serfs, were assertive defenders of their communal rights.[11] A closer look at the Hohenzollerns' security needs, moreover, reveals that, while their far-flung territories were vulnerable to attack, particularly from Sweden in the mid-seventeenth century, this threat had all but vanished by the early 1720s, precisely the moment when Frederick William I was building up the Prussian army to unprecedented levels. As for the importance of leadership from above, the usual emphasis in historical accounts on the personalities and policies of the Prussian rulers obscures the crucial issue of how they were able to gain support for their initiatives from society at large, particularly the Junkers. For it could not have been immediately apparent to the nobility that the radical changes being introduced by the Hohenzollerns were in the best interests of that hitherto traditionalistic landholding elite.

In this book I shall argue that what galvanized Prussian society in the early eighteenth century, what enabled the above factors to come fully into play, was an essentially cultural phenomenon: the propagation and pervasive acceptance of an ideology of unconditional service to the state.[12] This Prussian ideology came, of course, to exercise a fateful fascination for the modern German intelligentsia and, to a considerable extent, the German people as a whole. The full extremism of this mentality is captured by the historian Hans-Jürgen Puhle, who describes Prussianism as "the one-dimensional, often quite monomaniacal instrumentality, which was defined as 'state interest' and . . . which demanded, and increasingly also sought to achieve, often in an inhuman and repulsive way,

[11] William W. Hagen, "The Junkers' Faithless Servants," in R. J. Evans and W. R. Lee, eds., *The German Peasantry: Conflict and Community in Rural Society from the 18th to the 20th Centuries* (London, 1986).

[12] Thus proponents of this Prussianism, especially in the early decades of this century, would speak lyrically of a "feeling of commonality," of a willingness of individuals to "sacrifice themselves for the whole," of that great "inner freedom," that "freedom in obedience, which has always characterized the best exemplars of Prussian discipline." These phrases are taken from Oswald Spengler, *Preussentum und Sozialismus* (Munich, 1920), 31–32.

the subordination to itself of all other purposes and expressions of life [*Lebensäusserungen*]."[13]

Those contemporary writers and observers of eighteenth-century Prussia who were not bedazzled by its efficiency and military successes likewise used strong language to describe the oppressive atmosphere of internal control that resulted from the attempted organization of an entire society on the basis of this state-service ideology. Thus Lessing in 1769 characterized Prussia as the "most enslaved country of Europe."[14] To a surprising extent, however, modern historians have tended to underestimate the importance of this ideologically based political culture for that society. To be sure, the relationship between Frederick the Great's ideas on the nature of kingship and the political theory of the Enlightenment has been well explored. Much has also been written on the controversial question of how faithfully Frederick adhered to Enlightenment precepts in the actual governing of his kingdom.[15] And there has been a great deal of polemical comment on the effect of the Prussian ideology on subsequent German history.[16] But with few exceptions historical writing on Prussia has not focused directly on the central place of this ideology in the creation and successful functioning of eighteenth-century Prussia as a political system.

Perhaps the key reason for this neglect has been an understandable preoccupation with the consequences for nineteenth- and twentieth-century German history of Prussia's state institutions and political culture. In light of the politically charged nature of the historiography on Prussia, it is only to be expected that modern ideologies have strongly influenced the research strategies and interpretive orientations in this field – to the detriment, paradoxically, of the ideological component of early modern state building. Thus, on the one hand, most Marxist historians have assumed that the

13 Hans-Jürgen Puhle, "Preussen: Entwicklung und Fehlentwicklung," in H.-J. Puhle and H.-U. Wehler, eds., *Preussen im Rückblick* (Göttingen, 1980), 14.

14 Quoted in Hans Rosenberg, *Bureaucracy, Aristocracy, and Autocracy: The Prussian Experience, 1660–1815* (Boston, 1958), 41.

15 For a balanced discussion of the historiographical controversy over enlightened despotism, see Charles Ingrao, "The Problem of 'Enlightened Absolutism' and the German States," *Journal of Modern History*, 58, suppl. (December 1986): 161–80.

16 Two books that appeared in Germany during the great revival of interest in Prussian history in the early 1980s show how divergent assessments of the Prussian ideology can be. For an unabashed apologia, see Berthold Maack, *Preussen: Jedem das Seine* (Tübingen, 1980). For a very critical perspective, see Christian Graf von Krockow, *Warnung vor Preussen* (Berlin, 1981).

Prussian state arose in order to serve the class interests of the landowning Junker aristocracy, thereby excluding in an *a priori* way any independent role for ideology in the formation and maintenance of the Prussian political system.[17] On the other hand, bourgeois historians have generally followed the lead of the nationalistic "Prussian Historical School" of the late nineteenth century in its concentration on reconstructing in great detail the development of Prussia's military and bureaucratic institutions. Since the members of the Prussian school themselves never doubted the legitimacy of the Prussian state-building effort, the historiography they spawned has systematically failed to stress the need of the eighteenth-century Prussian polity for an ideology powerful enough to justify the unusual demands it was placing on all its subjects, nobles and commoners alike. Even postwar historians who have little sympathy for German nationalism or militarism have not been able to overcome this particular legacy of the Prussian School.[18]

Another influence at work here has been the tendency of historians, especially since World War II, to concentrate on the reign of the more sympathetic and articulate Frederick the Great and neglect that of his father, the dictatorial, fanatical, and seemingly "simple-minded" Frederick William I.[19] It was under the leadership of the latter, though, that a process of rapid institutional and social change produced a state system whose essential features remained intact until the Prussian military defeat at the hands of Napoleon in 1806.[20] Since it is during such dynamic periods of state formation that the importance of ideology is often most clearly evident, the relative lack of recent scholarly interest in the reign of Frederick William I has further contributed to the present inade-

[17] For a critique of this assumption and the literature based on it, see Klaus Deppermann, "Der preussische Absolutismus und der Adel: Eine Auseinandersetzung mit der marxistischen Absolutismustheorie," *Geschichte und Gesellschaft*, 8 (1982): 538–53.

[18] I am thinking here of perhaps the two most important postwar works on eighteenth-century Prussia: Büsch, *Militärsystem und Sozialleben* and Rosenberg, *Bureaucracy, Aristocracy, and Autocracy*.

[19] The characterization "simple-minded" is Behrens's: "In his simple-minded fashion Frederick William I . . . established the administrative foundations of Prussian absolutism." See Behrens, *Society, Government and the Enlightenment*, 56. This sentence captures perfectly the difficulty historians have had in accounting for the creative inspiration behind a political and social system that was in many ways more efficient and "modern" than any of its contemporaries – as Behrens herself would be among the first to claim.

[20] The element of continuity in the institutions of the Prussian state from the reign of Frederick William I to 1806 was so strong that in his structural–functional analysis of old-regime Prussia Otto Büsch was able to treat the entire period as one entity without undue distortion. See Büsch, *Militärsystem und Sozialleben*.

quate understanding of the origins and functional significance of the Prussian ideology.[21]

The work of the German historian Carl Hinrichs, however, has constituted a notable exception to this trend. Beginning in the 1950s, Hinrichs advanced the thesis that the origins and development of the Prussian state-service ideology can best be interpreted in the context of the Lutheran Pietist movement.[22] Especially in *Preussentum und Pietismus* (1971), Hinrichs identified important links between Pietism and some of the major institutional changes carried out by Frederick William I. But despite Hinrichs's professional eminence and the absence of any significant critique of his work, historians have shown a strong, almost instinctual resistance to accepting the full implications of his thesis.[23]

This reluctance to acknowledge the full impact of Pietism on the Prussian state stems in part from two deeply ingrained stereotypes that have prevented many people from conceiving of Lutheran Pietism as capable of playing such a dynamic political role. One of these has been the reputation of Lutheranism in general for political passivity and submissiveness to state authority.[24] In fact, Lutherans' willing subordination to the state in all worldly matters has long

[21] Though as a result of the work of the Prussian Historical School Frederick William I's significance is widely recognized, albeit in a general way, no complete, full-scale, scholarly biography has yet appeared in any language. The authoritative life begun by Carl Hinrichs takes the story only up to his ascension to the throne in 1713. Hinrichs, *Friedrich Wilhelm I., König in Preussen: Eine Biographie*, vol. 1 (Hamburg, 1941). One-volume postwar works in German, such as those by Gerhard Oestreich and Heinz Kathe, have been based on already existing research. Oestreich, *Friedrich Wilhelm I.: Preussischer Absolutismus, Merkantilismus, Militarismus* (Göttingen, 1977); Kathe, *Der "Soldatenkönig," Friedrich Wilhelm I., 1688–1740: König in Preussen* (Cologne, 1981). The last book-length treatment in English is Robert Ergang, *The Potsdam Führer: Frederick William I, Father of Prussian Militarism* (New York, 1941). Possible connections between the personality of that king and the psychological roots of the Nazi regime may very well have discouraged in-depth probing by German and perhaps other scholars. The *Resonanz* that the character of Frederick William I can still find among the German public was demonstrated, however, in the late 1970s, when the reissue of Jochen Klepper's long literary biography of Frederick William, *Der Vater: Roman eines Königs* (Munich, 1977), became a best-seller in the Federal Republic.

[22] See Carl Hinrichs, *Preussen als historisches Problem: Gesammelte Abhandlungen*, ed. Gerhard Oestreich (Berlin and New York, 1964); and his *Preussentum und Pietismus: Der Pietismus in Brandenburg-Preussen als religiös-soziale Reformbewegung* (Göttingen, 1971).

[23] For an example of an uncritical acceptance of Hinrichs's ideas, which yet remain unintegrated into the systematic account given of seventeenth- and eighteenth-century Prussia, see Hannsjoachim W. Koch, *A History of Prussia* (London and New York, 1978), 80–81.

[24] Laurence Dickey, in his recent work on the Protestant roots of Hegel's political philosophy, has encountered these same preconceptions. For his forceful criticism of the notion of alleged Lutheran political passivity, see Dickey, *Hegel: Religion, Economics, and the Politics of Spirit, 1770–1807* (Cambridge, 1987), 8–11.

been alleged as a major distinguishing factor between the German path of development and that of the "West," where Calvinism and influences from the radical Reformation have presumably served to prepare the way for modern capitalism and democracy.[25] This characterization of the Lutheran church has been so taken for granted that even a scholar as fine as Leonard Krieger simply dismissed the possibility of any Lutheran influence on the origins of the modern German political culture.[26]

The other stereotype pertains to the Pietist movement specifically. To this day the term "Pietism" unfailingly evokes an idea of quietistic spirituality unconcerned with politics and dedicated to the cultivation of a mystical inner life. This view of Pietism as otherworldly had already become firmly established by the end of the nineteenth century, when it was given even more credibility by no less a social theorist than Max Weber. In his *Protestant Ethic and the Spirit of Capitalism*, Weber acknowledged that Lutheran Pietism shared some of the qualities of "inner-worldly asceticism," whose importance in English Puritanism he so strongly emphasized. But Weber's final verdict on Pietism was that it lacked the doctrine of predestination, or some equivalent theological inducement, for the exercise of the "constant self-control" that made the Puritans' striving for external signs of grace so purposeful and efficacious. Weber further contrasted the supposedly mystical "emotionalism" of the Pietists with the "rationality" of the Puritans, concluding that Pietism was therefore less able than its English counterpart to contribute to the process of building the modern world – or, in Weber's own terminology, to furthering the process of "rationalization."[27]

In addition to having to overcome the effects of these deeply ingrained assumptions about Lutheran Pietism, Hinrichs's thesis has also been burdened by the shortcomings of his own exposition of that

[25] The consensus behind this interpretation within the early twentieth-century German academic world was so broad that it included both those, such as Ernst Troeltsch, who wanted Germany to become more "modern," i.e. more like the "West," and those of more strongly nationalist conviction who desired to preserve the alleged uniqueness of the German way. See Fritz Fischer, "Der deutsche Protestantismus und die Politik im 19. Jahrhundert," *Historische Zeitschrift*, 171 (1951): 73–76.

[26] Leonard Krieger, *The German Idea of Freedom: History of a Political Tradition* (Boston, 1957), 5–6.

[27] For Weber's views on Pietism, see Max Weber, *The Protestant Ethic and the Spirit of Capitalism*, trans. Talcott Parsons (New York, 1958), 128–39. For a critique of Weber's analysis of Pietism, see Richard L. Gawthrop, "Lutheran Pietism and the Weber Thesis," *German Studies Review*, 12 (1989): 237–47.

thesis. *Preussentum und Pietismus*, by far the most important work on the subject, was published posthumously and is a collection of essays rather than a systematically developed argument. Consequently, there are a number of aspects of the relationship between Pietism and the state-building efforts of Frederick William I not discussed by Hinrichs, notably the influence of Pietism on the Prussian bureaucracy. Even more significantly, Hinrichs does not address the issue of defining the nature of Frederick William's spirituality, which is crucial in determining the extent of the Pietist role in the transformation of Prussian society carried out by that king. For though the Pietists were prominent in many of the socializing institutions through which the doctrine of state service was inculcated, the king was the initiator, "the boss," the driving force behind the campaign to propagate this ideology. If, as some church historians have maintained, Frederick William was not a Pietist, then it is not difficult to argue either that the impact of Pietism was fairly limited or that Frederick William I merely used the Pietists to help him achieve objectives that had little or nothing to do with Pietism.[28]

This study seeks to overcome the various barriers that have limited the impact of Hinrichs's thesis. One way it does so is by providing the historical framework needed to illuminate the full significance of Pietism in the making of eighteenth-century Prussia. The aim of the first three chapters of this book, for example, is to clarify the relationship between the state building of Frederick William I, on the one hand, and the policies pursued by his two immediate predecessors, Frederick William the Great Elector (1640–88) and Frederick III(I) (1688–1713), on the other. The outcome of this comparison is crucial for the overall argument of this work. For if the achievements of Frederick William I's reign were essentially an elaboration upon those of the pre-1713 era,

[28] Recent works by Gerd Heinrich and Mary Fulbrook show just how significant – and how unclarified – the issue of Frederick William I's relationship to Pietism remains. Thus Heinrich questions "whether in Francke's lifetime the still small Pietist group in the state assumed an equal level of spiritual leadership [with the king] or whether it merely stimulated or supported the monarchs." Heinrich, *Geschichte Preussens: Staat und Dynastie* (Frankfurt/Main, 1981), 187. Similarly, Fulbrook, while acknowledging that after 1713 Prussia "differed from other absolutist states" as a result of the "'puritanism' and asceticism of the Prussian court" and while seeing this orientation of the court as contributing to "the development of a close relationship between precisionism [i.e. Pietism] and absolutism," does not attempt to account for the "puritanism" of Frederick William I and his entourage. Fulbrook, *Piety and Politics: Religion and the Rise of Absolutism in England, Württemberg and Prussia* (Cambridge, 1983), 167.

when the Pietists were *not* a major force in the Hohenzollern lands, then Pietism simply could not have been that crucial a factor in the process that ultimately produced Frederician Prussia.[29]

But if, in fact, there were fundamental discontinuities between the regime of Frederick William I and those of his predecessors, then the factors responsible for the successes of the latter would probably not account for the accomplishments of the former. I intend to show that such discontinuities did exist and that the Brandenburg-Prussian state between 1640 and 1713 differed in degree but not in kind from other seventeenth-century German territorial states. This preliminary analysis is crucial because it solidifies the argument that the crucial factor that made Prussia so different from its "ancestors and neighbors" was introduced into the Prussian polity during the reign of Frederick William I. And it was this element of discontinuity that also enabled Frederick William's regime to break through the constraints that would have inhibited further development of state power if the basic policies pursued by the Great Elector and Frederick III(I) had been continued.

Yet this new element, the characteristically Prussian sense of duty in serving the state, could not have been created *ex nihilo*; it had to appeal to cultural values already present in the German cultural milieu. Stereotypes about Lutheranism derived from nineteenth- and early twentieth-century experience notwithstanding, neither Reformation Lutheranism nor the Lutheran orthodoxy of the seventeenth century was inclined, theologically or politically, to endorse an ethic that placed an ultimate value on action for the good of the state. The middle chapters of the book serve the purpose of explaining how a works-oriented spirituality capable of undergirding such an ethic emerged from orthodox Lutheranism. After describing how in the seventeenth century a subjective, discipline-oriented piety became increasingly prevalent within the Lutheran tradition, I shall concentrate on the culmination of this trend, the Lutheran Pietist movement, which made its appearance in the

[29] As will be discussed below, the impression conveyed by most scholarly accounts is one of continuity, especially in the all-important relationship between the Junkers and the monarchy. Yet the foundations for this view are weak indeed. For a persuasive refutation of much of the conventional wisdom concerning the reign of the Great Elector, see William W. Hagen, "Seventeenth-Century Crisis in Brandenburg: The Thirty Years' War, the Destabilization of Serfdom, and the Rise of Absolutism," *American Historical Review*, 94 (1989): 302–35.

1670s. Deeply influenced by English Puritanism,[30] with all its intrusive moralism and emphasis on tangible results, Lutheran Pietism in its first two generations struggled to find the appropriate institutional means through which to impose moral "reform" on society.[31] Though convinced at first that they did not need, or want, the assistance of the state, the Pietists, especially under the leadership of August Hermann Francke, ultimately came to depend on the patronage of the Hohenzollerns, who allowed them to build up their own mini-society in the city of Halle. In this setting, the potentialities for social activism in early Pietism were fully realized, and Halle Pietism developed into an ideological and pedagogical force capable of fulfilling the role it was to assume in post-1713 Prussia.

The final section of this study examines the as yet only partially understood nature of the relationships between Halle Pietism, Frederick William I, and the creation of the Prussian political culture. My central contention here is that Frederick William, though not formally a disciple or follower of the Pietists, was motivated by a spirituality essentially similar to that of Halle Pietism. Demonstrating the existence of this deep affinity allows for a far more significant historical role for Pietism than Hinrichs could have ever asserted. For what happened in Prussia between 1713 and 1740 was more than simply a collaboration between the king and the Halle movement, in which the king gave the Pietists unprecedented and important opportunities for realizing their reform ambitions in society at large.[32] The even greater significance of these Pietist efforts, however, was that they powerfully reinforced and helped legitimate Frederick William I's fundamental restructuring of the administrative, military, and economic life of his kingdom – a

30 Hinrichs, though not unaware of the Puritan influence on Pietism, underestimated its significance – and, in the process, misinterpreted the nature of Pietism – by emphasizing instead the importance of "mystical spiritualism" in the development of Pietism. Hinrichs, *Preussentum und Pietismus*, 3–10.

31 In this context, "reform" is even more of a loaded word than it usually is. Even as judicious a historian as Robin Briggs was moved to assert that the analogous, seventeenth-century "catholic reform movement [in France] ... can be characterized, with only slight exaggeration, as one of the greatest repressive enterprises in European history." Briggs, *Communities of Belief: Cultural and Social Tension in Early Modern France* (Oxford, 1989), 230.

32 Making historians aware of this collaboration was the fundamental contribution of Hinrichs's work. Its nature, as Hinrichs presented it, is aptly captured in the following formulation by Heinrich: "In Prussia, the ruler and high office holders permitted [the Pietists] freedom of operation, took over reform ideas, and put them to trial in the great experiment of the *Lagerhaus* or in the reconstruction of East Prussia, in the course of which oppositional conservative or special interest forces were bloodlessly pushed aside." See Heinrich, *Geschichte Preussens*, 188.

restructuring that was *itself* based on Pietist concepts of God, self, and vocation.

The purpose of this book is therefore not only to prove the central role of Pietism in the crystallization of the Prussian political culture but also to show concretely just how integral that culture was in the creation of the institutions that gave the post-1713 Prussian state its power – and distinctiveness.[33] I shall accordingly present the "rise of Prussia" from an essentially sociocultural perspective, by emphasizing a state-sponsored pedagogical process of unusual depth and intensity.[34] Through the extensive network of institutions controlled by the Lutheran church and through the state's, i.e. the king's, ability to issue and enforce new rules governing the conduct of members of public bodies, the Pietists and Frederick William I were able to accomplish nothing less than a "cultural revolution."[35] For this great cultural reorientation of Prussian society was not only instrumental in a sudden upsurge of state power but must also have had profound, long-term effects, as yet unstudied, on such basic cultural factors as the Prussian people's work habits, child-reading practices, sex roles, schooling environments, and sense of identity.[36]

33 The only contemporary analogue to the regime of Frederick William I was that of Victor Amadeus II of Piedmont-Savoy, whose reign has been treated in Geoffrey Symcox, *Victor Amadeus II: Absolutism in the Savoyard State, 1675–1730* (Berkeley and Los Angeles, 1983). Although Symcox was unable to link Victor Amadeus II with any Catholic reform movement *per se*, one can still account for the unusual austerity and energy of that ruler by concluding that he applied with atypical consistency the values of post-Trent Catholicism to the practice of state building. I owe this suggestion to the late Professor Eric Cochrane.

34 Though not too long ago this methodological standpoint would have been regarded as unusual, a body of social theory now exists that sees states not merely as instruments of class domination or arbiters of divergent class interests but as deeply cultural phenomena. The most important theoretical work on the cultural dimension of the modern state is Philip Corrigan and Derek Sayer, *The Great Arch: English State Formation as Cultural Revolution* (Oxford, 1985). For a brief but significant essay that argues along similar lines, see Bernard S. Cohn and Nicholas B. Dirks, "Beyond the Fringe: The Nation State, Colonialism and the Technologies of Power," *Journal of Historical Sociology*, 1 (1988): 224–29. The importance of socialization institutions and ideological values as factors in state formation, as well as the cultural impact of state institutions, is recognized in Theda Skocpol, "Bringing the State Back In: Strategies of Analysis in Current Research," in Peter B. Evans, Dietrich Rueschemeyer, and Theda Skocpol, eds., *Bringing the State Back In* (Cambridge, 1985), 9–10, 20–21.

35 For an illuminating theoretical statement of the causal connection between "state formation" and "cultural revolution," see Corrigan and Sayer, *The Great Arch*, 1–13. Corrigan and Sayer, despite their debt to Marx, reject the relegation of "state formation" and "cultural revolution" to the status of being mere "superstructures." They furthermore regard "systematically ignoring ... the organized project of those with the social power to define [state forms]" – in the name of history "from below" – as simply "bad faith." *The Great Arch*, 9.

36 The complete social and cultural impact of the political, ideological, and religious mobili-

This emphasis on the close association between cultural transformation and the production of Prussian state power should therefore contribute to a broader understanding of modern German history. For the values and instruments of socialization forced on eighteenth-century Prussians were perpetrated, for the same reasons and in only somewhat modified form, on nineteenth- and early twentieth-century Germans. To what degree, and in what ways, was the German experience in this important area of life different from those of other modern European peoples, all of whom were likewise subjected to a disciplining, "civilizing" process indissolubly linked to the emergence of modern bureaucratic power structures?[37] Until this question is given more consideration, the history of the state–society relationship in a modernizing Germany will remain incomplete;[38] and our ability to assess the uniqueness of the modern German path will lack the necessary basis.

zation that produced eighteenth-century Prussia should be evaluated using the same kind of methodologies that have in recent decades been applied to Puritanism and seventeenth-century French Catholicism. For an exceptionally comprehensive evaluation of the latter's sociocultural significance, see Briggs, *Communities of Belief*. For the reasons why these perspectives on the relationship between religion and society have not been widely incorporated into the historiography of post-Reformation Germany, see Richard J. Evans, *Rethinking German History: Nineteenth-Century Germany and the Origins of the Third Reich* (London, 1987), 128–30.

37 I am consciously using the phrase "civilizing process" in the sense of the central theme in Norbert Elias, *The Civilizing Process*, trans. Edmund Jephcott (New York, 1978). For a valuable summary of Elias's views, as well as an important statement on the recent rediscovery of the significance of "mentalities," see Patrick Hutton, "The History of Mentalities: The New Map of Cultural History," *History and Theory*, 20 (1981): 237–59.

38 The recent historiographical debate over the German *Sonderweg* clearly illustrates this point. The participants in this controversy have neglected the possible role of culture as a causal factor, confining themselves to analyzing the political and economic aspects of modern Germany's "special way." To be sure, Geoff Eley acknowledges the importance of the cultural factor when he states that "ultimately the battle for 'modernity' is fought out in the hearts and minds of the bourgeoisie." See David Blackbourn and Geoff Eley, *The Peculiarities of German History: Bourgeois Society and Politics in Nineteenth-Century Germany* (New York, 1984), 48. Neither Eley nor his opponents, however, have taken the trouble to analyze in any depth modern German political culture, which is still generally viewed unproblematically as a "pre-industrial" legacy that for some unexplained reason was able to retain a powerful hold over the nineteenth-century German middle classes.

CHAPTER I

The German territorial state in the sixteenth and seventeenth centuries

INTRODUCTION

The story of a revolution always begins with its *ancien régime*. In the case of the transformation of Prussia under Frederick William I, this procedure is particularly necessary because the revolutionary character of that king's reign is frequently not emphasized by historians. Instead, it is customary to regard the four Hohenzollerns – Frederick William the Great Elector, Frederick III(I), Frederick William I, and Frederick II the Great – as a single group, with each ruler making a greater or lesser contribution to the development of Prussian absolutism. The assumption behind this approach is that the basic framework for what became the eighteenth-century Prussian state was established by the Great Elector in the aftermath of the Thirty Years' War and then gradually evolved under his successors until it attained its definitive form under Frederick the Great in the mid-eighteenth century.

This conception of early modern Prussian history has received support from the most ideologically diverse sources. The Prussian Historical School focused its abundant energies on the growth of the key state institutions, most of which, notably the War Commissariat, dated from the Great Elector's reign. Though the innovative character of Frederick William I's kingship was often recognized, especially by Gustav Schmoller, the politically conservative Prussian School's interpretation of the "rise of Prussia" inevitably stressed the formal continuity of the basic state structures.[1]

In the decades following World War II, both bourgeois and Marxist historians have reacted against the ideological and

[1] For an example of Schmoller's high valuation of the work of Frederick William I, see Gustav Schmoller, "Das Städtewesen unter Friedrich Wilhelm I.," in Schmoller, *Deutsches Städtewesen in älterer Zeit* (Bonn, 1922), 231–428.

methodological positions of the Prussian School by asserting that the Prussian state came into being in order to serve the class interests of the Junker aristocracy. This viewpoint, though, in its own way likewise assumes a fundamental continuity throughout the period 1640–1786. Following the lead of Hans Rosenberg, most recent writing finds the determining social basis for Prussian absolutism in a kind of social contract between the Hohenzollerns and the Junkers concluded in the 1650s. By terms of this agreement, the nobility, hard pressed by a labor shortage and a depression in the price of grain, allowed the Great Elector to levy the taxes needed to fund a standing army in return for the state's guaranteeing the Junkers' economic and legal position *vis-à-vis* their peasant serfs.[2]

From a European-wide perspective, this accord is regarded as part of the broader process by which the deterioration of the legal position of the East European peasantry in the sixteenth century, the so-called "second serfdom," produced social formations allegedly more oppressive than those in Western Europe and, consequently, political systems that were more authoritarian and militaristic.[3] The Junker–Hohenzollern alliance supposedly accomplished this linkage between serf-owning elite and absolutist regime in Prussia, thereby defining the essential character of the Prussian state for at least the next one hundred and fifty years. If this were indeed the case, the changes instituted by Frederick William I would have to be regarded as less revolutionary than those sponsored by the initiator of that alliance, the ruler commonly considered to be the founder of the uniquely Prussian form of state building – the Great Elector.

But should the eighteenth-century Prussian state be understood primarily as a product of the harsh realities of the serf-based economy in early modern East Central Europe? In these first three chapters, I shall critically evaluate this position by challenging the assumption of an essential continuity in the history of Prussian absolutism between the mid-seventeenth and late eighteenth centuries. To do this systematically, one must compare the state-building accomplishments of the Great Elector and Frederick III(I) with the achievements of their counterparts in the rest of the Holy

[2] See Hans Rosenberg, "The Rise of the Junkers in Brandenburg-Prussia, 1410–1653," *American Historical Review*, 49 (1943/44): 240. For a compelling critique of the assumptions behind this viewpoint, see Hagen, Seventeenth-Century Crisis in Brandenburg," esp. 333–35.

[3] Though his own position is more complex than this, for a strong statement of this point of view, see Anderson, *Lineages of the Absolutist State*, 195.

Roman Empire. For if one assumes that eighteenth-century Prussia differed qualitatively from the other German states and that there existed a direct line of development between it and the earlier regimes of 1640–1713, then a comparative analysis of the late seventeenth-century Hohenzollern state with other princedoms in Germany at that time should reveal fundamental dissimilarities between it and the presumably more typical pattern of German state formation. The purpose of this present chapter, therefore, is to present an analysis of seventeenth-century German absolutism that will serve as the basis for comparison. The two succeeding chapters will then examine the state building of the Great Elector and Frederick III(I), in light of the general characteristics identified below as basic to the configuration of absolutism in seventeenth-century Germany.

THE SIXTEENTH-CENTURY DRIVE TOWARD UNIFORMITY

The absence of a strong imperial government in early modern times favored the emergence of the so-called territorial states as regional political powers in the German lands. Even within these relatively small political units, moreover, the process of decentralization so characteristic of the late medieval period left an enduring mark. In the fourteenth and fifteenth centuries knights and towns in the various territorial princedoms organized themselves as self-governing corporations, or estates, which came to meet periodically in assemblies (*Landtage*) that claimed – and received – a large say in the conduct of affairs on the territorial level as well.[4] In some of the territorial states, to be sure, the reigning princes, by the seventeenth or eighteenth centuries, had acquired a monopoly on the right to enact legislation affecting the territory as a whole, as well as supreme judicial and administrative authority. Yet none of these "absolutist" polities, even eighteenth-century Prussia, was able, or inclined, to set aside the local governing institutions of the estates.[5] Hence

[4] Gerald Strauss, *Law, Resistance, and the State in Sixteenth-Century Germany* (Princeton, 1986), 246–49; Gerhard Oestreich, *Neostoicism and the Early Modern State*, trans. David McLintock (Cambridge, 1982), 189–91.

[5] This theme has been strongly emphasized in the recent literature. See for example, the essays in Peter Baumgart, ed., *Ständetum und Staatsbildung in Brandenburg-Preussen* (Berlin and New York, 1983). For an analytical discussion of the limits of "absolutism" in seventeenth-century Germany, see Richard L. Gawthrop, "The Social Role of the Seventeenth-Century German Territorial State," in Andrew C. Fix and Susan C. Karant-Nunn, eds., *Germania*

German territorial states throughout the early modern period all possessed "dualistic" structures, with princes and their estates sharing power in proportions that varied widely from state to state and in the same state over time.

Although it is thus misleading to describe the evolution of the post-medieval German state simply in terms of the progressive displacement of "dualism" by "absolutism" over the course of the sixteenth and seventeenth centuries in most of the larger princedoms, the institutions of the central government did assume ever greater responsibilities, and the distribution of power between prince and estates shifted most often in favor of the former. These stronger, more centralized political units arose in response to the disruptive social effects occasioned by the economic upswing that, beginning in the mid to late fifteenth century, produced a rapidly growing population, commercial prosperity, and rising prices.[6] Persisting throughout the sixteenth century, these economic trends created a need for greater state power because they had the destabilizing effect of weakening bonds of solidarity in both urban and rural German communities.

Thus in the cities and larger towns the substantial wealth acquired by successful merchants elevated them in terms of financial status far above the level of the rest of the urban population, whose numbers were growing but whose real wages were steadily declining. As the sixteenth century proceeded, it therefore became increasingly common for patriciates formed from the very rich families to achieve a corresponding ascendancy in the political realm and to exercise an uneasy dominion over municipalities formerly run in a far more democratic manner by the guilds.[7]

In the countryside, rising grain prices and growing urban centers meant that considerable profits could be made by those, be they noble or peasant, with a surplus to sell. Yet this linkage of the rural community to the market economy proved to be a mixed blessing. It

Illustrata: Essays on Early Modern Germany Presented to Gerald Strauss (Kirksville, Mo., 1992), 243–47.

6 Indeed, until the middle of the sixteenth century, the German economy led, rather than followed, the rest of Europe as a result of the central European mining boom and the leading role of the South German imperial cities in international trade and banking. For an overview of the sixteenth-century expansion with many references to German developments, see Peter Kriedte, *Peasants, Landlords, and Merchant Capitalists: Europe and the World Economy, 1500–1800*, trans. V. R. Berghahn (Cambridge, 1983), 18–60.

7 See Thomas A. Brady, Jr., *Turning Swiss: Cities and Empire, 1450–1550* (Cambridge, 1985), 11–16.

widened, if it did not create, the gap in the village between the well-off peasants able to produce surplus grain and sell it to urban consumers and those peasants with such small holdings that they had to buy much of their own food in the market, at ever higher prices. In addition, the opportunities for profit and the need to cover the steadily mounting costs of living prompted the nobility to attempt to exploit more intensively their rights to the land. Whether this "rent offensive" took the form of demanding peasant labor services or curtailing the village community's use of its common land, it posed a threat to the newly found prosperity of some peasants and to the very subsistence of others.[8]

In an atmosphere of increasing social tensions, serious efforts were made to reform the highly decentralized German political system. On the imperial level, the diet (*Reichstag*), consisting of princes, prelates, and imperial cities, had become an organized, periodically convened body by the late fifteenth century. In the early sixteenth century, those who sought to strengthen the central government of the Empire succeeded in enacting an imperial law code (the *Carolina*) and creating an imperial supreme court, though further initiatives were blocked by power struggles resulting from the conflicting interests of the emperor, the princes, and the imperial cities.[9] During this same period, in many territories in the Empire cooperation between the princes and their territorial estates became much more formalized, and the *Landtage* not only met more regularly but also assumed much more substantial legislative and administrative responsibilities. Finally, in southern Germany the Swabian League arose in the 1490s, comprised of the Emperor, the wealthy imperial cities, and some knights and princes. Though the League's composition and political agenda varied in the course of its forty-odd year history, it possessed enough coherence and commonality of purpose that by the early 1520s it appeared as though it might serve as the nucleus for the formation of a large south German state.[10]

These improvements in political organization could not prevent the explosion of the 1520s, though they ultimately contained it. The crushing of the uprisings of 1524–25 did not, however, put an end to

8 Peter Blickle, *The Revolution of 1525: The German Peasants' War from a New Perspective*, trans. Thomas A. Brady, Jr., and H. C. Erik Midelfort (Baltimore, 1981), 68–78.

9 For the motives behind the frequent opposition of the imperial cities to these "reforms," see Brady, *Turning Swiss*, 44, 69–70.

10 For the reasons why this possible outcome was never realized, see *ibid.*, 226–28.

the assertiveness of the lower orders of society nor reverse the economic forces that were jeopardizing their way of life. The fear of a recurrence of the events of the 1520s remained an important component in the mentality of German elites throughout the century. This perception of fragility in the social system simply intensified the religious-based view contemporaries already held of their own age as a time of extreme disorder, of evil barely under control, of a world coming to an end.[11] This resulting, generalized sense of insecurity pervaded mid to late sixteenth-century culture and gave rise to two related movements, each of which sought to bring order to society by imposing a clear, authoritative standard whose enforcement by the territorial governments would produce a much desired uniformity and predictability.[12]

One of these movements was the drive to overturn the traditional legal system based on custom and precedent, which had allegedly been proven inadequate, and replace it with a centralized system based on the procedures and precepts of Roman law. Although the creation of a central, consistent, impartial, territorial legal system was desired (at times) by all parties and although the territorial estates sometimes collaborated in the formulation of the new legal constitutions,[13] the princes gained substantial political advantages from the promulgation of these systematic juridical reforms. Ideologically, it enabled a prince to claim that his authority represented the "general good" that the imposition of such a definitive code alone could provide.[14] Socially, a prince's commitment to a legal *reformatio* attracted to his service a new, ambitious juristic elite, drawn from the middle classes and dedicated to extending the uniform, princely jurisdiction at the expense of all "ancient customs, freedoms, and traditions."[15] Particularly after mid-century these university-trained lawyers succeeded in gradually penetrating the preserves of the "old law" and opening up towns and rural districts to the prospect of direct administrative control by the territorial government. As they did so, the princely authorities began to issue

[11] The centrality of this eschatological perspective to Luther's spirituality is a central theme in Heiko Oberman, *Luther zwischen Gott und Teufel* (Berlin, 1982). See also Strauss, *Law, Resistance, and the State*, 98.

[12] I owe the idea of linking sixteenth-century legal reform and confessionalization in this way to Gerald Strauss.

[13] Strauss, *Law, Resistance, and the State*, 161–62; Oestreich, *Neostoicism and the Early Modern State*, 193.

[14] Strauss, *Law, Resistance, and the State*, 136f.

[15] *Ibid.*, 98.

an ever greater number of "police" ordinances, which were particularly directed at the towns and which sought to regulate the dress, morality, economic activity, and nearly every other aspect of the people's lives.[16]

An authoritarian drive toward uniformity also made itself felt in German religious life. Faced with the task of building their new churches into permanent ecclesiastical institutions, mainstream Protestant leaders saw themselves threatened on many fronts: from the radicals of 1525 and their Anabaptist successors, from the resurgence of Catholicism after mid-century, and from the splits in their ranks, the most momentous of which divided German Protestantism into a Lutheran majority and a Calvinist, or "Reformed," minority.[17] As the century wore on and the religious competition became increasingly intense, German clerics from all confessions not surprisingly turned for help to the territorial princes. In return for the prince's help in securing the complete triumph of their cause in his territory and in eliminating all traces of the opposing confessions, the dominant clerical groups ceded varying amounts of the central administrative control of their church to their prince.[18]

In this way the territorial princes secured the allegiance of another highly motivated elite, and the process of "confessionalizing" the various princedoms augmented the ruler's power in a number of ways.[19] In both Catholic and Protestant parts of Germany, enforcing religious discipline and preserving the true faith became responsibilities of the state power, thereby superimpos-

16 *Ibid.*, 137. For the tone and content of these ordinances, see the summary in Marc Raeff, *The Well-Ordered Police State: Social and Institutional Change through Law in the Germanies and Russia, 1600–1800* (New Haven, 1983), 167–69. For their impact on urban communities, see Heinz Schilling, "The European Crisis of the 1590s: The Situation in the German Towns," in Peter Clark, ed., *The European Crisis of the 1590s* (London, 1985), 147–50.

17 Interpreting these difficulties as signs confirming Luther's pessimistic eschatology, Melanchthon, for one, believed that concentrating power in the hands of the Christian prince was the only way to preserve order in the time remaining before the Judgment. Strauss, *Law, Resistance, and the State*, 224–30.

18 State control over the territorial church was greatest in those Protestant states, such as the Palatinate and Hesse-Cassel, which in the mid to late sixteenth century adopted the Reformed faith as an integral part of a dynamic, aggressive state-building program. See Heinz Schilling, "Die 'Zweite Reformation' als Kategorie der Geschichtswissenschaft," in Schilling, ed., *Die reformierte Konfessionalisierung in Deutschland: Das Problem der "Zweiten Reformation"* (Gütersloh, 1986), 428–32.

19 For the role of confessionalization as a "welcome instrument for the intensification of authority and for building up the state," see Heinz Schilling, "Between the Territorial State and Urban Liberty: Lutheranism and Calvinism in the County of Lippe," in R. Po-chia Hsia, ed., *The German People and the Reformation* (Ithaca, 1988), 266.

ing a most potent source of legitimation on the prince's traditional claim to rule on the basis of his being a patriarch to his subjects. This enhancement of the princely position quickly became part of imperial law when the Peace of Augsburg in 1555 conferred on all magistrates in the Empire the *ius reformandi*, the right of rulers to determine their subjects' religious confession and compel conformity to the established doctrine. To carry out this mandate, territorial princes commissioned their clerical leaders and legal advisers to draw up church constitutions (*Kirchenordnungen*), which laid down the bureaucratic structure and procedures through which the state would exercise control over the territorial church.[20]

Within this framework, the authorities vigorously pursued the goal of religious uniformity. At the elite level, *gymnasia* and even new universities were founded to ensure that future teachers, clergy, and other state servants were imbued with the appropriate confessional consciousness. More ambitious still was the unprecedented effort to educate the lower orders in the essentials of the faith. Village schools were established in great numbers, systematic catechization of the young became the prescribed norm, and periodic visitations of parishes by ecclesiastical superiors were designed to make sure that the expectations of church and state were being fulfilled.[21]

By the late sixteenth century the creation of centralized judicial and administrative systems, as well as the beginnings of a uniform territorial culture produced by confessionalization, had put at the disposal of German princes far more resources and far stronger means for wielding power than they had ever had. In an Empire fragmented politically and divided religiously, the dynamic process of confessionalization created, moreover, a dangerous potential for religious war from the 1580s on. Aggressive princes, most especially Maximilian of Bavaria (1597–1651), took advantage of the fears thus aroused and seized the political initiative from their estates, excluding them in varying degrees from participation at the highest levels of decision making. It was regimes of princes such as these that

20 For the texts, see Emil Sehling, ed., *Die evangelischen Kirchenordnungen des XVI. Jahrhundert*, 5 vols. (Leipzig, 1902–11).

21 For a brief treatment of this theme, see Richard Gawthrop and Gerald Strauss, "Protestantism and Literacy in Early Modern Germany," *Past & Present*, no. 104 (August 1984): 31–43. Characteristically, these pedagogical measures were pursued most seriously and most effectively in territories of princes committed to the Reformed faith. See Gerald Strauss, *Luther's House of Learning: Indoctrination of the Young in the German Reformation* (Baltimore, 1978), 291–93.

enacted the most ambitious legislation for creating territorial economies and limiting the autonomy of local governing bodies.

Yet despite the undeniable importance of energetic state-building efforts by the princes and their functionaries, it is also true that without the support of significant sectors of the population late sixteenth-century German territorial states would never have succeeded in extending their authority over society to the extent that they did. In most of the German lands the social instability caused by inflation and overpopulation induced both the better-off and the poor to turn for help to the state, albeit for different reasons. On the one hand, the growing numbers of landless laborers became increasingly dependent on the state for grain supplies and other forms of support.[22] On the other hand, the nobility, the urban patriciates, and the wealthy village elites received state sanction for their positions of dominance in the local communities.[23]

In return the states secured steady, sizable increases in taxation, but the way in which these levies were exacted placed definite limits on the ability of the sixteenth-century territorial states, and their seventeenth-century successors, to penetrate and transform the societies they governed. For in all cases the princes continued to rely on the estates for the actual collection of taxes rather than expanding the bureaucracy to the extent necessary to take on that responsibility.[24] Not surprisingly, as the state's fiscal needs increased, so did its dependence on the ever more complex system of tax collection run by the estates. This situation produced a conflict in priorities, since many of the targets of those state-decreed ordinances designed to eliminate special immunities and promote uniformity were often precisely those corporations and institutions through whose efforts state revenues were raised. Typically, the princely governments chose to sacrifice principle to expediency, permitting the survival of the privileged groups and allowing government offices on the district level to be filled by leaders of the local communities.[25] This

[22] This dependence was the most pronounced in the area of greatest overpopulation, i.e. the German southwest. See Thomas Willard Robisheaux, *Rural Society and the Search for Order in Early Modern Germany* (Cambridge, 1989), 196, 213.

[23] For a very good description of how this process worked in a smaller, "patrimonial" territory, see *ibid.*, 165–98.

[24] For the Bavarian case, see Rudolf Schlögl, *Bauern, Krieg und Staat: Oberbayerische Bauernwirtschaft und frühmoderner Staat im 17. Jahrhundert* (Göttingen, 1988), 214.

[25] Consequently, the gap between the legislative intentions embodied in the *Polizeiordnungen* and their actual enforcement remained substantial. This was true even in Maximilian's Bavaria. For the latter, see Strauss, *Law, Resistance, and the State*, 268.

kind of "dualistic" administration extended to ecclesiastical affairs as well, where it was very common for village pastors to be nominated by the local nobility and for these appointments to be approved routinely by the central consistory.

THE POWER OF THE SEVENTEENTH-CENTURY GERMAN TERRITORIAL PRINCE

Because indispensable administrative roles continued to be performed in this manner by local elites, the sixteenth-century drive toward political centralization ultimately encountered limits beyond which it could not go. Consequently, the estates continued to play a major political role despite the enhanced power of the princes. The Thirty Years' War (1618–48), however, threatened to disrupt the state–society relationship that had developed in response to the stresses of the preceding century. Particularly in regions plundered by hostile or "friendly" armies, the state – and its social allies – had to work hard to reestablish the credibility of the politically buttressed system of social control that had come into existence by the beginning of the war. The success of this political reconstruction was not a foregone conclusion as in many areas the complete absence of the customary civil authorities due to military occupation lasted up to ten years or even longer.[26]

Another potential source of discontinuity was the war's impact on the economy of the German lands. The effects of the war were serious enough: an aggregate population loss of about one third, heavy taxation, and a general impoverishment that greatly weakened the domestic market for both grain and industrial products. Prospects for long-term recovery were undermined, moreover, by the depletion of Germany's capital supply through the inflation that accompanied the outbreak of the war as well as by the demands of the competing war machines.[27] A final set of constraints on the economic recovery of the German lands was imposed by adverse trends in the European economy as a whole. In addition to lower prices for grain resulting from weak demand at home and abroad,

26 Robisheaux, *Rural Society and the Search for Order*, 222–23, 229–31. Hagen's work on Brandenburg demonstrates that this problem was not confined to the patrimonial states. Hagen, "Seventeenth-Century Crisis in Brandenburg," 314–16.

27 Theodore K. Rabb, "The Economic Effects of the War Reviewed," in Rabb, ed., *The Thirty Years' War* (Lexington, Mass., 1972), 74, 77.

German landowners also had to face the novel problem of labor shortages and correspondingly higher wage rates.[28] Merchants and artisans in German cities were confronted with the similarly disconcerting loss of traditional markets in Italy and East Central Europe due to English and Dutch competition or to depressed economic conditions in those areas. Despite all these obstacles, some regions and economic sectors shows signs of returning prosperity in the 1650s and 1660s, but the outbreak of war in 1672, which continued with only short intervals of peace for the next forty years, raised taxation to crushing levels and made a return to pre-1618 conditions, especially in the towns, more difficult still.[29]

The Thirty Years' War, commercial and industrial depression, and the resumption of almost uninterrupted warfare in the late seventeenth century inevitably modified the relationship between the princes and society. Or perhaps it would be more precise to say that the process of adjusting to the situation brought about by these factors altered the institutional forms through which the dominant social groups exercised their superiority. In many of the larger territorial states especially, the seventeenth century saw that apparently marked increase in the power of the princes that has led subsequent historians to label this period the "age of absolutism."

There was a certain amount of reality in this appearance of new-found princely power. The estates, the only constitutional body able to check the princes politically, were often seriously weakened by the adverse economic climate. This was especially true of the urban estates as many towns had lost their prosperity and even, in some cases, their civic consciousness and bourgeois identity.[30] But even the nobility, now more ascendant within the estates than ever

[28] Henry Kamen, "The Social and Economic Consequences of the Thirty Years' War," *Past & Present*, no. 39 (1968): 44–61; Kriedte, *Peasants, Landlords and Merchant Capitalists*, 65–70.

[29] In the case of Nördlingen, the impact of the wartime taxation of the late seventeenth century was even more detrimental than the effects of the Thirty Years' War. See Christopher Friedrichs, *Urban Society in an Age of War: Nördlingen, 1580–1720* (Princeton, 1979), 293.

[30] In towns in the eastern areas of the Empire, a large percentage of the inhabitants were forced to farm small plots to make ends meet; politically and socially, such towns were dominated by the local nobility. For a discussion of this phenomenon in the Habsburg lands, see R. J. W. Evans, *The Making of the Habsburg Monarchy, 1550–1700: An Interpretation* (Oxford, 1979), 84–85. Further west, the ruling patriciates often became so attached to the princely regime that they lost their sense of organic connection with the lower orders in their own communities. The result was political passivity on the part of the "subject" population. For the case of Koblenz, see Etienne François, *Koblenz im 18. Jahrhundert: Zur Sozial- und Bevölkerungsstruktur einer deutschen Residenzstadt* (Göttingen, 1982), 195–98.

before, were increasingly divided between those who were being coopted into the princes' service and those whose incomes came primarily from feudal dues, largely paid in kind, whose market value declined sharply after the 1630s.[31] The financial weakness of the estates made it difficult for them to make loans to the princes – one of the means by which the estates had previously been able to exert influence over the ruler. This function increasingly passed into the hands of the foreigners and court Jews with a corresponding loss of political leverage for the estates.[32]

In contrast, the political and financial position of the princes received powerful reinforcement throughout the last three quarters of the seventeenth century. The unprecedented military demands of the Thirty Years' War compelled the German states to increase their revenues, mostly through direct taxes on the peasantry, to levels undreamed of in the sixteenth century. Thanks to these additional resources, princes of the larger states for the first time had disposition over sizable military forces. Since the war ultimately resulted in the defeat of the Habsburgs and the failure of their attempt to rule directly over the Empire, the peace treaty of Westphalia (1648) sought to circumscribe Habsburg authority in Germany by granting sovereignty to the territorial princes. The political significance of this gain in legal status for the princes was enhanced by imperial legislation in 1654, which obliged the territorial estates to fulfill all taxes demanded by the prince to support fortresses and garrisons. It was also strengthened by the electoral agreement of 1658, which prohibited meetings by the estates not sanctioned by the ruler. And even though the coming of peace meant the reduction, or sometimes the dissolution, of the wartime armies, nominal levels of taxation were not significantly reduced in the larger territorial states, while deflation in those years made tax yields rise in real terms.[33]

When almost continuous warfare resumed in the 1670s, the princes had no difficulty in increasing taxes still further. The scope of the resulting permanent gain in state revenues is illustrated by

31 Schlögl, *Bauern, Krieg und Staat*, 363.

32 For the importance of this financial role played by the estates, see Oestreich, *Neostoicism and the Early Modern State*, 192.

33 A notable instance of rising taxation in even nominal terms in the years after 1648, besides Brandenburg-Prussia, was the Palatinate, where the state was faced with a heavy debt burden and continuing military commitments. See Volker Sellin, *Die Finanzpolitik Karl Ludwigs von der Pfalz: Staatswirtschaft im Wiederaufbau nach dem Dreissigjährigen Krieg* (Stuttgart, 1978), 207.

Bavaria, where the nominal rate of direct taxation on the peasantry in 1700 was three and a half times that levied on average during the decade 1611/20.[34] As the Empire was engaged in a protracted two-front war against Louis XIV's France to the west and the Ottoman Turks in the east, the estates could not contest the princes' claim that very high troop levels were required in such a time of national emergency. The size of the military forces that the princes could put into the field was further bolstered by the availability of West European subsidies, notably Dutch and English payments during the War of Spanish Succession (1701–13).

From an economic standpoint, the result of these trends was an extraordinarily rapid growth of the public sector at the expense of the rest of the economy. The state's control over a much larger share of society's wealth gave it, through its spending policies, the potential to shape to an unusual extent the pattern of social development during this period. Obviously, a major priority for many princes was the creation of a standing army, partly for security reasons, partly for the prestige and *gloire* it would bring to the prince's name.[35] Although military expenditure thereby lent weight to the prince's political pretensions, from the point of view of civil society the money spent on maintaining the army brought proportionately little benefit. To be sure, foreign subsidies covered some of these costs, some members of the native nobility found employment in the princely army, and in some cases the army's need for uniforms and other supplies stimulated select sectors of the local economy.

Typically, however, within the officer corps the majority of the regimental commanders were mercenary adventurers with no organic connection to their employer's territorial society. The potentially positive economic impact of the military establishment was limited, moreover, by the long-term absence from the territory of most of the troops owing to the almost non-stop character of the late seventeenth- and early eighteenth-century wars. While this absence for the most part spared the home front from the costs and social strains of hosting permanent garrisons, it also meant that most

34 Schlögl, *Bauern, Krieg und Staat*, 260–61. In Württemberg, tax rates in the late seventeenth century were four times what they were in 1618. Wolfgang von Hippel, "Bevölkerung und Wirtschaft im Zeitalter des Dreissigjährigen Krieges: Das Beispiel Württemberg," *Zeitschrift für historische Forschung*, 5 (1978): 444.

35 The cultural dimension to the pressure on the princes to acquire a standing army is emphasized by James Allen Vann. See Vann, *The Making of a State: Württemberg, 1593–1793* (Ithaca, 1984), 167.

of the military supplies procured by the commanders as well as the goods and services purchased by the common soldiers were provided by foreign enterprises. It is no wonder, then, that the estates so bitterly resented having to pay for such forces and that their recalcitrance on this issue was often the impetus behind a prince's decision to exclude the estates from his inner councils and govern in an "absolutist" manner.[36]

But not all or sometimes even most of the territorial prince's resources were spent on the military. In many cases a large proportion was also expended on the princely court. Magnificent palaces for the princes and stately residences for the court nobility, sumptuous clothes and decorations, elaborate ceremonies and lavish entertainments – all were intended to enhance a ruler's "representation" of himself and his dynasty. In a century even more status conscious than preceding ones, presiding over the most elegant court, with the highest ranking nobility in attendance, was the most tangible, visible way for a ruler to convey a sense of rank and authority.[37]

"Representation," while intended as a means of bolstering the prince's prestige within the aristocratic society of Europe, also had important social and economic impacts within the prince's own territory. For the court, far more than the military, offered opportunities for industrious and ambitious members of the local population. Although some luxury articles and individual artists were imported from abroad, the court provided employment for large numbers of skilled artisans, masons, architects, painters, actors, and musicians.[38] The nobility, of course, were attracted by the offices, officerships, and pensions that a ruler bestowed on his courtiers, as well as by the glamor associated with participation in the cult of the prince's person. By residing more or less permanently at court, the most influential families of the territory became "reeducated" to a

[36] For an account of such a confrontation in Württemberg in 1698–99, see *ibid.*, 164–70. F. L. Carsten makes the point, however, that standing armies and reasonably strong estate institutions could coexist. Carsten, *Princes and Parliaments in Germany: From the Fifteenth to the Eighteenth Century* (Oxford, 1959), 438.

[37] On the relationship between theatricality and display, on the one hand, and princely power, on the other, see James Van Horn Melton, "From Image to Word: Cultural Reform and the Rise of Literate Culture in Eighteenth-Century Austria," *Journal of Modern History*, 58 (1986): 98.

[38] For a discussion of the economic impact of the court on a *Residenzstadt*, see Edith Ennen, "Mitteleuropäische Städte im 17. und 18. Jahrhundert," in W. Rausch, ed., *Die Städte Mitteleuropas im 17. und 18. Jahrhundert* (Linz/Donau, 1981), 15f.

new ideal of nobility, which included both a highly cultivated and worldly sophistication and at least a formalistic sense of subordination to their benefactor.[39] Thus through the court a key section of the territorial nobility became economically dependent on the ruler and socially identified with the exclusivity of his regime.

In these ways, seventeenth-century German princes were able to use the greater resources at their disposal to present themselves to their peers as political and cultural potentates. Certainly the lavish style of the typical seventeenth-century court differed profoundly from its far more modest sixteenth-century predecessor.[40] Yet the substance of rulership in the modern sense, that is the capability of exerting direct control over the day-to-day workings of society, did not develop in that century at nearly the same pace as the growth in the rulers' tax receipts. The grassroots effectiveness of seventeenth-century German bureaucracies is an underexplored topic in the historical literature. It is nevertheless safe to say that the ability of some post-1648 states to project more power than their immediate forerunners was not based mainly on increased bureaucratic penetration of society but rather on intensified utilization, through the institution of the court, of the same techniques of governing through personal connections that had prevailed in the sixteenth century.[41]

An examination of late seventeenth-century economic policy in the territorial states confirms this view. Historians have traditionally regarded this period as constituting the beginning of an age of state intervention in the economy carried out in accordance with mercantilist theoretical principles. They identify the origins of this movement with the states' allegedly dynamic response to the catastrophic economic conditions created by the Thirty Years' War. They

[39] Jürgen von Kruedener, *Die Rolle des Hofes im Absolutismus* (Stuttgart, 1973), 76–80. I agree, however, with Briggs's conclusion that the "courtly rationality" emphasized by Kruedener and Norbert Elias had only a relatively superficial psychological impact on the nobles subject to it. The court culture's code of conduct required of them no "renunciation of hedonism in their general conduct" and only a "very limited" imposition of "superego controls." See Briggs, *Communities of Belief*, 408.

[40] Rudolf Vierhaus, "Höfe und höfische Gesellschaft in Deutschland im 17. und 18. Jahrhundert," in Ernst Hinrichs, ed., *Absolutismus* (Frankfurt/Main, 1986), 122–23.

[41] For strong statements regarding the weakness of seventeenth-century bureaucracies as pillars of state power, see Robisheaux, *Rural Society and the Search for Order*, 178–79, 232; Richard Dietrich, "Merkantilismus und Städtewesen in Kursachsen," in Volker Press, ed., *Städtewesen und Merkantilismus in Mitteleuropa* (Cologne and Vienna, 1983), 259; Rudolf Schlögl, *Bauern, Krieg und Staat*, 214. For a devastating analysis of the inadequacies of the Habsburg bureaucracy during this period, see Evans, *The Making of the Habsburg Monarchy*, 146–51.

further point to the founding of the German mercantilist school of thought, usually known as "cameralism," by J. J. Becher in the 1670s and 1680s. Becher's call for the establishment within the state bureaucracy of a separate "commercial college" charged with aggressively promoting trade and manufacturing in the Habsburg lands inspired bureaucrats throughout the Empire to attempt to establish such colleges in their own territories.[42] Becher's proposals to the Viennese court also embodied a new spirit that had appeared before 1700 in many German state bureaucracies. As Marc Raeff's comparative study of sixteenth-century and post-1648 police ordinances concludes, the late seventeenth-century legislation was based on a much more rationalistic and pragmatic approach to problem solving and assumed a much broader mandate for state-directed economic transformation than did the sixteenth-century ordinances.[43]

In practice, however, this new spirit was not to bear much fruit until well into the eighteenth century.[44] With respect to the efforts of German states to assist economic reconstruction after the Thirty Years' War, governments in southern, central, and western Germany indeed acted decisively in the immediate postwar period to prevent the nobility from buying out abandoned peasant holdings and thereby depriving the state of its tax base.[45] In protecting the peasantry from expropriation, the states were not, however, doing anything they had not already done many times in the course of the sixteenth century.[46] Beyond enforcing this long-standing policy and providing some peasants with building materials and short-term tax relief, the states did not have the resources or the personnel to

[42] Ingomar Bog, "Mercantilism in Germany," in D. C. Coleman, ed., *Revisions in Mercantilism* (London, 1969), 175–77.

[43] Raeff, *The Well-Ordered Police State*, 169–79.

[44] While the main reason for this was the lack of economic means and political will as described in this and subsequent paragraphs, it is also important to remember that late seventeenth-century economic thought was still dominated by traditionalistic ideas. In the words of Keith Tribe, "writing which addressed itself to the economic improvement of the state likewise displayed a dominating concern with 'proper household management' [i.e. successful reproduction of the existing social, moral, and economic pattern] rather than with wealth or accumulation for its own sake." Tribe, *Governing Economy: The Reformation of German Economic Discourse, 1750–1840* (Cambridge, 1988), 27.

[45] Kamen, "The Social and Economic Consequences of the Thirty Years' War," 56; Schlögl, *Bauern, Krieg und Staat*, 88f.

[46] Schlögl, *Bauern, Krieg und Staat*, 85. In Robisheaux's words, "these policies simply continued practices of domination dating back to the sixteenth century," Robisheaux, *Rural Society and the Search for Order*, 237.

implement a comprehensive, uniform, far-reaching agrarian program.[47]

Despite cameralist ambitions, moreover, the bureaucracies also faced formidable problems in stimulating trade and industrial development. In this area, the opposition of the guilds to almost any economic initiative was a difficult obstacle to overcome. Their prosperity having been destroyed in the course of the seventeenth century, the guilds responded to the weakness in consumer demand by refusing to update their antiquated techniques and using their political influence to minimize competition. In light of the protection given the guilds by imperial legislation and the guilds' role as tax collectors for the territorial state, state policy makers generally did not challenge the guilds' rights and in some cases even designed "mercantilist" legislation for the specific purpose of helping the guilds survive.[48] Prevented in this way from conducting a systematic restructuring of the urban economy, central bureaucracies sought to promote the development of non-traditional industries outside the guild system, especially those making luxury goods or products needed by the military. Foreign entrepreneurs were frequently recruited through privileges and concessions to run these businesses, which operated on the margins of the indigenous economy.[49]

Even these limited efforts, however, faced an uphill struggle in the late seventeenth century. In Catholic and most Lutheran states, the established churches refused to permit the settling of immigrants who did not adhere to the same confession as that of the territorial church.[50] And even if the right entrepreneur could be found, budgetary constraints often meant that these enterprises were undercapitalized; and the demands of the court and army frequently burdened them with excessive taxation. In short, most of these state-initiated ventures failed because of a willingness to allow short-term requirements for more state revenue to override the

[47] For a balanced assessment of the accomplishments and limitations of post-1648 state agrarian policy in Bavaria, see Schlögl, *Bauern, Krieg und Staat*, 90–96.

[48] Wilhelm Treue, "Wirtschafts- und Sozialgeschichte vom 16. bis zum 18. Jahrhundert," in Bruno Gebhardt, *Handbuch der deutschen Geschichte*, 8th edn, vol. II (Stuttgart, 1955), 380–82.

[49] Volker Press, "Merkantilismus und die Städte," in Press, ed., *Städtewesen und Merkantilismus in Mitteleuropa*, 8–9.

[50] For Bavaria, see Schlögl, *Bauern, Krieg und Staat*, 88; for Württemberg, where the estates, in alliance with the Lutheran church, prevented the government from admitting Huguenot refugees until 1699, see Wilhelm Söll, *Die staatliche Wirtschaftspolitik in Württemberg im 17. und 18. Jahrhundert* (Tübingen, 1934), 86.

investment needs of the local economy.[51] This "fiscalist" orientation, already present in the territorial administrations, was greatly strengthened during the period of protracted war (1672–1718).[52] Indicative of its impact on economic development was the fate of those "commercial colleges" established on Becher's Austrian model. Fiscalist opposition at princely courts led to the failure of all the colleges founded before 1700, including Becher's. Only after 1740 did the commercial colleges become numerous, long-lasting, and productively innovative.[53]

The inability, or reluctance, of territorial governments to abolish or restrict the powers of the guilds is a revealing example of the abiding strength of the corporate elements in German society during the early modern period. Despite much higher revenues and the imposing facade of court and standing army that those additional funds made possible, the princely regimes made little progress in dismantling the structure of privilege in their territories.[54] It is thus not surprising that in the so-called age of absolutism the territorial estates retained significant political power. In some of the larger polities, the estates were able to either resist absolutism completely (Mecklenburg) or regain their customary position after a period of absolutist rule (Württemberg). Even in the more typical cases in which the estates had lost ground compared to the sixteenth century, executive committees representing the estates played important advisory roles (Bavaria, Saxony, Hesse).[55]

In addition to their own strength, the territorial estates could count on outside help to defend the established order. Recent research has clearly identified a system of checks and balances

51 For specific examples, see Söll, *Die staatliche Wirtschaftspolitik*, 49–60, 77–81.

52 According to Jean Bérenger, the cameralist policies were "blocked by the wars of the end of the seventeenth century." See Bérenger, *Lexique historique de l'Europe danubienne, XVIe-XXe siècle* (Paris, 1976), 37.

53 Bog, "Mercantilism in Germany," 178–80.

54 It is possible that some of the princely regimes may have actually lost some of their control over local administration. For it has been recently demonstrated that in seventeenth-century Spain substantial growth in the financial resources of the central government and administrative decentralization were in fact quite compatible. See Helen Nader, *Liberty in Absolutist Spain: The Hapsburg Sale of Towns, 1516–1700* (Baltimore, 1990).

55 Carsten, *Princes and Parliaments*, 183–85, 233, 239–40, 414–15, 437. In some areas, the estates' position was bolstered still further by their success in attracting strong popular support when the prince converted to another form of Christianity. In Saxony, for example, when Friedrich August I embraced Catholicism in order to become king of Poland, the estates championed the religious cause of his Lutheran subjects and thereby turned the power of confessional sentiment against the prince. *Ibid.*, 244.

within the Holy Roman Empire, whereby neighboring princes, regional imperial organizations known as "circles," or the imperial courts would intervene on behalf of the rights of a *Landtag*, a territorial town, or even a peasant community.[56] Legally, these interventions were justified by the body of imperial law set forth in the Peace of Westphalia, which guaranteed the "constitution" of each territory. Invariably included in these territorial constitutions were historic agreements in which the princes had conceded specific privileges and immunities to their subjects; hence any attempt by a prince to do away with or infringe on such corporate rights usually succeeded in mobilizing the constitutional machinery of the Empire against him.[57]

Politically, this system of imperial protection was guaranteed and strongly supported by the Habsburg emperors. Prevented by the Peace of Westphalia from annexing territory in the Empire, the Habsburgs strove to use imperial institutions to prevent any territorial prince from becoming powerful enough to challenge their supremacy within the Empire. The Habsburgs therefore threw their weight behind the imperial circles, supported the independence of the imperial cities, helped imperial knights gain bishoprics in the Catholic church, and exercised considerable patronage through their court at Vienna.[58] The Habsburg position in the Empire was so strong that during the wars of 1672–1718 only a very few princes fought on the French side, while most sent contingents of troops to the Rhine or to the Turkish front in Hungary. What R. J. W. Evans calls the "limited hegemony" exercised by the Habsburgs over Germany during this period thus helped to limit the state-building options of the territorial princes, though it did compensate them

56 The classic description of this system is Mack Walker's. See Walker, *German Home Towns: Community, State, and General Estate, 1648–1871* (Ithaca, 1971), 11–33. On the ability of peasant communities to use the imperial judiciary to protect their rights, see Winfried Schulze, "Peasant Resistance in Sixteenth- and Seventeenth-Century Germany in a European Context," in Kaspar von Greyerz, ed., *Religion, Politics and Social Protest: Three Studies on Early Modern Germany* (London, 1984), 61–88.

57 Carol M. Rose, "Empire and Territories at the End of the Old Reich," in James A. Vann and Steven Rowan, eds., *The Old Reich: Essays on German Political Institutions, 1495–1806* (Brussels, 1974), 66–68; James A. Vann, "New Directions for Study of the Old *Reich*," *Journal of Modern History*, 58, suppl. (December 1986): 12–13.

58 On the role of the imperial knights, see Lawrence G. Duggan, "The Church as an Institution of the Reich," in Vann and Rowan eds., *The Old Reich*, 159–60; on the political role of the Habsburg court, see Volker Press, "The Habsburg Court as Center of the Imperial Government," *Journal of Modern History*, 58, suppl. (December 1986): 40–41.

with prospects for gaining honor and wealth in the emperor's service.[59]

In considering, then, the reigns of the two Hohenzollerns, the Great Elector and Frederick III(I), which extended from 1640 to 1713, it will be well to remember the basic character of the "typical" princely state in the Holy Roman Empire at that time. In essence, late seventeenth-century regimes exploited the administrative and legal system bequeathed by their sixteenth-century predecessors to claim a much larger share of society's resources. From the point of view of the Empire as a whole, this system generated the military power that ultimately stopped Louis XIV at the Rhine and ended for all time the Turkish threat to Central Europe. At the territorial level, significant internal restructuring of society was not an immediate consequence of the build-up of state power in the course of the seventeenth century. This was not simply the result of state funds' being spent mainly on far-away armies and on courts in whose activities only a select few could participate. On the basis of some recent research, one can also argue that the demographic losses of the Thirty Years' War and the resulting rise in real wages slowed down the decomposition of traditional society and eased the pressure on the territorial states to provide additional services to buttress, or supersede, long-standing corporate institutions.[60] Most of German society's constructive energy in the postwar period was directed, not at "modernizing" an economy and social system that had become "backward" by West European standards, but at consolidating or "reproducing" a hierarchical social pattern that had become more or less well formed by the early seventeenth century and which had been threatened with disintegration by the destructive effects of the Thirty Years' War.[61]

This struggle to achieve an internal "restoration" was complicated and to a considerable degree frustrated by the financial demands of near continuous warfare on every frontier of the Holy Roman Empire. Not the least of the difficulties was that the high level of public spending continually drained capital and purchasing

[59] Evans, *The Making of the Habsburg Monarchy*, 275–308.

[60] Schlögl, *Bauern, Krieg und Staat*, 362.

[61] See, for example, Robisheaux, *Rural Society and the Search for Order*, 228–43.

power from the private sector and was therefore an important factor in delaying recovery from the Thirty Years' War.[62] The same factor also underlay much of the postwar conflict between princes and their estates, for the taxes extracted from the peasantry by the territorial governments siphoned off revenue which ultimately would have gone to support the landowning nobility. Consequently, in the ranks of the aristocracy, the seventeenth century was a time not of continuity but of turnover, with the impoverishment of many older families and the rise of military commanders and others who succeeded in gaining favor at the princely courts.[63]

Yet the deeply conservative aspirations of Central European society during this period contributed heavily to the perpetuation of many of the essential features of the pre-1618 state–society relationship. The estates continued to possess a near monopoly on the actual conduct of local administration. Society remained divided into legally distinct, semi-autonomous institutional groupings; and unless a regime was unusually desperate for money, it tended to adopt a fairly passive attitude toward the dearly held traditional rights of the corporate entities in its territory. The princely governments did serve as mechanisms for coordinating and adjudicating the interests of the various categories of their subjects; but other, more traditional functions of the central authorities were at least as significant in providing a sense of unity for the territory as a whole.

Thus the person of the prince continued to be regarded as a quasi-sacred, patriarchal figure – a status only enhanced, or rather staged more formally, by the development of courtly institutions and culture. In like manner, common participation in the rites of the territorial church was still an important unifying force – hence the continuing importance of confessionalism even after the ending of the Religious Wars.[64] To be sure, the concentration of power achieved by the princes of the larger territories constituted a necessary prerequisite for the emergence of bureaucratic absolutism in the following century. But, as the case of Brandenburg-Prussia will

[62] According to a classic essay by Niels Steensgaard, a "crisis of distribution" resulting from this excessive public spending was an important, if not the key, factor in the persistently depressed economic conditions in many parts of Europe during the seventeenth century. See Niels Steensgaard, "The Seventeenth-Century Crisis," in Geoffrey Parker and Lesley M. Smith, eds., *The General Crisis of the Seventeenth Century* (London, 1978), 37–42.

[63] For the turnover in the top ranks of the nobility in the Habsburg lands in the early to mid-seventeenth century, see Evans, *The Making of the Habsburg Monarchy*, 93–94.

[64] Melton, "From Image to Word," 98.

illustrate, the coming of this more modern state form was not simply a continuation of the type of state that dominated the scene in seventeenth-century Germany.[65]

[65] Because of its lack of penetration into society, in practice the seventeenth-century German territorial state belongs in the category of a "traditional" as opposed to a "modern" state, as the latter even in its "democratic" forms is able to intervene in almost every conceivable aspect of everyday life. For an important discussion of the characteristics of the "traditional state," see Anthony Giddens, *The Nation-State and Violence: Volume Two of a Contemporary Critique of Historical Materialism* (Berkeley and Los Angeles, 1987), 35–82.

CHAPTER 2

Reformed confessionalism and the reign of the Great Elector

The state-building accomplishments of the sixteenth-century Hohenzollern electors lagged behind those of their counterparts in most of the rest of the Empire. During the era before the Thirty Years' War, none of the rulers of the Mark Brandenburg was able to counteract socioeconomic trends that in northeastern Germany and Poland worked against political centralization and thereby set this region apart from central, western, and southern Germany. The causal forces behind this regional differentiation are still controversial, but the process had clearly begun by the late fifteenth century with the weakening of the economic and political position of the East Elbian towns *vis-à-vis* the landed nobility.[1] This deterioration was in marked contrast to the situation in the German lands west of the Elbe River, where the cities and towns retained much, if not all, of their medieval autonomy until at least the 1590s and were therefore well placed to benefit from the economic expansion of the sixteenth century.

In Brandenburg, Mecklenburg, Pomerania, Poland, and ducal Prussia, however, this same period of time was characterized by the achievement of an almost total domination of society by the landed nobility. Profiting from rising grain prices and increasing opportunities for raw material exports to Western Europe, the Brandenburg Junkers, like other landowning elites in the Baltic area, were able to use their economic strength to compel the financially strapped central government to do their bidding. Thus by the mid-sixteenth century the nobility in Brandenburg had secured a monopoly on all important princely offices – middle-class jurists had little scope to operate here! – and had gained complete control over the collection

[1] For a detailed account of the decline of the Baltic towns in the fifteenth century, see F. L. Carsten, *The Origins of Prussia* (Oxford, 1954), 117–35.

of taxes and tolls.[2] Reflecting the wishes of the nobles, the electoral regime pursued a non-aggressive, insular foreign policy and adopted a very traditionalistic, highly ritualistic form of Lutheranism.[3] Even the apparent exception to this caution and passivity, the ambitious marriage policy, was designed, according to Hintze, "primarily" to increase the dynasty's income and certainly not as part of a grand strategy to build a powerful state out of the newly acquired lands.[4]

Naturally, the Junkers also used their strong political position to advance their economic interests. In West Elbian Germany the nobility's "rent offensive" in the sixteenth century largely failed on account of strong peasant resistance supported by the towns and territorial princes. In Brandenburg, not only were the electors financially dependent on the nobility, but they themselves were also the largest landowner in the Mark, thanks to the incorporation into the electoral domain of large amounts of church land confiscated during the Reformation.[5] The united front presented by the Junkers and the Brandenburg electors, combined with the impotence of the towns, enabled the nobles to impose heavy labor services on the peasantry and thereby increase substantially the size of the marketable surplus from their estates.[6] The nobility also benefited from electoral legislation that drastically undermined the economic viability of the towns. Most significant in this respect were the tax exemptions bestowed on Junker beer breweries and the permission granted landowners to bypass the local towns and sell their export items directly to foreign merchants, often without having to pay any duty at all.[7]

The long period of peace enjoyed by the Baltic region during the sixteenth century allowed the Junkers to pursue their entrepreneurial

2 *Ibid.*, 166–67. See also Peter-Michael Hahn, "Landesstaat und Ständetum im Kurfürstentum Brandenburg während des 16. und 17. Jahrhunderts," in Baumgart, ed., *Ständetum und Staatsbildung*, 62–63.

3 The retention in Brandenburg's Lutheranism of much of the traditional Catholic ceremonial is referred to in Bodo Nischan, "The Schools of Brandenburg and the 'Second Reformation': Centers of Calvinist Learning and Propaganda," in Robert V. Schnucker, ed., *Calviniana: Ideas and Influence of Jean Calvin* (Kirksville, Mo., 1988), 216.

4 Otto Hintze, "Calvinism and Raison d'Etat in Early Seventeenth-Century Brandenburg," in *The Historical Essays of Otto Hintze*, ed. Felix Gilbert (New York, 1975), 103.

5 Carsten, *The Origins of Prussia*, 166.

6 For an analysis emphasizing the limits to the Junkers' exploitation of their serfs in the manorial system that had emerged by the late sixteenth century, see William W. Hagen, "Working for the Junker: The Standard of Living of Manorial Laborers in Brandenburg, 1584–1810," *Journal of Modern History*, 58 (1986): 145–52.

7 Carsten, *The Origins of Prussia*, 170–72.

activities undisturbed. The early seventeenth century, however, brought a series of catastrophes to Brandenburg and a weakening of the Junkers' grip on society. The first signs of trouble appeared as early as 1600, when inflation had raised the price of imports so much that profits from the grain trade began to decline. Despite high prices for grain exports, the Junkers got ever more deeply into debt. A speculative boom in estates pushed the price of land to great heights but stimulated even more borrowing. The inflationary crisis and credit crunch of 1619–23 triggered a crash in land values and a large number of bankruptcies.[8]

And worse was to come. The commercial depression of the 1620s reduced Western Europe's demand for grain. When imperial troops occupied the Baltic coast in the mid-1620s, they further disrupted the grain trade by imposing embargoes on exports to the United Provinces. After the Swedes drove out the Habsburg forces, they in turn imposed, between 1629 and 1635, heavy tolls on exports from the East Prussian and Polish coasts. Twenty percent of Sweden's war costs were covered by these "Prussian" licenses.[9] From 1635 until 1648, Brandenburg had the dubious honor of serving as the major base of operations for the Swedish forces in Germany. The Mark consequently suffered more than its share of physical devastation, looting, depopulation, and wartime taxation. The final blow was the steep fall of grain prices in the 1640s. By the time the war was over, the population of the Mark had decreased by 50 percent, with some areas suffering as much as a 90 percent decline. Most of the provincial towns were in ruins, and a large percentage of the arable land lay abandoned.[10] In addition to these material losses, one must also take into account the disruptive effects of the war on the Mark's schools and churches, which resulted in a general, often dramatic decline in the educational and moral level of the population, including that of the elite groups of society.[11]

8 Rosenberg, "The Rise of the Junkers in Brandenburg-Prussia," 237–38. For an up-to-date analysis which downplays the extent of the crisis before 1618 but still emphasizes Junker indebtedness, see Hagen, "Seventeenth-Century Crisis in Brandenburg," 307–14.

9 Immanuel Wallerstein, *The Modern World System II* (New York, 1980), 207–08; Rosenberg, "The Rise of the Junkers in Brandenburg–Prussia," 239.

10 Schmoller, "Das Städtewesen unter Friedrich Wilhelm I.," 244–49; Selma Stern, *Der preussische Staat und die Juden*, vol. 1, pt. 1 (Tübingen, 1962), 34; Hagen, "Seventeenth-Century Crisis in Brandenburg," 314–15.

11 Friedrich Wienecke, "Die Begründung der evangelischen Volksschule in der Kurmark und ihre Entwicklung bis zum Tode Friedrichs I., 1540–1713," *Zeitschrift für die Geschichte der Erziehung und des Unterrichts*, 3, Heft 1 (1913): 42; Hugo Landwehr, "Die kirchlichen

Prospects for postwar recovery were not good. The depression in the grain market was to last until the very end of the century due to slack demand throughout Europe and the postwar emergence of England as a major grain exporter. The impact of these unfavorable conditions in the international markets was intensified by much higher production costs resulting from the manifold effects of the war on the estate-owner's operations. Not only did devastated lands need to be rebuilt, animal herds replenished, and villages resettled, but the social preeminence of the Junkers also had to be reestablished after a breakdown during the war of the system of social control by which the nobility had previously kept their peasants in a state of subjugation.[12]

The nobles' natural inclination was to reassert their authority through coercive measures sanctioned by state legislation from the prewar era. Working against this tendency, though, was the extreme shortage of labor, which not only raised the rates Junkers had to pay their wage laborers but also compelled them to offer favorable terms to peasants in order to induce the latter to reoccupy and reconstruct the abandoned farmland. The landowners' bargaining position *vis-à-vis* the peasantry was further weakened by competition from the state, whose domains were similarly in need of peasant labor.[13] In this situation, the nobility was more dependent on the cooperation of the electoral regime than at any time since the establishment of its political and economic ascendancy.

In seeking to exploit this opportunity to reverse the long-term weakness of the Hohenzollern state, the elector Frederick William, the Great Elector (1620–88, reigned 1640–88), possessed at least one great advantage: a larger amount of land than any German prince except the emperor. Even though his predecessors may not have succeeded in increasing electoral power within their lands, their marriage diplomacy greatly increased the number of lands held by the Hohenzollern dynasty. In addition to the Mark Brandenburg, Frederick William inherited in 1640 the Duchy of Prussia (later called East Prussia), the Duchy of Cleve–Mark on the lower Rhine, the small territories of Minden and Ravensberg in north-central Germany, and a strong claim to the Duchy of Pomerania. As a result

Zustände der Mark unter dem Grossen Kurfürst," *Forschungen zur brandenburgischen und preussischen Geschichte*, 1 (1888): 184–87.

12 Hagen, "Seventeenth-Century Crisis in Brandenburg," 315.

13 *Ibid.*, 315–18.

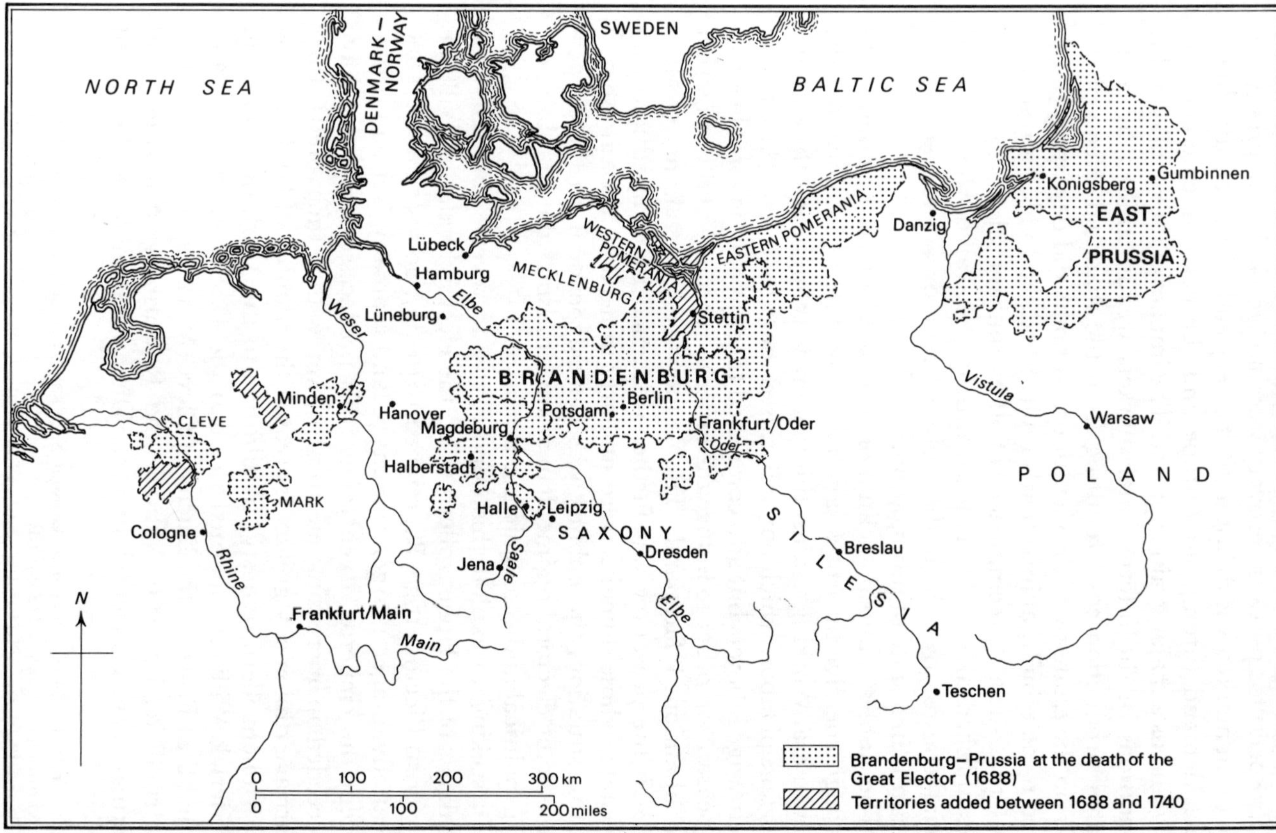
NORTH SEA
DENMARK – NORWAY
SWEDEN
BALTIC SEA
Lübeck
Hamburg
MECKLENBURG
WESTERN POMERANIA
EASTERN POMERANIA
Danzig
Königsberg
Gumbinnen
EAST PRUSSIA
Elbe
Weser
Lüneburg
Stettin
BRANDENBURG
Minden
Hanover
Berlin
Potsdam
Frankfurt/Oder
Oder
CLEVE
Magdeburg
Halberstadt
MARK
Halle
Leipzig
SAXONY
Cologne
Jena
Saale
Dresden
Breslau
SILESIA
Vistula
Warsaw
POLAND
Rhine
N
Frankfurt/Main
Main
Elbe
Teschen
0 100 200 300 km
0 100 200 miles
Brandenburg–Prussia at the death of the Great Elector (1688)
Territories added between 1688 and 1740

Map 1

of the Peace of Westphalia, however, Pomerania was partitioned, with the victorious Swedes receiving the western part of Pomerania, including the mouth of the Oder River and the port of Stettin. Frederick William had to content himself with sparsely populated eastern Pomerania. As compensation for the loss of western Pomerania, the Great Elector received the former bishoprics of Magdeburg and Halberstadt, though these territories did not formally become his until 1680.

The crucial test for Frederick William, in the years following the Peace of Westphalia, was whether he would succeed in asserting his authority over these territories. Not only were they scattered over a seven hundred mile stretch from the Rhine to the Lithuanian districts of East Prussia, but the territories at the two extremes had closer ties to foreign powers than to Berlin. Most of Cleve-Mark had been occupied by the Dutch during the Thirty Years' War, and strong economic and cultural links between the two neighbors had developed.[14] East Prussia, outside the Holy Roman Empire, was a fief of the King of Poland, to whom Frederick William had to pay homage as a vassal. In the event of an attempt by Frederick William to restrict the rights of the East Prussian estates, the estates could appeal over the head of their duke Frederick William to the King of Poland, who would almost certainly rule in favor of their cause.[15]

Even within Frederick William's home territory, the Mark Brandenburg, his power was not very great. Although he did not have to contend with such powerful vassals as the Polish high nobility, who had their own private armies and miniature courts,[16] the Great Elector was in basically the same political position as the King of Poland, who also ruled over a large, sparsely populated territory dominated by a fiercely independent landed aristocracy. Despite the relative disarray of the Junkers in the immediate postwar period, Frederick William, unlike the princes west of the Elbe, did not have the advantage of inheriting a comparatively well-developed, centralized administrative system from his sixteenth-century predecessors. If he was to gain a position of dominance over the estates in his widely scattered territories, he needed to act quickly to secure a

[14] Ferdinand Schevill, *The Great Elector* (Chicago, 1947), 99.

[15] *Ibid.*, 97.

[16] This point is heavily emphasized in Marxist historiography in order to account for the different historical paths taken by Brandenburg-Prussia and Poland. See for example, Wallerstein, *The Modern World System II*, 227.

much higher level of revenue from his impoverished lands and use it to build up from scratch an army and bureaucracy strong enough to enable him to impose his will on society. Failure to develop such an instrument of princely power would have ensured that at best the Junker-dominated estates would have reestablished their control over the electoral government in the manner of, say, Mecklenburg. At worst, it could have led to a virtual disintegration or partition of the state comparable to that which actually occurred in eighteenth-century Poland.

Fortunately for Frederick William, he was able to draw on ideas, people, and resources from outside East Elbia to assist him in his state-building task. The conduit that connected the elector to the wider world was the adherence of his house to the Calvinist faith, which become official in 1613 with the public conversion of Frederick William's grandfather, John Sigismund (1608–19).[17] The Hohenzollern dynasty's switch from Lutheranism to the Reformed confession was part of a larger movement in the late sixteenth and early seventeenth centuries in which a number of Lutheran princes throughout Germany converted to Calvinism – a phenomenon historians now refer to as the "Second Reformation."[18]

In that time and place, a prince's decision to join the Calvinist cause stemmed from dissatisfaction with Lutheranism's tendency to compromise – theologically with Catholicism, and politically with the emperor and the territorial estates. Thus the Calvinist princes on the eve of the Thirty Years' War took the initiative in allying with the Dutch Republic to counter the spread within the Empire of a reinvigorated Catholicism and the Habsburg power allied to it. In order to maximize their strength for the coming showdown with Catholicism, the Reformed regimes domestically tended to pursue the goal of administrative centralization more strenuously than their Lutheran or Catholic counterparts. Typical features of the state apparatuses created by the Reformed princes were the more complete subordination of the church to the state and a more intensive

[17] Whether the motivations behind this conversion were spiritual or political has long been debated. For a summary of the religious beliefs of John Sigismund, see Wolfgang Gericke, ed., *Glaubenszeugnisse und Konfessionspolitik der brandenburgischen Herrscher bis zur Preussischen Union, 1540 bis 1815* (Bielefeld, 1977), 22–29. I tend to agree with Hintze's conclusion that, while John Sigismund was long inclined to convert to the Reformed faith, the timing of the conversion was politically determined. Hintze, "Calvinism and Raison d'Etat," 105.

[18] For a comprehensive recent discussion, see Schilling, ed., *Die reformierte Konfessionalisierung, passim.*

use of the confessional church to impose a stricter moral discipline on the population at large.[19]

In terms of this standard, to be sure, the Second Reformation in Brandenburg did not measure up very well. By 1615 the combined resistance of the Lutheran church and the Brandenburg estates compelled John Sigismund to grant official toleration to Lutheranism, thereby giving up any hopes he may have had of converting the bulk of the population to Calvinism.[20] Nor, except during the temporary, wartime dictatorship of the minister Count Schwartzenberg, were John Sigismund (1608–19) and his successor George William (1619–40) able to wrest much power from the hands of the estates. But important connections, confessional and dynastic, between the Hohenzollern house and the international Reformed network did develop during this period. Thus the University of Frankfurt/Oder, at that time the only university in Brandenburg, became Reformed in the 1610s with the appointment of three Reformed theologians, all of whom were educated or had taught at Calvinist centers of learning in western Germany, France, England, or the Dutch Republic.[21] The forging of ties with Western Europe also motivated the marriage policy of the Hohenzollerns. George William's bride was a princess from the Palatinate, the leading Reformed territory in the Empire; and in 1631 John Sigismund's much younger half-sister married the heir to the Palatinate electorate.

Not surprisingly, therefore, Frederick William, the son of George William, was raised with the expectation that he would assume an important leadership role in the European-wide Calvinist move-

19 Schilling, "Die 'Zweite Reformation' als Kategorie der Geschichtswissenschaft," in *ibid.*, 428–32. With respect to church–state relations in the tradition of Continental Calvinism, Klaus Deppermann points out that a strong tendency of the Reformed church toward acceptance of, and active collaboration with, an absolutist state extended beyond the German Calvinists to include the French Huguenots, who were strongly royalist, especially after the accession of Henry IV and the promulgation of the Edict of Nantes. Deppermann, "Die Kirchenpolitik des Grossen Kurfürsten," *Pietismus und Neuzeit*, 6 (1980): 100.

20 Nischan, "The Schools of Brandenburg and the 'Second Reformation,'" 227.

21 *Ibid.*, 224. For an essay suggesting that the Reformed religion had a far greater impact on seventeenth-century (and subsequent) German culture than has hitherto been recognized, see Klaus Garber, "Zentraleuropäischer Calvinismus und deutsche 'Barock'-Literatur: Zu den konfessionspolitischen Ursprüngen der deutschen Nationalliteratur," in Schilling, ed., *Die reformierte Konfessionalisierung*, 317–48. The long-standing neglect by historians of Calvinism's influence in Germany is yet another consequence of the view, so strongly asserted by Ernst Troeltsch and others, that Germany's "special path" was the result of a supposedly radical divergence between the Calvinism of the West and the Lutheranism of the German lands. See above, p. 8.

ment. His most crucial formative experiences occurred during his teens, which he spent mainly in the Dutch Republic. From 1634 to 1638 Frederick William was enrolled at the University of Leiden, then the foremost university in Europe.[22] During his stay in the Low Countries, the young Hohenzollern prince also frequented the military camp of Prince Maurice of Orange, whose innovations in the organization and drilling of troops played an important role in the development of large standing armies throughout Europe over the next one hundred years.[23] While in the Netherlands, Frederick William was a member of the entourage of his uncle, Frederick V, Elector of the Palatinate, who had led the anti-Habsburg forces in Bohemia in 1618 and who had been in exile since 1620. Finally, the heir to the Brandenburg electorate further solidified his family's ties to the international Reformed movement by marrying Louise Henrietta, daughter of the Prince of Orange and granddaughter of William the Silent.

Frederick William emerged from these years a committed Calvinist, regarding the Reformed faith as "alone grounded on the true Word of God."[24] Convinced that he was one of a small group of the "elect," chosen by God to be saved, Frederick William possessed a personal faith that led him to strive to demonstrate the reality of his election to others through a life dedicated to the achievement of practical goals.[25] Since Frederick William's vocation was to be a Reformed prince in an age of religious war, his strong sense of mission realized itself through his adoption of the aggressive diplomatic and state-building policies characteristic of Second Reformation princes. The same motivation also led him to promote vigorously the expansion of the Reformed church within Brandenburg-Prussia; for since the prince believed that the eternal welfare of his people was entrusted to him, it was only natural for him to feel that the Calvinist faith "must be spread and nurtured in all our lands."[26]

22 Heinz Schneppen, *Niederländische Universitäten und deutsches Geistesleben von der Gründung der Universität Leiden bis ins späte 18. Jahrhundert* (Münster, 1960), 66–67.

23 Schevill, *The Great Elector*, 82.

24 "'Politisches Testament' des Grossen Kurfürsten," in Gericke, ed., *Glaubenszeugnisse und Konfessionspolitik*, 176.

25 Gericke, ed., *Glaubenszeugnisse und Konfessionspolitik*, 37–39; Jürgen Regge, *Kabinettsjustiz in Brandenburg-Preussen: Eine Studie zur Geschichte des landesherrlichen Bestätigungsrechts in der Strafrechtspflege des 17. und 18. Jahrhunderts* (Berlin and Munich, 1977), 46.

26 "'Politisches Testament' des Grossen Kurfürsten," in Gericke, ed., *Glaubenszeugnisse und Konfessionspolitik*, 176.

The first step that the new elector needed to take in expanding the size and influence of the Reformed church in his territories was that of broadening its institutional scope. Even though his grandfather's conversion took place in 1613, during the twenty-seven-year period that ended with Frederick William's ascension to the electoral dignity in 1640, the only institutions in all Brandenburg-Prussia that had become Calvinist were the court, the Berlin cathedral, and the University of Frankfurt/Oder.[27] The rest of the country, except for the Calvinist portion of the population of Cleve-Mark, had remained solidly Lutheran. The Great Elector sought to build up the institution of the Calvinist church in his lands primarily by distributing throughout his territories Calvinist clerics formally known as "court preachers" (*Hofprediger*). These functionaries had much more far-reaching duties than their titles would seem to suggest. They staffed local parishes of the Calvinist church, which were founded in Berlin and nineteen other towns in Brandenburg-Prussia.[28] They also trained the teachers of Calvinist schools and carried out periodic inspections of these institutions, whose purpose was not only to prevent immigrants' children from being assimilated into the rest of the population but also to provide elementary training for prospective state bureaucrats.[29]

Besides strengthening the state-sponsored Reformed church institutionally, Frederick William worked hard to increase the size of the Reformed population in his lands, promoting by every possible means the immigration of Calvinist refugees into Brandenburg-Prussia. The inducements he offered included partial self-government and a separate judicial system for Reformed communities, as well as tax relief and other economic privileges.[30] In the first decades of the Great Elector's reign, immigrants consisted mostly of wealthy, well-educated, or high-ranking individuals, who came from countries as far apart as Scotland and Silesia.[31] They came to serve under

27 Otto Hintze, "Die Epochen des evangelischen Kirchenregiments in Preussen," in Hintze, *Regierung und Verwaltung; Gesammelte Abhandlungen zur Staats-, Rechts- und Sozialgeschichte Preussens*, ed. Gerhard Oestreich (Göttingen, 1976), 72.

28 Rudolf von Thadden, *Die brandenburgisch-preussischen Hofprediger im 17. und 18. Jahrhundert: Ein Beitrag zur Geschichte der absolutistischen Staatsgesellschaft in Brandenburg-Preussen* (Berlin, 1959), 16.

29 *Ibid.*, 44–53.

30 Martin Preetz, "Die deutschen Hugenottenkolonien: Ein Experiment des Merkantilismus" (Phil. Diss., U. Jena, 1930), 12.

31 Ernst Opgenoorth, *"Ausländer" in Brandenburg-Preussen als leitende Beamte und Offiziere, 1604–1871* (Würzburg, 1967); Thadden, *Die brandenburgisch-preussischen Hofprediger*, 79–83.

Frederick William for reasons ranging from shared ideological commitment to sheer adventurism.

Later, after 1672, as the resumption of almost continuous warfare on the continent led to increased harassment of entire Protestant communities by Catholic governments, Brandenburg-Prussia received substantial numbers of refugees from France, the Palatinate, the upper Rhine region, and the Habsburg lands – a flow that reached its high point in the 1680s and 1690s. Most significantly, as a result of Louis XIV's persecutions, twenty thousand Huguenots made their way to Brandenburg-Prussia.[32] Six thousand of them settled in Berlin, so that in 1690 every third Berliner was said to speak French.[33] To help fill his underpopulated, war-damaged lands, the Great Elector took in several thousand non-Calvinist refugees as well, including Waldensians from southern France and Bohemian Brethren from the Czech lands.

The vital importance of these newcomers is evident from an examination of the new bureaucratic elite in Brandenburg-Prussia that had already begun to take shape in the 1650s. To be sure, Frederick William tried to reduce his dependence on foreign recruits by nurturing a home-grown Calvinist elite. In 1654 he founded the Reformed University of Duisburg in order to train lawyers and bureaucrats for service in the Brandenburg-Prussian state. But Frederick William's efforts to produce large numbers of domestically trained civil servants foundered on the unending financial difficulties of the University of Duisburg and the inability of the University of Frankfurt/Oder to recover from the almost total devastation of Frankfurt during the Thirty Years' War.[34] As a result, jurists needed by the growing bureaucracy were usually of foreign origin.

The connecting bonds among the bureaucratic elite were the Reformed religion, personal loyalty to the elector, and absence of ties to the Lutheran estates. As one would expect, most of the rank and file bureaucrats were from the middle classes, while at the higher levels of the bureaucracy, the percentage of aristocrats increased sharply, though commoners were by no means excluded. The Great Elector, in fact, was served by a series of non-noble

32 Albrecht Prüfer, "Französische Kirche zu Berlin, 1672–1966," *Der deutsche Hugenott*, 30 (1966): 34–35.

33 Eduard Wechssler, "Preussengeist und calvinisch-stoicische Erziehung," *Zeitschrift für Geschichte der Erziehung und des Unterrichts*, 23 (1933): 223.

34 Opgenoorth, *"Ausländer" in Brandenburg-Preussen*, 20.

confidants – Friedrich Jena, Franz Meinders, and Paul Fuchs.[35] Nevertheless, Frederick William by inclination preferred the service of nobles, and his parvenu regime needed the prestige of titled officeholders. In the early decades of his reign, Frederick William dispatched high-ranking nobles of foreign origin to East Prussia and Cleve-Mark to act as governors (*Statthalter*) in these two provinces where his authority was most tenuous. The Great Elector also recruited princes of small German Calvinist states, bringing into his service Count Waldeck and Prince Johann Georg von Anhalt-Dessau.[36] The membership of the highest central body of the new bureaucracy, the Privy Council, established in 1651, was representative of the heterogeneous character of the new elite: most of the Council's leading members were foreigners, roughly three-quarters of the membership belonged to the nobility, and nearly all at first were Calvinists.[37]

Foreigners, or men trained in foreign lands, were important also in the officer corps of Frederick William's new standing army. Throughout the seventeenth century, the key figures in European armies were the colonels or regimental commanders, i.e. military entrepreneurs who sold their services to the warlord granting the most lucrative concessions. As the nobility of Brandenburg-Prussia in most cases did not have enough capital to recruit and provision regiments,[38] the Great Elector, whose own financial resources were at first quite modest, was forced to pick up regimental commanders wherever he could get them. A few colonels joined his army because of religious convictions. Others joined because they had been released by the Swedish or Habsburg armies in the course of postwar demobilizations.[39] And younger sons of the not so prosperous nobility of Brandenburg and eastern Pomerania were wont to seek their fortunes in military service. Many of them learned the military trade in foreign armies, acquired some capital along the way, and then returned to serve as colonels in the Brandenburg army. Native

35 Rosenberg, *Bureaucracy, Aristocracy, and Autocracy*, 67.

36 Opgenoorth, *"Ausländer" in Brandenburg-Preussen*, 28–38.

37 Martin Lackner, *Die Kirchenpolitik des Grossen Kurfürsten* (Witten, 1973), 305; Rosenberg, *Bureaucracy, Aristocracy, and Autocracy*, 66.

38 Friedrich von Schrötter, "Das preussische Offizierskorps unter dem ersten Könige von Preussen," *Forschungen zur brandenburgischen und preussischen Geschichte*, 27 (1914): 97.

39 Opgenoorth, *"Ausländer" in Brandenburg-Preussen*, 20. Among those who joined the Great Elector's army after Sweden's demobilization of 1661 was Landgraf Friedrich II von Hessen-Homburg, whose role in the battle of Fehrbellin (1675) inspired Kleist's drama "Prinz Friedrich von Homburg."

commoners, many of them educated outside of Brandenburg-Prussia, also became officers, especially in the engineering and artillery corps. The quality of the Brandenburg army received a tremendous boost with the arrival of the Huguenot refugees, many of whom had been high-ranking officers or highly trained military engineers and technicians in the French army. In all, some 2,300 Huguenots entered the Brandenburg-Prussian army, and in 1688 the 328 Huguenot officers constituted 31 percent of the army's officer corps.[40]

Immigrants also played a major role in Frederick William's plans for economic development. Perhaps to an even greater extent than in other parts of Germany after the Thirty Years' War, the East Elbian core of the Hohenzollern princedom suffered not only from a quantitative shortage of labor but also from such qualitative deficiencies as entrepreneurial spirit and technical skill.[41] Jews had been permitted to enter Brandenburg-Prussia since 1650, but large numbers arrived only after an electoral edict of 1671 granted extensive legal protection. Exact statistics are lacking, but the evidence assembled by Selma Stern suggests that thousands of Jews from Poland and the Habsburg lands took advantage of the edict's liberal provisions and migrated to the Hohenzollern territories.[42] While the Jewish immigrants settled down as traders, many of the Gentile immigrants, especially the Huguenots, established themselves as practitioners of specialized crafts, many of them new to the Mark Brandenburg. Foreigners were also recruited for entrepreneurial ventures as native merchants in the coastal cities of eastern Pomerania and East Prussia refused to participate in the Great Elector's schemes for acquiring colonies and pursuing overseas trade. The Hollander Benjamin Raule was by far the most important of these adventurers.[43]

But all Frederick William's efforts to recruit a loyal and competent elite would have been in vain had he not succeeded in raising the tax revenues needed to settle immigrants, pay the bureaucracy, maintain the army, and subsidize the entrepreneurs. Only the

[40] Schrötter, "Das preussische Offizierskorps," 101, 104, 114.

[41] Kurt Hinze, *Die Arbeiterfrage zu Beginn des modernen Kapitalismus in Brandenburg-Preussen* (Berlin and New York, 1963), 42–47.

[42] Stern, *Der preussische Staat und die Juden*, vol. I, pt. I, 9–14.

[43] Wilhelm Naudé and Gustav Schmoller, eds., *Acta Borussica: Die Getreidehandelspolitik und Kriegsmagazinverwaltung Brandenburg-Preussens*, vol. II (Berlin, 1901), 78–81; Opgenoorth, *"Ausländer" in Brandenburg-Preussen*, 25–26.

indigenous estates could approve the necessary taxes. Between 1653 and 1667 a series of confrontations between the Great Elector and the estates of Brandenburg, East Prussia, and Cleve-Mark eventually produced compromise settlements.[44] The continuing political strength of the nobility is reflected in the terms of these agreements. Negotiations with the Brandenburg *Landtag* in 1653 resulted in Frederick William's having to confirm nearly all the old privileges of the Junkers, notably those governing the legal relationship with their peasants. On the economic front, the elector granted once more to the nobility those tax immunities that enabled the land-owning elite to undersell town breweries and trade with foreign merchants with only minimal restrictions. Politically, the elector had to promise to consult the estates on all important decisions, though, significantly, he refused to accede to the estates' demand that he appoint only native noblemen to state offices.[45]

The fiscal concessions extracted from the Junkers in return were relatively modest, but they sufficed to allow Frederick William to capitalize on a favorable opportunity to intervene in international power politics in the late 1650s. After securing in 1653 the right to levy war taxes ("contributions") on the peasantry of Brandenburg for a period of six years, the elector quickly recruited an army that reached 22,000 men during the Northern War of 1655–60.[46] At first allied with Sweden against Poland, Frederick William switched sides in 1658 with the encouragement of the Dutch, who sought to limit Sweden's expansion in the Baltic now that the Habsburgs were no longer a threat in that region.[47] With the diplomatic support of the great powers, Frederick William secured at the Peace of Oliva sovereignty over East Prussia as his reward for helping to check Sweden.

This diplomatic gain, in turn, had two highly desirable consequences for Frederick William: no longer a vassal of the King of Poland, the elector could more readily control the internal affairs of East Prussia; and as a sovereign prince in a territory outside the Holy Roman Empire, Frederick William now had the right to grant

44 For a complete account, see Carsten, *The Origins of Prussia*, 179–252.

45 *Ibid.*, 187–89; Hagen, "Seventeenth-Century Crisis in Brandenburg," 319. For an abridged but readily accessible text of the agreement, see the "Revers des Kurfürsten Friedrich Wilhelm für die kurmärkischen Stände ... 1653," in Peter Baumgart, ed., *Erscheinungsformen des preussischen Absolutismus: Verfassung und Verwaltung* (Germering, 1966), 9–25.

46 Carsten, *The Origins of Prussia*, 270.

47 Wallerstein, *The Modern World System II*, 229.

titles of nobility to those who served him.[48] Success in war and the existence of a strong army by his side also gave the elector greatly increased bargaining power in negotiations with the estates, as well as the ability to increase or extend existing taxes without the consent of the estates. These increased financial resources, in turn, enabled Frederick William to attract more immigrants, as well as increase the size of his bureaucracy and army.[49]

The participation of Brandenburg–Prussia in the Northern War was therefore a major breakthrough for Frederick William, and the pace of his state-building efforts accelerated after 1660. Although he had formally conceded to the estates and provincial governments most of their customary rights, the Great elector from the early 1660s on systematically used his newly acquired position of strength to undermine or circumvent these rights. In church matters, this policy took the form of restricting the ability of the Lutheran church to interfere with the further development of the Reformed community in Brandenburg-Prussia. In many respects, to be sure, Frederick William continued in this area the conciliatory policies of his father and grandfather, the purpose of which was to achieve an interconfessional understanding based on a sense of harmony and parity between the two Protestant faiths.[50] The problem with the Reformed conception of the compatibility of the two evangelical faiths was that most Lutherans did not share it. Their customary stance was to condemn the Reformed theology as heresy and, with the strong support of the estates, to resist with all their strength the introduction into their communities of the Calvinist church and indeed all the non-Lutheran faiths of the various immigrant groups.

The passivity of John Sigismund and George William, by voluntarily limiting the scope of the Reformed penetration of society to a

[48] Gerhard Oestreich, *Friedrich Wilhelm: Der Grosse Kurfürst* (Göttingen, 1971), 51; Rosenberg, *Bureaucracy, Aristocracy, and Autocracy*, 139–40.

[49] Carsten views the Northern War of 1655–60 and its aftermath as the decisive period of the Great Elector's reign. Only as a result of the advantages gained by Frederick William from the war could he take the initiatives on the domestic front that produced the regime that took shape in the 1670s and 1680s. See Carsten, *The Origins of Prussia*, 207.

[50] This Reformed effort to find common ground with the Lutherans even extended to matters of theology; for despite inevitable differences on such issues as the nature of communion and the Lutheran retention of traditional ceremonial, the Calvinist church in the Hohenzollern lands adopted a soteriology quite close to the Lutherans' own and thereby greatly de-emphasized the importance of the doctrine of predestination. For the position of John Sigismund on this point, which was accepted by all his successors, see the "Confessio Fidei Johannis Sigismundi, 1614," in Gericke, ed., *Glaubenszeugnisse und Konfessionspolitik*, esp. 129–30.

handful of institutions, made possible an uneasy truce. But the aggressive expansion of the Reformed church carried out by Frederick William aroused intense opposition from the Lutheran party, backed up by the leading orthodox Lutheran theologians based in the universities of nearby Saxony. Already a major source of conflict between elector and estates at the Brandenburg *Landtag* in 1653, the controversy over the relationship between the two confessions came to a head in the early 1660s. Following up his success in the Northern War, the Great Elector overcame the vehement resistance of the East Prussian estates and established Reformed institutions in that province for the first time. Simultaneously, Frederick William launched a major effort to compel the Lutheran clergy to renounce doctrines central to their confession. With the aid of the estates, the Brandenburg Lutherans were ultimately able to force the elector to back down, even to the point of permitting the Lutheran party to express their doctrinal point of view so long as it was done without rancor or recrimination. The regime, though, retained the power to impose censorship if this standard were violated.[51]

The outcome of these confrontations was that the estates failed to prevent the institutional expansion of the Reformed church, while the Great Elector failed to force the Lutheran clergy to accept the notion of the fundamental affinity of the two churches. Frederick William consequently realized that the orthodox mentality of the Lutheran establishment could not be changed in the short term, so he adopted a policy of increasing the state's administrative control over the Lutheran (and all other) churches and using it to force the various confessions to live at peace with one another.[52] As early as 1637 a Reformed court preacher sat on the Lutheran consistory of Brandenburg. Under the Great Elector, every provincial consistory had at least one Reformed member. In 1665 the elector appointed a Reformed court preacher to be president of the Brandenburg consistory, while at the same time the *Statthalter* were placed in charge of the consistories in their respective provinces.[53] As a result of these measures, the institutional autonomy of the Lutheran church quickly crumbled. By the 1680s it had become customary for the

[51] Depperman, "Die Kirchenpolitik des Grossen Kurfürsten," 104–13.

[52] Hintze, "Die Epochen des evangelischen Kirchenregiments in Preussen," in *Regierung und Verwaltung*, 73–74; Otto Hintze, "Staat und Gesellschaft unter dem ersten König," in *Regierung und Verwaltung*, 399.

[53] Landwehr, "Die kirchlichen Zustände der Mark," 204–07, 209, 216–18.

Lutheran consistories to refer important matters to the electoral Privy Council, one of whose members came to specialize in church affairs.[54]

Binding the clergy's judicial authority to the central bureaucracy was only one part of a broader effort by the Great Elector to limit the judicial power of the old order. The absence of up-to-date imperial legal codes, the application in practice of a mixture of Roman and Germanic law, and the lack of uniform procedures made it easier for the elector and his legal agents, the fiscals, to carve out a place within the legal system for the new central administration.[55] Electoral decrees establishing and regulating the new bureaucratic and military institutions had no legal precedent and rested ultimately on force. As these institutions encroached more and more on the daily lives of the people of Brandenburg-Prussia, jurisdictional conflicts between the electoral regime and provincial governments became increasingly frequent.[56] In the ensuing legal battles, the fiscals served as the watchdogs of the electoral edicts. In crucial cases, the fiscals called on the elector to appoint an investigative commission to review the case. As the territorial lord was generally acknowledged as the source of all law and justice, there was little that the provincial governments could do to prevent these commissions, which naturally represented the interests of the elector, from deciding these cases in favor of the fiscals.[57]

These juridical labors made possible the expansion of the central bureaucracy. Under the leadership of Dodo von Knyphausen, an East Frisian Calvinist recruited by the Great Elector, the electoral domain administration made some headway. Revenues from the elector's domains, which constituted about 30 percent of the total land area of Brandenburg-Prussia, had always been the major source of income for the electors. What the elector actually received, however, was only a fraction of the revenue generated by the domains. The rest was appropriated by the local nobility, either by direct coercion or by levies made by representatives of the provincial

[54] Hintze, "Die Epochen des evangelischen Kirchenregiments in Preussen," 78. The elector tried to use the influence he thus gained over the administration of the Lutheran church to put in office clergy whose attitude toward the Reformed church was more conciliatory than that of the orthodox group. This strategy had only limited success because the nobility retained the right to appoint pastors on their lands and they as a group tended to favor orthodox Lutheranism for largely political reasons.

[55] Regge, *Kabinettsjustiz in Brandenburg-Preussen*, 100–01.

[56] Eberhard Schmidt, *Fiskalat und Strafprozess* (Berlin and Munich, 1921), 54.

[57] Hintze, "Staat und Gesellschaft unter dem ersten König," 397–98.

governments. With the help of the fiscals, Knyphausen succeeded in weakening the grip of the local estates on the domain officials.[58]

Knyphausen also reformed the method of administering the domains. Instead of having his officials directly administer the land under their jurisdiction, which was usually the equivalent of several estates per official, he instituted a system of leasing manageable portions of the domain land to tenant farmers for a term of six years. The relatively short term of the leases enabled the state in theory to replace incompetent or lazy tenants and to adjust the rents to market conditions. Although Knyphausen was eventually able to institute the new leasing system throughout Brandenburg-Prussia, the vagueness of the leases' provisions, lax enforcement, and low grain prices resulting from the agricultural depression precluded a significant rise in rents received from the domain lands.[59] But the tighter central control over the domains, reflected in the preparation by Knyphausen of the first general domain budget in 1689, resulted in a considerable increase in domain revenues from non-agricultural sources. Tolls, as well as revenues from beer brewing, the salt monopoly, and other regalian rights, accounted for a rise in domain revenues from 400,000 Taler in 1640 to 850,000 Taler in 1688.[60]

Far more spectacular was the growth in the revenues collected by the war commissariat. The Brandenburg estates had granted the elector the right to levy contribution taxes on the peasantry in 1653 and excise taxes on the towns in 1667. At first the impact of these concessions was felt only during times of war; in peacetime the tax commissars supervising their collection were dropped from the electoral payroll.[61] In 1670, for example, the proceeds from the two war taxes were a very modest 18,000 Taler.[62]

The breakthrough came with the rapid expansion of the army during the Dutch–French war of 1672–79. A permanent war com-

58 *Ibid.*, 371, though Hintze overstates the effectiveness of Knyphausen's administration.

59 *Ibid.*, 391; see also August Skalweit, *Die ostpreussische Domänenverwaltung unter Friedrich Wilhelm I. und das Retablissement Litauens* (Leipzig, 1906).

60 Ernst Klein, *Geschichte der öffentlichen Finanzen in Deutschland, 1550–1870* (Wiesbaden, 1974), 45; Hintze, "Staat und Gesellschaft unter dem ersten König," 371.

61 Yet the sums collected during the Northern War were very high, especially in light of the very short interval of time that had passed since the devastations of the Thirty Years' War. On a per capita basis, the tax rates were probably higher than at any time in the seventeenth century. See Hagen, "Seventeenth-Century Crisis in Brandenburg," 321, 325.

62 Schmoller, "Das Städtewesen unter Friedrich Wilhelm I.," 256–58; Klein, *Geschichte der öffentlichen Finanzen*, 45.

missariat, charged with collecting funds for the army and with handling many of the administrative matters arising from the existence of the army, emerged in the early 1670s. Its degree of organization, far higher than that of the domain bureaucracy, was reflected in the formation in 1674 of a central treasury for revenues from the contribution and excise taxes.[63] By 1680 the excise tax had been introduced in every town in Brandenburg; and by 1684 the excise in Brandenburg was being collected by the tax commissars, rather than by the towns themselves. By 1688, the excise system, with collection carried out by tax commissars, had also taken hold in Minden, Magdeburg, Halberstadt, and eastern Pomerania.[64] Together with more regular collection of the contribution tax, the development of the excise tax system enabled revenues from the two war taxes in 1688 to reach 1.6 million Taler.[65]

Though this astronomical rise in state revenues was mainly the result of new tax levies combined with an improved collection system, to a certain, debatable extent it was also a product of electoral policies promoting economic development.[66] In the 1660s, Frederick William, using his own capital, initiated the construction of the Mullroser canal in order to link the Oder and Elbe rivers via Berlin, where Frederick William installed docking facilities and a crane. The purpose of this project was to attract to the Mark Brandenburg a significant share of the east-west inland transit trade between Hamburg and the Low Countries, on the one end, and Bohemia, Silesia, Saxony, and Poland, on the other.[67] But merely building the canal would not necessarily have achieved the elector's goal. Shortly after the completion of the canal in 1669 came the large-scale Jewish immigration. Thanks to the Jews' commercial connections throughout Eastern Europe, Berlin and the other towns along the canal became the beneficiaries of an expanded commerce. The Jews were also instrumental in reviving the market at Frankfurt/Oder, which for the first time since the outbreak of the

63 Hintze, "Staat und Gesellschaft unter dem ersten König," 375.

64 Hugo Rachel, "Der Merkantilismus in Brandenburg-Preussen," *Forschungen zur brandenburgischen und preussischen Geschichte*, 40 (1928): 227. For a detailed account of the introduction of the excise in the various provinces, see Hugo Rachel, ed., *Acta Borussica: Die Handels-, Zoll- und Akzisepolitik Preussens*, vol. 1 (Berlin, 1911), 510–85.

65 Klein, *Geschichte der öffentlichen Finanzen*, 45.

66 Hagen, for example, argues that the heavy taxes imposed by the Great Elector worked to stifle any general trend toward economic recovery from the Thirty Years' War. Hagen, "Seventeenth-Century Crisis in Brandenburg," 335.

67 Rachel, "Der Merkantilismus in Brandenburg-Preussen," 225.

Thirty Years' War was able to compete again with fairs at Leipzig and Breslau.[68]

The tax commissars, backed up by the army, protected the Jews from persecution by the local authorities. They likewise helped to settle the non-Jewish immigrants from western Germany, the Low Countries, and France, who began arriving in large numbers after 1672. The new residents were not only numerous; in many cases they were well-to-do. Schmoller estimates that the Huguenot families coming from Metz brought with them a total of two million Taler and that the average Huguenot entered Brandenburg-Prussia with at least three hundred Taler. If these figures are correct, the twenty thousand Huguenot immigrants alone were responsible for a capital inflow of six million Taler into Brandenburg-Prussia. The immigrants' skills were of comparable value. Artisans from Liège brought technical knowledge of armaments manufacturing, Walloon immigrants contributed their skill in tobacco cultivation, and the Huguenots introduced into Brandenburg-Prussia at least a dozen highly skilled crafts.[69]

The special privileges offered to these immigrants were part of a systematic policy favoring manufacturing. In 1686 Frederick William put into operation near Halle a salt manufacturing enterprise that became a profitable state monopoly. In 1687 the elector issued a series of edicts intended to use the excise system to discourage exports of raw materials, especially wool, and imports of manufactured items. Although these edicts did not stop wool exports or imports of mass-produced textiles, they did enable the new craft industries in Brandenburg-Prussia to take the place of a portion of luxury goods imports.[70] In the last decade of the Great Elector's reign, the tax commissars attempted to expand their jurisdiction over municipal affairs to the point of attempting to "reform" the native guilds in order to increase industrial productivity. Although the commissars' intervention against the worst guild abuses set useful precedents and actually did some good in isolated cases, the major effect of these efforts at exerting control over the local

68 Stern, *Der preussische Staat und die Juden*, vol. 1, pt. 1, 50–52. For an informative discussion of the state of the Jewish community in Brandenburg-Prussia in the years around 1700, see Stefi Jersch-Wenzel, *Juden und "Franzosen" in der Wirtschaft des Raumes Berlin/Brandenburg zur Zeit des Merkantilismus* (Berlin, 1978), 58–69.

69 Schmoller, "Das Städtewesen unter Friedrich Wilhelm I.," 291.

70 Rachel, "Der Merkantilismus in Brandenburg-Preussen," 227, 229; Hintze, "Staat und Gesellschaft unter dem ersten König," 387, 417.

economy was to provoke unrest and resistance among the guilds.[71] The failure to make fundamental changes in the guild system shows clearly the domestic limitations of the Great Elector's regime, which could never mobilize the energies of the bulk of the population and which depended so heavily on immigrants and social outsiders.

The regime also failed to acquire a position within the European state system sufficiently strong to enable the Great Elector to realize his dream of acquiring a share of the colonial trade – a dream inspired by Frederick William's teenage observations of the workings of the Dutch economy. The elector, to be sure, was given an opportunity to put his plans into action when during the Dutch–French war of 1672–79, the French induced the Swedes to attack the Holy Roman Empire, most of whose princes were fighting on the Dutch side. Showing surprising strength against the forces of a great power, the army of the Great Elector defeated the Swedes at Fehrbellin in 1675. Later in the same year, Brandenburg's forces conquered Stettin, and within three years almost all of western Pomerania was in Hohenzollern hands.

After seizing Stettin, Frederick William, in partnership with Benjamin Raule, then set in motion the schemes that culminated in the founding of the Africa Company in 1682. By the mid-1680s a slave station had been set up on the coast of what is now Ghana. In order to supply export articles with which to purchase slaves, Frederick William in the late 1670s and early 1680s liberally subsidized a large metal-working factory near Krossen and several wool textile factories in Berlin. At the same time he also sponsored a sugar refinery in Berlin, presumably to process the sugar received in exchange for the slaves delivered to the New World by the Africa Company.[72] Clearly, the elector was seeking to fashion his own version of the "triangle trade," which would have enabled Brandenburg-Prussia to supply its home market and much of Eastern Europe with colonial products.

This attempt to use state power to imitate the economic policies of England, France, and the Netherlands never stood a chance of success. The export and finishing industries, lacking both capital

[71] Gustav Schmoller, "Das brandenburgisch-preussische Innungswesen von 1640 bis 1800, hauptsächlich die Reform unter Friedrich Wilhelm I.," in Schmoller, *Umrisse und Untersuchungen zur Verfassungs-, Verwaltungs- und Wirtschaftsgeschichte besonders des preussischen Staates im 17. und 18. Jahrhundert* (Leipzig, 1898), 348–52.

[72] Rachel, "Der Merkantilismus in Brandenburg-Preussen," 225–26; Henri Brunschwig, *L'expansion allemande outre-mer du XVe siècle à nos jours* (Paris, 1957), 35.

and an adequately skilled labor force, failed almost immediately after being founded. As if having to overcome all the internal obstacles to the creation of the required industrial base were not difficult enough, the Great Elector also had to contend with intractable opposition from the great powers. Although the Dutch were willing to support Brandenburg-Prussia as a counterweight to Sweden, they would not tolerate a new commercial competitor, particularly one based in the Baltic region.[73] The Dutch West India Company, backed by the Dutch government, simply refused to share its East European market with a local firm, such as the Africa Company of Brandenburg-Prussia, that sought to obtain colonial products directly from their source and bypass Dutch middlemen. As a result, in the peace negotiations of 1679, when the French insisted that western Pomerania and Stettin be returned to Sweden, the Dutch raised no objections. The Africa Company, not able to use Stettin, could not withstand constant Dutch harassment and was all but out of business by the early 1690s.[74]

Although pursuit of overseas trade and colonies was the highest aspiration of the Great Elector's economic program, well over half of state expenditures under Frederick William were channeled into a large, standing army. The elector needed the army, above all, to realize his goal of wresting Stettin from the Swedes. The army also served to reinforce electoral control over territories far from Berlin, especially East Prussia, and to intimidate the provincial estates.[75] Moreover, if Brandenburg-Prussia were unable to acquire the mouth of the Oder River, the army would be the primary instrument in pursuing an alternative strategy of pushing Hohenzollern claims to territories in Silesia and the Rhineland. Accordingly, from a force numbering 4,000 men in the early 1640s, the army of Brandenburg-Prussia reached a strength of 22,000 during the Northern War of the late 1650s, stabilized at a peacetime level of 12,000 between 1660 and 1672, and expanded again during the war of 1672–79 to over 45,000 men under arms.[76]

[73] Thus whenever East Prussian or Pomeranian merchants, on prodding from the elector, attempted to sell grain directly on the Dutch market, the Dutch, who had long handled the transport and marketing of Baltic grain, quickly emptied their warehouses to undersell them. See Naudé and Schmoller, eds., *Die Getreidehandelspolitik*, vol. II, 83.

[74] Rachel, "Der Merkantilismus in Brandenburg-Preussen," 229.

[75] Carsten, *The Origins of Prussia*, 208.

[76] *Ibid.*, 280; Curt Jany, *Geschichte der Königlich Preussischen Armee bis zum Jahre 1807*, vol. I (Berlin, 1928), 274.

The great importance and large size of the army necessitated tight electoral control over it. For a seventeenth-century state like Brandenburg-Prussia, securing control over its army was no easier a task than enforcing its will on civilian society. In most seventeenth-century armies, the colonels were in charge of the personnel and finances of their regiments, and they negotiated with a state on equal terms. Despite this tradition, the Great Elector gained considerable success in undermining the autonomy of the colonels. Under a series of negotiated agreements between the colonels and Frederick William, the former, in return for high regular salaries, conceded to the elector the right to appoint the subordinate officers of their regiments.[77] The most important of these subordinates, the company commanders (usually captains) were given greater administrative authority over their units and were made more directly responsible to the war commissariat in bookkeeping matters.[78] Another diminution of the colonels' authority was the placement with each regiment of full-time legal officials and clergy. These auditors and army chaplains were in part subordinate to two new electoral bodies established in the 1680s and 1690s, the General Auditor's Office and the Military Consistory. I say "in part" because the colonels still appointed and paid the salaries of the auditors and army chaplains.[79] But by the end of Frederick William's reign the colonels had lost much control over day-to-day operations of their regiments to their captains and to the central authorities, especially the war commissariat.

Following the decisive setback to the elector's overseas and colonial plans in 1679, the army gradually acquired economic importance in its own right. As early as the war of 1672–79, Brandenburg-Prussia received 1.5 million Taler in subsidies from the Spanish and Dutch.[80] Partly as a result of these subsidies, the army had grown to become such a powerful force that, when the war ended, the elector was reluctant to demobilize it. Since the domestic economy of Brandenburg-Prussia was still very weak, it was neces-

[77] Schrötter, "Das preussische Offizierskorps unter dem ersten Könige von Preussen," *Forschungen zur brandenburgischen und preussischen Geschichte*, 26 (1913): 429–35.

[78] *Ibid.*, 483, 487; Fritz Redlich, *The German Military Enterpriser and His Work Force: A Study in European Economic and Social History*, vol. II (Wiesbaden, 1965), 78–79.

[79] Werner Hülle, *Das Auditoriat in Brandenburg-Preussen* (Göttingen, 1971), 36–37; for the army chaplains, see J. Langhäuser, *Das Militärkirchenwesen im kurbrandenburgischen und Königlich Preussischen Heer: Seine Entwicklung und derzeitige Gestalt* (Metz, 1912), 22–24.

[80] Klein, *Geschichte der öffentlichen Finanzen*, 45.

sary for the elector to rely on foreign subsidy payments to keep his large army basically intact. Thus it was more than just Frederick William's anger at his erstwhile allies in the war of 1672–79 that induced him to conclude a secret alliance with France. The annual subsidies he received from Louis XIV, which increased from 100,000 Taler in 1681 to almost 200,000 Taler in 1684, enabled him to keep his peacetime strength at 25,000 men, with a considerable reserve of men on furlough.[81]

This arrangement lasted until 1685 when France cut off diplomatic relations and subsidy payments to Brandenburg-Prussia after Frederick William began so actively and so openly recruiting Huguenot refugees after the Revocation of the Edict of Nantes. But almost immediately thereafter, in 1686, the Great Elector concluded an alliance with the emperor, who subsidized the dispatch of a large Brandenburg contingent to Hungary for a campaign against the Turks. In 1688 the major scene of hostilities shifted to Western Europe with the outbreak of a war between France, on the one side, and England, the Netherlands, and the Habsburgs, on the other. In return for Dutch and imperial subsidies, the army of Brandenburg-Prussia joined that of most other German princes in countering and eventually containing Louis XIV's first attempt to conquer Germany. Although Sweden, the Great Elector's arch-enemy, was also a member of the anti-French coalition, Frederick William's anti-French policy was based on the calculation that only a weakening of France would prevent a repetition of the humiliation of 1679.[82] Frederick William had his eyes on Stettin until the end of his days.

[81] Jany, *Geschichte der Königlich Preussischen Armee*, vol. 1, 273–74; Carl Hinrichs, "Der Grosse Kurfürst, 1620–1688," in Hinrichs, *Preussen als historisches Problem*, 247.

[82] Hinrichs, "Der Grosse Kurfürst," 251–52.

CHAPTER 3

The nature of the pre-1713 Hohenzollern state

HARMONY AND RECONCILIATION? THE POLICIES OF FREDERICK III(I)

The accession in 1688 of Frederick William's son, Frederick III(I), who reigned until 1713, assured that there would be no radical changes in the Great Elector's policies. Like his father, Frederick not only demonstrated from an early age a strong commitment to the Reformed faith but also experienced a personal sense of election from God that he came to regard as the source of the political triumphs that he was to enjoy in his life.[1] The new elector's allegiance to his confession was likewise made manifest by a series of actions that marked him as a late example of a "Second Reformation" German prince. Viewing the Reformed religion as the "true" form of the Christian religion, Frederick worked to expand the network of Reformed churches and clergy in his lands, took in large numbers of Huguenot and other Calvinist immigrants, and charged his successors to continue his work in this respect.[2] Politically, Frederick as a matter of policy favored persons of Reformed background for positions at court and in his administration. In foreign affairs, Frederick adopted the last policy direction his father had taken, allying firmly and loyally with the Protestant powers, the Dutch Republic and Great Britain, against the persecutor of the Huguenots, Louis XIV.[3]

In light of Frederick's tendency to let favorites manage the day-to-day running of the government, continuity with the past was

[1] "Auszug aus dem Testament des Kurprinzen Friedrich ... 1684," in Gericke, ed., *Glaubenszeugnisse und Konfessionspolitik*, 183; "Haupt Testament Sr. Majestät König Friedrichs I. ... 1707," in *ibid.*, 187.

[2] *Ibid.*, 183, 187.

[3] For the strongly confessional orientation of Frederick's foreign policy, see Richard Dietrich, ed., *Die politischen Testamente der Hohenzollern* (Cologne and Vienna, 1986), 60, 62–63.

further assured by his initial willingness to let his father's advisers, most notably Eberhard Danckelmann, carry on the Great Elector's policies. During this period, which lasted until Danckelmann's fall in 1697, the greater portion of the Huguenots were settled and the constructive work of the war commissariat and the domain administration was continued.[4] Even the most notable initiative of the Danckelmann administration, the founding of the University of Halle as a Lutheran university in 1692, can be viewed as a continuation of the rivalry between Saxony and Brandenburg-Prussia, initiated by Frederick William, for regional supremacy and for leadership within German Protestantism as a whole. Therefore, not only did Danckelmann and Paul Fuchs, the minister of cultural and religious affairs, recruit for the Halle faculty such distinguished secular thinkers as Ludwig von Seckendorff and Christian Thomasius; but they also worked simultaneously to attract to Brandenburg-Prussia the leaders of Lutheran Pietism, the only dissident movement within the Lutheran church able to compete, academically and spiritually, with Saxon orthodoxy. Thus the founder of Pietism, Philipp Jakob Spener, settled in Berlin and became an important figure at Frederick's court; and Spener's chief protégé, August Hermann Francke, was appointed Professor of Near Eastern Languages at the University of Halle.[5]

To a large extent, the welcoming of the Pietists was a continuation of the Great Elector's policy of seeking to nurture within the Lutheran church of Brandenburg-Prussia individuals and movements less hostile to the Reformed church than the hard-core orthodox party.[6] Yet the depth of the commitment of Frederick's government to the University of Halle – to the point of making a *Lutheran* university the leading university in the Hohenzollern lands – constituted an unprecedented recognition of the limits of

4 Hintze, "Staat und Gesellschaft unter dem ersten König," 417.

5 Carl Hinrichs, "König Friedrich I. von Preussen: Die geistige und politische Bedeutung seiner Regierung," in Hinrichs, *Preussen als historisches Problem*, 266–67.

6 The most significant precedent for the Hohenzollerns' promotion of irenical, non-orthodox movements within Lutheranism was the Great Elector's appointing of followers of the Lutheran theologian Georg Calixt to professorships on the theological faculty at the University of Königsberg in the early part of his reign. In the early 1660s, the Königsberg Calixtians supported Frederick William in his political and religious conflict with the East Prussian estates. Deppermann, "Die Kirchenpolitik des Grossen Kurfürsten," 109; see also Johannes Wallmann, "Zwischen Reformation und Humanismus: Eigenart und Wirkungen Helmstedter Theologie unter besonderer Berücksichtigung Georg Calixts," *Zeitschrift für Theologie und Kirche*, 74 (1977): 344–70.

Reformed confessionalism in Brandenburg-Prussia. In this sense, the favor shown this university is symptomatic of how Frederick, while adhering in the main to the course marked out by his father, introduced characteristic modifications that gave his regime its special stamp. For behind these changes was Frederick's desire to promote a reconciliation between the dynasty and those traditional, corporate elements of society who felt alienated from the system of rule established so largely through the confrontational methods used by the Great Elector.[7]

In the critical area of interconfessional relations, Frederick's desire for harmony led him not only to practice toleration of Lutheranism but also to pursue the goal of institutional unification of the Lutheran and Reformed churches.[8] The way in which the elector (later king) and his chief collaborator in this effort, the Berlin court preacher Daniel Ernst Jablonski, sought to accomplish this goal provides an important clue as to how Frederick approached the mission of overcoming internal divisions within his realm. Frederick strongly supported Jablonski's efforts to unify the two Protestant faiths through the creation of an umbrella church modelled on the national church of Brandenburg-Prussia's English ally.

What Jablonski saw as the key to creating an eventual Lutheran-Reformed union, and what undoubtedly induced Frederick to back his plans, was the adoption of the Anglican liturgy by both churches. For despite Frederick's pride in his Reformed heritage, he apparently believed that the theological differences between his church and that of the Lutherans were not significant enough to rule out a unity through common liturgy, i.e. a unity based on ceremony and ritual.[9] This vision led Frederick to have the Book of Common

[7] That this was a conscious aim of Frederick's from the beginning is demonstrated by his telling a Saxon envoy in his first days as ruler that he intended to create a "loveable government." Quoted in Linda and Marsha Frey, *Frederick I: The Man and His Times* (Boulder and New York, 1984), 51.

[8] Frederick's writings make clear that not only domestic considerations lay behind the unity scheme but also the long-standing desire within the German Reformed Church to present a united Protestant front in order to resist the still ongoing recatholicization of Central Europe. See his "Haupt Testament . . . 1707," in Gericke, ed., *Glaubenszeugnisse und Konfessionspolitik*, 188.

[9] In Gericke's words, "For this ruler, despite his emphatically Reformed standpoint, the differences between both religious parties were fundamentally meaningless." See Gericke, ed., *Glaubenszeugnisse und Konfessionspolitik*, 50. This statement encapsulates those tensions in Frederick's position between Reformed confessionalism and some never fully developed alternative – tensions that the elector/king himself was not able to confront directly, much less resolve. The emphasis on liturgy as a means of fashioning a unity transcending confessional distinctions is significant not only because of its parallel in intended function to

Prayer translated into German in 1704 and introduced in his own chapel and the Berlin cathedral. One final reason for his regime's bestowing so much favor on the Pietists, at least initially, was the expectation that, being themselves indifferent to dogma in general and confessional polemics in particular, the Pietists would support the government's unity effort from within the Lutheran church.[10]

Though the Pietists ultimately refused to cooperate in the negotiations for union and though the relationship with the Anglican church soured as the alliance with England deteriorated in the final years of Frederick's reign, the unsuccessful campaign for unity did result in the regime making some ecumenical gestures to court the Lutheran church. In addition to the new Lutheran university at Halle, many Reformed churches in the cities became "simultaneous churches," that is to say they performed both Lutheran and Reformed services. Another important precedent was set when Crown Prince Frederick William's bride, Princess Dorothea of Hanover, was allowed to keep her Lutheran faith.[11]

Yet regardless of the limited amount of good will these gestures may have generated, they did not suffice to induce Lutheran participation in a dialogue over possible union or to moderate the grassroots Lutheran antipathy toward the Reformed religion. If anything, the large numbers of Calvinist immigrants that arrived in the country in the first years of Frederick's reign exacerbated the hostility of the Lutheran populace. Even those newcomers who were in desperate straits received little help from local authorities and had to bear abuse and mockery from the members of the community. For the latter "saw in the misery of the refugees the just punishment of God for their false belief."[12]

the ritualistic ceremonial at Frederick's court but also because of what it reveals about the depth of his traditionalism.

10 For the most detailed account of Jablonski's attempts to unify the two churches, see Walter Delius, "Berliner Unionsversuche im 17. und 18. Jahrhundert," *Jahrbuch für Berlin-brandenburgische Kirchengeschichte*, 45 (1970): 24–38, 52–67.

11 *Ibid.*, 49–50; Hintze, "Die Epochen des evangelischen Kirchenregiments in Preussen," 76. The limits of this ecumenism are evident, however, from Frederick's emphatic statement, in his Testament of 1707, that all the children from the Crown Prince's marriage, girls as well as boys, would be raised in the Reformed faith and "in no way be educated in the Lutheran religion." See his "Haupt Testament ... 1707," in Gericke, ed., *Glaubenszeugnisse und Konfessionspolitik*, 188–89.

12 For this and other difficulties facing the immigrants, see Deppermann, "Die politischen Voraussetzungen für die Etablierung des Pietismus in Brandenburg-Preussen," *Pietismus und Neuzeit*, 12 (1986): 43–44. A similar example of deeply rooted anti-Reformed confessional animosity, which occurred during the reign of the Great Elector, was the Lutheran clergy's public praying for a Swedish, i.e. Lutheran, victory at Fehrbellin in 1675. See

Just as Frederick sought to rely on benevolent actions and the acceptance of a common liturgy to achieve confessional unification, so he attempted to overcome the political division between the estates and his government through similarly paternalistic and traditionalistic methods. Thus, after Danckelmann's fall in 1697, when the direction of government policy was set even more in accordance with Frederick's personal priorities, the constant challenges of the estates' legal rights by the central bureaucracy largely ceased. Instead of pursuing his father's strategy of attacking the privileges of the nobility and provincial governments head on, Frederick attempted to obtain the voluntary cooperation of the traditional elites by offering them the chance to participate in life at his court.[13]

To a much greater extent than his predecessors, therefore, Frederick worked to fashion the Berlin court into an institution capable of defining a complex, but orderly hierarchical world within whose categories all members of the territorial elite could find a place. Despite his personal feelings of ambivalence about the artificiality of court life, Frederick structured his own daily life around its rituals and took very seriously his role of arbiter of relationships among the actors on the courtly stage. Frederick oversaw the publication of the first Hohenzollern ordinance that systematically ranked the various court offices. In the fifth such *Hofrangordnung* issued during Frederick's reign, the tendency toward elaboration of social distinctions had reached such a point that no fewer than 141 degrees of hierarchy were spelled out by that ordinance.[14]

Given Frederick's preoccupation with the court, it is not surprising that the primary aim of his regime was to enhance the prestige of that institution. Little expense was spared in creating luxurious settings, props, and costumes for the courtly ceremonies – all in highly self-conscious imitation of the styles of Versailles. Diplomatically, Frederick after 1697 boldly and successfully exploited a favorable international situation to pursue recognition by the great powers of his assumption of the title of king in the one land where he was fully sovereign, East Prussia. On January 14, 1701, in the East

Walter Wendland, "Studien zum kirchlichen Leben in Berlin um 1700," *Jahrbuch für brandenburgische Kirchengeschichte*, 21 (1926): 157.

13 Regge, *Kabinettsjustiz in Brandenburg-Preussen*, 129–30; Hintze, "Staat und Gesellschaft unter dem ersten König," 316.

14 Frey, *Frederick I*, 52–53.

Prussian capital, Königsberg, Frederick crowned himself King in Prussia, amidst prolonged sumptuous ceremonies and celebrations, the total cost for which came to the enormous sum of 6 million Taler.[15] Intended to add still more lustre to the court and contribute to the image of Brandenburg-Prussia as a center of culture, was the founding of the Berlin Academy of Sciences in 1700, whose prime instigator was the great philosopher Leibniz.[16]

Yet just as the union initiative failed to attract the Lutheran clergy, so Frederick's court for all its brilliance remained largely incapable of forging meaningful connections between the dynasty and the native nobility.[17] The king's final hope for encouraging a greater sense of internal harmony was to do what he could to bring about an economic recovery that would restore prosperity to lands burdened by the wars and high taxes of the preceding reigns. In addition to trusting that his "mildness" in governing would provide his subjects with a less restrictive economic environment,[18] Frederick also sought to attract substantial foreign capital in the form of subsidy payments advanced in return for the services of the Brandenburg-Prussian army.

[15] For an account of the diplomatic campaign that won the acquiescence of the great powers to Frederick's royal title, see *ibid.*, 56–61. According to Hintze, Frederick crowned himself – the first time in Western history since Charlemagne that a Christian prince did not receive a crown from a cleric. Hintze, "Staat und Gesellschaft unter dem ersten König," 399. Until 1701, Frederick's title was Frederick III, Elector of Brandenburg, Duke of Prussia, etc. After 1701, Frederick was Frederick I, King in Prussia, Elector of Brandenburg, etc. Hence when I refer to his reign as a whole, I use the appellation "Frederick III(I)."

[16] Leibniz's academy movement was a later, more public form of the secret societies founded in the early seventeenth century by Protestant German literati who aspired to overcome the intellectual restrictions imposed by confessionalization. Frederick's sponsorship of the Berlin Academy was a fitting gesture not only because his wife Sophie Charlotte had close ties with Leibniz but also because his father had belonged to a secret society, the *Fruchtbringende Gesellschaft*, that was an important forerunner of the scientific academies. Gerhard Oestreich, "Fundamente preussischer Geistesgeschichte: Religion und Weltanschauung in Brandenburg im 17. Jahrhundert, *Jahrbuch Preussischer Kulturbesitz* (1969): 37.

[17] As the Freys point out, the court was in fact dominated by those who adhered at least nominally to the Reformed religion and by nobles either of foreign origin or from the kingdom's peripheral provinces. Frey, *Frederick I*, 136–37. Why Frederick's court was not able to attract Junker families from the core provinces is not explained, but certainly the elector/king's preference for Reformed councillors (and favorites!) must have operated as a strong deterrent.

[18] Frederick's desire to act benevolently toward his subjects was an important part of his self-image as a ruler. Thus in February 1713, in his last meeting with Crown Prince Frederick William, Frederick, aware of his son's character and anticipating perhaps what was to come, "advised him ... to govern his people with mildness." See Elézar de Mauvillon, *The Life of Frederick William I, late King of Prussia, Containing many Authentick Letters and Pieces*, trans. William Phelips (London, 1750), 77.

Though the Great Elector had also done this in the last decade of his reign, Frederick III(I) was in the position to carry out this practice on a much greater scale. For in the War of Spanish Succession, which broke out in 1701, the defection of Spain to the side of France reduced the size of the armed forces available to defend the Low Countries and Central Europe against the French. Moreover, the high stakes of this war – on the line was nothing less than control of trade, including the slave trade, with Spain's New World empire – made both sides, especially the Grand Alliance, willing to pay a high price for use of a large, experienced army. Frederick I was in the enviable position of having such a force at his disposal, and his diplomats drove a hard bargain for its services. Not only was the Habsburg emperor forced to recognize Frederick as King in Prussia, but the English and Dutch also had to pay sizeable subsidies to maintain the 31,000 Brandenburg-Prussian troops fighting in Italy and the Low Countries. By 1710 these subsidy payments had reached 1.5 million Taler a year.[19] During the entire reign of Frederick III(I), some 14 million Taler in subsidies flowed into Brandenburg-Prussia, most of it after 1700.[20]

The main beneficiaries of this capital inflow were the Berlin court and the luxury industries that supplied its needs. During the period 1705–10 state expenditures amounted to about 5.3 million Taler a year. Out of that sum, about 600,000 Taler went for the king's personal use, 180,000 for the use of the rest of the royal family, 400,000 for other court expenditures, 150,000 for stipends and pensions, and 50,000 for maintaining the royal palace.[21] Thus a total of almost 1.4 million Taler, more than half the amount of all state expenditures in 1688, was spent on personal consumption by the privileged elite in the capital. Indicative of the sudden escalation of such expenditures after 1697 are the excise taxes paid by Berlin's Jews, who controlled much of the trade in luxury goods. In 1696, when Danckelmann was still in power, the Jews paid 8,614 Taler in excise taxes. In 1705 the figure was 117,437 Taler.[22] With this much money in circulation, Berlin became a fortune-seeker's paradise. The city's population, less than 20,000 in 1690, exploded in the next

[19] Max Braubach, *Die Bedeutung der Subsidien für die Politik im spanischen Erbfolgekriege* (Bonn and Leipzig, 1923), 124–25.

[20] Klein, *Geschichte der öffentlichen Finanzen*, 48.

[21] *Ibid.*, 47.

[22] Stern, *Der preussische Staat und die Juden*, vol. 1, pt. 1, 126.

twenty years and reached 55,000 in 1710.[23] The growth of Berlin was so great that it absorbed all the grain surpluses produced by farmers in the city's hinterland.[24] A dependable market for grain enabled these parts of the Mark Brandenburg to prosper. For the first time since the Thirty Years' War, there was even enough money available to finance primary schools in some of the villages and towns in the Mark.[25]

Unfortunately, the sources for the funds supporting these high levels of state expenditure were not all so benign as subsidies from abroad. The clique that came to dominate Frederick I and his court by 1702 – the notorious trio of Wittgenstein, Wartensleben, and Wartenberg – looked on the lands of the monarchy merely as sources of revenue for the court. Not concerned with promoting the long-term health of the economy, the "3 W's" used every conceivable method to squeeze money from the provinces. Extraordinary head taxes, each of which raised 200,000 Taler, were levied eight times during Frederick III(I)'s reign. The excise tax was extended to bread and beer. As head of the central domain administration, Wittgenstein mercilessly raised the price of the salt sold by the state-run monopoly.[26] The postal service was similarly exploited.[27]

Even seemingly constructive measures were actually fiscalist in nature. Higher excise rates for imported luxury items served as pretexts for officials to extort bribes. Funds collected for a state-administered fire insurance scheme were embezzled.[28] A far-reaching reform of the leasing system on the royal domains was sponsored by Wittgenstein only because it promised a large, initial increase in revenue. As it turned out, corruption in the domain administration was so great that effective implementation of the

23 Naudé and Schmoller, eds., *Die Getreidehandelspolitik*, vol. II, 159. The sources give many different figures for Berlin's 1690 population, ranging from 14,000 to 21,000. The figure of 14,000 is based on the work of Süssmilch, a mid-eighteenth-century Prussian cameralist. Given the Huguenot immigration to Berlin in the late 1680s of some 5,000 or 6,000 persons, a population of 14,000 is possible only if there had been minimal growth between the mid-1650s, when there were 6,000 Berliners, and the mid-1680s. For this reason, I estimate the population of Berlin in 1690 to have been about 18,000. The figures usually cited for the population of Berlin in 1710 are much more consistent with one another.

24 *Ibid.*, 115.

25 Wienecke, "Die Begründung der evangelischen Volksschule in der Kurmark," 49, 58.

26 Klein, *Geschichte der öffentlichen Finanzen*, 47; Hintze, "Staat und Gesellschaft unter dem ersten König," 368.

27 Hintze, "Staat und Gesellschaft unter dem ersten König," 417.

28 Reinhold Dorwart, "The Earliest Fire Insurance Company in Berlin and Brandenburg, 1705–1711," *Business History Review*, 32 (1958): 199–200.

reform plan proved to be impossible. Meanwhile, low grain prices and extortionate taxation had forced many peasants to flee the land, either to the cities and towns of Brandenburg-Prussia or to Poland.[29]

Thus not only did the consumption boom in Berlin and its environs do little to help economic recovery in the rest of Brandenburg-Prussia, but the regime's corrupt fiscalism also contributed to the same negative result. In addition, during Frederick's reign the social problems he inherited from his father, particularly those confronting the municipalities, became increasingly difficult to manage. The main source of the towns' difficulties was the misery and destitution created by the existence of the army. Like all seventeenth-century armies, the army of Brandenburg-Prussia was far larger than the state could afford. The victims of the resulting underfunding were the common soldiers. Members of society's lowest classes, recruited from all over Germany by means of deceit or force, the soldiers were quartered mainly in camps in the countryside, though they were also garrisoned for short periods in the larger towns and cities. Except for rudimentary military training, soldiers received no other form of education. Setting aside the Huguenot officers, the moral standards of the officer corps were very low, so that the officers could hardly have served as role models for their men.[30]

In addition to morally degrading surroundings, the soldiers never received adequate food, clothing, or housing.[31] Their medical needs were attended to by untrained barber-surgeons, who were paid only a little more than bearers of the regimental colors.[32] Except for the interlude of 1697–1701, this army was fighting continuously for a twenty-five year period beginning in 1688. The surviving casualties of war – the wounded, widows, and orphans – received no help from the state. Since most of these people lacked marketable skills and were considered outcasts by society, they had no recourse other than begging. Thousands of these beggars congregated in Berlin and the other cities. The strain on the cities' social service network

29 Hintze, "Staat und Gesellschaft unter dem ersten König," 392, 407.

30 Schrötter, "Das preussische Offizierskorps," *Forschungen zur brandenburgischen und preussischen Geschichte*, 27 (1914): 97. As the colonels appointed the regimental chaplains, moreover, the military clergy's ability to raise the level of morality in the camps was limited.

31 Redlich, *The German Military Enterpriser*, vol. II, 192–96.

32 *Die Kriegschirurgen und Feldärzte Preussens*, vol. I (Berlin, 1899), 25.

had already produced a state of crisis in the periods 1675–79 and 1691–95.[33] After 1701, the problem got out of control.

Virtually nothing was done to alleviate the resulting health problems. Medical practice in Brandenburg-Prussia lagged far behind the level achieved in the cities of southern Germany in the sixteenth century. To be sure, in 1685 the Great Elector issued an edict establishing a College of Medicine, whose purpose was to supervise medical practicioners and apothecaries in accordance with the more advanced South German regulations.[34] But this edict was not even printed until 1692, and in any case the College of Medicine lacked the means of enforcing the codes of conduct that it prescribed. No institutes or clinics were set up to train qualified medical personnel. Consequently, the edict had little effect.[35]

Until the 1690s, moreover, no serious effort was made to provide even a measure of poor relief to the indigent multitudes. Hospitals and other charitable institutions set up by the church were the customary providers of poor relief. But their effectiveness had been impaired by the loss of their endowments during the Thirty Years' War, and the social activism of the Lutheran church was stifled in any case by the religious policies of the Great Elector. In order to build up the Calvinist church in Brandenburg-Prussia, Frederick William not only sought to curtail Lutheran polemical writings but also used his ecclesiastical authority to limit institutional initiatives within the Lutheran church. Characteristically, no general visitations, i.e. inspections of conditions in the church's parishes, were carried out by the Lutheran consistories between 1640 and 1688, since Frederick William feared that negative findings would lead to reform movements within the Lutheran church that he could not control.[36]

33 Willi Grün, *Speners soziale Leistungen und Gedanken: Ein Beitrag zur Geschichte des Armenwesens und des kirchlichen Pietismus in Frankfurt a. M. und in Brandenburg-Preussen* (Würzburg, 1934), 42–44, 46.

34 Karl-Dietrich Remme, "Beitrag zur Entwicklung des Medizinalwesens in Brandenburg-Preussen im ausgehenden 17. und zu Beginn des 18. Jahrhunderts" (Med. Diss., F. U. Berlin, 1954), 22. See also Reinhold Dorwart, "The Royal College of Medicine and Public Health in Brandenburg-Prussia, 1685–1740," *Medical History*, 2 (1958): 13–14.

35 Dorwart, "The Royal College of Medicine," 15.

36 Landwehr, "Die kirchlichen Zustände der Mark," 188. Another possible reason for the policy of avoiding general visitations was the recognition on the part of the regime that, given the tense nature of relations between the two confessions, a call for a general visitation by the elector would be interpreted by the orthodox Lutheran party as the first step of an aggressive electoral policy of transforming Lutheran institutions along Calvinist lines. Nischan, "The Schools of Brandenburg and the 'Second Reformation,'" 217–18.

The confessional impasse during the reign of the Great Elector, combined with a lack of funds, thus prevented any significant revival in social institutions run by the Lutherans, be they schools or hospitals. As the Lutheran hospitals could not handle the growing numbers of destitute persons, Frederick William took initiatives that brought the state into this area. The elector issued prohibitions on begging and sought to keep beggars from entering towns by increasing police forces at the town gates. Since these coercive measures did not begin to correct the causes of the beggar problem, they were completely ineffective.[37]

After adhering at first to the Great Elector's welfare policies, Frederick III(I) adopted a more constructive, if ultimately unsuccessful, approach to the social problems he inherited. As part of his conciliatory policy toward the estates and the Lutheran church, Frederick supported a wide range of reforms involving the Lutheran church. By 1710 a general visitation in Brandenburg-Prussia was under way, but well before that date the Pietists, led by Spener in Berlin and Francke in Halle, had already founded and staffed numerous primary schools in Berlin and its environs.[38] But the Pietists' major initiative was in the field of poor relief. In 1693 Spener proposed to the state authorities a scheme of poor relief similar to the one he had introduced in Frankfurt/Main in the 1670s. Adopted and implemented in Berlin after 1695, Spener's plan put beggars to work as spinners and carders of wool and paid them wages for their labor. To house these people and force them to attend religious services, the state built a large facility, the Grosse Friedrichshospital, which opened in 1701. A state agency, the Commission for the Poor, established in 1699, was designed to oversee the program.[39]

For several years after 1695, the poor relief program in Berlin succeeded in clearing the beggars from the streets. But following the outbreak of war in 1701, the number of beggars again exceeded the ability of charitable institutions to take care of them. Since space in the hospitals did not increase after 1701, Frederick's regime had to resort ever more frequently to the police measures relied on by his father.[40] Moreover, the police in Berlin were hampered in carrying

37 Grün, *Speners soziale Leistungen und Gedanken*, 44–45.

38 Wienecke, "Die Begründung der evangelischen Volksschule," 50–51.

39 Grün, *Speners soziale Leistungen und Gedanken*, 47–59, 66–70, 72–75; Wendland, "Studien zum kirchlichen Leben," 186–88.

40 Grün, *Speners soziale Leistungen und Gedanken*, 64.

out their duties by the general hostility of the population toward them. In particular, soldiers stationed in the Berlin garrison frequently beat up policemen, since the policeman's job entailed harassing the many beggars who happened to be ex-soldiers.[41] The effectiveness of the poor relief program was further undermined by the inability of the central authorities to force other towns to adopt Spener's plan. The inmates of the hospitals in Berlin, who disliked the hard labor and intensive catechization they encountered in these institutions, fled in large numbers to other towns, where they could resume the easier life of begging.[42]

All the factors that undermined the credibility of Frederick's government – his preoccupation with the Berlin court, the corrupt fiscalism, and an inability to respond effectively to worsening social problems – became all too apparent in the subsistence crisis of 1708–10. This disaster was in part a consequence of the changes in society that the policies initiated by the Great Elector had produced. For a long period after 1640, to be sure, the Hohenzollern lands were not especially vulnerable to widespread famine. Frederick William had generally permitted the nobles to export grain, except in times of extreme scarcity.[43] Until the 1690s, this policy was generally beneficial because the cities were still fairly small and could rely on their own food production to meet most of their needs.

But after immigrants, ex-soldiers, and ex-peasants had swelled the population of the towns and cities of Brandenburg-Prussia from the 1680s on, the problem of feeding urban residents during times of famine presented itself for the first time. During the famine of 1697–98, the Danckelmann administration succeeded in imposing effective grain export embargoes, and a serious crisis was prevented.[44] But plentiful harvests between 1700 and 1708 induced complacency on the part of most of the central bureaucracy, most notably on the part of domain director Wittgenstein. Proposals to build magazines, where grain, bought at low prices in years of abundance, could be stored for distribution in times of famine, were not taken seriously by Wittgenstein.[45] Instead, Wittgenstein applied

41 *Ibid.*, 71.

42 *Ibid.*, 59.

43 He did this not solely as a concession to the Junkers, since the Hohenzollerns' domains also earned money from grain exports and since exports from the nobles' lands yielded customs revenues to the state.

44 Naudé and Schmoller, eds., *Die Getreidehandelspolitik*, vol. II, 134.

45 *Ibid.*, 157, 160–70.

himself to taking as much money as he could from the peasantry in order to underwrite the rapidly rising costs of the royal court.

When famine and plague struck the eastern part of Brandenburg, eastern Pomerania, and East Prussia after the extremely cold winter of 1708–09, Wittgenstein was still preoccupied with securing revenue for the court. Since the famine was severe and affected most of Europe, the price of grain soared everywhere; and Western Europe's demand for grain from the Baltic region reached its highest level since the Thirty Years' War. Wittgenstein, consequently, permitted the grain-producing region around Magdeburg and Halberstadt, which had not been affected by the famine, to export large quantities of grain in order to fetch the high prices prevailing in the Western European market.[46] At the cost of expropriating grain from the peasants and siphoning off some of the grain exports from Magdeburg and Halberstadt, Wittgenstein managed to feed Berlin. But these policies left the Pomeranian and East Prussian peasants, already impoverished by heavy taxation, without grain and without the means to buy any food at all. Even from these hardest hit areas, however, some grain was exported to feed Swedish and Polish troops battling in Poland.[47] Although 250,000 people in East Prussia – 40 percent of the province's population – died from the famine and plague, export of grain from East Prussia was not prohibited until April 1710. And this prohibition applied only to export by land, not by sea.[48]

Although the state profited handsomely from these grain exports, Frederick I could not ultimately ignore the calamity unfolding around him. In the fall of 1710 Frederick I asked the leaders of the anti-Wittgenstein faction at court to submit a report on the state of his kingdom.[49] In December the king dismissed Wittgenstein and Wartenberg. A new regime, dominated by the crown prince and his supporters, came to power, although a radical change in policy could not occur until the death of Frederick I in 1713 and the ascension to the throne of Frederick William I.

46 *Ibid.*, 180.

47 *Ibid.*

48 Fritz Terveen, *Gesamtstaat und Retablissement: Der Wiederaufbau des nördlichen Ostpreussens unter Friedrich Wilhelm I., 1714–1740* (Göttingen, 1954), 18; Naudé and Schmoller, eds., *Die Getreidehandelspolitik*, vol. II, 184.

49 W. Michaelis, "Die Staatskrise Preussens in den Jahren 1709–10: Der Ruin des Landes, seine Ursachen und der Reformbeginn," *Geschichte in Wissenschaft und Unterricht*, 24 (1973): 157–58. See also Klaus-Ludwig Feckl, *Preussen im spanischen Erbfolgekrieg* (Frankfurt/Main, 1979), 158–65.

THE PRE-1713 HOHENZOLLERN STATE IN COMPARATIVE PERSPECTIVE

The ignominious events of 1708–10 should not obscure for us the accomplishments of the Great Elector and Frederick III(I). Motivated and sustained by the cause of Reformed confessionalism, these rulers established and maintained a state system that generated enough military force to block any further expansion by mid-seventeenth-century Sweden and made a major contribution to the ultimate defeat of Louis XIV. This achievement was all the more remarkable in light of the weakness of the sixteenth-century Hohenzollern princes and, indeed, of the absence of any tradition of centralization in the East Elbian region.

In terms of the relationship between the post-1640 Hohenzollern regimes and their contemporary counterparts, much of the "greatness" of Frederick William and his son, besides the military success of the former, consisted precisely in their ability to raise their princedom from political insignificance to a position of comparable rank to territorial states such as Bavaria and Saxony. In order to accomplish this in a relatively compressed time frame, the Great Elector and Frederick III(I) had to be somewhat more aggressive in their internal policies than most other princes in the Empire. The intrusive power of the pre-1713 Hohenzollern state manifested itself especially in its ability to settle an unusually large number of immigrants, mostly Calvinists, despite the opposition of the estates and the established Lutheran church. In addition, although the states of Saxony and Württemberg were able to levy general excise taxes for a period of time, only in Brandenburg-Prussia was the excise both permanent and collected mainly by a princely bureaucracy.[50] As a result of this added capability for extracting tax revenue from society, the Great Elector and Frederick III(I) were able to raise larger armies and attract higher subsidy payments than any German prince except the emperor.[51]

50 Carsten, *Princes and Parliaments*, 439. As the failure to transform the guild system illustrates, however, it is easy to exaggerate the effectiveness of the pre-1713 bureaucracy and to underestimate its dependence on the local estates for the performance of its tasks. As a case study of one section (*Hauptamt*) of East Prussia indicates, before the 1720s the war commissars visited the towns only occasionally, and political control in the municipalities remained securely in the hands of the local elite. Hannelore Juhr, *Die Verwaltung des Hauptamtes Brandenburg/Ostpreussen von 1713 bis 1751* (Berlin, 1967), 118–26.

51 To compare the relative troop contributions of the various German princedoms to the War of Spanish Succession, see Braubach, *Die Bedeutung der Subsidien*, 170–71.

Important as they were, however, the distinctive features of this political system did not constitute a revolutionary departure from seventeenth-century norms. The rootedness of Frederick William and Frederick in their time is demonstrated by their very confessionalism and by their conception of the nature of rulership, which in the final analysis was the traditional, patrimonial one. To be sure, the fact that their confessionalism was of the Reformed type meant that, like the rulers of the Palatinate, they pursued adventurous, risky foreign policies and sometimes departed from tradition to procure from domestic sources the power they needed to back up their diplomacy.[52] This tendency, also exhibited by seventeenth-century Catholic leaders such as Maximilian of Bavaria and Cardinal Richelieu, was reflected in the Great Elector's emphasis on the autonomy of the military from the rest of a state structure still partly controlled by the estates.[53]

Yet the decisive point is that for Frederick William the army – and, by extension, state power in general – was not an end in itself, as was the case with his grandson, but a means to an end. For both he and his son Frederick envisaged a prince's role in traditionalistic terms, i.e. as a patriarchal ruler who serves his people through dispensing justice, governing in council, and working for peace and the welfare of his subjects.[54] Commitment to these principles certainly lay behind Frederick's attempt to reconcile the estates to his government in the name of "harmony." That even his father's allegiance to the older conception of rulership was much more than mere posturing is shown by Frederick William's will, in which he partitioned "his lands" among his sons – a not uncommon practice among sixteenth- and seventeenth-century Protestant (mostly Lutheran) princes.[55] A more telling indication of Frederick

[52] Schilling regards this kind of brinkmanship as a common trait of "Second Reformation" rulers. See Schilling, "Die 'Zweite Reformation' als Kategorie der Geschichtswissenschaft," 431–32.

[53] "Politisches Testament des Grossen Kurfürsten," in Dietrich, ed., *Die politischen Testamente der Hohenzollern*, 201–03.

[54] *Ibid.*, 199. See also the "Erste Ermahnung Kurfürst Friedrichs III. an seinen Nachfolger," in *ibid.*, 212, 214. Georg Küntzel finds the traditional goals of rulership as enunciated by the Great Elector comparable to the ideas of the conservative late sixteenth-century Lutheran social thinker Melchior von Ossa. See Küntzel, *Die drei grossen Hohenzollern und der Aufstieg Preussens im 17. und 18. Jahrhundert* (Stuttgart and Berlin, 1922), 74.

[55] For a discussion of the significance of this action, see Dietrich, ed., *Die politischen Testamente der Hohenzollern*, 44–47, 69–70. For a recent study showing that the widespread loyalty of Protestant princes to the principle of partible inheritance lasted well into the seventeenth century, see Paula Sutter Fichtner, *Protestantism and Primogeniture in Early Modern Europe*

William's archaic view of his own political creation can hardly be imagined.

In characterizing the pre-1713 Hohenzollern regime, then, it is perhaps most accurate to say that it embodied in acute form the tensions and contradictions of large seventeenth-century German territorial states, which, while retaining patriarchal and confessional forms of legitimation, frequently violated in practice the norms attendant upon traditional rulership. Thus while the Great Elector built up an impressive army by pushing customary constitutional limitations to the maximum, he also in the process created in unusually intense form a sense of estrangement on the part of the estates toward the princely government.

In other words, the political system developed by the Hohenzollerns after 1640 displayed in a somewhat heightened manner not only the strengths of the seventeenth-century German princedom but also its characteristic weaknesses. For in Brandenburg-Prussia the gap between the dynasty and indigenous elites, which throughout the German lands constituted a source of ultimate weakness for the state, was if anything greater than elsewhere. The extraordinarily heavy taxes spawned a corresponding degree of resentment on the part of the Junkers because even though the nobles themselves were largely tax exempt, by extracting a sizable percentage of the peasant surplus, the state thereby restricted the amount of feudal dues that the estate-owners could collect from their peasants.[56] At the same time, the Junker families were not usually able to compensate for the limited income from their farming operations by obtaining well-paying electoral offices, as was the case for at least a portion of their counterparts in the other princely states. The reason for this – both rulers' systematic preference for members of the Reformed faith, often foreigners, for positions at court – shows again how the same policy that strengthened the Hohenzollern state in one way, weakened it in another.[57] Thus despite Frederick III(I)'s attempts to ease confessional tensions and improve relations with the estates, it is no wonder that the Junkers as a whole felt no loyalty toward the Hohenzollern state and no obligation to serve it.[58]

(New Haven, 1989). Upon his accession Frederick was able to prevent the partition from occurring and firmly established thereby the principles of primogeniture and indivisibility in Hohenzollern family law. See Frey, *Frederick I*, 39–41.

56 Hagen, "Seventeenth-Century Crisis in Brandenburg," 326.

57 Dietrich, ed., *Die politischen Testamente der Hohenzollern*, 37, 64.

58 Hintze, "Staat und Gesellschaft unter dem ersten König," 405.

The alienation felt by the estates toward the regime was not diminished by the failure of state policies to restore economic well-being. Once again in a kind of exaggerated conformity with the experience of other territorial states, the Hohenzollerns' mercantilist efforts foundered for lack of funds and a lack of a serious commitment to restructuring the economy. The Great Elector's performance was particularly dismal in this respect, almost in inverse proportion to the grandiosity of his plans. For whereas most parts of Germany benefited from almost twenty-five years of peace after the Thirty Years' War, Frederick William led his country into a major war only eight years after the Peace of Westphalia had been signed, thereby reversing the process of recovery.[59] After 1660, when he had gained enough control over his lands to carry out a systematic economic program, his plans to reproduce the Dutch model in Brandenburg-Prussia proved to be ill-conceived and unrealistic.[60] To be sure, his canal-building did increase the transit trade through Brandenburg, and some of the enterprises run by immigrants prospered.[61] On balance, though, during his reign the countryside and the portion of the urban economy controlled by the guilds received little constructive help in overcoming the effects of periodic wartime devastation and heavy taxation.

Nor was Frederick III(I)'s record that much better. Though the country was spared from hostile invasion and the subsidy-fed growth of Berlin boosted the immediate hinterland's economy, Frederick's regime knew only four years of peace and exhibited in a blatant form the evils of fiscalism, which rendered counter-productive even the most promising initiatives. The fiscalism became so severe after 1702 that constructive economic policies could not be carried out; hence

59 Hagen, "Seventeenth-Century Crisis in Brandenburg," 322.

60 Even in basing a recovery plan on emulating the Dutch model, Frederick William was not alone among German princes. Characteristically, it was another German Calvinist ruler, Karl Ludwig, elector of the Palatinate, who acted on a similar vision. In 1652 Karl Ludwig refounded Mannheim and gave the city extensive privileges, including freedom from all princely tariffs and tolls, with the hope that it would become the Amsterdam of the Rhine valley. Sellin, *Die Finanzpolitik Karl Ludwigs von der Pfalz*, 205–06.

61 The author of the best study available on the pre-1713 immigration to Brandenburg-Prussia concludes that there were definite limits, especially in the short and medium term, to the economic stimulation brought about by the arrival of the Jews and Huguenots. Besides the severe structural, systemic problems of the economy within which they sought to operate, the immigrants were also hindered in making a quick and successful adaptation to their new home by the religious-inspired hostility of the indigenous population, which the regime could not always control. See Jersch-Wenzel, *Juden und "Franzosen" in der Wirtschaft des Raumes Berlin/Brandenburg*, 87–88, 244–47.

nothing was done to prevent foreigners from supplying most of the goods demanded by the court and army. As a result, a high percentage of the capital that flowed into Brandenburg-Prussia quickly left the country and ultimately provided jobs for skilled workers in such places as Saxony, the Dutch Republic, and France. The inability of consumption spending by a small elite to bring about a broad-based prosperity was illustrated by the fate of the easternmost provinces in 1708–10.[62] But even in Berlin itself, Frederick's Baroque buildings stood side by side with rubble left over from the Thirty Years' War, and the contrast in wealth between Wittgenstein's coterie and the growing numbers of beggars in the streets could not have been more glaring.[63]

From this comparative perspective, the pre-1713 Hohenzollern polity did not differ fundamentally from the type of political system common among the larger late seventeenth- and early eighteenth-century German territorial states. An impartial observer in 1713 would have predicted, moreover, that, barring some radically new policy direction, the Hohenzollern regime in the coming years would come to resemble its compatriots in the Empire even more closely. For as we have seen, the growth in state power under the Great Elector and his son was heavily dependent on immigrants and capital inflows from Western Europe. But the final defeat of Louis XIV in 1713 ended the favorable market for the services of the Brandenburg-Prussian army, and the coming of peace was also likely to bring about a relaxation in the persecution of Calvinist minorities by Catholic monarchs. In addition, the security requirements for the Hohenzollern state were bound to ease, especially in light of the definitive defeat of the Swedes by the Russians at Poltava in 1709. At the time of his death in early 1713, Frederick III(I) planned to reduce drastically the size of his army; even in a much more unsettled time, 1690, he envisioned a peacetime army of only 20,000 soldiers.[64]

Any such diminution in the intensity of Hohenzollern state-building enterprise would have led, in turn, to a greater assertiveness on the part of the estates. Far from viewing the state as their instrument or ally, the Junkers, had they been given the chance, would have done everything possible to limit its power. The nobility

[62] Feckl, *Preussen im spanischen Erbfolgekrieg*, 154.
[63] Hintze, "Staat und Gesellschaft unter dem ersten König," 415.
[64] Dietrich, ed., *Die politischen Testamente der Hohenzollern*, 61.

of Brandenburg-Prussia were well aware that in every other East Central European land, be it Mecklenburg, Poland, Bohemia, or Hungary, the indigenous elites had far more "freedom" then they. Thus instead of geopolitical and socioeconomic forces impelling further centralization after 1713, all the signs seemed to be pointing the other way.

But we know from hindsight that between 1713 and 1740 the Prussian army doubled in size and the economy became productive enough to enable the state to keep this much larger army in the field without the benefit of foreign subsidies. A state that failed in its attempt to pursue a foreign policy independent of the Habsburgs before 1713 waged three victorious wars against the Habsburgs in the generation after 1740. This chapter has shown that the rapid development of the Prussian state between 1713 and 1740 cannot have resulted from a continuation or intensification of the state-building strategies of the Great Elector and Frederick III(I). It has also made clear, by inference, that for Brandenburg-Prussia, or for any of the other early eighteenth-century territorial states, to break through existing limits to further growth in state power, it was necessary above all to restructure the economy to create additional resources in the private sector. Taxing at still higher levels the economies of the Hohenzollern lands and the other German princedoms would only serve to prolong the economic depression and diminish long-term productive capacity.

But an attempt by a seventeenth- or early eighteenth-century German princedom to impose significant structural transformation by decree not only would have aroused the opposition of the estates but also would have foundered on the unwillingness of a bureaucracy, composed mainly of local notables, to carry out an unduly radical centralization.[65] To defeat the inevitable resistance to such measures as setting aside guild privileges and abrogating local economic controls, the prince or king needed, therefore, to enlist the active collaboration of a significant portion of the local elites in his territory. Procuring such support for initiatives of such a non-traditional sort required nothing less than a broader, more modern

[65] When Eberhard Ludwig, Duke of Württemberg (1692–1733), and Friedrich August I of Saxony (1694–1733) attempted to push toward a centralization that went beyond the standards of the seventeenth century, the decisive obstacle to the realization of their plans was the traditionalistic character of their bureaucracies. See Vann, *The Making of a State*, 176–78; Dietrich, "Merkantilismus und Städtewesen in Kursachsen," 259.

definition of the state's role and the acceptance of that definition by leading elements of society. Such an acceptance would necessarily entail, however, a renunciation by the nobility of much of their corporate autonomy and an unprecedented willingness to subordinate their personal inclinations to the state.[66] Only a powerful spiritual or ideological impetus could overcome the nobility's reluctance to embrace such change, especially as its deeply ingrained traditionalism was so strongly reinforced by an imperial political culture profoundly opposed to extraordinary concentrations of power at the territorial level.[67]

The ability of the Hohenzollern monarchy to articulate a more modern ideological legitimation for its rule and induce its Junker elite to participate in the creation of a new political culture based on that ideology was an indispensable factor in its rapid growth in power after 1713. Since the cultural and psychological means for achieving that end were derived from German Protestantism, especially from Lutheran Pietism, it is to the story of the Pietist movement that we now shall turn.

[66] As Briggs points out with respect to the prototypical case of Louis XIV's France, the court culture did little to promote among the nobility an ethos of self-sacrifice based on instinctual repression. See above, p. 28, n. 39. In fact, the tendency on the part of court nobles was rather to strive to "establish frontiers between themselves and other social groups" by elaborating "a style of fashionable behavior" based on hedonistic values. Briggs, *Communities of Belief*, 408. In other words, there was a marked discontinuity between the psychocultural milieu at the typical seventeenth-century absolutist court and the more austere, work-oriented atmosphere prevalent at the Prussian court under Frederick William I and also at the "Enlightened" courts throughout mid to late eighteenth-century Europe.

[67] For the latter, see Vann, "New Directions for Study of the Old *Reich*," 12–13.

CHAPTER 4

Lutheran confessionalism

PROMETHEAN SPIRITUALITY AND THE EMERGENCE OF THE MODERN STATE

The pressure on seventeenth-century European states to increase their military capability resulted largely from the competitive nature of the European state system. The insecurity attendant from the inability of any power to establish a hegemonic position in Europe was particularly acute between the late sixteenth and early eighteenth centuries. The nearly constant warfare of that period reflected the impact of successive bids to achieve dominance, first by Spain and then by France, as well as the political rivalries and religious tensions generated by the splitting of the Roman church into three major confessions. Still another, at first less obvious source of conflict was the growing international economic rivalry, which increasingly compelled European states to defend with force lucrative assets such as colonies or trading privileges in which they themselves had heavily invested. But despite often spectacular increases in the size of armed forces achieved by seventeenth-century European states, as we have seen in the case of the German princedoms, the states were usually able to acquire the resources to pay for their armaments through an intensification of traditionalistic forms of rule, without having to initiate fundamental social changes within their territories.[1]

Although the diminishing of confessional animosities by the early eighteenth century and the simultaneous defeat of Louis XIV's expansionary policies had the effect of stabilizing international

[1] J. H. Shennan argues that a lack of internal transformation in seventeenth-century society at all commensurate with the surge in external state power was not just a German but a continental European phenomenon. See Shennan, *The Origins of the Modern European State, 1450–1725* (London, 1974), 112–13.

relations somewhat, the process of state building that had achieved such momentum in the crisis-ridden seventeenth century accelerated, if anything, in the more prosperous and less warlike eighteenth. The further growth in state power was due, in part, to the negative impact of eighteenth-century economic trends on traditional, still largely autonomous communities. Especially destabilizing for the latter were the marked, indeed revolutionary, demographic growth that began in the 1720s and the concomitant penetration by the market economy into previously self-sufficient rural areas.[2] As the guild-dominated towns and self-governing rural communes gradually lost their social cohesion, their leading groups needed the state even more than before both to uphold their own local primacy and to supply new forms of social control that would compensate for the ongoing dissolution of the older order.[3] To be sure, the process by which the inflationary expansion of the eighteenth century favored the expansion of state control over subject communities was in many respects a replay of the sixteenth-century state–society relationship described above.[4] What distinguished the eighteenth-century dynamic, however, was not only the greater power of the economic forces in question but also the social role of the local elites, who by the eighteenth century tended to be even more culturally and socially separated from the rest of their communities and hence much more amenable to economic and political initiatives originating from outside their localities.[5]

Yet the dynamism of eighteenth-century states stemmed from more than their ability to exploit the effects of socioeconomic change. Especially in the latter half of the century, the state-building enterprise assumed an unprecedentedly self-conscious character, which was reflected in the emergence of two qualities now regarded as constituting the essence of the modern state. With

[2] For an extended analysis of this eighteenth-century phase of economic expansion, see Kriedte, *Peasants, Landlords and Merchant Capitalists*, 101–57.

[3] This is a central theme in James Van Horn Melton's excellent study on educational reform in eighteenth-century Central Europe. See Melton, *Absolutism and the Eighteenth-Century Origins of Compulsory Schooling in Prussia and Austria* (Cambridge, 1988), esp. 145–68.

[4] See above, pp. 16–23.

[5] Culturally, this separation took the form of participation in a non-communal print culture. Socially and economically, as Freidrichs has shown in the case of Nördlingen, many urban patriciates by the mid to late eighteenth century had lost their paternalistic sense of connection with the craft guilds and had adopted instead a pro-capitalist, "pro-development" outlook. See Friedrichs, *Urban Society in an Age of War*, 296–97. That many smaller urban communities did not experience this trend until well into the nineteenth century is, of course, demonstrated in Walker, *German Home Towns*, *passim*.

respect to political theory, this period witnessed the ever more frequent assertion and increasingly broad acceptance of the doctrine of sovereignty, according to which the state was conceived to be an abstract entity above and distinct from both the person of the monarch and society as a whole.[6] Along with this non-traditional image of the state as an autonomous and superior agency, eighteenth-century European states developed correspondingly novel capacities for manipulating, mobilizing, and bestowing a new form of unity upon the societies in their charge. The crucial change in this area was the sustained effort made to transform inherited semi-traditionalistic administrative structures into impersonal, intrusive bureaucracies dedicated to imposing state control over the day-to-day activities of their subjects at the expense of customary social patterns.[7]

Despite the momentous nature of this attempt, successful in the long run, to bind society to the state through this new institutional instrument, historians and sociologists alike have viewed this debut of modern bureaucracy in an unproblematic fashion. Even Max Weber, for all his awareness of the centrality of bureaucracy in what he called the "rationalization" of Western society, conspicuously failed to formulate a systematic explanation for the birth of the characteristically modern administrative organization. In an essay that presents his fullest treatment of this problem, Weber contended merely that "the decisive reason for the advance of bureaucratic organization has always been its purely technical superiority over any other form of organization."[8] In explaining what he meant by "technical superiority," Weber, to be sure, repeatedly and insightfully compared modern bureaucracy to capitalist enterprise in that both types of institutions transact their business in an "objective" manner, according to "calculable rules" and "without regard

6 Shennan, *The Origins of the Modern European State*, 113–14.

7 The linkage of the "notion of impersonal administrative power" with the emergence of the concept of sovereignty in "late [i.e. eighteenth-century] absolutism" is also made by Giddens, *The Nation-State and Violence*, 4. The centrality of bureaucratic administrative capability to the modern state is also emphasized by Michael Mann, who views the distinctive quality of the modern state, be it democratic or authoritarian, as that of possessing a high degree of "infrastructural coordination," which he defines as "the capacity of the state actually to penetrate civil society, and to implement logistically political decisions throughout the realm." See Mann, "The Autonomous Power of the State: Its Origins, Mechanisms and Results," in John A. Hall, ed., *States in History* (Oxford, 1986), 113.

8 Max Weber, *From Max Weber: Essays in Sociology*, ed. and trans. H. H. Gerth and C. Wright Mills (New York, 1958), 214.

to persons."[9] Yet Weber did not go much beyond this, leaving the impression that the historical appearance of bureaucracy was the result of a natural, evolutionary process that was partly a product of "economic conditions" and partly a result of the ambitions of early modern European princes.[10]

Such a casual treatment of this issue begs many questions, not the least significant of which was posed by Weber himself: why, despite its "indubitable technical superiority" has "bureaucracy everywhere been a comparatively late development"?[11] Weber's failure to attempt a serious probe of the origins of bureaucracy contrasts strongly with his recognition that the triumph of modern capitalism happened not only because of some inherent "superiority" but also because of the role of a non-material factor, the Protestant ethic, in overcoming economic traditionalism.[12] An important legacy of this omission in his sociological system has been the virtual absence of any discussion by subsequent writers of a cultural dimension to the emergence of the modern form of state organization.[13]

Yet the parallels between the "spirit of capitalism" and the mentality permeating bureaucratic institutions could hardly be more evident. Beyond the traits of rationality, impersonality, and calculability noted by Weber, the modern mind-set prevailing in both economic and political realms is animated by a Promethean desire to obtain control over natural processes and human commu-

[9] *Ibid.*, 215. See also p. 221, where Weber describes the development of public bureaucracies in terms of the "concentration of material means of management." Weber's understanding of the process of bureaucratization is thus directly analogous, by implication, to the Marxian view of capitalism as tending to develop by means of a concentration in relatively few hands of the economic "means of production."

[10] *Ibid.*, 224–27. Weber's approach in effect makes bureaucratic rationalization a given that really does not need to be accounted for in terms of other historical factors. This same assumption lies behind the largely descriptive treatment given to the historical development of the Prussian School historians. For the historiographical implications of their legacy, see above, p. 6.

[11] Weber, *From Max Weber*, 224. To be fair to Weber, it is possible that had he lived longer he might have addressed this issue more fully in a projected work on the sociology of the state.

[12] The importance of the Weber thesis today is not nearly so much in its actual interpretation of the connection between the theology of predestination and its alleged behavioral consequences as in its recognition that a critical part of the explanation for the unique destiny of the West lies in the interactions between Christianity and capitalism in the early modern period. See Gawthrop, "Lutheran Pietism and the Weber Thesis," 237–45.

[13] An exception has been George L. Yaney's book on agrarian reform in late nineteenth- and early twentieth-century Russia, in which the author identifies a psycho-cultural force, which he calls the "urge to mobilize," behind the bureaucratic initiatives he studies. See Yaney, *The Urge to Mobilize: Agrarian Reform in Russia, 1861-1930* (Urbana, Ill., 1982), esp. 6–9.

nities in order to transform them in ways that increase the "yield" they can provide the entrepreneur/bureaucrat. What was (and is) revolutionary about this kind of willful manipulation of social and physical environments has been its single-minded concentration on the immediate enhancement of wealth/power with a corresponding lack of consideration for the environmental, social, and cultural restraints imposed by, or embodied in, custom and tradition.[14]

This relatively uninhibited "will to power" represented such a radical departure from previous norms that it could not have been simply created *ex post facto* to justify what was politically or economically necessary. Rather it resulted from a centuries-long process of change in European culture that by the early to mid-eighteenth century had produced a recognizably modern mentality, or sensibility, that, once crystallized, began to redefine the essential character of all spheres of thought and activity.[15] That the European states, too, experienced the transforming impact of this cultural force would naturally result from the states' tendency to embody the fundamental values of their societies in order to maintain their legitimacy.

Any adequate explanation for the appearance of the modern bureaucratic state, either as a general phenomenon or in a particular case, must take into account this interdependence between the political order and the central value system. An emphasis on the connection between cultural change and eighteenth-century state building is especially necessary because the polity that the post-seventeenth-century European state was to replace, the traditional state, rested on a cultural basis antithetical to the nature of modernity. Articulated and institutionally maintained by the various branches of the church, traditional Christianity supplied for over a millennium the inspiration that had shaped the formation of European culture. A crucial component of that tradition was derived from the incorporation of Platonist metaphysics into Christian theology by the Church Fathers. Throughout the medieval period, therefore, the Church held the purpose of human existence to be the transformation of self through knowledge of metaphysical truth and

[14] For an exceptionally acute critique of this mentality, see Wendell Berry, *A Continuous Harmony: Essays Cultural and Agricultural* (New York, 1970), 86–168.

[15] The most characteristic and most studied aspect of this change is the Scientific Revolution. For the pioneering study that sought to find the same spirit in other areas of human endeavor, see Paul Hazard, *La crise de la conscience européenne, 1680–1715*, 2 vols. (Paris, 1935).

a simultaneous moral purification. One was to strive for the contemplative goal of achieving the closest possible union with that eternal divine order which both suffused and transcended the world perceived by the senses.[16]

The character of premodern European states was reinforced by this traditional Christianity in two fundamental ways. The source of legitimacy for the premodern ruler was not the functional utility of the state but the status of the monarch's person. In Christianized Europe, an integral part of that personal status was the sense of sacredness that the ecclesiastically sanctioned ruler held in the sacred, hierarchical order that governed all creation. Because of the mystical connection between the ruler and ruled, the premodern state was able to present itself as an intermediary, almost sacramental institution whose subjects could participate through their obedience to its will in a cosmic unity and harmony.[17] This widely diffused and deeply embedded popular devotion to the sacred, strengthened and given focus by the church, helps explain how the premodern state was able to use this method of legitimation to receive loyalty (and taxes) from communities that were in most respects self-sufficient and autonomous.

The other effect of traditional Christianity on the premodern polity was to place limits on the ambitions rulers may have had to increase their direct control over communities some distance from their courts. On the political level, the cultural constraints placed by tradition on such behavior included, of course, whatever personal sense of accountability to God the monarch may have felt for any arbitrary abuses of power. The medieval religious culture also gave strong ideological reinforcement to the consensus prevailing in society at large that subjects' customary rights and privileges formed an integral part of the divinely upheld order.[18]

Most important of all, however, were the inhibitions to bureaucratization posed by the very character of traditional Christianity. This belief system set a greater store on the quality of one's being

[16] For an account of the synthesis made in late antiquity between Greek philosophy and Christian spirituality, see Werner Jaeger, *Early Christianity and the Greek Paideia* (Cambridge, Mass., 1961).

[17] For a recognition of the importance of this cultural component to traditional monarchical rule, see Benedict Anderson, *Imagined Communities: Reflections on the Origin and Spread of Nationalism* (London, 1983), 25–28, 40.

[18] For the importance of the latter factor in seventeenth-century Germany, see Martin Heckel, *Deutschland im konfessionellen Zeitalter* (Göttingen, 1983), 212–14.

than on worldly accomplishments, focused on eternity and the "perpetual present" rather than on the temporal past and future, and ascribed greater weight to ultimate purposes rather than the cause-and-effect functioning of creation.[19] Identifying itself with these traditionalist positions, the medieval church used its extensive array of pastoral and pedagogical institutions to uphold and propagate these values, which were antithetical to those associated with the restless activism of modern bureaucratic and capitalist endeavor.[20]

Thus the metaphysical quality of traditional Christianity, while strengthening the personal authority of premodern monarchs, also constituted an important obstacle to political modernization. Since the modern, bureaucratic state ultimately prevailed, the traditional Christian spirituality must have either lost its hold on society or else been transformed into a type of religion capable of supplying a strongly anti-traditional cultural impetus to the building of a modern political system. Any account of the cultural side to the triumph of the eighteenth-century bureaucratic state must, therefore, begin with the fate of the deeply rooted religious values inherited from the Middle Ages. It has long been customary to see the era of the Reformation and confessionalization as constituting *the* period in which the traditional spirituality declined and in which more modern forms of Christianity were introduced. Pushed too far, however, this ingrained tendency among historians has had the consequence of overstating both the modernity of the sixteenth-century reformers and the degree of continuity between their ideals and achievements, on the one hand, and those of their eighteenth-century successors on the other.

With respect to German Lutheranism, in particular, this kind of interpretation has led to the difficulties, now widely recognized, associated with views positing a direct linkage between Luther and

19 For the profound significance of these contrasts, see Huston Smith, *Beyond the Post-Modern Mind*, 1st edn (New York, 1982), 142–45, 153–54, 157–58.

20 Thus, for example, the qualitative medieval conception of time and eternity was "wholly alien" to the "idea of a sociological organism moving calendrically through homogeneous, empty time," a conception basic to the ability of the modern state to affirm its very identity as an achievement-oriented organization. See Anderson, *Imagined Communities*, 30–31. In a related insight, Giddens sees the dominance of tradition in the premodern state as related to an absence of "the 'opening out of the future' and the 'seizure of the past,'" which is intimately connected with the "organized mobilization of information" indispensable to the modern state. See Giddens, *The Nation-State and Violence*, 76.

the development of the modern German state.[21] This chapter seeks to confirm the inadequacy of such perspectives by showing that it was only at the very end of the seventeenth century, within the Lutheran Pietist movement, that there emerged the kind of fully Promethean spirituality capable of contributing so substantially to the bureaucratization of post-1713 Prussia. What emerged, in other words, was a Christianity that, upon repudiating the values associated with the traditional metaphysical order, redefined the religious quest as primarily an endeavor in which all spiritual, social, and natural resources must be utilized for the self-conscious build-up of human power.[22]

By elucidating the origins of this spirituality, I shall also demonstrate that it is simply not correct to assume, as has so often been done, that Pietism constituted a mere continuation or intensification of Luther's basic religious outlook; for this position not only minimizes crucial differences between Luther and the Pietists but also ignores the legacy of the intervening period of almost one hundred and fifty years.[23] The essential modernity of Pietism, rather, especially that of what became Prussian Pietism, arose in response to the state of church–society relations in seventeenth-century Protestant Germany. Since the dynamics of this relationship are not widely known, I shall begin with an analysis of the tensions between traditionalistic and modernizing tendencies within the Lutheran community in the confessional era.

TENSIONS IN LUTHERAN CONFESSIONALISM

From almost the very moment of Luther's break with the Roman church, the Reformation has been perceived as a profound upheaval,

[21] For a critique of the deeply embedded notion that Luther played the role of "Father" of modern German political authoritarianism, see the essays in James D. Tracy, ed., *Luther and the Modern State in Germany* (Kirksville, Mo., 1986). For a brief, but suggestive account that traces this belief to the tendency of late nineteenth- and early twentieth-century authors to invoke Luther's authority to buttress the authority of the modern German nation-state, see Thomas A. Brady, Jr., "Luther and the State: The Reformer's Teaching in its Social Setting," in Tracy, ed., *Luther and the Modern State*, 41–43.

[22] For a discussion that probes the mythological and theological depths of the Promethean spirituality, see Thomas Merton, *The New Man* (New York, 1978), 15–34. Another illuminating essay by Merton on this theme is his "Prometheus: A Meditation," in *A Thomas Merton Reader*, ed. Thomas P. McDonnell (Garden City, N.Y., 1974), 338–44.

[23] Part of the reason for this common error is simply what James Tracy has called "the curious dearth of studies of religious life in seventeenth-century Germany." See Tracy, "Luther and the Modern State: A Neuralgic Theme," in Tracy, ed., *Luther and the Modern State*, 18.

a radical break with the medieval past, the portent of a new age. In recent decades, some historians have begun to interpret the nature of this discontinuity in a new way. Instead of focusing on the institutional break-up of the Western church and the differences between the various confessions, they emphasize how post-Reformation Catholic and Protestant faiths alike disavowed traditions of theology and piety inherited from the Middle Ages and how they articulated an alternative vision of the human–divine relationship that became the basis for the subsequent development of the major Western churches.[24]

It is indeed the case that beneath all the theological conflicts of the sixteenth and seventeenth centuries Catholic and Protestant reformers shared a common anti-traditionalism, although the depth and intensity of this attitude varied considerably among and within the different confessions. One crucial, across-the-board change was the tendency to exalt the omnipotence of God at the expense of the authority of the various intermediaries – the saints, the dead, the living community, the church – that gave late medieval piety such a prolixity of possible spiritual relationships.[25] As in eighth-century Byzantium, this desire to limit the availability of the holy to a comparatively few sources led to, among other things, the physical destruction of the sacred art whose symbolism embodied and expressed the spiritual status of these entities.[26] What set apart the iconoclasm of early modern Europe was that, partly due to the existence of a capitalistic publishing industry based on the technology of the printing press, the process of simplifying Christianity's symbolic content turned into a devaluation of sacred symbolism as such in favor of the printed word.[27] Thereby reinforced by the very nature of the medium in which its message was presented, the iconoclastic tendency present to greater or lesser extent in the sixteenth-century reformers constituted a powerful assault upon that

[24] For an analytic treatment of early modern Western Christianity in which this position is persuasively argued, see John Bossy, *Christianity in the West, 1400–1700* (New York, 1985).

[25] *Ibid.*, 92–95.

[26] For Byzantine iconoclasm, see Kallistos (Timothy) Ware, *The Orthodox Church* (Harmondsworth, 1984), 38–43. One of several recent scholarly works emphasizing the importance of iconoclasm in early modern Christianity is that of Carlos M. N. Eire, *War against the Idols: The Reformation of Worship from Erasmus to Calvin* (Cambridge, 1986).

[27] Bossy, *Christianity in the West*, 95–97. For the long-term, sociocultural significance of "print capitalism," see Anderson, *Imagined Communities*, 41–49. For the vital role played by sacred art and symbolism in sustaining a traditional spirituality, see Seyyed Hossein Nasr, *Knowledge and the Sacred* (Albany, N.Y., 1989), 253–74.

incarnational, sacramental, late medieval piety in which "the sacred was manifested through the material ... [and was] located in places and objects.[28]

There was, of course, a corresponding cultural impetus behind the drive to concentrate political authority in the hands of the princes; and, as we have seen, sixteenth-century polities, especially in Protestant areas, did much to promote catechization campaigns designed to instill in the people a rudimentary conceptual understanding of the new spirituality.[29] Despite the considerable religious and sociopolitical energies devoted to this effort, however, it would be naive to assume that the comparatively "disenchanted," less personalistic world view simply prevailed from the moment of its historical appearance. For it is no more accurate, in the cultural realm, to neglect the resistance to the anti-traditional elements introduced by the Reformation than it is to overlook the ability of the decentralized political structures inherited from the Middle Ages to prevent the emergence of a truly modern, bureaucratic state until well into the eighteenth century.

In describing the actual nature of Lutheran confessionalism in the early modern period, it is important, moreover, not to oversimplify the motivations of the sixteenth-century reformers. One of the genuine advances in recent understanding of the Reformation has been the recognition of just how strongly Protestant and Catholic reformers alike were influenced by Renaissance humanism – and not just in the area of textual criticism but in such matters as ideals of decorum and civility, pedagogical goals and methods, and social policy in general.[30] Yet on another level, the fundamental character of the Reformation was that of a movement seeking to reaffirm the faith of Christendom over and against the skepticism inherent in humanism. In the sixteenth century, this quest for the absolute still required the embrace of an objective, metaphysical truth that mattered more than any transformation in the social or natural order.[31]

[28] R. W. Scribner, "Interpreting Religion in Early Modern Europe," *European Studies Review*, 13 (1983): 92.

[29] See above, p. 21.

[30] For a demonstration of the pervasiveness of Erasmus's influence in the formation of the Puritan social agenda, see Margo Todd, *Christian Humanism and the Puritan Social Order* (Cambridge, 1987).

[31] For the limits to sixteenth-century skepticism, see Lucien Febvre, *The Problem of Unbelief in the Sixteenth Century: The Religion of Rabelais*, trans. Beatrice Gottlieb (Cambridge, Mass., 1982).

Even Luther, for all his hostility to scholasticism, regarded the grace-imparted, saving faith as constituting a "mystical union" with God, the beginning of the believer's continuing love toward, and hence knowledge of, the Creator.[32]

The tension in the Lutheran reformers between humanist and iconoclast attitudes, on the one hand, and the priority given to metaphysical certitude, on the other, was inevitably reflected in their educational and pastoral efforts.[33] Although Luther's ultimate goal was to purify the church's teaching and not to fashion a more sober, literate, and self-disciplined populace, it was not unreasonable of him and his fellow reformers to expect energetic preaching and teaching of the Word to have a transforming impact on popular behavior. But the sixteenth-century pedagogical initiatives, despite the large numbers of schools founded and visitations conducted, produced only modest results among the population at large.[34] Although many factors contributed to this outcome, perhaps the most critical was the reluctance, especially in the rural areas, to abandon customary, "superstitious" beliefs and communal rituals, which generally offered people more effective aid and comfort than the message being presented by the reformers.[35]

The leaders of sixteenth-century Lutheranism sooner or later came to view this popular resistance as yet another sign of the impending end of time, a perception given emphatic sanction by Luther's own apocalyptic eschatology and powerfully reinforced by

[32] For a valuable discussion of this point, see Peter Erb, "Introduction," in Johann Arndt, *True Christianity*, trans. Peter Erb (New York, 1979), 8.

[33] William J. Bouwsma's recent biography of Calvin, whose central theme is the conflict within the founder of the Reformed church of well-nigh contradictory allegiances to humanist and scholastic world views, gives striking confirmation that this tension was not confined to the Lutheran confession. See Bouwsma, *John Calvin: A Sixteenth-Century Portrait* (New York, 1988).

[34] For a heavily documented demonstration of this finding, see Strauss, *Luther's House of Learning*, *passim*. For a similar verdict on a comparable campaign by the Catholic church in seventeenth-century France, see Briggs, *Communities of Belief*, 267 and *passim*.

[35] For a recent summary of the causes of the ineffectiveness of the reformers' pedagogy, see Gerald Strauss, "The Reformation and Its Public in an Age of Orthodoxy," in Hsia, ed., *The German People and the Reformation*, 208–13. The point emphasized here is explained more fully in Keith Thomas, *Religion and the Decline of Magic* (New York, 1971), 74–77. According to Walter J. Ong, another cultural barrier to the acceptance of the reformers' message was the incompatibility of the "flat," linear presentation of "facts" in the catechisms and textbooks with the paradoxical, proverbial manner of communication characteristic of peasant oral culture. See Ong, *Orality and Literacy: The Technologizing of the Word* (New York, 1982), 134.

the continuing internal instability of German society.[36] This heightened fear of the coming cataclysm had the long-term consequence of dampening the clerical elite's remaining expectations of meaningful social change and accentuating, instead, the desire to pursue a policy of preventing the spread of false doctrine and maintaining social stability. The sense of living in the Last Days supplied all the motivation necessary for the secular and ecclesiastical authorities to proclaim, and to some extent enforce, ordinances aimed at ensuring conformity to existing social norms.[37] In focusing so much on external behavior and outward loyalty, however, the leadership of the Lutheran church tended not to demand much of a commitment to living a "righteous life" in imitation of Christ. Thus sixteenth-century prayer books, instructional booklets, passionals, and catechisms instructed believers merely to assent to the truth of the Word of God, receive the sacraments, carry out their vocational labors, and trust in God's forgiveness.[38]

With the arrival of the new century, the actual and potential threats to the position of the Lutheran establishment became more serious than before. In light of the extraordinary importance placed by that leadership on a coherent, correct doctrine, the church hierarchy was especially nervous about the continued adherence on the part of some of the laity to spiritualist doctrines, such as those of Valentin Weigel, which taught that salvation and a sense of oneness with God could be achieved through the cultivation of personal illumination rather than through the biblical Word as mediated by the clerical authorities.[39] A related, much more public expression of spiritual discontent was the surge of intense eschatological

[36] For an invaluable guide to Lutheran apocalypticism in the sixteenth and early seventeenth centuries, see Robin Bruce Barnes, *Apocalypticism in the Wake of the Lutheran Reformation: Prophecy and Gnosis* (Stanford, 1988).

[37] Strauss, "The Reformation and Its Public," 204–05. The more humanist-influenced Calvin, in contrast to Luther, held out some hope for the earthly future – a difference between the two main Protestant traditions that had important long-term consequences. See Barnes, *Apocalypticism*, 33.

[38] F. Ernest Stoeffler, *The Rise of Evangelical Pietism* (Leiden, 1965), 187. For a demonstration that the actual nature of piety among the laity in sixteenth-century Strasbourg did not exceed these expectations, see Miriam U. Chrisman, *Lay Culture, Learned Culture: Books and Social Change in Strasbourg, 1480–1599* (New Haven, 1982), 260–64.

[39] For an analysis of how analogous forms of spiritual dissent were generated in the Anglican church by its imposition of typically Protestant limitations on incarnational piety, see David Zaret, *The Heavenly Contract: Ideology and Organization in Pre-Revolutionary Puritanism* (Chicago, 1985), 96–104. See also Barnes, *Apocalypticism*, 29–30.

expectancy among the population at large, especially in the urban communities.[40] Although the theological basis for this phenomenon was fully in accord with Luther's own teaching, the quest for knowledge of the precise date of the Second Coming led authors in this field to draw on non-biblical prophetic traditions, as well as alchemy and other esoteric disciplines.[41]

By the 1610s the profusion of prophetic voices was creating a problem for the Lutheran authorities. Not only was it a question of internally disciplining those writers whose often popular works set forth unorthodox, sometimes chiliastic scenarios, but in a time of increasingly competitive interconfessional rivalries the external reputation of the church was also at stake. In bidding to regain the allegiance of Central Europe's elite groups for the Catholic church, the Jesuits were particularly effective in blaming the restlessness of the lower orders on the permissiveness of the Protestants toward popular prophecy and divination.[42]

The Lutheran establishment had to confront these internal difficulties at a time of mounting social crisis, exacerbated after 1618 by often horrific wartime conditions. Not surprisingly, the seventeenth-century Lutheran church, in tandem with other institutions in German society at that time, became increasingly obsessed with the preservation or restoration of stability and security.[43] Already in the 1610s, leading Lutheran theologians were launching what proved to be largely successful attacks on chiliasm, in particular, and the questing for prophetic knowledge, in general.[44]

This ongoing process of suppressing speculation based on personal readings of the biblical text was complemented by the simultaneous effort by Lutheran academics to produce definitive interpretations

40 For the urban character of this movement, see Barnes, *Apocalypticism*, 10. For the social crisis facing urban communities in the late sixteenth century, which for many *Bürger* constituted the end of the social world as they had known it, see Schilling, "The European Crisis of the 1590s: The Situation in the German Towns," in Peter Clark, ed., *The European Crisis of the 1590s* (London, 1985), 135–51.

41 Barnes, *Apocalypticism*, 230–31.

42 Evans, *The Making of the Habsburg Monarchy*, 109–11, 394–96.

43 An analogous, contemporary movement was the Laudian reaction in the Anglican church. For an analytical overview, see Todd, *Christian Humanism and the Puritan Social Order*, 206–60.

44 Barnes, *Apocalypticism*, 240, 247. For more information, especially regarding the key role of Johann Gerhard in the orthodox campaign against chiliasm, see Johannes Wallmann, "Zwischen Reformation und Pietismus: Reich Gottes und Chiliasmus in der lutherischen Orthodoxie," in Eberhard von Jüngel, Johannes Wallmann, and Wilfried Werbeck, eds., *Verifikationen: Festschrift für Gerhard Ebeling zum 70. Geburtstag* (Tübingen, 1982), 190–94.

of Scripture. To achieve this latter aim, Lutheran orthodoxy came to rely not on the historical and critical methods of humanism, but on a renewed use of Aristotelian logic and scholastic philosophy.[45] With these traditional disciplines' providing an authoritative epistemological and metaphysical framework, seventeenth-century Lutheran scholastics labored to subsume theology – and all other branches of knowledge – within great dogmatic *summae*, which often were thousands of pages in length. In the view of Johann Gerhard, the leader of this movement, only such an integration of Christian theology with what was "universally true" could provide an adequate understanding of "what faith receives, to what it is attached, and to what end it should be directed."[46]

Theologically, this neo-scholasticism was intended to be a buttress against the relativism implicit in both spiritualism and those theologies that placed more emphasis on ethical behavior than on achieving knowledge of the divine. In terms of its contemporary social significance, Gerhard's emphasis on the primacy of metaphysical truth had the related effect of underpinning a resurgence in the principle of hierarchy as *the* basis of the socio-spiritual order.[47] Like other privileged groups in seventeenth-century German society, the clergy exploited this resurgence in traditionalist ideas to enhance their position as a corporate body. This preoccupation with status led to the repudiation of any claims on the part of the laity to spiritual equality with the clergy – the "priesthood of all believers" notwithstanding. Out of this same mentality also arose the need on the part of the clergy to publicly and ostentatiously dramatize their exalted position in the hierarchical scheme of things. "Representation" on the part of the clergy sometimes took the form of pastors' employing their sermons as media for intimidating displays of erudition. The same drive to accentuate clerical rank and precedence likewise manifested itself in the reintroduction of the practice of auricular confession as well

45 Martin Heckel, *Deutschland im konfessionellen Zeitalter*, 219. Although the neo-scholastic theologians, entrenched in the Saxon universities, were dominant within the Lutheran establishment, a vigorous dissident movement, led by Georg Calixt and based in the University of Helmstedt, articulated an alternative, methodologically humanist, ethically oriented theology. See above, p. 61, n. 6.

46 See Jörg Baur, "Johann Gerhard," in Martin Greschat, ed., *Orthodoxie und Pietismus* (Stuttgart, 1982), 102.

47 Heckel, *Deutschland im konfessionellen Zeitalter*, 212–14, 221–23.

as in the widespread revival in the worship service of pre-Reformation liturgy and clerical vestments.[48]

Along with a fiercely polemical stance toward the other confessions of the Western church, this resurgence of traditionalism has often been viewed as the characteristic feature of this "orthodox" period in the history of Lutheranism. Effective as neo-scholastic dogma and high ceremonial were in strengthening the authority of the clergy, the extraordinary social stresses of the time demanded, however, an intensification of all forms of control – not just of the more traditionalistic ones. Thus the sixteenth-century pedagogical enterprise, with its aim of educating the laity in both the principles of the faith and the basics of Christian conduct, was far from being abandoned in the seventeenth century. Networks of schools that were disrupted or destroyed by the Thirty Years' War and by later wars in the century were painstakingly reconstructed as part of the broader process of "reproducing" the social system as it had existed before 1618.[49]

In certain areas of Lutheran Germany, moreover, church leaders sought to build on the already existing church–state collaboration in the enforcing of socio-religious norms. The civil authorities frequently responded to such demands for "reform" by issuing decrees on church discipline, promoting catechization campaigns, declaring special days of repentance, and even mandating a stricter observance of the Sabbath.[50] With respect to the larger territorial states, these measures seem to have been pursued with the greatest zeal in Württemberg and in Hanoverian lands.[51] The most innovative reform program of this type was carried out in the small state of Saxe-Gotha under Duke Ernest the Pious (d. 1675), whose admin-

[48] According to R. J. W. Evans, *The Making of the Habsburg Monarchy*, 286, the traditionalism of Saxon Lutheranism was manifested through that church's use of "auricular confession and quasi-conventual religious houses ... some whole services in Latin, vestments and liturgical colours, sacring bells and incense, elevation of the Host and fine church plate, even a residue of canon law." For the Laudian revival of ceremonialism in the Anglican church as a means of reinforcing clerical authority, see Todd, *Christian Humanism and the Puritan Social Order*, 227.

[49] See above, p. 33.

[50] Hans Leube, *Die Reformideen in der deutschen lutherischen Kirche zur Zeit der Orthodoxie* (Leipzig, 1924), 142–43. Leube's works continue to be the only comprehensive studies in existence on the phenomenon of "Reform Orthodoxy."

[51] For an important discussion of the judicial institution in Württemberg charged with enforcing these measures, the *Kirchenkonvent*, see Martin Brecht, *Kirchenordnung und Kirchenzucht in Württemberg vom 16. bis zum 18. Jahrhundert* (Stuttgart, 1967), 75–80. For the Hanoverian lands, see Reinhold Ruprecht, *Der Pietismus in den Hannoverschen Stammländern* (Göttingen, 1919), 3–7.

istration went well beyond the standards of the day in aiding widows and orphans, providing scholarships for university students, and seeking comprehensive improvements in public health.[52]

These institutional initiatives, important as they may have been in holding German society together through the great crises of the seventeenth century, did not, however, depart fundamentally in form or content from their sixteenth-century models.[53] What was really different about the new century's pedagogical effort to achieve greater social discipline stemmed from a growing awareness in the Lutheran church that securing the people's external assent to orthodox belief had effected little real change in their behavior.[54] By the early decades of the seventeenth century, the perception of an unacceptable gap between professed belief and everyday conduct clearly was held by most orthodox theologians as well as by those reformers usually viewed as forerunners of Pietism.[55] The impetus for this change came, moreover, not merely from the leadership of the Lutheran church. It was also to a considerable extent a response to an ongoing shift in spiritual focus among the spiritually inclined minority of the laity from apocalyptic expectancy to a concern with one's own personal, interior life.[56]

The most significant public expression of this more introspective piety was the famous devotional book by Johann Arndt, *Das wahre*

52 Lowell C. Green, "Duke Ernest the Pious of Saxe-Gotha and His Relationship to Pietism," in Heinrich Bornkamm *et al.*, eds., *Der Pietismus in Gestalten und Wirkungen: Martin Schmidt zum 65. Geburtstag* (Bielefeld, 1975), 181.

53 For a detailed account of the reforms instituted in the 1650s by Duke August of Braunschweig-Wolfenbüttel, in the course of which it becomes clear how little they went beyond sixteenth-century aims and methods, see Friedrich Koldewey, *Geschichte des Schulwesens im Herzogtum Braunschweig von den ältesten Zeiten bis zum Regierungsantritt des Herzogs Wilhelm im Jahre 1831* (Wolfenbüttel, 1891), 95–112.

54 According to Udo Sträter, this awareness was a cause of concern for all the confessions in the early seventeenth century. See Sträter, *Sonthom, Bayly, Dyke und Hall: Studien zur Rezeption der englischen Erbauungsliteratur in Deutschland im 17. Jahrhundert* (Tübingen, 1987), 119.

55 The influential Gerhard, for example, took the position that a commitment to leading a "righteous life" (*heiliges Leben*) was a necessary complement or fulfillment of correct doctrine. For Gerhard's personal commitment to "inner piety" (*Innerlichkeit*), which was decisively influenced by Johann Arndt, see Baur, "Johann Gerhard," 100–02. For the motivations behind the reform activity of the important Württemberg church leader, J. V. Andreae, who was later to exert an important influence on Spener, see Brecht, *Kirchenordnung und Kirchenzucht*, 72–73.

56 For the way in which the Thirty Years' War itself contributed to the discrediting of apocalypticism among the laity, see Barnes, *Apocalypticism*, 249–50, 257–58. For an extremely suggestive analysis of the social and psychological factors behind the spontaneous emergence of this same *dévot* mentality in seventeenth-century France, see Briggs, *Communities of Belief*, 410–11.

Christentum, or *True Christianity*, first published in 1605–09.[57] Even though *True Christianity* was only one of several such edificatory works that appeared at about the same time, its appeal was unique; several hundred thousand copies were sold during the seventeenth century – a figure that almost certainly exceeded the number of Bibles sold in Germany during the same period.[58] At the root of Arndt's success lay the author's ability to present, within a Lutheran doctrinal framework, spiritual concepts drawn from traditional mystical sources in an accessible way which inspired readers to cultivate a personal love of God.

Arndt's work can be viewed as accomplishing on the devotional level what Gerhard was trying to do theologically – namely, to amplify and make more concrete Luther's notion of faith as a mystical union with God. Yet the emphasis in Arndt on the "life of love" was so much greater than in earlier Lutheran writers that it necessitated some important theological alterations to mainstream Lutheranism as the latter had developed by this time. Arndt's chief innovation in this area was the grafting onto Luther's doctrine of justification the more experiential concept of "rebirth," or *Wiedergeburt*. Effected by God's grace, this spiritual transformation, in Arndt's conception, enabled believers to cast off their old, sinful nature and become "new people," able to imitate the life of Christ. As was the case with Christ, the love of the "reborn" was to focus not only on God but also on their neighbors – a charity born of a faith brought to life by the *Wiedergeburt*.[59] *True Christianity* gave powerful spiritual support to those seeking to remake themselves in God's image by leading exemplary lives devoted to charity and good works. As such, it constituted by far the single most important influence on Lutheran piety in the seventeenth century.[60]

Despite the power, timeliness, and broad impact of Arndt's message, it initially aroused strong opposition from some leading Lutheran theologians, who were eventually able to launch a major

57 For a widely available, though substantially abridged English translation, see Johann Arndt, *True Christianity*, trans. Peter Erb (New York, 1979).

58 Rolf Engelsing, *Analphabetentum und Lektüre: Zur Sozialgeschichte des Lesens in Deutschland* (Stuttgart, 1973), 43.

59 Arndt, *True Christianity*, esp. 117–19, 125–26.

60 According to Johannes Wallmann, Arndt's works in the seventeenth and eighteenth centuries went through "hundreds" of editions and "far eclipsed" in influence the writings of Luther himself. Clergy even had to remind their parishioners to read the Bible as well as Arndt. See Wallmann, *Kirchengeschichte Deutschlands seit der Reformation*, 3rd edn (Tübingen, 1988), 111.

attack against Arndt shortly after the latter's death in 1621. The reasons for their stand reveal many of the characteristic fears besetting the orthodox establishment. Given the obsession with maintaining "pure doctrine," it is not surprising that in some quarters the centrality for Arndt of the *Wiedergeburt* would be condemned as leading to a devaluation of Luther's key concept of justification and, even more to the point, as giving aid and comfort to those adhering to "spiritualist" doctrines of personal illumination. Such critics also found disturbing – for much the same reasons – the metaphysical foundation of *True Christianity*. Arndt set forth in that work a conception of reality, derived from Neoplatonism, that featured the same microcosm–macrocosm motif so prominent in both the writings of the great alchemist Paracelsus and those of other unorthodox seekers whose influence the Lutheran establishment was working so hard to limit.[61]

But after only a few years of controversy along these lines, the theological faculties of Wittenberg, Leipzig, and Strasbourg officially endorsed Arndt, praising above all the power of his writings to move people to repentance.[62] Reflective of the new Lutheran concern for the "righteous life," the feelings of solidarity with Arndt on the part of the clerical community were so strong, moreover, that the academic theologians were moved to undertake the unusual step of formally modifying Lutheran doctrine. As a result of Gerhard's efforts, both the rebirth and the sanctification following from it were incorporated into the generally accepted body of orthodox dogma.[63] This doctrinal revision had its desired impact of shielding Arndt's extremely popular writings from any subsequent polemical attack by giving them orthodoxy's full seal of approval.

The qualitiative impact of the devotional movement spawned by Arndt's work epitomized the Janus-faced character of seventeenth-century Lutheranism. Although typically regarded as the beginning of modern, "subjective" forms of Lutheran spirituality, such as Pietism,[64] the type of mystical spirituality pervading *True Christianity* had always been an integral part of ancient and medieval Chris-

61 Barnes, *Apocalypticism*, 239. See Arndt, *True Christianity*, 231–71.
62 Leube, *Die Reformideen*, 44.
63 Stoeffler, *The Rise of Evangelical Pietism*, 219.
64 In Stoeffler's view, it was Arndt, not Spener, who was the "father" of Lutheran Pietism. See *ibid.*, 202.

tianity. Indeed, in certain decisive ways Arndt's piety was diametrically opposed to that subjectivism so characteristic of modernity, which gives supreme ontological status to perspectives derived from the thoughts and emotions of the human subject. Like his almost exact contemporary, St. Francis de Sales, Arndt was, for example, thoroughly traditional in his understanding of his role as author. Thus the essential content of *True Christianity* was derived not from descriptions of, or direct generalizations from, Arndt's personal religious experiences but from his ability to arrange in an effective, persuasive way insights derived from traditionally accepted sources of wisdom and revelation.

In addition to the objectivity of Arndt's writings, the traditionalism of Arndt is also manifest in his emphasis on the believer's capacity to experience the presence of God in the center of his or her being. In Arndt's own words, "What can we seek externally in the world if we have internally in ourselves everything and the whole Kingdom of God?"[65] Arndt's stress on the connectedness between the human and the divine also worked to break down that opposition to the diffusion of the sacred so fundamental to the iconoclastic impulse of the Reformation.[66] It was perfectly consistent, moreover, with the already mentioned tendency in seventeenth-century Lutheranism to place a high value on the liturgy and sacraments.[67] The seventeenth-century liturgical setting came to be adorned by the outpourings of lyric poets, hymn writers, and composers of large-scale musical works – most of them inspired by the work of Arndt.[68] This creative activity, finally, was of such quality and depth that it culminated in a sacred art no less universal in stature than that of Johann Sebastian Bach.[69]

[65] Arndt, *True Christianity*, 222. This and the quotation in the following footnote are taken from Book 3 of *True Christianity*, which was strongly influenced by the medieval mystic Johannes Tauler.

[66] "Although God, by His general presence, is in all things, and not bound up with them, but in an inconceivable way fills heaven and earth, in a special and characteristic way He is in the enlightened soul of man in which He lives and has His seat. There, in His own image and likeness, He enacts those works that He Himself is." *Ibid.*

[67] For Arndt's own high esteem of the sacraments, see *ibid.*, 231.

[68] Wallmann, *Kirchengeschichte Deutschlands*, 110.

[69] The theological books in Bach's personal library included volumes by Arndt, Gerhard, and Heinrich Müller (a follower of Arndt), along with a Bible with commentary by Abraham Calov (a strictly orthodox theologian). In other words, Bach's spiritual perspective was based on a synthesis between the ancient mysticism of Christianity and the highly metaphysical doctrinal system characteristic of seventeenth-century Lutheran orthodoxy. See Walter Blankenburg, "Johann Sebastian Bach," in Greschat, ed., *Orthodoxie und Pietismus*, 313.

And yet the movement for an "active," "living" faith given such impetus by Arndt's writings also furthered in some ways the modernizing tendencies within Lutheranism. For as the century progressed, Arndtian piety did gradually acquire a more subjective character. In other words, there occurred a gradual shift away from an "inwardness" (*Innerlichkeit*) cultivated in order to achieve a greater unity with God as present in, and knowable through, all reality, including the self, to an "inwardness" that regarded self-analysis as the main source of metaphysical certainty.[70]

Part of the reason for this outcome was the repudiation by orthodox theologians, even by those who otherwise supported him, of Arndt's Neoplatonic cosmology in favor of their doctrinally safer, albeit much less mystical Aristotelian neo-scholasticism.[71] Detached thereby from its metaphysical framework, which had provided the basis for its "objectivity," Arndt's original message was therefore susceptible to being overlaid in time by accretions that subtly modified its perspective.

The most important source for this process of gradual alteration was a growing body of translated writings from English Puritan authors. These words, the first officially approved translations of which appeared in Lutheran Germany in the 1630s, appealed to those Lutherans who, while seeking a more devout life, tended to be less disposed to seek the "full union [with God] through love" central to Arndt's own vision.[72] Instead, these pious Germans seemed to be interested above all in proving to themselves that they were indeed justified or reborn, which to Arndt was simply the first stage of the spiritual life.[73] The Puritan devotional literature catered precisely to this need for assurance of salvation by supplying concrete spiritual techniques, rules of conduct, and standards for self-

[70] This same distinction is made in somewhat different language by Johannes Wallmann, who views Bach as characteristic of the former variety of *Innerlichkeit* and Spener as representative of the latter. See Wallmann, "Geistliche Erneuerung der Kirche nach Philipp Jakob Spener," *Pietismus und Neuzeit*, 12 (1986): 12–13.

[71] Barnes, *Apocalypticism*, 239. Arndt, *True Christianity*, 221, believed that "Scripture, Christ, man, and *the whole of nature* agree and ... [that] everything in one eternal living source, which is God Himself, flows together and leads to God" (my emphasis). Arndt's need to defend this position from criticism by contemporaries is evident from the brief apologetic passage at the beginning of Book 4, which is a detailed exposition of his view of the natural world. For the *apologia*, see *ibid.*, 231.

[72] Arndt, *True Christianity*, 221.

[73] Wallmann, *Kirchengeschichte Deutschlands*, 121–22.

evaluation that were incorporated into devotional material produced by Arndt's successors.[74]

Especially in the long run, what was most significant about these Puritan books was their highly self-conscious, "extraordinarily modern" character.[75] These works introduced into the Lutheran world a new type of spirituality which had first emerged in Western Christianity in full-blown form within the Reformed tradition to which the Puritans belonged.[76] Permeating the latter's writings was a self-analytical, psychologizing mode of piety, non-existent in Calvin himself, which resulted from an apparent loss of assurance in the ability of faith simply to comprehend the actuality of its own existence.[77] Hence to achieve the all-important sense of certainty of salvation, an important section of the Reformed church, beginning with Beza and including most of the Puritan leadership, advised believers to examine their actions to determine whether or not the latter proceeded from grace and a saving faith. Thus originated, in the words of Charles Cohen, that "emphatic link between grace and works, identifying the performance of holy duties as a pre-eminent sign of election, [which] transforms assurance from a concomitant of faith into an act of perception."[78]

Thus, in terms of its lay-clergy relationship, its doctrine, and,

[74] The works of the Puritan writer, Joseph Hall, for example, exerted a significant influence over Christian Scriver's *Gottholds Zufällige Andachten*, one of the most widely read Lutheran devotional books in the second half of the seventeenth century. See Sträter, *Sonthom, Bayly, Dyke und Hall*, 10.

[75] *Ibid.*, 119. Sträter here notes that in diagnosing the spiritual health of the soul and prescribing appropriate cures the Puritan books used the terminology of analysis and experiment then being introduced into the natural sciences.

[76] Sträter and others have noted, though, that the Puritan devotional writings were in many respects dependent on Jesuit and other Counter-Reformation forerunners. See *ibid.*, 58–59, 117–21.

[77] "For Calvin, assurance is identical to faith ... Faith is knowledge [as it also was for Luther, see above p. 90], the apprehension of Christ's redeeming sacrifice thrust on the mind by the Spirit ... One need go no further for assurance than to contemplate the redeemer." Charles L. Cohen, *God's Caress: The Psychology of Puritan Religious Experience* (New York, 1986), 9.

[78] *Ibid.*, 10. In this connection, J. Samuel Preus makes an important observation when he points out that seventeenth-century Puritan spirituality was characterized by an unprecedented "reification of inner religious events," a change in spirituality that provided the "generative context" for the subsequent appearance of the very term "religious experience," hitherto never used. See Preus, "The Reified Heart in Seventeenth-Century Religion," in M. Despland and G. Vallée, eds., *Religion in History: The Word, the Idea, the Reality* (Waterloo, Ont., 1992), 45–46. It is only an apparent paradox that the modern tendency to emphasize in a Cartesian manner the individual spiritual subject was accompanied from the very beginning by the reduction of the soul to an object whose very faith could be analyzed on the basis of empirical observation.

especially, its piety, the seventeenth-century Lutheran church witnessed no resolution to the tensions between traditionalistic and modernizing impulses that had already existed in the sixteenth century. If anything, in the crisis atmosphere of the seventeenth century, each of the contradictory tendencies seemed to achieve a greater intensity, resulting in a complexity not unfitting for a "baroque" age. As it was, what we would regard as traditional and modern standpoints continued to coexist, both in particular individuals and the church as a whole, in a kind of contrapuntal, yet fundamentally static unity.[79]

The resulting sense of stalemate within the Lutheran community was compounded by the divisions caused by almost constant polemical battling over the nature of "pure doctrine."[80] It was likewise reinforced by the emergence in the seventeenth century of a more confused, complicated relationship between church and state than had existed before the Thirty Years' War, when a much clearer unity of purpose characterized the collaboration between religious reformers and the secular authorities. Though the princely regimes at bottom remained attached to confessionalism as a potent means of maintaining control over their territories, in light of the post-1648 relaxation of religious tensions within the Empire the degree of commitment on the part of most princes to their territorial churches slackened. Given the comparative indifference of the secular authorities to the internal workings of the church and given the latter's ambivalence to the secular tone and open immoralities at the princely courts, it is not surprising that the Lutheran hierarchy tended to go its own way and concentrate its energies on enlarging its own sphere of corporate autonomy within the traditional order.

For despite Luther's theologically based renunciation of independent clerical power, during the confessional period the Lutheran church, even in theory, never understood its role as one of subser-

[79] For the inconsistencies of J. V. Andreae's position, for example, see Brecht, *Kirchenordnung und Kirchenzucht*, 79.

[80] One of the main themes of Spener's reform manifesto, the *Pia Desideria*, was the urgent need to de-emphasize theological polemics because of their tendency to absorb so much of the time and energy of the clergy for so little benefit. See Philipp Jakob Spener, *Pia Desideria*, trans. Theodore G. Tappert (Philadelphia, 1964), 49–54. For the analogous situation in seventeenth-century France, where a comparable drive to achieve doctrinal uniformity within the Catholic church likewise produced only a debilitating fragmentation, see Briggs, *Communities of Belief*, 222.

vience to the state.[81] In practice, the church was largely able to overcome its apparent lack of legal autonomy by politically aligning with the estates or by playing off the prince and the estates against each other. This loosening of ties with the central authority had consequences for the spiritual orientation of the Lutheran community; for in joining forces with the estates the church could not but be influenced by the corporate traditionalism of its allies. Socially grounded in the increasingly hereditary character of the clerical profession,[82] the Lutheran establishment exhibited a strong tendency to cling to tradition as *the* fundamental value, especially in those territories ruled by either Catholic or Reformed princes.

Yet there were also those among the leadership of the Lutheran church who held out hope that the old church–state partnership could be not only fully reconstituted but also raised to a higher level of effectiveness. To be sure, those whose expectations as to the standards of communal behavior had been heightened by the influence of Arndtian piety tended to criticize the existing interpenetration of church and state as "caesaropapist," judging it to be as inimical to the propagation of the faith as the papal power overturned by the efforts of Martin Luther.[83] But even the harshest clerical critics felt they had no choice but to look to the state as their natural ally in any campaign to inculcate a culture of discipline into the population at large.[84] Although this sense of reliance on the state stemmed to some extent from the precedent of past collaboration, the reluctance of even the most ardent reformers to consider any alternative strategy came most fundamentally from the deeply hierarchical view of reality prevalent among seventeenth-century Lutheran clerics. From this traditionalist perspective, reform could

81 The commitment of orthodox Lutheranism (as opposed to Calixtianism, Halle Pietism, and the *Aufklärung*) to pursuing an independent role for the church within the power structure is emphasized by Wallmann, "Zwischen Reformation und Humanismus," 369–70. This is consistent with the finding that despite Luther's emphasis on patriarchal, hence princely, authority, his social vision accorded divine sanction to the entire existing pattern of social relations; hence the net effect of his teaching was to place strong limits on the power of the prince to intervene in society for the purpose of disturbing that pattern. See Brady, "Luther and the State," 35–36.

82 Heckel, *Deutschland im konfessionellen Zeitalter*, 218, who estimates that by the seventeenth century some three-quarters of all Lutheran clergy were sons of pastors.

83 For the strong views of J. V. Andreae along these lines, see Brecht, *Kirchenordnung und Kirchenzucht*, 63–65.

84 This was true both of Arndtian Lutherans, such as Andreae, and those reformers, such as Theophil Grossgebauer, who were strongly influenced by English Puritanism. For one of the most compelling books written in the orthodox period, see Grossgebauer, *Wächterstimme aus dem verwüsteten Zion* (Frankfurt/Main, 1661).

proceed only as a result of initiatives emanating from the secular and clerical elites of society acting in concert.

As we have seen, though, even when the orthodox reformers did secure enough support from Lutheran territorial governments to institute some modifications and extensions of the existing ecclesiastical system, the net effect was merely to intensify the legalism and externality of the pedagogical and judicial pressure being applied to the people.[85] Though satisfactory to those clerics whose primary objective was to tighten their control over the laity, this outcome merely intensified the frustrations of those reformers who remained truest to the original Arndtian ideal of a holier community based on genuine acceptance by its members of a "living faith." It was as an attempt to realize this latter ideal that Philipp Jakob Spener took the decisive step of advocating a reform from below based on a widespread adoption by the laity of a works-oriented, strongly Puritan piety. With the publication in 1675 of Spener's reform proposals in his *Pia Desideria*, the Lutheran church would now have to face a movement that, on the one hand, offered a new way to achieve the long-standing goal of "improving" lay morality but that, on the other hand, also seemed to threaten the stability that the orthodox party had striven so hard to achieve.

[85] This is Brecht's verdict on the impact of the *Kirchenkonvent* in Württemberg. See Brecht, *Kirchenordnung und Kirchenzucht*, 77–78.

CHAPTER 5

Spenerian Pietism

THE *PIA DESIDERIA*

As was the case with the first two decades of the seventeenth century, a growing crisis in international relations and ensuing outbreak of general war contributed heavily to making the period from the late 1660s through the 1680s a time of crisis and change of direction within the Lutheran church. After only about twenty years of comparative peace, the Holy Roman Empire was once again beset by aggressive external enemies and subject to the surge in social misery that accompanied the return of war. Unlike the similarly stressful period at the beginning of the century, however, the general mood among Lutheran clergy and laity in the 1670s and 1680s was not one of apocalyptic expectancy but rather one of seeking to strengthen the church in whatever ways were required to meet the challenges posed by Catholic France and the Muslim Turks.[1]

Indicative of this new willingness to change – and the widespread, popular character of this sentiment – was the veritable explosion of interest in the translated writings of English Puritan authors. Well into the 1660s, the works of only a small number of Puritan writers, no more than a dozen, had been translated. The appearance of many of these editions came about, moreover, as a result of initiatives by church leaders, such as Johann Schmidt of Strasbourg, who made sure in some cases that prior to publication the texts had been "purified" of theological "errors" stemming from the Reformed origin of these works. Although the impact of the initial editions was

[1] Symptomatic of the preoccupation with the Turks, as they once again in the early 1660s showed signs of threatening Central Europe, was Spener's using for the subject of his doctoral dissertation the prophecy (Revelation 9:13–21) customarily regarded in orthodox Lutheran scholarship as the biblical passage most clearly foretelling the rise of Islam. Hartmut Lehmann, "Der Pietismus im Alten Reich," *Historische Zeitschrift*, 214 (1972):73.

by no means insignificant, beginning in the 1660s popular demand for Puritan tracts and sermons became so intense that the ecclesiastical authorities were no longer able to control the translation process. New translations of more than one hundred different English authors appeared in German book stores in the 1670s and 1680s alone as large numbers of private printers became active in this field and commissioned translations without bothering to secure approval of the local clergy. The haste to profit from the extraordinary appeal of these writings sometimes led to badly done translations, but the very atmosphere of chaotic improvisation in the publishing trade suggests the urgency of the public's desire for more rigorous spiritual teachings and for a religious renewal based on those teachings.[2]

Appearing in 1675, Philipp Jakob Spener's *Pia Desideria* set forth proposals for reforming the church that, while carefully reaffirming the essentials of the Lutheran tradition, embodied the moralistic Puritan sensibility then in vogue. For the difficult tasks of formulating such a delicate synthesis and launching a reform movement designed to achieve the aims enunciated in it, Spener was perhaps uniquely qualified. Raised in a pious Alsatian household, where both Arndt's works and the early Puritan translations were part of the family library, Spener as a young man received at the University of Strasbourg a thorough grounding in Luther's theology from his mentor, Johann Konrad Dannhauer (1603–66). Then, as if to compensate for his one-sided Lutheran academic training, Spener travelled and studied for two years in the Reformed areas of France and Switzerland, including Geneva. His learning, piety, and his lifelong habit of cultivating high-level contacts enabled him to rise quickly in the Lutheran ecclesiastical world. In 1666, at the age of thirty-one, Spener became senior of the Lutheran clergy in Frankfurt am Main. From this position of authority, he embarked on a ministry that sought, above all through pedagogical means, to bring about a renewal in the Frankfurt church. Thus in the early 1670s, Spener began to meet regularly with members of his Frankfurt parish to read and discuss the Bible and devotional literature. In addition to the formation of this conventicle, or *collegium pietatis*,

[2] The phenomenon of "massive" circulation of Puritan translations in the last third of the seventeenth century was noted in the 1920s by Leube, *Die Reformideen*, 166, 169. The subject was not, however, thoroughly investigated until Udo Sträter's important study. For the information given here, see Sträter, *Bayly, Sonthom, Dyke und Hall*, 8–18.

Spener's reform efforts also included an expansion in the catechization programs directed at the young and a successful revival of the practice of confirmation.[3]

The fruits of this theological training and pastoral experience are evident in the *Pia Desideria*, which in keeping with the times introduced important novelties, even though Spener took pains to emphasize the elements of continuity with mainstream Lutheran tradition by frequently citing works of his orthodox predecessors. Spener, of course, shared the concern, common to most Lutheran theologians and church officials, regarding the apparent gap between the external adherence of the population to correct doctrine and the persistent lack of evidence that the church's teachings were raising the common level of morality.[4] That Spener had some new ideas as to how to solve this problem was evident, however, from his proposing the widespread imitation of the conventicle he had organized at Frankfurt, which had very few precedents in seventeenth-century Lutheranism.[5] The rarity with which orthodox Lutherans had experimented with this kind of gathering was in part due to the prevalent desire on the part of the clergy to preserve their privileged status by monopolizing spiritual functions in their parishes. In strong contrast to this widely held attitude of clerical exclusiveness, Spener explicitly called for the realization of Luther's concept of the "priesthood of all believers."[6] In doing so, Spener

[3] The best treatment of Spener's early career and the development of the ideas that found expression in the *Pia Desideria* is Johannes Wallmann, *Philipp Jakob Spener und die Anfänge des Pietismus*, 1st edn (Tübingen, 1970). *The* comprehensive biography is still Paul Grünberg, *Philipp Jakob Spener*, 3 vols. (Göttingen, 1893–1906).

[4] The degree to which the pedagogical goals of seventeenth-century Lutheran reformers were actually achieved in terms of their impact on the mentality of the bulk of the population has not been systematically studied. Preliminary findings are mixed and inconclusive. In Brecht's view, the *Kirchenkonvent* in Württemberg, as an instrument of social discipline, was, for all its legalism and externality, "extremely active and effective" between 1660 and 1690. Brecht, *Kirchenordnung und Kirchenzucht*, 80. A different impression – one of continued strong popular resistance to the inculcation of clerical values – emerges from Hans-Christoph Rublack, "'Der Wohlgeplagte Priester': Vom Selbstverständnis lutherischer Geistlichkeit im Zeitalter der Orthodixie," *Zeitschrift für historische Forschung*, 16 (1989): 1–30.

[5] Such precedents as there were are discussed in Wallmann, *Philipp Jakob Spener*, 269–70.

[6] So pervasive was the emphasis on clerical authority in Lutheran Germany that, prior to Spener, those seventeenth-century Lutheran clerics who used this concept as the foundation of a program of reform were almost always spiritualists, such as Joachim Betke, who existed on the margins of the institutional church. For Betke, see Margarete Bornemann, *Der mystische Spiritualist Joachim Betke (1601–1663) und seine Theologie* (Berlin, 1959). By contrast, the Puritans as a group consistently sought to create among the laity an active commitment to personal and communal "reform," seeing the pastor's role as being "a guide, not a spiritual magistrate, a functionary, not an intermediary." Todd, *Christian Humanism and the*

went completely against the grain of well over one hundred years of Lutheran practice, arguing that only with active lay participation could the proposed reforms succeed and that the current problems of the church were largely the result of neglecting the "universal priesthood."[7]

Inseparably linked with Spener's unusually deep commitment to reactivating the spiritual energies of the laity was his equally atypical conviction that God had foreordained the occurrence of a tangible improvement in the level of faith and morality in the Lutheran church at that time. This type of outlook was rarely present in seventeenth-century Lutheranism. Even though the expectancy of the imminent end was no longer so fervently or literally held as in the first decades of the century, the eschatological perspectives of all orthodox Lutherans, including that of Arndt, were pessimistic with respect to the earthly prospects for the Christian community.[8] To be sure, the optimistic, chiliastic views that had surfaced at the height of the apocalyptic movement in the church had survived orthodox repression and had found expression throughout the century in the spiritualist subculture.[9] But there is no evidence that Spener's eschatology was derived from this source; and even if Spener had been influenced by spiritualist writings, he could not have simply reproduced their argumentation lest he be condemned and ostracized without further ado by the vigilant watchdogs of orthodoxy.

The most probable source of inspiration for Spener's confidence in the future was, rather, the same that gave his work much of its innovative character – namely, English Puritanism. In Part 1 of the *Pia Desideria*, Spener compellingly restated the standard criticisms by seventeenth-century Lutherans of their own church, concluding that the "spiritual misery" afflicting the civil authorities, clergy, and laity was so extreme that God could not permit it to continue much longer.[10] Part 2 of that same work, entitled "The Possibility of Better

Puritan Social Order, 220. This latter position was much closer to Spener's than that of the German spiritualists, who were much more radical in their opposition to hierarchy than Spener.

7 Spener, *Pia Desideria*, 92–94.

8 Wallmann, *Philipp Jakob Spener*. For a more detailed demonstration of the effectiveness of the orthodox anti-chiliastic polemic, see Wallmann, "Zwischen Reformation und Pietismus," 195–205.

9 Hinrichs, *Preussentum und Pietismus*, 9.

10 Spener, *Pia Desideria*, 40. Spener was particularly influenced in his (negative) evaluation of the state of the seventeenth-century Lutheran church by the impassioned critique of Theophil Grossgebauer. See Wallmann, *Philipp Jakob Spener*, 155–56.

Conditions in the Church," reveals, however, that Spener drew a radically different conclusion from the familiar Lutheran critique of existing conditions. In this section, Spener cited biblical prophecies of the conversion of the Jews and the fall of the papacy – based on Romans 11:25–26 and Revelation 18 and 19 respectively – as proof that "God promised his church here on earth a better state than this."[11]

These same prophecies had been widely used in the same way as support for reform demands by English Puritan and sectarian groups since the publication of an English edition of Joseph Mede's *Clavis Apocalyptica* in 1642.[12] As Johannes Wallmann has demonstrated, Spener, in the early 1670s, was in possession of a copy of the Latin version of Mede's work.[13] This linkage with Puritan eschatology is confirmed by Spener's call for a "limited perfection" comparable to that achieved by the early, pre-Constantinian church.[14] Such a position is identical to the meliorist eschatology common in later Calvinism, according to which "a limited triumph of the Gospel and a churchly flowering could be confidently expected before the Last Day."[15]

Spener's meliorism sought to detach eschatological energy from concentration on the apocalypse and redirect it instead to the realization of an expected "churchly flowering." The "Proposals to Correct Conditions in the Church," Part 3 of the *Pia Desideria*, were intended to initiate that process of rejuvenation. Since Spener believed that any good in people was the result of the power of the Word of God, he reasoned that "the more at home the Word of God is among us the more we shall bring about faith and its fruits."[16] It was in seeking to encourage "more extensive use of the Word of God among us" that Spener had established the conventicle at Frankfurt, which in the *Pia Desideria* he compared to those "ancient and

[11] Spener, *Pia Desideria*, 76–77. Spener's reasoning here was that either improvement in the Lutheran church would help bring about these events or else the simple occurrence of these events would produce new, zealous converts to Lutheranism, whose impact on the church would be rejuvenating.

[12] E.L. Tuveson, *Millennium and Utopia: A Study in the Background of the Idea of Progress* (New York, 1964), 75–86.

[13] Johannes Wallmann, *Philipp Jakob Spener*, 330.

[14] Spener, *Pia Desideria*, 80–84.

[15] Robin Bruce Barnes, "Prophecy and the Eschaton in Lutheran Germany, 1530–1630" (Ph.D. dissertation, University of Virginia, 1980), 15. The chiliasm of many of the German spiritualists, by contrast, was considerably more radical than the meliorist position of Spener.

[16] Spener, *Pia Desideria*, 87.

apostolic kinds of church meetings" modelled on the exchange of prophecies among those attending the gathering described in 1 Corinthians 14.[17] Although Spener carefully stipulated that the pastor be present and lead the meeting, in the Frankfurt *collegium* a discussion format was adopted that allowed sharing of knowledge among all participants and consequently a more in-depth learning about Scripture than was possible either through sermons or unsupervised Bible reading at home. The give and take between minister and congregation in these meetings also helped to break down hitherto insuperable status barriers between pastor and congregation, on the one hand, and between members of the various social classes among the laity, on the other.[18]

As Spener came to realize the usefulness of the *collegium* he became convinced that conventicles should serve as nuclei for the reform of entire congregations.[19] Through the conventicles, at least select members of the parish would form the habit of reading the Bible, meditating on it, and then discussing it with others. As soon as a small group could be "won for such activities," each member could then teach the Word to others not in the group, "especially those under his own roof."[20] By "getting the people to seek eagerly and diligently in the book of life for their joy ... they will become altogether different people." If in this way enough people became, in Spener's words, "altogether different," the church would be "visibly reformed"; and the prophecies of improvement would be fulfilled.[21]

From Spener's perspective, therefore, the Lutheran church was being offered an opportunity by God to share in the glorious future prophesied for the Christian peoples; and for this desired reform to occur in Lutheran Germany it had to begin at the parish level with the spiritual transformation of individuals' lives. The basic change in the soul called for by Spener was the "rebirth," introduced into

17 *Ibid.*, 89.

18 See Lehmann, "Der Pietismus im alten Reich," 82; Martin Greschat, "Christliche Gemeinschaft und Sozialgestaltung bei Philipp Jakob Spener," *Pietismus und Neuzeit*, 4 (1977–78): 312; and Wallmann, "Geistliche Erneuerung der Kirche," 31–32.

19 Wallmann points out that Spener's method of reform through the conventicle, by selecting out the more pious members of the parish and offering them spiritual training, was in clear opposition to the long practiced orthodox idea of reform, by which pedagogical and judicial measures were to apply equally to all members of the parish. Wallmann, *Philipp Jakob Spener*, 32.

20 Spener, *Pia Desideria*, 94.

21 *Ibid.*, 91, 95.

Lutheran spirituality by Johann Arndt. Like Arndt, Spener emphasized the hold of Satan over the corrupt soul of the unconverted person. Only the individual's repentance and the intervention of God's grace could lead to the deep inner change signaling a saving rebirth. By appropriating the doctrine of rebirth, Spener guaranteed for his movement a strong measure of continuity with the Arndtian tradition. Spener made his connection with Arndt apparent to all by publishing the *Pia Desideria* originally as a preface to a book of sermons by Arndt, the *Postille*. Spener's followers felt a similar affinity. *True Christianity* remained by far the most popular devotional work among Pietists throughout the movement's history.

Yet Spener's spirituality was considerably less mystical in orientation than Arndt's. It is indicative of the differences between the two that Spener, influenced as a student by the natural-law theories of Grotius, was anti-Aristotelian and unsympathetic toward qualitative metaphysics in general.[22] Compared to Arndt, Spener placed little emphasis on knowledge of God, contemplative prayer, or unity with God following rebirth. Removing the rebirth from any metaphysical context made it easier for Spener to prune away all speculative, potentially unorthodox accretions to the doctrine.[23] Thus stripped of the cosmological significance given it by Arndt, the rebirth became, in Spener's theology, simply a prelude to the holy life. Spener's attitude toward mystical theology – and hence toward any, to him, excessive preoccupation with the process of rebirth or subsequent striving for mystical unity with God – was ambivalent. While heartily recommending the *Theologia Deutsch* and the writings of Tauler as far more useful for students than contemporary polemical treatises, he nevertheless called these works "simple little books" and cautioned that they "can and may be esteemed too highly" as "something of the darkness of their age still clings" to them.[24]

What did excite Spener's wholehearted interest was the opportunity for advancing in piety available to those who had already experienced rebirth. Having undergone a real change in their lives brought about by God's grace, the reborn in Spener's view were to experience that love of God, born of gratitude, that is "the fountain,

22 Greschat, "Christliche Gemeinschaft und Sozialgestaltung," 305.

23 Martin Schmidt, "Speners Wiedergeburtslehre," in Martin Greschat, ed., *Zur neueren Pietismusforschung* (Darmstadt, 1977), 30–31.

24 Spener, *Pia Desideria*, 110, 112. On this issue, too, Spener differed fundamentally from the spiritualists, who stressed in no uncertain terms the quest for mystical unity with God.

the source, of all that the new [i.e. reborn] person ever does."[25] Yet in keeping with the Puritan side of Spener, it is also clear that the regenerate believer must also be sure that this feeling of love for God is real, that it is not a self-deception. For Spener, the surest sign of a person's true love for God was obedience to God's commands, especially to the great New Testament injunction to love one's neighbor.[26] For the conscience can with "relative ease and certainty" test whether the believer has diligently organized his or her life in "accordance with God's commands" and even whether this obedience has been performed with a "sincere, upright heart."[27]

Those who have been spiritually reborn, then, should ideally observe themselves constantly, and observe one another, to make sure that despite temptations and difficulties they will be increasingly able to conform to all the biblical precepts, "without exception."[28] In addition, theology faculties at the universities, pastors, school teachers, and fathers should themselves be "true Christians" in this sense, so that they can fulfill their all important roles as moral exemplars for those under their supervision. Although the pious behavior of such teachers would impart the most important lessons, Spener also urged that spiritual mentors should provide "concrete suggestions" that would help their charges learn how to pray, carry out spiritual examinations, resist carnal temptations, become ever more virtuous, and ultimately develop into teachers themselves.[29]

As the lives of more and more people in the Lutheran church

[25] Philipp Jakob Spener, *Der neue Mensch*, ed. Hans-Georg Feller (Stuttgart, 1966), 19. Charles L. Cohen demonstrates that it was the love of God that follows conversion, not anxiety stemming from the doctrine of predestination, which was the central motivating emotion in Puritan spirituality. See Cohen, "The Saints Zealous in Love and Labor: The Puritan Psychology of Work," *Harvard Theological Review*, 76 (1983): 455–80.

[26] Spener, *Der neue Mensch*, 28. Although love of neighbor and the holy life were of great importance to Arndt, "love of God," for him, was not restricted to, or fully realized in, this more earthly, external dimension. "Insofar as it [the soul] knows God, it loves Him and insofar as it loves Him, it desires to have Him for itself completely. This is the true mark of love, that it has the beloved completely, is united completely with the beloved, and changes itself completely into the beloved." *True Christianity*, Book 2, Chapter 13. Though this chapter is only summarized in the contemporary English translation, this particular passage is quoted in Erb, "Introduction," in Arndt, *True Christianity*, 12.

[27] Spener, *Der neue Mensch*, 93. Needless to say, Arndt did not place nearly this much emphasis on believers' empirically testing the actual existence of their love for God.

[28] *Ibid.*, 26.

[29] Spener, *Pia Desideria*, 112–13. Although the context for this particular admonition of Spener's was a discussion of how university programs in theology should be reformed, these recommendations reflect Spener's vision of the type of spiritual training that he wished everyone would receive.

became transformed in this manner, Spener believed that the reform of society at large would then proceed as a direct consequence of the broadening and deepening of commitment to this moralistic Christianity. Characteristically, Spener envisioned a gradual amelioration of the worst social evils, among which he included drunkenness, litigiousness, lack of ethical behavior in the workaday world, and, above all, the widespread practice of begging.[30] In overcoming these maladies, the church, revitalized by conventicles, was to play the leading role. Spener believed that the church should influence people in the community to mobilize the necessary resources to meet the needs of their neighbors.[31] Spener pointed out that in the early church "there was no need of begging among the brethren"; and he also invoked in this context the New Testament principle of the community of goods.[32]

Notwithstanding this use in his argument of the radical precedents set by the first Christians, Spener was not advocating an immediate total transformation of either church or society. Rather, he urged a step-by-step reform that would result from the repentance, conversion, and charitable activity of ever larger numbers of individuals. Trusting the church's ability to perform this providential mission on its own, he rejected that notion of the church's dependence on state assistance characteristic of all previous Lutheran attempts to impose moral discipline on society.[33] This same confidence in the possibility of reforming the church also led him subsequently to resist any desire of Pietist conventicles to separate from the established church.[34] Spener's acceptance of the existing institutional structure of society extended to the state and social class system as well. Since the third estate was not yet imbued with a truly

[30] *Ibid.*, 58–60. To get a sense of how perfectly Spener's social reform agenda and methodology conformed to those of the Puritans, see, for the latter, Todd, *Christian Humanism and the Puritan Social Order*, 147–75, 192–205.

[31] In the Frankfurt conventicle, Spener directed the spiritual energies of the group toward actions, such as the establishment of a workhouse, intended to help the neediest of the community. See Wallmann, "Geistliche Erneuerung der Kirche," 31.

[32] Spener, *Pia Desideria*, 61.

[33] The fact that Spener's position constituted such a complete break with Lutheran precedent is emphasized by Martin Kruse, *Speners Kritik am landesherrlichen Kirchenregiment und ihre Vorgeschichte* (Witten, 1971), 175. This stand of Spener's did not, however, imply opposition, in principle, to the institution of the territorial state church or preclude possible cooperation with the secular authorities. With respect to this point, see Wallmann, "Geistliche Erneuerung der Kirche," 17.

[34] Lehmann, "Der Pietismus im alten Reich," 77.

Christian ethic, its rule, to Spener, would hardly be preferable to that of an absolutist prince.[35] If the ideals of self-denial and love of one's neighbor were to become paramount in society (and, in Spener's eschatology, God had promised that they would), action directed toward changing external structures could only detract from the saving work of persuading others to repent, experience rebirth, and help their neighbors. Whether the secular and ecclesiastical authorities would permit the "saving work" to proceed in the manner envisaged by Spener was, of course, another question.

THE FATE OF THE MOVEMENT

Spener's respect for the existing institutional order of society notwithstanding, his reform proposals contained more than enough departures from customary norms to make highly likely their rejection by the principalities and powers of his time. Yet, at least initially, the forces of opposition were not strong enough to prevent either the wide circulation and discussion of Spener's ideas or the growth of a loose network of followers who looked to Spener as the leader of a reform movement whose members, from the early 1690s on, were known as "Pietists."

The strength of Spener's movement came, to a yet to be determined extent, from that popular mood, receptive to puritanical values and initiatives, which pervaded Lutheran towns and cities in the 1670s and 1680s. A better understood factor in the initial development of Pietism was the importance of Spener's own leadership style and abilities. Besides the wide recognition for his authority as a scholar, pedagogue, and church leader, Spener's effectiveness as a leader was enhanced by the effort he expended to build a consensus for his program. Having long maintained an extensive correspondence and having developed friendships with people representing the entire range of theological opinion within the Lutheran church, Spener did not neglect to send copies of the *Pia Desideria* to dozens of church officials and theologians in advance of its publication and ask for their reactions to it. It was characteristic of Spener's humility and willingness to entertain other points of view

35 Hans Leube, *Orthodoxie und Pietismus: Gesammelte Studien*, ed. Dietrich Blaufuss (Bielefeld, 1975), 142–45. Until the Laudian persecution, the Puritans, despite their implicitly anti-hierarchical standpoint, were similarly conversative – disinclined, that is, to oppose the social status quo. See, Todd, *Christian Humanism and the Puritan Social Order*, 204–05.

that, when the *Pia Desideria* was published separately, shortly after its initial appearance as the preface to Arndt's *Postille*, Spener had two of the lengthier responses he had received included with it, even though the authors of those treatises disagreed somewhat with some of his key ideas.[36]

Spener's inclusive way of maintaining good relations with people holding a wide variety of viewpoints helped to minimize negative reaction to the *Pia Desideria*. For almost fifteen years, moreover, his influence served to prevent a polarization within the church between his supporters and those of more orthodox sentiments.[37] Under these circumstances, Spener's movement steadily gained more adherents within the ranks of the Lutheran clergy. Especially significant was its penetration into the academic world, reflected in the fact that by the early 1690s Pietist professors dominated or strongly influenced the theological programs at the universities of Giessen and Jena, the latter one of the largest and most prestigious in Germany.[38] This meant that, in accordance with the principles laid down in the *Pia Desideria*, students at these institutions were not only trained in academic theology but were also instructed in how to achieve a more "active Christianity" in their own lives.[39] Having gained this kind of foothold in these institutions, the Pietist movement was thus in a position to replenish its ranks with recruits from the next generation.

Outside the church, the Pietists gained at least the neutrality and sometimes the active support of the political authorities in most of the Lutheran areas. Though part of the reason for this was Spener's ability to diffuse much of the potential opposition from within the church, the priority placed by the Pietists on helping those in need

36 See Kurt Aland, *Spener-Studien* (Berlin, 1943), 63–65, which also contains a long list of names of the persons who responded in writing to Spener's solicitation.

37 This need to prevent a catastrophic rupture within the church, as well as Spener's own personal conviction that the desired reform should be carried out *within* the church, accounted for Spener's continuing efforts during this period to dissuade his own followers from taking such provocative steps as forming conventicles outside the established church. That he was not always successful in this respect is indicated by Martin Kruse, "Preussen und der frühe Pietismus," *Jahrbuch für Berlin-Brandenburgische Kirchengeschichte*, 53 (1981): 10.

38 For more information about the theological faculty at Jena, who were to train many of the students who later were to find positions in the Prussian service during the reign of Frederick William I, see Max Steinmetz, ed., *Geschichte der Universität Jena, 1548/58–1958: Festgabe zum vierhundert-jährigen Universitätsjubiläum*, vol. 1 (Jena, 1958), 194–99.

39 For Spener's suggestions for a reform of university theology programs, see Spener, *Pia Desideria*, 103–15.

resulted in what were widely perceived as positive social initiatives designed to alleviate the severe social problems resulting from the non-stop warfare of this period. Most especially, in the course of the 1670s Spener convinced the Frankfurt authorities to establish an orphanage–workhouse in order to provide regular poor relief and catechetical instruction to the city's beggars.[40] A large number of cities, including Augsburg, Darmstadt, Nuremberg, Leipzig, Jena, Hanover, and many others, followed Frankfurt's example and closely copied the regulations drawn up by Spener for the Frankfurt workhouse. Governments of the larger territories, always alert to possibilities for increasing revenues, also sponsored a limited number of workhouses as prospective money-making ventures and as centers for training more productive citizens.[41] These new institutions, of course, often provided both jobs for young Pietist clergy and teachers, as well as settings in which Pietist pedagogical principles could be applied to the inmates.[42]

In addition to appreciating the utility of these Pietist workhouses, some territorial rulers also valued the Pietists' relative indifference to confessional distinctions. In the eyes of such princes, Pietism constituted a faction within the Lutheran church that, unlike the orthodox majority, was not opposed to the immigration of non-Lutheran refugees – an important source of capital and skills for the impoverished German polities.[43] Though actual sympathy for Pietism did not run very deep at the worldly courts, such pragmatic considerations helped soften otherwise hostile perceptions on the part of many of the courtiers.

Much more natural allies of the Pietists were those among the German elites who disliked or resented the extravagant, hedonistic court culture.[44] Many of these people, like Spener himself, were raised in families strongly attached to the Arndtian devotional

40 Kurt Aland, "Der Pietismus und die soziale Frage," in Aland, ed., *Pietismus und moderne Welt* (Witten, 1974), 101–04.

41 See Lehmann, "Der Pietismus im alten Reich," 53–54; Ruprecht, *Der Pietismus in den Hannoverschen Stammländern*, 193n; and Dietrich Blaufuss, *Reichsstadt und Pietismus: Philipp Jakob Spener und Gottlieb Spizel aus Augsburg* (Neustadt, 1977), 25. This wave of workhouse establishments was the German equivalent to the phenomenon of the "Great Confinement" in mid to late seventeenth-century France noted by Michel Foucault, Orest Ranum, and others.

42 For some of the obstacles facing these institutions in particular and the Pietist relief program in general, as exemplified by the experience of the city of Berlin in the 1690s and 1700s, see above, pp. 70–71.

43 For the case of Württemberg, see Lehmann, *Pietismus und weltliche Ordnung*, 50.

44 Lehmann, "Der Pietismus im alten Reich," 84. See also, Vann, "New Directions," 12–18.

movement. With his scholarly prestige, diplomatic skill, and knowledge of heraldry (his avocation), Spener was especially adept at finding patrons for his movement among pious members of the nobility, many of whom gave Pietists jobs as pastors in villages over which they exercised the right of patronage (*Patronatsrecht*).[45]

Even though all of these factors were able to sustain Spenerian Pietism for a time, the movement's existence was always precarious. While leaders of the orthodox party continued to have no objections to "building" or even "improving" the church, they never ceased suspecting Pietism of being a vehicle for a new Reformation, an unacceptably radical (to them) transformation of both the doctrine and institutional structure of the church.[46] Fear of heterodox spirituality had formed a strong component of the mainstream Lutheran mentality since the 1520s, and it was indeed the case that Spener's puritanical variant of Arndtian piety was not the only spiritual alternative to orthodoxy in late seventeenth-century Germany.[47] From the perspective of the more rigid members of the orthodox party, the Pietist leaders, including Spener himself, too often failed to dissociate themselves emphatically enough from chiliasts or spiritualists, who probably formed a considerable percentage of their supporters among the non-elite population.[48]

If these tensions between Spener's group and their traditionalistic opponents were ever to escalate into open conflict, moreover, the secular authorities would almost certainly side with orthodoxy. The Pietists would inevitably be viewed as the party disrupting the social status quo, and the hold of the premodern princely states on society was too tenuous for them to tolerate religious movements that could serve as potential rallying points for the numerous dissatisfied elements among their subject populations. Confessional solidarity was simply too important a part of the established order to risk for the sake of a movement for which most of those of the highest status had in any case little real sympathy. Urban patriciates, court nobles, and princes lived in accordance with an ethic prizing conspicuous consumption, a way of life Pietist preachers rarely hesitated to

[45] Aland, "Der Pietismus und die soziale Frage," 122–23.
[46] Leube, *Orthodoxie und Pietismus*, 36–38.
[47] For the spiritualist subculture and its points of contact with Pietism, see Martin Schmidt, *Pietismus* (Stuttgart, 1972), 123–37.
[48] Ruprecht, *Der Pietismus in den Hannoverschen Stammländern*, 6.

criticize.[49] Compared, therefore, to the possible threat posed by Pietism to the public order and to the court culture, the value to most seventeenth-century princes of workhouses, industrious workers, or even economic development was hardly sufficient for them to support the Pietists over their orthodox adversaries.[50]

Although the Duke of Hesse-Cassel banned conventicles as early as 1678,[51] the tension between Pietism and the Lutheran establishment did not turn into intense wide-ranging conflict until the early 1690s. A takeover of the University of Leipzig by Pietist students precipitated the crisis. A closer examination of the incident reveals how it confirmed the worst fears of the ecclesiastical authorities with respect to the potentially subversive nature of the Pietist movement. In 1686, his standing within the Lutheran leadership still at a very high level, Spener left Frankfurt to accept a prestigious appointment as head court chaplain and consistory member in Electoral Saxony, the heartland of the orthodox establishment. Although there were tensions from the beginning between Spener and the worldly elite at court, serious troubles began only in the spring of 1689, when August Hermann Francke, an advanced student of biblical languages at the university and a protégé of Spener's, delivered a series of lectures on New Testament exegesis. Following the pedagogical principles for theological study set forth in the *Pia Desideria*, Francke sought to demonstrate to his hearers how to apply biblical teachings to everyday spiritual concerns – a complete break from the orthodox method of theological instruction, oriented as it was toward metaphysics and dogma.

Even more disturbing to the professoriate than Francke's exegetical approach, however, was the response his lectures provoked – a spontaneous, powerful "revival" affecting a large proportion of the theology students at the most orthodox Lutheran university in

49 The most famous example is the conflict between Spener and the Saxon court after his appointment in 1686 as *Oberhofprediger*. See Lehmann, "Der Pietismus im alten Reich," 80. Similarly, relations between the ducal court and the Württemberg Pietists foundered repeatedly on the latter's opposition to ducal immorality. See Lehmann, *Pietismus und weltliche Ordnung*, 59, 62.

50 Not coincidentally, the 1670s and 1680s witnessed the first bloom of the cameralism of Becher and his followers, which, "forward-looking" like Pietism, was also in at least latent conflict with the (same) powerful cultural and political forces of the day and was similarly unable to prevail against them, in the short and medium term. See above, pp. 29–31.

51 Wilhelm Diehl, *Die Schulordnungen des Grossherzogtums Hessen*, Monumenta Germaniae Paedagogica, vol. XXXIII (Berlin, 1905), 106. For a more detailed account, see Heinrich Streitz, "Das antipietistische Programm der Landgrafschaft Hessen-Darmstadt von 1678," in Bornkamm *et al.*, eds., *Der Pietismus in Gestalten und Wirkungen*, 444–65.

Germany. Although the theology faculty immediately prohibited Francke from giving any more *collegia* on biblical topics, his friends, especially Johann Caspar Schade, continued to hold public meetings in which academic concerns increasingly took second place to Pietist preaching and discussion of edificatory works. Students ceased attending regular lectures and formed numerous conventicles, few of which were led by academically qualified individuals. Worse still from the point of view of both university officials and the secular authorities, the movement spread to the townspeople. Schade took the revolutionary step of permitting women from town to attend his *Kolleg* – the first known participation by women in the academic life of a German university. As was not the case with the earlier conventicles, moreover, the uncontrolled situation in Leipzig allowed the interjection of "enthusiasm" (*Schwärmerei*) into the Pietist milieu, with several important visionaries, most of them female, appearing in Middle and North Germany in the early years of the 1690s.[52]

All of these events, above all perhaps this public emergence of spiritualist prophets, set off the strongest possible reaction against Spener's movement among orthodox circles throughout the German lands.[53] The heavy polemical weaponry of Lutheran orthodoxy was now directed against the Pietists, unleashing an intense controversy that in its acute form lasted about two decades and a division within the church that lasted even longer than that. Not surprisingly, this split within the Lutheran community had adverse political consequences for the Pietist movement. In March 1690 the elector of Saxony responded to the Leipzig conflict by prohibiting conventicles, forcing Francke and Schade into exile, denying scholarships to Pietist students, and thereby crushing the Pietist movement in Saxony.[54] In the course of the 1690s, likewise responding to orthodox pressure, Lutheran governments elsewhere initiated repressive measures wherever the Pietist movement had gained widespread support. In Hamburg, for example, where the Pietists had founded three schools for the poor and amassed a con-

52 For what is still by far the best account of the Leipzig movement, see Leube, *Orthodoxie und Pietismus*, 170–211.

53 For the especially divisive character of the spiritualism issue, see Wallmann, "Geistliche Erneuerung der Kirche," 32–33.

54 Leube, *Orthodoxie und Pietismus*, 202.

siderable following, the expulsion of Johann Heinrich Horb, Spener's brother-in-law, in 1693 put an end to Pietism as an open, public movement.[55]

A most revealing example of the fears of the authorities with respect to the Pietist movement was the case of Württemberg. In that duchy, where an aggressive territorial government was seeking to promote educational reform and economic development, where a large segment of the social elite (the *Ehrbarkeit*) identified Pietism with a long-sought restoration of traditional values in society, and where the chair of the consistory was a friend of Spener's, Pietist initiatives found no official response during the entire period 1690–1710, except for the establishment of a workhouse in 1705. The reason: a strong tendency on the part of Württemberg Pietists, alienated from the power structure by the immoralities at court and driven to desperation by repeated devastations of the country by French armies, to form conventicles outside the established church. Although the government was not strong enough to enforce its ban on the separatist conventicles, its concern with checking their influence outweighed the desirability of enacting such Pietist-sponsored measures as the introduction of confirmation and reform of the confessional.[56]

Lacking decisive backing from the secular governments in most of the Lutheran territories, the Pietists thus could not secure legal sanction for their conventicles. The tight restrictions placed on the Pietists' ability to transform society gradually produced, in turn, a change in the nature of the Pietist movement itself. Spenerian Pietism had combined the concept of spiritual rebirth with an optimistic social activism based on conventicles operating within the established church. By about 1710, Pietist groups in most of Lutheran Germany had decided that conditions in the world were deteriorating, rather than improving, and therefore abandoned the attempt to initiate broad social change. Instead, in the character of mid to late sixteenth-century Anabaptism, they tended to gather in small communities without attempting to proselytize among society at large. As such, they constituted an important subculture in eighteenth-century Germany, tolerated in practice by regimes no

[55] Dieter Klemenz, *Der Religionsunterricht in Hamburg von der Kirchenordnung von 1529 bis zum staatlichen Unterrichtsgesetz von 1870* (Hamburg, 1971), 94–97.

[56] Lehmann, *Pietismus und weltliche Ordnung*, 36–54.

longer threatened by them.[57] It was these Pietist groups who contributed so heavily to the German Romantic movement and from whose lack of concern for "the world" originated the quietistic associations that still cling to the very term "Pietism."

The activist strain in Pietism did not die out, however. In Brandenburg-Prussia, where Frederick III(I) welcomed the Pietists exiled by the persecutions of the 1690s, it lived on because of the unique political and religious situation in that territorial state. With the Palatinate devastated and/or occupied by the French during this period, the Hohenzollern territories constituted the only stronghold of Reformed confessionalism among the larger German states. At the height of the persecutions of Calvinist communities in Western Europe, Frederick's government was committed like no other German state to accepting Reformed immigrants, despite the problems that policy caused between the electoral regime and a Lutheran church that, embracing the overwhelming majority of his subjects, had proven to be such a thorn in the side of Frederick and his father. As a result, the regime in Berlin saw in the Pietists a group within the Lutheran church that would be much more accommodating toward the Huguenot refugees, much less hostile to the Reformed faith in general, and perhaps quite useful to the state as a counterweight to the heavily orthodox Lutheran leadership.[58]

Yet even in Brandenburg-Prussia, Spenerian Pietism did not survive in its original form. There, its activism eventually became closely intertwined with the state-building process and, while gradually abandoning the conventicle, found new vehicles in institutions that were to have a far greater impact on society. This fundamental reorientation in Spenerian Pietism, carried out by August Hermann Francke, not only enabled the activist form of Pietism to survive and prosper in Brandenburg-Prussia but also contributed decisively to the transformation of the Brandenburg–Prussian state itself.[59]

[57] *Ibid.*, 50; Leube, *Orthodoxie und Pietismus*, 229–35. The history of these "non-church" or "radical" Pietists has not been adequately researched or conceptualized. For a penetrating historiographical assessment of these groups, see Hans Schneider, "Der radikale Pietismus in der neueren Forschung," *Pietismus und Neuzeit*, 8 (1982): 15–42 and 9 (1983): 117–51.

[58] For Spener's support for the policy of accepting immigrants and the importance of the relatively non-confessional character of Pietism for the subsequent development of the Pietist–Hohenzollern collaboration, see Deppermann, "Die politischen Voraussetzungen für die Etablierung des Pietismus," 46–50. For other factors behind Frederick's support of Pietism, see above, pp. 61–63.

[59] For reflections on the unlikely concatenation of circumstances by which the Pietist–Hohenzollern collaboration produced the Prussia of Frederick the Great, see Hartmut Lehmann, "Pietismus und soziale Reform in Brandenburg-Prussia," in Oswald Hauser, ed., *Preussen, Europa und das Reich* (Cologne and Vienna, 1987), 119–20.

CHAPTER 6

From Spener to Francke

PIETISM AND THE HOHENZOLLERN STATE TO 1700

By early 1691 Spener's relationship with the Elector of Saxony had deteriorated so seriously that he left the country. Spener did not remain unemployed for long, however; for in June he received from the Brandenburg-Prussian state a dual appointment as provost at Berlin's St. Nicholas church and as a member of the Lutheran consistory of Brandenburg. Yet it would be a mistake to suppose that a working partnership between the Hohenzollern regime and the Pietists followed automatically from Spener's appointment. The Pietists, for their part, initially had reservations about too close an association with the Brandenburg-Prussian state. For one of the most important characteristics of the early Pietist movement was precisely its desire to *loosen* the bonds between church and state that had tightened during the confessional era. Spontaneous action arising from conventicles within the church would, it was felt, first renew the Lutheran community and then serve as an instrument for social transformation "from below."

Nor, despite the many political and religious reasons for supporting Pietism, was it by any means assured that the Brandenburg-Prussian state's backing for that movement would long endure. What would always remain a possible source of conflict between the Pietists and the Hohenzollern state were the latter's periodic attempts to pursue a goal first set forth by Frederick III(I): the union of the Lutheran and Reformed faiths. Although Spener was willing to work with Reformed clergy and regarded such a union as theoretically possible, he always suspected that the intense Reformed campaign on behalf of union stemmed from essentially political motives. Spener's approach toward negotiations for union was therefore cautious and circumspect. His own method for healing the split between the two churches – that both churches do penance for the sins that brought on the division – was not likely to find favor among the more zealous members of the Reformed party.[1]

A rift between Spener and the Reformed leaders over the union issue could have left the Pietists dangerously isolated in the event of a Pietist–orthodox confrontation. The latter was, indeed, a virtual certainty. Any significant Pietist activity in Brandenburg-Prussia, especially the introduction of conventicles, was bound to incite immediate, vehement opposition from an orthodox leadership well informed about recent events in neighboring Saxony. The ultimate arbiter in such a crisis, Frederick, was much more inclined than his father, moreover, to take a conciliatory stance toward the traditional elites. If, at the moment of decision, the ties between Pietism and the state were for any reason less than solid, Frederick would have been at least tempted to extricate himself from an awkward situation by repudiating Spener and his followers.

Thus even in Brandenburg-Prussia the position of Pietism was precarious. Spener, however, worked hard to overcome all obstacles to the survival of Pietism in the Hohenzollern realm. Through his organizational work in the church and his diplomatic activity at court, Spener succeeded in quickly assembling the nucleus for a strong Pietist movement in Brandenburg-Prussia. His most obvious contribution consisted of recruiting leading Pietists, many of them forced to leave their homelands during the persecutions of the 1690s, and using his influence to find jobs for them in Brandenburg-Prussia. In 1692 Spener helped persuade the Berlin authorities to appoint Pietists to the two professorships on the theological faculty of the newly established University of Halle. The successful candidates were Joachim Justus Breithaupt, then on the verge of being forced out of his position as senior pastor at Erfurt, and Paul Anton, a leader of the Leipzig students in 1689–90. As noted earlier, August Hermann Francke was also able to join the Halle faculty, as professor of Near Eastern languages. In addition to placing these and other exiles in prominent posts, Spener trained a new generation of Pietist leaders in his *Collegium Biblicum*, a Bible-study group that met twice a week in Berlin. Among the participants were Joachim Lange, Ferdinand Lichtscheidt, Heinrich Lysius, Lampertus Gedicke, and Johann Porst.[2] The last three, in

[1] Delius, "Berliner Unionsversuche im 17. und 18. Jahrhundert," 16, 21, 32.
[2] Wendland, "Studien zum kirchlichen Leben," 166–69.

particular, figured prominently in the later history of Prussian Pietism.

Spener not only assembled this formidable group of activists but also introduced an important change in tactics appropriate to the situation he was facing. To take away from the orthodox Lutherans their most ready pretext for launching a potentially destructive conflict, Spener de-emphasized the importance of the conventicle in his Berlin ministry.[3] That this change in policy reflected a fundamental reorientation in the character of his movement is evident from Spener's simultaneous decision to stake the future of Pietism on close collaboration with the Hohenzollern regime.[4] Spener looked to the Brandenburg-Prussian state as an indispensable partner not only because its support would enable him to nurture Pietism in the Hohenzollern territories but also because its protection would allow him to work in an uninhibited way to help Pietists outside Brandenburg-Prussia during a time of general persecution.[5]

Spener, therefore, did everything in his power to maintain the Berlin regime's good will toward the Pietists. He successfully avoided a controversial role in the negotiations for union of the confessions, managing to state his reservations persuasively while retaining the respect of all parties.[6] From 1695 on he actively assisted the state in an effort to reform its welfare policies.[7] Most importantly, he won over to his side an impressive array of army officers and government officials. These included the head of the domain administration (Samuel von Chwalkowski), the minister of cultural and ecclesiastical affairs (Paul von Fuchs), a prominent general (D. G. von Natzmer), two privy councillors (von Katsch and von Schweinitz), and a member of the high nobility (Freiherr Carl Hildebrand von Canstein).[8] These men not only provided

3 This shift away from his earlier vision of a renewal based on spontaneous change at the parish level was Spener's response to the unrelenting opposition of the orthodox clergy in the 1690s. See Blaufuss, *Reichsstadt und Pietismus*, 136n; Lehmann, "Der Pietismus im alten Reich," 80.

4 Deppermann, "Die politischen Voraussetzungen für die Etablierung des Pietismus," 50.

5 Johannes Wallmann, "Philipp Jakob Spener in Berlin, 1691–1705," *Zeitschrift für Theologie und Kirche*, 84 (1987): 74–75, 77–78. In this same article (pp. 82–83), Willmann goes on to describe how Spener also used the opportunity offered by the existence of his safe haven in Berlin to launch a polemical campaign on behalf of his melioristic chiliasm, which he had hitherto felt compelled to downplay because his exposition of this eschatology in the *Pia Desideria* had met with such a lack of positive response from the Lutheran establishment.

6 Delius, "Berliner Unionsversuche im 17. und 18. Jahrhundert," 32–33, 47.

7 See above, pp. 70–71.

8 Wendland, "Studien zum kirchlichen Leben," 163–65.

access to the highest levels of the central administration but also made large financial contributions to Pietist causes. Especially generous was Canstein, whose commitment to Spener's work was so great that, on the latter's death in 1705, he assumed the responsibility of representing Pietist interests at the Berlin court.[9]

Despite Spener's role in establishing a strong foothold for Pietism in Brandenburg-Prussia, he left unresolved the question of how the Pietist movement there would bring about the desired reform of church and society. This issue was especially troubling to his more militant junior colleagues. Members of a generation that matured during the fierce polemics and intense confrontations of the late 1680s and early 1690s, these younger Pietists found Spenerian reform, especially in its attenuated, post-1690 form, to be too limited in scope and purpose.[10] This younger generation was aiming to create as quickly as possible a "truly Christian" society. As a result of their commitment to dramatic change, they were more willing than their mentor to challenge the status quo and were less inhibited about tampering with, or devising alternatives to, existing institutions.

In the course of the 1690s, two strategies for promoting radical reform became manifest in the Pietist movement – each one associated with a strong personality among Spener's younger followers. Johann Caspar Schade, whose *Kolleg* had constituted the core of the Leipzig student movement of 1689–90, applied his abilities as a charismatic preacher to the task of bringing about a spiritual transformation in his parish. Permeated by a general dissatisfaction with "this world," Schade's preaching, with its heartfelt sighs, sobs, and freely flowing tears profoundly moved his audiences.[11] In addition to his sermons, Schade's ministry consisted of numerous household visitations and frequent gatherings of his followers in private homes.[12]

Schade, however, may have poured so much into the evangelistic aspect of his ministry as to leave him with little energy or desire to

[9] For a detailed account of Spener's relationship with Canstein, see Peter Schicketanz, *Carl Hildebrand v. Cansteins Beziehungen zu Philipp Jakob Spener* (Witten, 1967), 17–19, 26–61. See also Klaus Deppermann, *Der hallesche Pietismus und der preussische Staat unter Friedrich III.(I.)* (Göttingen, 1961), 66, 155–57.

[10] Lehmann, "Der Pietismus im alten Reich," 86–87.

[11] Wendland, "Studien zum kirchlichen Leben," 174–76.

[12] Georg Simon, "Der Berliner Beichtstuhlstreit, 1697–1698," *Jahrbuch für Berlin-Brandenburgische Kirchengeschichte*, 39 (1964): 48–50.

attend to the more routine tasks of his office. This was particularly the case with the hearing of confessions and the granting of absolution, the customary procedure through which the church then enforced moral discipline. Confessional practice in the late seventeenth-century Lutheran church still retained many features of its medieval forebear, with absolution being given after the recitation of prescribed answers to a standard set of questions and after the payment of a small sum of money to the pastor. Too scrupulous to carry out this duty in such a mechanistic manner, Schade apparently did not have the psychological stamina to give his personal attention to the sins of every member of his congregation.[13] Early in 1697, therefore, Schade refused to hold individual confession any longer, replacing it with a form of "generalized" confessional, a procedure that did not require him to absolve individuals directly without closely examining their consciences.

As Schade's immediate supervisor, Spener forbade this general confessional. Schade, in reply, refused to hold any kind of confessional, thereby occasioning complaints from anxious parishioners. In May 1698 Spener petitioned Fuchs to prohibit gatherings in Schade's house. Two months later, stripped of his post and aware that many of his former followers had turned violently against him, Schade died from a high fever.[14] Although Schade's unstable personality undoubtedly contributed to his undoing, his almost exclusive reliance on a revivalist emotionalism, combined with an unwillingness to manipulate existing church institutions for his own purposes, meant that Schade simply had not built up a solid enough base to mount a successful challenge to the ecclesiastical status quo.

The reasons for Schade's failure to develop a viable new direction for the Pietist movement become clearer when his career is contrasted to that of his fellow radical, August Hermann Francke. Raised in Gotha, where his father was a councillor at the court of Ernest the Pious, Francke, under the influence of his sister, was exposed to Arndt's writings as a teenager. Gifted in the study of biblical languages, he experienced as a university student a growing conflict between the values of his upbringing and the worldly attractions offered by his calling. After a brief period of atheistic

[13] *Ibid.*, 50–51; Wendland, "Studien zum kirchlichen Leben," 178–79.

[14] Wendland, "Studien zum kirchlichen Leben," 176, 179–81; Simon, "Der Berliner Beichtstuhlstreit," 81–85. For an explanation of Spener's motives for opposing Schade, see Wallmann, "Philipp Jakob Spener in Berlin," 80–81.

doubt and despair, he underwent a dramatic conversion and went on to play a crucial role in the "awakening" of the Leipzig student body in 1689–90.[15]

In the spring of 1690, J. J. Breithaupt, as senior of the Erfurt clergy, invited him to give a guest sermon in that city; and Francke so impressed his hearers that they demanded he remain as a deacon, a post he filled until orthodox opposition forced him to leave in the fall of 1691. The controversy surrounding Francke's ministry in Erfurt stemmed in part from his refusal to discount any reputed vision or prophetic revelation, however dubious or potentially unorthodox. This practice of Francke's, an extension of the Pietist tendency to encourage private devotions among the laity, continued even after he assumed his Halle professorship in early 1692. In that year he joined in the defense of Johann Wilhelm Petersen, who had lost his job as superintendent in Lüneburg for publicly endorsing the visions of a woman living in his house. The spiritualist Petersen visited Francke in Halle, where the religious atmosphere in Francke's circle was still sufficiently unconventional to foster the conversion of a young law student, Hochmann von Hohenau, and start him on a celebrated career of itinerant preaching and periodic incarceration.[16]

Francke's presence would thus have been provocative almost anywhere in northern Germany in the early 1690s, but political conditions in Halle, where he assumed his professorship in the spring of 1692, guaranteed him an extremely hostile reception from the local authorities. Halle was subject to the jurisdiction of the provincial government (*Regierung*) at Magdeburg in the so-called Old Mark. The latter had been incorporated into the Brandenburg-Prussian state only in 1680. Its *Regierung*, dominated by five magnate families, stubbornly resisted relinquishing any of its authority to the central government in Berlin.[17] As was typically the case in areas where the estates exercised dominant political control, the orthodox

[15] The main source for Francke's early spiritual development is Francke's own account of his conversion in his "Lebenslauf." For the complete text, see A. H. Francke, "August Hermann Franckes Lebenslauf," in *Werke in Auswahl*, ed. Erhard Peschke (Witten, 1969), 5–29.

[16] Joachim Böhme, "Heinrich Julius Elers, ein Freund und Mitarbeiter A. H. Franckes" (Phil. Diss., F. U. Berlin, 1956), 12–13.

[17] Hinrichs, *Preussentum und Pietismus*, 217–18. Deppermann describes the local regime as a "noble republic" (*Adelsrepublik*), a term commonly used in connection with early modern Poland. Deppermann, "Die politischen Voraussetzungen für die Etablierung des Pietismus," 48.

Lutheran establishment was well entrenched and totally opposed to any interference with its religious monopoly. Indicative of the attitude of the estates of Magdeburg was their bitter opposition to the new university at Halle, not least because they had to pay the salaries of both Pietist theologians and jurists like Christian Thomasius, an early Enlightenment thinker who advocated both absolutism and religious toleration.[18]

The intense antipathy to Pietism on the part of the local elites was not the only difficulty facing Francke. He also had to confront a challenging pastoral responsibility, for his professorial appointment was combined with a pastorate position in the surrounding community. Halle in 1692 was suffering from the effects of a prolonged economic depression. The city's troubles had begun during the Thirty Years' War, when an imperial army plundered the town and damaged its salt works so severely that they were never rebuilt. With the basis of its former prosperity in ruins, the problems affecting Halle's postwar economy were intensified by its cession to Brandenburg-Prussia in 1680. As a Hohenzollern enclave surrounded by the territories of Saxony, Brandenburg-Prussia's main regional rival, Halle could no longer trade with its natural hinterland. The city's misfortunes culminated in the plague of 1681–83, which reduced Halle's population from thirteen thousand to fewer than six thousand. In the demographic recovery following the plague, one of the babies born in 1685 was Georg Friedrich Händel. But even if the import of those tidings could have been appreciated by the community, it would not have lifted the burden of a stagnant economy and a staggering municipal debt, which had reached 4.6 million Taler by 1688.[19]

The impact of such depressed conditions on the level of civic morale was predictably severe. The school system was in terrible shape, with no poor or free schools at all. Most of the city's young people roamed the streets with nothing to do. Joined by many of

[18] For a collection of articles that gives a comprehensive picture of recent research on Thomasius, see Werner Schneiders, ed., *Christian Thomasius, 1655–1728: Interpretationen zu Werk und Wirkung* (Hamburg, 1989). The fiscal battle over the university was part of a larger struggle for revenues between the Magdeburg *Regierung* and the Berlin regime, in which the latter usually prevailed. The taxes paid by the region to the electoral (royal) government increased from 156,000 Taler in 1681 to 450,000 Taler in 1710. Deppermann, "Die politischen Voraussetzungen für die Etablierung des Pietismus," 49.

[19] Deppermann, *Der hallesche Pietismus und der preussische Staat*, 71; See also E. Heinicke, "Die wirtschaftliche Entwicklung der Stadt Halle unter brandenburg-preussischer Wirtschaftspolitik von 1680–1806" (Jur. Diss., U. Halle, 1929), 18, 22.

their elders, they spent much of their time in the "sin resort" of the suburb Glaucha, where Francke's new parish was located. Out of two hundred dwellings in Glaucha, thirty-seven were taverns, and many of these were also brothels. Every citizen of Glaucha had the right to manufacture and sell spirits. Francke's predecessor, quite at home in the local taverns, had been dismissed for committing adultery in the confessional.[20] Francke's job was to "clean up" Glaucha, and on his performance rested more than just the success or failure of that particular mission. Francke's and the other Pietists' credibility at the University of Halle was riding on the outcome.

The Pietists were not alone, however, in their struggle. The Berlin authorities had placed the Pietists in Halle as part of a comprehensive strategy designed to integrate the Old Mark more completely into the Hohenzollern realm. The two-fold purpose behind a whole series of steps taken by the governments of the Great Elector and Frederick III(I) had always been to promote economic development in the region and simultaneously weaken the political power of the estates in Magdeburg. Thus the Great Elector had settled Jews and Huguenots in Halle and introduced the excise tax there. Between 1686 and 1692, through privileges granted by the central government to individual immigrants, seventeen textile establishments had been founded in the city.[21] Most recently, the Berlin regime had chosen Halle as the site for the new university in large part because of the economic stimulus it would provide the city.

The process by which Frederick's government selected Francke for his dual assignment illustrates the high priority it was continuing to give to the Halle-Magdeburg area. Francke's name was suggested by Christian Friedrich Krautt, brother of the top financier at court and a powerful figure in his own right. Final approval for the appointment was required from Veit Ludwig von Seckendorff, chancellor of the new university, and Eberhard Danckelmann, prime minister and *de facto* head of the government. Both men attended in person a sermon by Francke before arriving at their decision.[22]

Without connections of this kind with the highest levels of the Brandenburg-Prussian state, Francke would never have achieved

[20] Wolf Oschlies, *Die Arbeits- und Berufspädagogik August H. Franckes: Schule und Leben im Menschenbild des Hauptvertreter des halleschen Pietismus* (Witten, 1969), 14–15.
[21] Heinicke, "Die wirtschaftliche Entwicklung der Stadt Halle," 25, 27–28.
[22] Deppermann, *Der hallesche Pietismus und der preussische Staat*, 66–68.

long-term success in Halle. State support, however, did not ensure his effectiveness as pastor at Glaucha, where his ministry found an immediate, positive response. His preaching had such a profound emotional impact on his parishioners that two hundred and fifty people reportedly came daily to church to hear him pray. Demanding a personally experienced life of faith from his entire congregation, Francke also established catechism classes for children, instituted rigorous confirmation procedures for adolescents, and made extensive use of the Bible in church services.[23] Like Schade, Francke personally disliked the institution of the confessional, and he strongly disagreed with what he regarded as Spener's abandonment of Schade in the 1697–98 controversy over the use of the confessional.[24] Unlike Schade, however, Francke exploited the confessional as a means for settling family feuds, disciplining tavern owners, and forcing the upper class to take more responsibility for the town's well-being.[25] Francke thus not only worked to inculcate piety but also took the initiative in actively opposing those social forces which threatened to hinder the effectiveness of his pastoral mission.

Francke's tactics (and successes) quickly aroused against him a hostile coalition of innkeepers, orthodox clergy, and those whom he had refused to absolve in the confessional. Their campaign of opposition brought forth a strong counter-attack by Francke, who denounced the orthodox clergy of Halle in a sermon delivered on July 3, 1692. In order to heal this open split in the Halle clergy, the Berlin authorities stepped in and appointed a special investigatory commission chaired by Seckendorff, the chancellor of the University of Halle. In the light of Seckendorff's commitment to retaining Francke and Breithaupt on the faculty of his university, the outcome of the investigation was never in doubt. The head of the orthodox party fled to Leipzig, and a compromise largely favoring the Pietists

23 Erich Beyreuther, *August Hermann Francke, 1663–1727: Zeuge des lebendigen Gottes* (Marburg, 1956), 118–22, 126–31.

24 Helmut Obst, *Der Berliner Beichtstuhlstreit: Die Kritik des Pietismus an der Beichtpraxis der lutherischen Orthodoxie* (Witten, 1972), 62. For Francke's critique of the confessional, see A. H. Francke, "Kürzer und einfältiger Entwurf von den Missbräuchen des Beichtstuhls," in *Werke in Auswahl*, 92–107.

25 Beyreuther, *August Hermann Francke*, 124–27. In Catholic France, moralistic reformers advocated using the confessional as the chief instrument for disciplining and "improving" the laity. As Briggs points out, however, the great limitation to this approach was that without "some kind of coercive backing" from the secular power, such as Francke was to receive ultimately from Berlin, such ostracisms would inevitably be ineffective and instead serve merely to call attention to the individual pastor's "lack of real power." Briggs, *Communities of Belief*, 329.

was accepted by both sides in November 1692.[26] In addition to affirming the state's support for the Halle Pietists, the commission's investigation had the effect of compelling Francke to place himself above even the suspicion of adherence to heterodox doctrines. Under the tutelage of Seckendorff and Spener, Francke, beginning in late 1692, distanced himself more and more from Petersen in particular and spiritualism in general, concentrating his energies henceforth on his pastoral labors and university teaching.[27]

The settlement of 1692 secured Francke's position only temporarily. The estates, represented by the provincial government in Magdeburg, were far from ready to accede to the presence of Pietists in Halle. Their resistance could quite possibly have persuaded Berlin to abandon Francke, were it not for the latter's energy and initiative in struggling against the social problems of the Halle community. Aware from his pastoral work that children from poorer families were almost totally ignorant of the catechism, Francke resolved to do whatever was necessary to improve primary education in the city. On a very modest initial capital of 4 Taler, he opened a "poor school" (*Armenschule*) around Easter of 1695, employing as teachers university students who received a free meal in exchange for two hours a day of teaching. The school gained a good reputation in such a short time that by June of that year middle-class and noble families were entrusting their children's education to Francke and his student assistants. By the end of 1695, three distinct schools had come into being: the poor school, a Latin school for middle-class children, and a *Paedagogium* for the sons of the nobility. Gifted pupils from poorer families could, however, attend the Latin school on scholarship, and class distinctions on the whole were not rigorously observed.[28]

26 Beyreuther, *August Hermann Francke*, 133; see also Deppermann, *Der hallesche Pietismus und der preussische Staat*, 77–84; and Gustav Kramer, *Neue Beiträge zur Geschichte August Hermann Franckes* (Halle, 1875), 73–75.

27 For Francke's distancing himself from spiritualism, see Deppermann, *Der hallesche Pietismus und der preussische Staat*, 67, 80, 86; and Hinrichs, *Preussentum und Pietismus*, 219. For Spener's role in helping Francke through this crisis, see the correspondence between the two in Gustav Kramer, ed., *Beiträge zur Geschichte August Hermann Franckes enthaltend den Briefwechsel Franckes und Speners* (Halle, 1861), 208–83.

28 A. H. Francke, "Die Fusstapfen des noch lebenden und waltenden liebreichen und getreuen Gottes," in *Werke in Auswahl*, 32–34. There is an interesting parallel between Francke's schools and those of the contemporary French reformer J. B. de la Salle, whose schools, intended for the urban poor, featured a practical curriculum taught so effectively that more well-to-do families were soon enrolling their children in them. In pointed contrast to the Halle schools, however, the influence of la Salle's institutions was "far less

No sooner had the *Armenschule* opened its doors than Francke realized that the social environment encountered by the children outside the classroom undermined or even offset the morality and discipline taught in school.[29] As this was especially true of orphans and homeless children, Francke decided in November 1695 to accept custody of nine orphans and kept taking in more until by the end of 1698 there were about one hundred.[30] Such a large group of orphans, though housed at first in improvised accommodations scattered throughout the city, ultimately required the construction of a single, large dormitory. Having sent his assistant, Georg Neubauer, in 1697 to the Netherlands to inspect the physical plant and governing regulations of orphanages there, Francke decided to build an imposing stone orphanage at a cost in excess of twenty thousand Taler.[31] Most of the money was raised from private donors, with the largest contributions coming from the Berlin circle of patrons recruited by Spener. Baron von Canstein, henceforth the single most important financial contributor to Halle Pietism, donated as an outright gift the hefty sum of 8,000 Taler.[32]

An undertaking on the scale of Francke's orphanage needed the blessing of the regime in Berlin. The same patrons who supplied most of the capital also lobbied successfully for direct assistance from the state, vitally important not only for the immediate goal of building the orphanage but also for the future development of the entire complex of institutions attached to the orphanage. The legal basis for this support was a series of comprehensive "privileges," the most important of which were granted in April and September 1698. These enactments "annexed" the orphanage complex (also referred to as the Halle *Anstalten*) to the University of Halle, thereby placing it under the immediate legal jurisdiction of Berlin. As director of the orphanage, Francke was empowered to name his staff and successor. The edicts enabled the orphanage to operate a printing press, bindery, bookstore, and apothecary, as well as to maintain on its premises a tailor, shoemaker, blacksmith, and carpenter.

than it may have been," owing to the hostility of the clerical hierarchy and an absence of state support. Briggs, *Communities of Belief*, 272–73.

29 Francke, "Die Fusstapfen des noch lebenden ... Gottes,", 35.

30 Heinz Welsch, "Die Franckeschen Stiftungen als wirtschaftliches Grossunternehmen: Untersucht auf Grund der Rechnungsbücher der Franckeschen Stiftungen" (Phil. Diss., U. Halle, 1956), 12.

31 Oschlies, *Die Arbeits- und Berufspädagogik*, 21–24.

32 Welsch, "Die Franckeschen Stiftungen," 41.

Although the purpose of these industrial and commercial provisions was partly to provide orphan apprentices with opportunities to learn a trade, they were also designed to give financial security to the orphanage. The Halle *Anstalten* were also exempted from the excise tax and from the duty of quartering soldiers. To help with building of the orphanage, the state promised to make free deliveries to the construction site of wood and chalk, plus one hundred thousand building stones and thirty thousand roofing shingles. The privilege of September 1698, moreover, allowed Francke to conduct fund drives throughout the electoral realm and entitled him to one-tenth of the receipts from all fines under fifty Taler levied in the Magdeburg region.[33]

Although the settlement of 1692 had temporarily frustrated the desire of the local elites to be rid of Francke, they continued to harass him to the maximum possible extent. The clergy of Halle not only cast aspersions on Francke's character and doctrine but also sought to undermine his disciplinary authority by granting absolution to those of his parishioners whom he had excommunicated as part of his confessional practice. As Francke's activities broadened in scope and elicited increasing electoral support, the number of interest groups who felt threatened by him grew correspondingly. The privileges of 1698, for example, provoked a bitter quarrel between Francke and the guilds of Halle, who objected to the prospective competition from orphanage artisans and above all to the provision that permitted orphans without birth certificates to be admitted to apprentice associations with no questions asked. As such a procedure would impugn the "honor" of the guilds, their opposition was uncompromising; and eventually the Berlin government ordered Francke to refuse entry into the orphanage to foundlings and bastards.[34]

The provincial authorities also became more heavily involved in the resistance to Francke. In a well-coordinated campaign, orthodox clergy throughout the Old Mark so strongly opposed the privileges of 1698 that they forced Francke to give up his legal right to conduct fund drives in their parishes. In addition, officials appointed by the Magdeburg *Regierung* and charged with collecting

33 *Ibid.*, 39–40; see also Deppermann, *Der hallesche Pietismus und der preussische Staat*, 100–06.

34 Deppermann, *Der hallesche Pietismus und der preussische Staat*, 114–17. This incident illustrates the strength and independence of the guilds prior to the reign of Frederick William I. See above, pp. 55–56.

excise taxes ignored the freedom from the excise promised to the orphanage and persisted in attempting to collect the tax. When a direct electoral order ended their resistance on this point, they contrived other ways to use their position to impede the construction of the orphanage. Finally, the provincial government itself delayed forwarding the tithes due Francke from all fines under fifty Taler and even then did not hand over the full amount.[35]

In order to counter such attacks from the orthodox clergy and other elements of the regional establishment, Francke needed even stronger backing from the elector. Francke was well aware that the regime in Berlin lacked a consistent internal policy in the sense that, while it strove to maintain and expand on the centralizing tendencies of the Great Elector, it sought at the same time to effect a reconciliation with the estates, at whose expense any such increase in the power of the central government had to occur. Francke also knew that he had received substantial support from the elector, especially once he had established the orphanage and its network of schools. For in addition to the privileges for the orphanage, the state had already granted Francke relief from his pastoral duties in 1695, placed him in charge of the local welfare administration in 1697, and made him the third theology professor on the Halle University faculty in 1698.

Francke, therefore, was certain that, if it came to a showdown between him and the Magdeburg *Regierung*, the Hohenzollern regime would decide in his favor. Consequently, Francke decided to provoke a confrontation in order to strengthen his position. When Francke denounced the Halle clergy in a sermon on February 2, 1699, and in a "confession" (*Bekenntnis*) submitted to the electoral authorities shortly thereafter, he was attempting to force Berlin to end its ambiguous policy and choose definitively between him and his adversaries. Just before delivering his incendiary sermon, he is reported to have said, "I can not imagine anything but a great storm coming from this."[36]

As Francke had predicted, the result of his attack was indeed an

35 Hinrichs, *Preussentum und Pietismus*, 221–22. As Klaus Deppermann aptly remarks in this context, "in the world of Frederick III, there were not yet many traces of 'Prussian obedience.'" Deppermann, *Der hallesche Pietismus und der preussische Staat*, 113.

36 Hinrichs, *Preussentum und Pietismus*, 223. For extensive quotations from the *Bekenntnis*, in which Francke accused his clerical opponents of abetting the prevalent corruption in society through their neglect of the poor, their refusal to disturb the "fleshly security" of their parishioners, and their own worldliness and complacency, see *ibid.*, 223–27.

intense controversy. Because the Halle clergy were strongly supported by the Magdeburg *Regierung*, the Berlin government was at first reluctant to intervene and did little to resolve the dispute for over a year.[37] Then, in March 1700, the Magdeburg estates launched a full-scale assault on the theological faculty at the University of Halle and Francke's orphanage complex. To undermine the position of the former, the estates demanded both the repeal of an electoral edict prohibiting pulpit polemics against the Halle theologians and the authority to eliminate "spiritualist" influences from the Halle faculty, thereby raising once again the issue of the doctrinal orthodoxy of Francke, Breithaupt, and Anton. The estates' petition to the elector further alleged irregularities on the part of Francke in his handling of the orphanage finances. The intent behind this particular accusation was clearly to persuade the elector to allow the local authorities to assume control over the Halle *Anstalten*.[38] Just as Francke had hoped, the provincial estates had thus been goaded into attacking those institutions in which the Hohenzollern state had invested considerable capital and prestige, thereby putting the Berlin authorities in the position of having to choose between unequivocal endorsement of Halle Pietism and capitulation to the estates.

In response, Frederick, on the suggestion of Spener, appointed two special commissions: one to settle the quarrel between Francke and the Halle clergy, the other to investigate the finances of the Halle *Anstalten*. The composition of the commissions and the results of their proceedings reflected the priorities of the Berlin regime. In regard to the dispute between the clerical parties, the central government clearly wished for compromise and reconciliation. To be sure, the commission, headed by D. Johann Fischer, general superintendent of the Lutheran church in Latvia, contained two Pietist sympathizers and only one representative of the Magdeburg estates, one Stösser Edler von Lilienfeld. The formula of reconciliation imposed on both sides in June 1700 was, nevertheless, a *status quo ante* compromise, rather than a ringing vindication of Francke. The estates' demands of March 1700 were rejected: Francke and the Halle theological faculty were declared orthodox in belief, while the orthodox were forbidden to impugn their Pietist counterparts and were also admonished to introduce stricter confes-

[37] *Ibid.*, 227; See also Deppermann, *Der hallesche Pietismus und der preussische Staat*, 121–25.
[38] Hinrichs, *Preussentum und Pietismus*, 228–30.

sional procedures and better instruction in the catechism. But Francke was likewise forced to acknowledge that his opponents were "righteous servants of God" and that some of his accusatory statements were "overly hasty" and rested on "gossip."[39]

The outcome of the investigation of the Halle *Anstalten* was much more clearly a triumph for Francke. Having no intention of placing the orphanage under the control of the estates, the Berlin authorities solicited Francke's suggestions regarding the composition and agenda of the commission. All four members of the commission were high-ranking officials; only one of them, Privy Councillor Dieskau, also belonged to the Magdeburg estates. In its deliberations, the commission concentrated primarily on the failure of the Magdeburg *Regierung* to carry out the provisions of the privileges granted to the orphanage in 1698. The report of the commission not only brushed aside the estates' accusations of alleged mismanagement by Francke but also solidified his position as director of the *Anstalten*. Reflecting the conviction that the Pietist institutions at Halle were assisting the economic development of the region, the commission's findings prepared the way for the granting of additional privileges to the orphanage and the *Paedagogium* in 1702 and 1703.[40]

On balance, the commissions of 1700 dealt a decisive rebuff to the concerted campaign of anti-Pietist harassment on the part of the Halle clergy and the Magdeburg estates. Unlike the settlement of 1692, moreover, that of 1700 marked the end of serious opposition to Pietism from the local elites. One reason for this was a change in attitude on the part of the great families of the region. The head of one of these families, Privy Councillor Dieskau, after examining the books of the orphanage complex, adopted the pro-Francke view of the rest of the commission. He himself later became a patron of the orphanage. In the years after 1700, other members of the elite gradually came to share Dieskau's view that both the university and the orphanage were an economic boon to the area.[41]

Electoral intervention in the religious controversies in Halle also

[39] *Ibid.*, 228–29.

[40] *Ibid.*, 230.

[41] *Ibid.*, 231. Another factor contributing to the pacification of the provincial ruling groups was the appointment of Fischer, who was chair of the commission that in 1700 had imposed a settlement on the feuding Halle clergy, as superintendent of the Lutheran church in Magdeburg. His strongly anti-Pietist predecessor had died in September 1699, in the midst of the Pietist–orthodox controversy. Fischer's presence as leader of the provincial church was bound to reduce the incidence of hostile action toward Pietism on the part of his subordinates.

promoted an eventual settlement by inducing Francke to modify Spenerian Pietism further in order to make it more palatable to both central government and local elites. The strongly anti-Pietist environment in Halle had forced Francke into such a dependence on state support that the latter's will became an important factor in shaping the development of Francke's strategic vision. Thus Francke not only came to follow Spener's policy of de-emphasizing conventicles, despite an initial inclination to rely heavily on them; but he also did everything in his power to demonstrate to all parties his respect for the institutional continuity and formal theology of the Lutheran church.[42] A major reason for the permanence of the compromise of 1700 was an apparent acceptance among the orthodox party in the Magdeburg area of the notion that the Halle Pietists' most fundamental concern was not to propagate an alternative theology but to carry out concrete reforms in the churches and schools.[43]

Francke's commitment to transforming church and society had lost none of its intensity, however. By establishing the Halle *Anstalten*, Francke had succeeded in devising a new institutional means for the realization of Pietist goals. As we have seen, the need of the Hohenzollern state for the pedagogical and social services provided by the *Anstalten* was a major factor in its strong support for the Pietist cause in Halle. But as advantageous as Francke's schools became to the Brandenburg-Prussian state, they served Pietist purposes equally well. A state-sanctioned school system, operating with curricula devised by Francke himself, would greatly increase the numbers of young people exposed to the Pietist message. The permanence of the school as an institution, and its authoritarian character, stood in sharp contrast to the conventicle, dependent as the latter was on the spontaneous participation of parish members as well as on the leadership of a Pietist pastor, whose work could always be undone by a non-Pietist replacement.[44]

42 Deppermann, "Die politischen Voraussetzungen für die Etablierung des Pietismus," 50.

43 By 1710, Francke's attitude toward "special revelations" had undergone a complete change, reverting to the "standpoint of orthodoxy," i.e. one of condemning all heterodox or non-conformist testimonies as being "from the devil." In this respect, Francke, characteristically, had come to take a more authoritarian position than Spener, who throughout his life rejected the "either/or" approach of orthodoxy and retained an open mind on the validity of such personal illuminations. See Wallmann, "Geistliche Erneuerung der Kirche," 33–36.

44 There was an enormous difference between the restrictive environment in the schools of the Halle *Anstalten* and the voluntarist spirit of Spener's Frankfurt *collegium*, which in Spener's view of it "was to have fluid boundaries ... [and] be an open body (*offener Kreis*)." *Ibid.*, 27.

By 1700, then, Francke had built up his institutional power to the point where neither the Halle clergy nor the Magdeburg estates could hope to dislodge him, even if they had so desired. But despite the significance of this achievement, Francke's successful effort to establish himself in Halle constituted merely a preliminary stage in the fulfillment of his life-work. Freed from the struggle against the local elites, though not necessarily from future tensions with the Berlin regime, Francke exploited to the full the position he had gained in the settlement of 1700 and built the Halle *Anstalten* into a powerful educational, economic, and missionary organization. Before describing the growth of the *Anstalten*, however, we must seek to uncover Francke's deepest motivations by examining more closely his distinctive form of Pietist spirituality. Only then will a full explanation both of Francke's early success and the subsequent dynamism of the Halle Pietist movement become possible.

A PROMETHEAN SPIRITUALITY: THE PIETY OF AUGUST HERMANN FRANCKE

Of all the offshoots of Spenerian Pietism, the religious position represented by August Hermann Francke is usually viewed as truest to Spener's original inspiration. Historians of Pietism have commonly portrayed Spener and Francke as the dual bulwarks of mainstream, or "clerical," Pietism – the strand within the movement characterized by a desire to remain within the established church and by a rejection of esoteric or heterodox forms of mysticism. The linkage of Francke with Spener has been so widely assumed that I am aware of no study devoted to a systematic comparison of the two men.[45] The differences in tactics discussed above have not entirely escaped notice; but when historians do address these differences, they either ascribe them to contrasting temperaments or view them as resulting from Francke's attempt to apply Spener's ideas within the pedagogical framework of the Halle *Anstalten*.[46]

45 The widespread use of the term "spener-hallescher Pietismus" has had the inevitable result of minimizing the originality of Francke. For a strong statement on the baneful effects of this tendency, see F. Ernest Stoeffler, *German Pietism during the Eighteenth Century* (Leiden, 1973), 12.

46 This type of contrast with Francke is implicit, for example, in Greschat, "Christliche Gemeinschaft und Sozialgestaltung," 310–11. Another reason for the lack of comparative studies of the two is the high degree of specialization among scholars of Pietism.

Current interpretations, with their tendency to regard Spener and Francke as theological twins, therefore do not attempt to identify spiritual factors that would help explain why Francke pursued the social activism inherent in the *Pia Desideria* so much more aggressively than Spener himself.[47] It is true that Francke's combative personality and the challenging religious and political environment at Halle contributed greatly to the unprecedented dynamism of Francke and the Halle *Anstalten*. But any comprehensive explanation of Francke's accomplishments must take his spirituality into account as well. Despite numerous points in common with Spener's theology, Francke's religious outlook differed from it in fundamental ways, and these divergences had a direct bearing on Francke's more activistic approach to social problems.

The first step toward clarifying these differences between Spener and Francke is to examine the precise nature of Spener's personal influence on Francke. Beginning in 1682 at age sixteen, Francke enrolled in a series of universities: first at Erfurt near Francke's hometown of Gotha, then for three years at Kiel, and finally at Leipzig. From July 1686 on Francke played a leading role in the *collegium philobiblicum* at Leipzig. When Spener, who had only recently come to Saxony as the new head court chaplain, visited the *collegium* in early 1687, its primary purpose was to provide students with linguistic training in Greek and Hebrew. As a result of Spener's recommendations, the focus of the *collegium* changed, so that its members now devoted more attention to the personal applications of the scriptural passages on which they were working.[48] Although Francke found this new orientation appealing, he did not seek to cultivate any ties with Spener at that time and in the fall of 1687 left Leipzig to study exegesis in Lüneburg under the learned Superintendent Caspar Hermann Sandhagen.

Shortly after arriving in Lüneburg, Francke underwent the conversion that remained the central religious experience of his life. Only after this conversion did Francke begin to gravitate toward the Spenerian circle.[49] In 1688 he spent a considerable period of time

[47] The only (partial) exception I have found is a brief passage contrasting Spener and Francke's spiritualities in Kruse, "Preussen und der frühe Pietismus," 15–16. A study that does an excellent job in deducing Francke's social activism from his spirituality is Klaus Schaller, "Pietismus und moderne Pädagogik," in Aland, ed., *Pietismus und moderne Welt*, 161–84. Even Schaller, however, makes no attempt to contrast Francke with Spener.

[48] Beyreuther, *August Hermann Francke*, 30–42.

[49] Erich Beyreuther, *Geschichte des Pietismus* (Stuttgart, 1978), 132.

in Hamburg as house guest of, and collaborator with, Johannes Winkler, one of Spener's most loyal and active followers. Returning to Leipzig at Christmas of that year, Francke made immediate contact with Spener and stayed with him in Dresden for the first two months of 1689. As a result of this visit, Spener became Francke's spiritual mentor and began to help Francke give constructive expression to the religious energies released by his conversion. Spener subsequently provided political support and spiritual counsel during the Leipzig "days" of 1689–90 and during Francke's early years at Halle.

The most decisive event in Francke's spiritual development – his conversion – had, therefore, already taken place before Spener became a significant factor in his life. Francke's conversion in itself, moreover, had no precedent in Spener's life and was of a fundamentally different nature from anything Spener had ever experienced.[50] What happened to Francke in Lüneburg in October 1687 was the earliest important example of a "born-again" conversion within Lutheran Pietism. According to Francke's own account, from the time when he matriculated at Leipzig in 1684 he had experienced intense spiritual conflict. Outward appearances would have suggested that Francke's university career was progressing smoothly and successfully, but he was troubled by strong feelings of guilt for desiring worldly fame as a scholar and, in pursuit of that aim, for working to please others (rather than God) in order to gain favor with them.[51] Francke left Leipzig for Lüneburg in order to work out this conflict in a retreat-like setting and thereby "secure more completely my primary goal of becoming a righteous Christian."[52]

On arriving in Lüneburg, however, Francke became obsessed with his lack of "true faith" and yielded to skepticism toward the Holy Scriptures. His doubts, in turn, produced despair: a denial of belief in God and a sense that his whole life was a sin and a gross horror.[53] In a state of extreme anxiety, Francke called on God in prayer to save him from his misery. At that moment Francke directly experienced God's "fatherly love"; and "as quickly as one can turn over one's hand all my doubt had gone away, [and] I was

50 Wallmann, *Philipp Jakob Spener*, 88–89.
51 Francke, "August Hermann Franckes Lebenslauf," 23.
52 *Ibid.*, 25.
53 *Ibid.*, 26.

assured in my heart of the grace of God through Christ Jesus."[54] From this point on, Francke perceived himself to be of a "totally different" disposition than heretofore. His preconversion life was like a dream from which he had awakened. Learning, reason, and this world, all of which had previously exerted power over him, he now repudiated in scatological language. Assuming that the world would oppose him "for pursuing Christianity more seriously than it would deem necessary," Francke placed himself in God's hands with intense feelings of joy and gratitude.[55]

As Spener never personally experienced the type of radical discontinuity associated with Francke's conversion, the two men not surprisingly held to different conceptions of the nature of the rebirth. Spener, having never fundamentally doubted his faith, never questioned, as Francke did, "whether even the Holy Scriptures are God's Word since the Turks believe the same of their Quran and the Jews of their Talmud."[56] Spener, to be sure, experienced periods of doubt and lack of belief, but even in his youth he interpreted them as tests of an already existing faith, not as indicators of an absence of true belief.[57] Spener thus did not assume the necessity of a single, decisive break with one's own past, so that in his view rebirth tended to occur over time. For the same reason, Spener refused to schematize the process of rebirth, believing that each person must experience it in his or her own fashion. Nor did Spener require any evidence of a "conversion" for admission to his conventicles or make people's conversions the explicit goal of such groups, for he clearly considered the rebirth something of a mystery and therefore not subject to analysis or pedagogical manipulation.[58]

Francke, characteristically, had no qualms about using his clearcut conversion as the basis of his teaching and sermonizing on the subject of rebirth.[59] He deliberately encouraged people to engage in

[54] *Ibid.*, 27–28.

[55] *Ibid.*, 28–29.

[56] *Ibid.*, 26.

[57] Wallmann, *Philipp Jakob Spener*, 89–90. After demonstrating that Spener never underwent a "born-again" conversion, Wallmann observes that "in the question of conversion, in which Pietism has overwhelmingly followed August Hermann Francke, a contrast of great proportions opens up between the two most significant men of early Pietism."

[58] Wallmann, "Geistliche Erneuerung der Kirche," 28.

[59] See, for example, Francke's sermon "Vom rechtschaffenen Wachstum des Glaubens," in *Werke in Auswahl*, 273–92. In this sermon, which according to Peschke "offers the best insight into the basic intentions of his piety and theology," Francke sets forth the goal of "growth of faith" and the four stages by which that goal is to be achieved. These consist of *Gründung*, characterized by repentance (*Busse*); *Kräftigung*, in which God intervenes "at the

a "struggle to repent" (*Busskampf*) as a preliminary to conversion. Francke conceived of the *Busskampf* as a conflict within the soul between the "old self" (or "state of nature") and the "new self" (or "state of grace").[60] To weaken the hold of the "old self," the pastor was to preach the Law and the Last Judgment, thereby instilling a fear of God and creating such anxiety that the "old self" would be forced to call on God for help. Francke therefore preached the *Busskampf* insistently, regarding it as the only way that unconverted individuals could be induced to allow God to grant them the grace needed for the triumph of the "new self."[61] He not only assumed that the *Busskampf* constituted *the* precondition for conversion but also regarded an unconverted person as by definition an unbeliever, a "child of the world," separated by an abyss from those reborn as "children of God."[62]

But for both Spener and Francke, rebirth was only the first step on the path to righteousness. The developing relationship of the reborn Christian with God was really their central concern; and, in formulating their ideas on this subject, both men relied heavily for inspiration on the devotional works of English Puritan writers. Because of this common influence, Francke advocated for the "children of God" many of the same practices as Spener in the latter's descriptions of the "living faith" of the "new person." These acts of "obedience to God's commands" included prayer, Bible reading, renunciation of sinful diversions, and service to one's neighbor through acts of charity.

proper time" and consoles the believer with forgiveness of his or her sins; *Stärkung*, in which the actual, continual experience (*Erfahrung*) of God will strengthen the believer's faith and produce the "true fruits of righteousness"; and *Vollbereitung*, understood either as a level of faith sufficiently strong that the believer can take on any struggle in a knightly and successful way or as the final sacrifice of death.

60 For the profound difference between this anthropology of Francke's, which posits these two mutually opposed "selves," and that of Luther, in which the tension in the believer between "flesh" and "spirit" is not definitively resolved in this life (*simul peccator – simul justus*), see Friedrich de Boor, "A. H. Franckes Beitrag zu einer umfassenden Interpretation der Römerbriefvorrede Luthers," *Theologische Literaturzeitung*, 107 (1982): 654.

61 For the conformity of Francke's emphasis on the *Busskampf* to the classic Puritan paradigm of the conversion experience, see the description of the latter in Cohen, "Saints Zealous in Love and Labor," 465–69.

62 Erhard Peschke, *Studien zur Theologie August Hermann Franckes* (Berlin, 1964), 66–68. Francke held that the difference between the unconverted and the "children of God" was as absolute as that "between heaven and earth." He regarded anyone who refused to make this distinction, by definition, as "still a child of the world." While Spener, in the final analysis, would make the same distinction, he would be much less ready than Francke to put particular individuals in one category or the other. See above, p. 136, n. 43.

Despite this seeming continuity with Spener's moral prescriptions, Francke's concept of "living faith" rested in fact on a different emotional basis. This difference manifested itself on the level of theology in opposing interpretations of the relationship between faith and "spiritual experience" (*geistliche Erfahrung*). For Spener, faith could exist separately from the actual experience of faith in God; in Wallmann's words, Spener "does not want to make faith itself dependent on the feeling of faith."[63] In other words, for Spener the conscience is able to discern more easily whether the believer's acts of obedience are performed out of a genuine love for God arising from a spiritual rebirth.[64] The knowledge or assurance gained thereby becomes part of the person's permanent conception of self, subject to periodic reexamination, to be sure, but largely protected from the emotional stresses associated with periods of temptation and apparent absence of God.

Francke, however, made the believer's faith, or assurance of faith, much more dependent on the "living experience" of faith – i.e. on a direct perception of union with God's will while engaged in actions presumed to further God's plan for the world. In Francke's mysticism of action, once the Christian had passed through "the narrow doorway of the rebirth," the more "living experience" of faith the person received, the more his or her faith would be "strengthened, purified, and proven."[65] Francke's conception of the postconversion life was thus one of God working through the completely passive and receptive self of the believer.[66] The continual experience of being God's pliant instrument was the primary means by which the faith and assurance of salvation on the part of the individual would "grow."[67]

63 Wallmann, *Philipp Jakob Spener*, 89.

64 See above, pp. 110–11.

65 Francke, "Vom rechtschaffenen Wachstum des Glaubens," 281. For a learned discussion of the radical divergence between Luther's understanding of faith and Francke's emphasis on "experience of faith" as the foundation for assurance of salvation, see de Boor, "A. H. Franckes Beitrag zu einer umfassenden Interpretation der Römerbriefvorrede Luthers," 655–56.

66 "The tendency among spiritual men to imagine themselves as hollow, empty beings entirely governed and moved by a remote supernatural agency from outside and above themselves ... indeed pays homage to the idea that God is infinitely above man. But it entirely ignores the equally important truth of God's immanence within man." Merton, *The New Man*, 32. To get a sense of the enormous distance separating Francke and Arndt on this point, compare this characterization of Francke's position with the passage already quoted from Arndt. See above, p. 98, n. 66.

67 Francke, "Vom rechtschaffenen Wachstum des Glaubens," 282. For the pivotal significance of the concept of "experience" in Francke's theology, see also Schaller, "Pietismus und moderne Pädagogik," 168.

Francke's much greater dependence on "experience," understood in this sense, as compared with Spener's more cognitive, *a priori* faith, ensured periodic crises of faith on the part of the believer. Since no one can consistently perceive God's directing hand in the way Francke so insistently emphasized, reborn Christians of Franckean vintage would inevitably experience doubt and a sense of isolation during those "dry periods" when God's grace did not seem to be working through them. Francke's counsel to his followers was that God at such moments was hiding from the individual, deliberately producing a crisis in belief similar in nature to that preceding conversion. God's purpose was ultimately pedagogical, namely, to prevent a return to the egoism of the "old self" and bring about a further strengthening of faith.[68] In response to these "temptations" (*Anfechtungen*) sent by God, Francke recommended perseverance, prayer, and "serf-like" submission to God's Law.[69] The believer could then expect that obedience to the Law, particularly the law enjoining love of one's neighbor, would be followed, sooner or later, by the renewed sensation of grace.[70]

Even though Spener's conception of spiritual growth also emphasized suffering and obedience through loving one's neighbor, the especially emotional nature of Francke's spirituality resulted in an imperative to action far more passionate and totalistic than in the case of Spener. Thus Francke's commitment to performing in God's service extended to every waking hour.[71] As a result, not only did he condemn idle leisure, as Spener had done before him, but he also incorporated vocational labor into the domain of activity through

68 Peschke, *Studien zur Theologie August Hermann Franckes*, 47–49.

69 Merton's description of the God-believer relationship in the "Promethean theology" is as follows: "it comes to seem [in this kind of theology] as if God *did not want us to be free* . . . as if man saves himself and arrives at divine union by bartering his freedom for God's grace. The price of happiness is . . . the acceptance of a slave-status [and the punishments that go with it] in the household of a God who is powerful enough to make slavery worthwhile." Merton, *The New Man*, 27 (author's emphasis).

70 Peschke, *Studien zur Theologie August Hermann Franckes*, 88–89.

71 Departing once more from Spener, who never devoted much attention to the "proper use of time," Francke repeatedly stressed the iniquity of wasting even a quarter of an hour so long as there was good to be done for one's neighbor. For illustrative passages, see August Hermann Francke, *Lebens-Regeln*, ed. Georg Helbig (Berlin, 1938), 25–26, 38. For Francke's definitive work on the utilization of time, see A. H. Francke, *Der rechte Gebrauch der Zeit* (Halle, 1713). See also G. Bondi, "Der Beitrag des hallischen Pietismus zur Entwicklung des ökonomischen Denkens in Deutschland," *Jahrbuch für Wirtschaftsgeschichte* (1964): 28–33.

which the children of God served their neighbors.[72] Spener, by contrast, never formulated a consistent position on the role of occupational work in a Christian's life because he could not resolve a conflict he perceived between love for one's neighbor and the ascetic teaching that one should not honor the world.[73]

It was through his characteristic radicalism that Francke overcame this theological barrier to his aim of discerning divine meaning in the most mundane vocational activity. To be sure, he shared on one level Spener's, and much of traditional Christianity's, negative judgment of "this world," with the corresponding view of life as being essentially a preparation for eternity.[74] But, unlike Spener, Francke drew a radical, modern conclusion from this "contempt for the world": namely, that the creation was simply an object in need of being "improved upon" by the human subject as part of the latter's quest for the attainment of personal salvation.[75] Thus, assuming that believers could continue to maintain their subjective sense of acting in conformity with God's will, working diligently in the world was in fact the best way for them to demonstrate their obedience to God's Law. Francke did not hesitate to claim that God would reward such diligence in the future life with a "very important and substantial wage" in proportion to the amount of service rendered here on earth.[76]

72 Even within the Puritan tradition, making, as Francke did, a "life of mundane labor" into "the pivotal expression of godly love" constituted "the most extreme formulation" of the idea that "human beings are intermediaries in whose service the divine itself is served." Cohen, "Saints Zealous in Love and Labor," 475. Even Richard Baxter's activism, paradigmatic in Weber's analysis of the "Protestant ethic," "did not ... dismantle the barrier between secular occupations and works of piety and charity." Bossy, *Christianity in the West*, 151.

73 Greschat, "Christliche Gemeinschaft und Sozialgestaltung," 318. The same tension is also apparent in early Puritan devotional writers. See Böhme, "Heinrich Julius Elers," 171. In keeping with a certain restraint in Spener's work ethic, there are some indications in his writings that, while his spirituality was not nearly so mystical as Arndt's, he did value meditation on the divine qualities of God as an aspect of a believer's love for God. Spener, *Der neue Mensch*, 34.

74 Traditional Christianity, while following biblical injunctions to cultivate detachment from a world permeated by sin, also affirmed in the main, however, the equally biblical position that the natural and social orders are part of God's creation and that He is present and immanent in them. That this was Arndt's view is clear from a passage already quoted. See above, p. 99, n. 71. For a summary of Luther's similar view, see W. D. J. Cargill Thompson, *Studies in the Reformation* (London, 1980), 57–59.

75 For an insightful analysis of the deleterious consequences of this sort of religious individualism, see Berry, *A Continuous Harmony*, 6–12. Berry regards this type of spirituality as playing a causal role in the development of the typically modern contempt for nature and for the inherent value of human community.

76 Peschke, *Studien zur Theologie August Hermann Franckes*, 94.

By thereby giving occupational work eschatological significance, Francke completed the process, begun by Spener, of dissociating ascetism from its traditional role as an aid to contemplation. Francke redefined the primary purpose of prayer as an aid to action as can be seen in his interpretation of the story of Mary and Martha, in which Jesus commends the praying Mary rather than the restlessly active Martha (Luke 10:38–42). Instead of following the monastic tradition of understanding Mary's praying as contemplative meditation, Francke praises Mary for using prayer with her work to restrain any tendency toward an excessive, egotistical passion for work.[77] Thus for Francke prayer was primarily focused on the self, as an aid for helping to keep reborn Christians from succumbing to the temptations that would inevitably arise from their immersion in worldly activities.[78]

Francke also sought to help his followers remain obedient to God in their work by devising a comprehensive code of conduct, his *Lebens-Regeln*. These "rules for living" went well beyond the exercises in piety prescribed by Spener in laying down detailed rules and regulations governing all aspects of life, including everyday social interaction. The thoroughgoing severity of Francke's rules is illustrated by the following stricture against laughter: "not all laughter is forbidden; but it is quite easy thereby to sin and leave the heart open to a dangerous dissipation of its vital energy" (*Sinn*).[79] The need for constant vigilance against such "dissipation" made Francke regard as harmful any deviation from what he considered to be the believer's "permanent personality." This attitude led him to oppose even temporary alterations in identity. Thus any form of play acting – no matter how edifying the content of the play – drew Francke's wrath because it threatened the compulsiveness and rigidity of his ascetic regimen.[80]

There was a great tension in Francke's work ethic. On the one hand, Francke regarded the life of the "child of God" as characterized by an apparently "interior" process, the "growth of

[77] Francke, *Lebens-Regeln*, 28–29.

[78] In his analysis of John Bunyan's spirituality in particular, and Puritan spirituality in general, Preus emphasizes the Puritans' regard for the self as *the* "text" that had to be "read" by the believer, with the Bible and such works as *Pilgrim's Progress* serving as "instruments" for this task. Preus, "The Reified Heart," 48–51. It was only consistent for prayer to be used to the same end.

[79] Francke, *Lebens-Regeln*, 35.

[80] Wolfgang Schmitt, "Die pietistische Kritik der 'Künste'" (Phil. Diss., U. Köln, 1958), 25–26.

faith," in which the believer in a step-by-step fashion turns his or her heart away from "the world" in the quest of the ideal of well-nigh superhuman self-control embodied in Francke's "rules for living."[81] On the other hand, Francke so closely connected "growth in faith" with the experience of serving one's neighbor that failure to accomplish much manifest good for other people was a sure sign of a lack of God-given faith. Thus, for a faith as experiential as Francke's, tangible evidence of the impact of the reborn Christian's work on the immediate human environment, such as the success of the Halle *Anstalten*, was needed to provide empirical verification of the presence of God's grace.[82] The hand of God, in other words, needed to be discerned externally in the world, as well as internally in the soul, for the reborn Christian to be convinced of the reality of his or her faith.[83]

Given the gap between the "fallen" world and the high moralistic standards of the reborn Christian, the effectiveness of the latter's ministry was inevitably evaluated from the perspective of how much it contributed to the "improvement" of the world. In other words, the command to "love thy neighbor" meant to work for the ever closer conformity on the part of society at large to the precepts set forth in Francke's rules. In light of Francke's passionate, total commitment to such ethical action, obeying God's will in this sense justified the most extraordinary measures. As will become evident in the next two chapters, Francke and his Halle group did not hesitate to violate even strong Lutheran precedent, if such action produced an advancement in what they regarded as the material and spiritual well-being of the people.

Such an emphasis on concrete results also encouraged the instrumental thinking and pragmatism that became fundamental to Halle Pietism. Thus in Francke's writings "useful" (*nützlich*) was virtually synonymous with "good," and the boundary between material and spiritual utility was often blurred. In employing different variations of the phrase "for the good of thy neighbor," for example, Francke characteristically used *Wohl* ("well-being" or "prosperity") and *Nutzen* ("utility") interchangeably with *Gut* and

81 Peschke, *Studien zur Theologie August Hermann Franckes*, 98–101.

82 See also Schaller, "Pietismus und moderne Pädagogik," 169.

83 It is thus only an apparent paradox that Francke's piety, the most self-oriented and "individualistic" of all the Lutheran writers so far examined, was also the most radical in its "reformism," in its demand for a transformation of the external world.

its derivatives.[84] The believer's work had to be both "pleasing to God and useful to humanity."[85]

The existential necessity for the Halle Pietists to strive for tangible progress suggests a final contrast between Francke and the author of the *Pia Desideria*. Spener, for all his opposition to Aristotelianism and qualitative metaphysics, derived his confidence in the future of the church from a non-subjective form of knowledge – his meliorist eschatology. This particular interpretation of traditional prophetic sources constituted for Spener an objective assurance that God was at that moment working for improvement in the Lutheran church. Hence Spener, despite pursuing a reform program that relied heavily on pedagogical measures designed to promote spiritual growth in a largely Puritan sense, exhibited a genuine humility born of the recognition that it was God, not he, who was assuming the primary burden for accomplishing that task.[86]

Although the Halle Pietists shared Spener's optimism, the absence of any form of chiliasm or millenarianism in Francke and nearly all his followers implies that their positive vision for the future rested on a different kind of relationship between God and the believer.[87] According to Francke, the reborn needed no external form of knowledge, such as eschatological doctrine, in order to perceive the will of God.[88] As with the knowledge that brings assurance of genuine conversion, knowledge of God's precise intentions was seen as being transmitted to Francke and his followers in the course of their loyal execution of the divine commands. There was, then, despite his public commitment to orthodox doctrine, a subtle form of illuminism or spiritualism in Francke's claiming to know God's will with such certainty in so many particular situations – an ability that led the Halle Pietists to view themselves as God's uniquely privileged agents, empowered to override tradition and institute a new,

84 For the centrality of the notion of *nützlich* in Francke's theology, see Stoeffler, *German Pietism during the Eighteenth Century*, 45–46.

85 Francke, *Lebens-Regeln*, 27.

86 Spener, *Pia Desideria*, 78.

87 Stoeffler, *German Pietism during the Eighteenth Century*, 54. The only major figure in the Halle group adhering to a chiliastic eschatology was Joachim Lange, who worked in Berlin for many years under Spener's tutelage before finding a position at Halle.

88 In Francke's words, "God Himself has taught me to distinguish nature and grace, light and darkness, illusion and spiritual force" (*Kraft*). The believer, he goes on to say, needs merely not to resist the working of God's spirit in him or her, and God will clearly communicate His will to that person. See A. H. Francke, "Bekenntnis eines Christen," in *Werke in Auswahl*, 368.

more spiritually "advanced" order.[89] Thus whereas for Spener reform was bound to happen anyway and the Christian merely had to choose whether to participate, Francke and his colleagues tended to identify *themselves* as the reform. The Halle Pietists believed that riding on their ability to serve – and convert – their neighbors was nothing less than the fate of God's plan for the whole human race.

Francke exuded boldness and confidence in making such claims on behalf of his reform movement.[90] After all, for him knowledge obtained from God through His grace was "more certain than what my bodily eyes see, ears hear, and hands feel."[91] The very boundlessness of his sense of responsibility, as well as the obsessive way he sought to execute it – the "driven" quality of Francke, in other words – suggests, however, that the preconversion fear of meaninglessness and its accompanying despair were never very far from the surface of his consciousness. This, in turn, implies that his conversion, instead of constituting the beginning of a spiritual journey through which Francke would have eventually confronted these feelings as part of a genuinely mystical death of self, seems to have initiated, instead, a valiant, grandiose, and perhaps ultimately futile attempt to escape his own sense of emptiness and vulnerability.

A brief review of his spirituality indicates that the "dynamism" commentators have always found so remarkable in Francke stemmed from a drive to experience ever greater assurance and vitality through performing "God's work" as an antidote to this abiding feeling of internal weakness.[92] In Francke's own terminology, the "growth in faith" following conversion brought the "child of God" ever closer to perfection, but the process could never be consummated – or interrupted for even a quarter of an hour. "Standing still" was equivalent to retrogressing, a sliding backward toward the void characterized by Francke as the "old self."[93] The

89 Peschke, *Studien zur Theologie August Hermann Franckes*, 69–70.

90 In addition to the programmatic writings to be discussed in the next chapter, see A. H. Francke, *Nicodemus, or a Treatise on the Fear of Man*, abridged by John Wesley (Dublin, 1749). In this work, Francke argues that the "child of God" need not and must not fear any person or human institution standing in the way of the execution of "God's will."

91 Francke, "Bekenntnis eines Christen," 368.

92 In describing the Puritans' zeal to perform divinely commissioned work, Cohen uses much the same language. The individual thus feels a "desire to escape one's helpless [preconversion] state"; conversion "answers these desperate wishes for power"; the saints receive power as "a manifestation of God's love, and the sensation of this love that redeems and energizes them gratifies the Elect." Cohen, "Saints Zealous in Love and Labor," 480.

93 Francke, "Vom rechtschaffenen Wachstum des Glaubens," 274.

ascetic regimen could never be relaxed, for the sense of certainty acquired from conversion was always threatened: by the unregenerate (and never vanquished) "old self" from within and by the existence of "children of the world" from without. Even in God there could be no real refuge, for Francke had so little detachment with respect to his emotions that he projected his anxieties indiscriminately onto all persons, human and divine. Thus in Francke's words, "even God has His hours of temptation and humiliation."[94]

Such a desperate cosmic Manichaean struggle, in which Francke viewed God as personally affected by the ebb and flow of the battle, required constant work, limitless sacrifice, the mobilization of ever greater resources for "the cause." No victory could ever be final; no peace could ever be attained. Francke's was a truly Promethean spirituality, an obsession with power, action, and domination, fueled by the vision of an infinite challenge to be faced. In formulating the goals for his Halle *Anstalten*, Francke proposed to plant "a garden, from which can be expected a tangible improvement (*reale Verbesserung*) in all estates, inside and outside Germany, in Europe and all remaining parts of the world."[95] Clearly implied in the substance of this proposal and indeed in the whole thrust of his spirituality was that Francke would never allow himself to rest until such a transformation had actually taken place.

[94] Francke, "Bekenntnis eines Christen," 369.

[95] A. H. Francke, "Projekt zu einem Seminario universali," in *Werke in Auswahl*, 108.

CHAPTER 7

Halle Pietism I: ideology and indoctrination

FRANCKE'S REFORM VISION

One feature of Pietism that set it apart from earlier Lutheran movements was its expectation that the creation of new institutional forms within the established order would serve as the basis for an all-embracing reform of society. Because "reform" meant the spread of a particular form of piety, the personal religious orientation of the founder of Pietist institutions played a determining role in shaping the character of these organizations. Even though Spener and Francke shared a common spiritual ancestry and were close political allies, Francke's conversion experience and his Promethean emphasis on action resulted in an aggressive militancy that was not present in Spener. Not surprisingly, Francke's *Anstalten* in Halle displayed greater coherence and tighter discipline than Spener's widely scattered and loosely coordinated network of conventicles. Points of difference between the two men, moreover, went beyond organizational style to include goals and tactics. Spener believed that reform of the Lutheran church would, eventually and in some unspecified way, bring about the desired change in society. The more radical Francke worked for the simultaneous transformation of both the church and the social order. Francke envisioned the Halle *Anstalten*, therefore, as a model society, complete with institutions for socialization and economic activity, whose expansion would begin a reform of the entire world.

The years immediately after 1700 afforded Francke the opportunity to develop a strategy for accomplishing his mission. With the orphanage built and local opposition to his institutions defeated, Francke sketched the basic elements of his reform plan in a series of writings completed in 1704. Although the first of these, the "Segensvolle Fusstapfen" (1700) was largely a narrative account of the beginnings of the *Anstalten*, the "Projekt zu einem Seminario universali" (1701) and the much longer "Grosse Aufsatz" (1704) both contained what became Francke's standard analysis of the evils of society and the method for eliminating them. As might be expected, Francke's view of contemporary society closely corresponded to his conception of the "unconverted" individual. All the major social groups, according to Francke, were corrupted by their natural egoism and selfishness. "In the worldly estates, the devil has his kingdom, army, and government among the kings, princes, lords, and all the authorities," he wrote in a typically sweeping condemnation.[1]

Francke, of course, did not conclude from this diagnosis that Christians should simply withdraw into their private devotional lives and prepare for the world to come. Rather, for reasons already discussed, he sought to initiate a process of external transformation by identifying conditions in society responsible for the existing corruption. One factor he seized upon was the "terrible" education given to young people, who therefore "grow up to be raw, dissolute, and wild, without true knowledge and fear of God, without discipline and godly admonishment."[2] A second source of evil in society was the neglect of widows, orphans, and the poor, a neglect of both their immediate material needs and their underlying afflictions. Francke finished his prognosis of society's ills by protesting against a situation in which "such a multitude of people is left without discipline, without instruction, without supervision and order, given over to leisure, as a result of which they are occasioned to engage in thievery, whoring, murder, and street robberies, as well as many other horrors and sins."[3]

Francke's prescription for remedying this state of affairs called for strong measures designed to spread a culture of discipline among the population. In particular, Francke recommended educating the young, caring for the poor and helpless, training God-fearing preachers, putting virtuous persons in positions of authority, and

[1] "August Hermann Franckes Schrift über eine Reform des Erziehungs- und Bildungswesens als Ausgangspunkt einer geistlichen und sozialen Neuordnung der Evangelischen Kirche des 18. Jahrhunderts 'Der grosse Aufsatz,'" ed. Otto Podczeck, *Abhandlungen der sächsischen Akademie der Wissenschaften: Philosophische-historische Reihe*, 53, Heft 3 (Berlin, 1962): 71. Francke's often vehement critique of the greed, sensuality, and avarice of the upper classes was paralleled in the contemporary writings of French Catholic moralists. See Briggs, *Communities of Belief*, 318–20.

[2] Francke, "Der grosse Aufsatz," 76.

[3] *Ibid.*, 79–81.

directing the population from idleness into productive activity.[4] In his view, the primary responsibility for such tasks fell to the clergy, which Lutheran social theory categorized as the "teaching estate" (*Lehrstand*). Though implicated most heavily in the lack of order in society, the teaching estate would also initiate the sought-after improvement.[5] Francke declared that God had provided the teaching estate "a gateway to the betterment of the here described corruption" – namely, the orphanage at Halle, the schools attached to it, and the University of Halle itself.[6] Francke, moreover, imposed no theological restrictions on these providential instruments for the rebirth of society. Rejecting any form of predestination, Francke maintained that God had issued a "general call to grace," granting salvation to whoever experienced rebirth and served his or her neighbor. Institutions such as the Halle *Anstalten* were intended to carry out God's purpose in this respect by preparing for conversion people from every sort of moral and social background and providing them with opportunities to help convert others.[7]

Thus from the perspective of Francke's theology, the schools and university at Halle had unlimited potential to accomplish God's saving work. But while the "door for betterment" was open to all, crossing the threshold did not mean that the individual was free to pursue his or her spiritual development without restriction. In fact, although Francke and his co-workers did not believe in predestination, they none the less regarded themselves as an elite group with the power to direct and control the souls entrusted to them.[8] They legitimized this position, not by birthright or clerical office, but by the knowledge of God's commands made possible by their postconversion "experience" of God. They claimed to possess, as many modern ideologues have done, a type of knowledge that was simultaneously empirical and absolute. They based their claims of authority on their grasp of what Robert Jay Lifton, in his work on Chinese thought reform, called a "sacred science." For a body of doctrine to constitute a "sacred science" in Lifton's sense, it must have a claim to absolute metaphysical truth and be capable of combination with a body of all-encompassing moral principles. The

[4] *Ibid.*, 82.
[5] *Ibid.*, 73, 75.
[6] *Ibid.*, 87.
[7] Böhme, "Heinrich Julius Elers," 171–72; see also Peschke, *Studien zur Theologie August Hermann Franckes*, 68.
[8] Böhme, "Heinrich Julius Elers," 172.

combination of the two, yielding in the Pietists' case their notion of "God's commands," produces a system of thought with ethical imperatives that in the eyes of its proponents are applicable to "all men at all times."[9]

Francke and his inner circle claimed to be "merely" media through which God transmitted His wishes for the betterment of humankind. Yet behind this apparent self-deprecation was an attitude diametrically opposed to true humility: namely, the Halle group's self-conscious assertion that their own ascetic regimen constituted *the* standard for all human conduct, a "law" as comprehensive in its particularity as the Old Testament codes themselves. The consequences of this kind of presumption are penetratingly expressed by Thomas Merton:

> If I set myself up inexorably as a law to my brother, then I cannot help trying to interfere with his life by occult violence, malice, and deceit. I set myself up as a potential *power* to which I demand some form ... of homage and submission. I set myself up, in particular, as a virtuous example which defines and identifies my brother's sin – for that in which he differs from me becomes at once "sin." Note what I do in this: I arrogate to myself the right to *make him a sinner*. I take to myself the awful power which Paul ascribed to the law, of *bringing to life sin in my fellow man* [author's emphases] (Romans 7:8–10).[10]

Having done precisely this, Francke and his assistants did not hesitate to use highly intrusive pedagogical methods to "do good" to the children and students with whose personal development they were entrusted. To be sure, Francke acknowledged that "the work of education is beyond all powers of natural man" and that "it must be carried out through God's spirit." But later in the same passage, he asserts that human cooperation is necessary for God's plan to be realized and that the teacher who achieves the best results is he who in prayer "most earnestly ... struggles with God" in order that the souls of the pupils "may be saved from corruption."[11] As self-proclaimed experts in using prayer to extract transforming power from God, the Halle Pietists confidently assumed the role of intermediaries between God and their school-age flock.[12] They believed

[9] Robert Jay Lifton, *Thought Reform and the Psychology of Totalism* (New York, 1963), 427–28.

[10] Thomas Merton, *Love and Living*, eds. Naomi Burton Stone and Brother Patrick Hart (New York, 1979), 213.

[11] A. H. Francke, *Pädagogische Schriften*, ed. H. Lorenzen (Paderborn, 1957), 8.

[12] Note how this role is consistent with a Promethean-type relationship with God on the part of a believer who must go to extraordinary lengths to gain grace from a God apparently hostile or indifferent to the good of humanity. See above, p. 143, n. 69.

that this posture justified their manipulation of the educational environment in accordance with their "sacred science."

There was another reason for the confidence of the Halle Pietists. As we have seen, in Francke's theology, the "children of God," obliged to "grow in faith" by working for their neighbor's good, needed to experience positive results to confirm the reality of God's presence in their lives. The successful development of the Halle *Anstalten* during the three decades after 1700 furnished in abundance the very sort of external evidence required to assure them that their institutions were indeed beneficiaries of grace.

The purpose of the next two chapters is to describe the pedagogical workings of the orphanage complex and uncover the reasons for its dynamic material growth. As a result of the latter, Francke was able to extend his sphere of control beyond the immediate environment of the orphanage and the university. In pursuit of his "world reform," Francke made pioneering advances in vocational education, familiarized himself with the latest medical knowledge, exhibited extraordinary entrepreneurial skill, and coordinated missionary activity on three continents. Historians have frequently been struck by the apparent polarity between Francke's modernity and universalism, on the one hand, and his emphasis on oppressive discipline on the other.[13] If one does not, however, accept the conventional view of "modernity" as synonymous with "progress" or "freedom," what was most significant about Francke's world was precisely the way it was able to combine very tight internal control with a capacity for seemingly indefinite expansion.

THE SCHOOLS OF THE HALLE *ANSTALTEN*

Indoctrination in Lutheran schools did not originate with August Hermann Francke. The reformers of the sixteenth century included a strong component of religious education in the curricula of the expanding school systems. This training sought to impart the fundamental principles of the Lutheran faith by having pupils memorize Luther's Shorter Catechism. In light of the pessimistic

[13] This theme is prominent, for example, in Rosemarie Ahrbeck, "Zum Prinzip der Selbsttätigkeit und seiner gesellschaftlichen Funktion in A. H. Franckes Pädagogik: Ein Beitrag zur Standortbestimmung A. H. Franckes in der Geschichte des didaktischen Denkens," *Jahrbuch für Erziehungs- und Schulgeschichte*, 17 (1977): 56–79. For a subtle probing of this same tension, see Lehmann, "Pietismus und soziale Reform," 107–08.

eschatology bequeathed to the church by Luther himself, indoctrinating school children in this manner was designed to give them the means for resisting the evils of the day, especially the blandishments of "heresies" such as Catholicism or Calvinism. As Gerald Strauss has shown, however, this catechism campaign did not succeed in forcing a significant percentage of the German people to internalize the moral values taught by the church.[14]

Although such a complex phenomenon requires a multi-faceted explanation, one reason for the inability of these schools to change the traditional behavior patterns of the population was the existence of a distinct limit to the depth and intensity of the religious instruction given there. The pupils were required to master only the catechism; teaching them the Bible in German was not, to say the least, one of the priorities of sixteenth- or seventeenth-century German education.[15] In addition to providing only a rather narrow understanding of the faith, early Lutheran schools generally failed to make clear to the children how the doctrines learned from the catechism would apply to concrete situations in their adult lives. Thus, for most people, the religious knowledge acquired in such schools was insufficient to offset countervailing pressures toward "immorality" found in the family, the street, and the workplace.

Francke was determined that the impact of his schools on pupils' lives would not be so superficial. Francke's efforts to educate the orphans of Glaucha made him immediately aware of the corrupting influences of the social environment. It took only a few months for Francke to develop his characteristic response to this threat. By first boarding the children in Pietist households and then building a self-contained orphanage complex, Francke strove to create a pedagogical institution that would insulate his charges from the dangers of "this world." Within the confines of the orphanage, Francke and his staff were in a position to monitor all communication with and between the orphans, to exercise what Lifton calls "milieu control."[16] The Pietists imposed a similarly restrictive discipline in each of the schools of the Halle *Anstalten*: the "poor" (later called "German") schools; the Latin school, which trained mostly middle-

[14] Strauss, *Luther's House of Learning*, *passim*. See also above, pp. 90–91.

[15] For an analysis of the reasons for the authorities' aversion to using the Bible in the schools, see Gawthrop and Strauss, "Protestantism and Literacy in Early Modern Germany," 31–43.

[16] Lifton, *Thought Reform and the Psychology of Totalism*, 420.

class youths for university study; and the *Paedagogium*, a boarding school for upper-class boys. Only within such a controlled setting did Francke believe he could inculcate the puritanical values which would lead to the social transformation he envisioned.

Francke's program of indoctrination, then, was far more ambitious than its sixteenth-century counterparts in its systematic attempt to change the personal natures of its pupils. This effort began with respect to each child as soon as he or she entered the orphanage or enrolled at one of the Pietist schools. The physical isolation of the children from their former environments was reinforced by a form of psychological pressure placed on them by Francke's staff to renounce their "old selves." In theory, this process, called by Francke "breaking the will," was to be carried out with as much compassion as possible; pupils who had difficulty adjusting to the new regimen were to be treated gently.[17] Nevertheless, the purpose of this initiation procedure was the fundamentally coercive one of forcing the children to develop the habit of unconditional obedience to the commands of their teachers and supervisers.[18] According to Francke's pedagogical theory, breaking the child's "natural will" as quickly as possible was the necessary first step in leading him or her away from the snares of the world toward the goal of subordination to the divine will.[19] Only after such an initial reorientation could the children begin to internalize the values of the Halle *Anstalten*.

The next step in the process of imposing these values on the pupils was an intensive exposure to Pietist spirituality in the classroom. In all the schools more time was devoted to religious instruction than to any other subject, and the method of this instruction was quite systematic.[20] Pupils had to memorize portions of the catechism,

[17] Oschlies, *Die Arbeits- und Berufspädagogik*, 112. Oschlies concedes Francke's good intentions in this respect but adds, "undoubtedly in practice everything was not so benign as Francke describes it here."

[18] Many of the practices of the Halle *Anstalten* bear a strong resemblance to those of the "total institutions" studied by Erving Goffman. Thus, in discussing initiation procedures, Goffman emphasizes the importance such institutions place on making the new inmate show "extreme deference" to staff members as quickly after arrival as possible, so that "thereafter he will be manageable." Goffman, *Asylums: Essays on the Social Situations of Mental Patients and Other Inmates* (Garden City, N.Y., 1961), 89.

[19] Rosemarie Ahrbeck, "Zur Dialektik von Ziel und Methode in Franckes Pädagogik" in Rosemarie Ahrbeck and Burchard Thaler, eds., *August Hermann Francke, 1663–1727* (Halle, 1977), 40; see also Klaus Schaller, "Pietismus und moderne Pädagogik," 174.

[20] For the German schools, training in religion consumed roughly four of the seven daily school hours. For these schools' complete curriculum plan, see Elisabeth Gloria, *Der*

verses in the Bible, psalms, or long passages from the New Testament and recite them before their classmates. Teachers would then discuss with the children the meaning of the recited material and encourage them to restate it in their own words. As part of the same discussion, the teacher would also question the class in order to extract examples of how the text applied to everyday situations. On Wednesdays and Saturdays, classes in the German school would repeat what they had covered during the two previous classdays.[21]

The Latin school and the *Paedagogium* did not follow this repetitive pattern quite so strictly. In these more advanced schools the many hours of basic religious instruction were supplemented by introductory classes in theology, church history, and biblical history. But even in these schools readings used in foreign-language instruction, the second most time-consuming field of study in the curriculum, were limited almost exclusively to the Bible. Only in Latin classes was this not the case.[22]

In all three schools, recitation and discussion of sacred texts constituted only part of the effort devoted to religious training. Twice daily, class members read the Bible aloud to one another under a teacher's supervision. A time for prayer preceded both morning and afternoon sessions; and the school day closed with a prayer hour, attended by all the children, which included singing hymns, reading the Bible, and public catechization of small groups of pupils. Finally, on Sundays everyone was obliged to attend two church services and undergo catechization. The Sunday sermon, Bible readings, and hymns formed an integral part of the religious material studied during the preceding and following weeks.[23]

The main purpose of this schoolhouse drilling was to exhort the child to practice ascetic self-denial and charity toward his or her neighbor. Exhortation in Pietist values was also accomplished by means of having the teachers themselves embody the norms of the institution.[24] As one would expect, Francke employed only "born-again" Christians as teachers because they alone could serve as

Pietismus als Förderer der Volksbildung und sein Einfluss auf die preussische Volksschule (Halle, 1933), 37.

21 A. H. Francke, *Schriften über Erziehung und Unterricht*, ed. Karl Richter (Leipzig, 1880), 219–21..

22 *Ibid.*, 264, 267.

23 *Ibid.*, 222–25, 266–67, 270.

24 It is the group whom Goffman calls "lower staff" that must "personally present" the behavioral requirements of the institution to the inmates. Obviously the message presented is more powerful if the messengers themselves seem to live by it. Goffman, *Asylums*, 114.

moral exemplars for the children.[25] Admonition in and of itself, however, could not ensure that the pupils would actually apply what they had learned to their own behavior. As is the case in any program of intensive indoctrination, the Pietists' exhortatory appeals had to be supplemented by coercion.[26] The providential mission of the Halle *Anstalten* and the possession of a "sacred science" by the orphanage's staff was held to justify the use of harsh methods in overcoming any obstacles to what the staff believed to be God's plan.[27]

One aspect of this coercion was, of course, the creation of the controlled environment itself in order to shield the young people from contaminating worldly influences. Such influences also had to be eliminated from the curriculum, whose every lesson plan required prior approval from the school inspector or from Francke himself.[28] But besides tightly controlling the children's milieu, the staff of the *Anstalten* schools did not hesitate to exercise their coercive power by breaking any internal resistance to the precepts so forcibly presented in the classroom. Those who broke the rules were, therefore, swiftly punished; for, although in theory Francke criticized excessive use of the rod and advocated admonition for first offenses, in practice, corporal punishment was quite prevalent in the *Anstalten*. The most stubborn offenders were placed in a detention room with bread and water.[29]

The existence of resistance to the authority of the teachers was due in part to the cultural gap between the Pietist instructors' middle-class standards of cleanliness and propriety, on the one hand, and the upbringing received by children of often impoverished parents, on the other.[30] The bulk of the coercion was necessitated, however, by the nature of the institutional rules laid down by Francke. Designed to introduce the pupils to the life of a "child of God," these

25 Ahrbeck, "Zur Dialektik von Ziel und Methode," 39–40.

26 Lifton formulates the interrelationship between exhortation and coercion in this way: "the use of coercion ... [stimulates] excessive guilt and shame so that these in turn create an inner exhortation; and the use of exhortation ... [stimulates] negative conscience so powerfully that it becomes in effect a form of self-coercion." Lifton, *Thought Reform and the Psychology of Totalism*, 441.

27 Oschlies, *Die Arbeits- und Berufspädagogik*, 115.

28 *Ibid.*, 107. Textbooks, needless to say, were also carefully monitored. As many as possible were written by the staff of the *Anstalten* and published by the orphanage press. *Ibid.*, 119–22.

29 Ahrbeck, "Zum Prinzip der Selbsttätigkeit," 71–72.

30 Gloria, *Der Pietismus als Förderer der Volksbildung*, 31.

rules prescribed a highly regimented routine for the children. Orphans, pupils boarding at the *Anstalten*, and pupils from town all had to rise early and attend school or church services seven days a week, fifty-two weeks a year.[31] Those living on the grounds had to perform chores or do homework in the remaining hours of the day.

This constant activity was intended partly to accustom the youngsters to the uninterrupted alternation of prayer and work integral to Francke's concept of the Christian life. It also had the effect of restricting play. Francke's opposition to leisure was so intense that he refused to permit any form of free-wheeling sport or bodily exercise in which youthful exuberance might expend itself without achieving some pedagogical purpose.[32] If even the most innocent forms of childhood play aroused Francke's suspicion, it goes without saying that he prohibited such diversions as dancing, attending plays, reading unedifying books, and writing secret letters.[33]

Enforcing rules such as these required continuous surveillance of the children, "who should always be in the presence of their teachers."[34] Francke in fact regarded "careful inspection" as the "actual focal point [*nervus*] of education."[35] The staff of the *Anstalten* extended the scope of their supervision well beyond the classroom to include manners and demeanor of the children outside class, behavior in church, censorship of private reading, and contacts with friends outside the orphanage complex. Particularly to enforce this last rule, teachers required the support of a child's parents. Frequent teacher–parent conferences sought to enlist the cooperation, or at least the neutrality, of parents toward the teacher's disciplinary role.[36] To prevent the rapid turnover of teachers from disrupting continuity in the treatment of any particular child, dossiers were kept on all the children. Four times a year teachers were also required to submit reports on the piety, behavior, and scholastic achievement of each of their pupils, thereby adding a bureaucratic

[31] *Ibid.*, 31; Ahrbeck, "Zur Dialektik von Ziel und Methode," 41.

[32] Gerd Lukas, "Über die Stellung August Hermann Franckes zum Körper und seiner Übung als Ausdruck des Einflusses christlichen Lehren," in Ahrbeck and Thaler, eds., *August Hermann Francke, 1663–1727*, 67.

[33] Werner Piechocki, "A. H. Franckes sozial- und schulhygienische An- und Einsichten," in *August Hermann Francke: Das humanistische Erbe des grossen Erziehers* (Halle, 1965), 49. See also Gloria, *Der Pietismus als Förderer der Volksbildung*, 34.

[34] A. H. Francke, *Pädagogische Schriften*, ed. Gustav Kramer (Langensalza, 1885), 226.

[35] *Ibid.*, 179.

[36] Oschlies, *Die Arbeits- und Berufspädagogik*, 107–11; Gloria, *Der Pietismus als Förderer der Volksbildung*, 32, 34.

dimension to the task of maintaining discipline within the *Anstalten*.[37]

Francke intended this harsh regimen and strict supervision to train the pupil's will in the practice of asceticism and in the duty of obedience to God's will. In keeping with Francke's piety, however, the schools in the orphanage complex also sought to cultivate a child's understanding. According to Francke, knowledge was intrinsically neither good nor bad and could be quite useful to a person with a properly trained will.[38] If the will possessed a fundamentally pious orientation, the intellect could seize upon and accept sound teachings, making it easier for the will, in turn, to follow the right path without coercion.[39] Hence Francke insisted that children not only memorize the catechism and selected biblical verses but also learn how to use the Bible as a kind of reference book to assist the will in its spiritual growth.[40]

Francke emphasized a similarly active approach to the more worldly disciplines. As we have seen, in Francke's spirituality, a "child of God" could "grow in faith" only by performing charitable works for the good of others. In this context, knowledge, particularly of a practical nature, could provide an invaluable service to the properly trained will. For those Christians who possessed sufficient worldly skills to enjoy material prosperity were also in the best position to "produce something useful" for their neighbors.[41] In his pedagogy, then, Francke strove to inculcate both "true righteousness" (*wahre Gottseligkeit*) and what he called *christliche Klugheit*, which may be translated as "Christian practical wisdom."

According to Francke, to be taught in the schools of the orphanage complex, a subject had to have "use in everyday life."[42] Although the curricula of the different schools thereby varied considerably, the depth and intensity of the training in practical sub-

[37] Gloria, *Der Pietismus als Förderer der Volksbildung*, 34.

[38] Ahrbeck, "Zum Prinzip der Selbsttätigkeit," 72–73.

[39] Oschlies, *Die Arbeits- und Berufspädagogik*, 107.

[40] For an illuminating discussion of Francke's notion of the Gospels as a source of rules for the will, see Schaller, "Pietismus und moderne Pädagogik." 174. For an analysis of the same tendency in English Puritanism, along with many valuable insights into the process of secularization, see the forthcoming essay by J. Samuel Preus, "Secularizing Divination: Spiritual Biography and the Invention of the Novel," *Journal of the American Academy of Religion*, 59 (1992). Preus emphasizes here the importance for the Puritans of "particular stories of biblical individuals," who served as *exempla* in comparison with which believers could judge themselves.

[41] Oschlies, *Die Arbeits- und Berufspädagogik*, 107.

[42] Quoted in Ahrbeck, "Zum Prinzip der Selbsttätigkeit," 72.

jects offered at the *Anstalten* were unprecedented in the history of German education.[43] A strong emphasis on mathematics in all the schools demonstrated this commitment to teaching practical knowledge.[44] Even more striking were the educational goals of both the Latin school and the *Paedagogium*: cultivation of a good *German* writing style, training in calligraphy, initiation into economics and jurisprudence, as well as introductory work in geography, botany, anatomy, and medicine.[45] In the *Paedagogium* pupils also had to learn French, master several mechanical disciplines, and gain experience in such trades as copperplate engraving, glasscutting, drawing, and woodworking. Francke intended this exposure to artisanal skills to illustrate the practical utility of such subjects as geometry and optics and serve to familiarize upper-class youngsters with the sorts of activities they would some day supervise.[46]

Francke's insistence that pupils gain a rational understanding of material presented to them dictated the methods by which the worldly disciplines were taught. Francke admonished his teachers to do everything possible to hold the children's attention. In the two upper schools, not more than three non-religious subjects were taught at once, so that the pupils could more easily concentrate and make progress. Francke also sought to stimulate interest by employing methods intended to channel the children's play instincts into learning.[47] In both upper schools, for example, botany class was held in the summer, so that frequent field trips could supplement classroom presentation.[48] In the *Paedagogium*, one hour a day was devoted to "recreational exercises," during which the *Realien* were taught in a number of unorthodox ways. It was during this hour that

43 The *Paedagogium* served as the model for the first *Realschule*, founded in Berlin by Hecker, who joined the staff of the Halle *Anstalten* shortly before Francke's death in 1727. See Oschlies, *Die Arbeits- und Berufspädagogik*, 69.

44 In all the schools, mathematics was taught by means of examples from well-known areas of everyday life. *Ibid.*, 76.

45 Ahrbeck, "Zum Prinzip der Selbsttätigkeit," 73.

46 Rosemarie Ahrbeck-Wothge, "Über Franckes 'Lehrart,'" *Jahrbuch für Erziehungs- und Schulgeschichte*, 3 (1963): 21; R. Ahrbeck-Wothge, "Zu Fragen der Arbeitserziehung und der Allgemeinbildung bei A. H. Francke," in *A. H. Francke: Festreden und Kolloquium aus Anlass der 300. Wiederkehr seines Geburtstages 22. März 1663* (Halle, 1964), 122.

47 The contrast between this empathetic approach, much praised by historians of pedagogy, and the relentless severity of the institutional discipline was bound, however, to have created difficulties, either for the teacher, who thereby had to adopt a different persona, or for the pupils, whose response to the learning environment in the classes on practical subjects was bound to have been inhibited by the harsh authoritarianism that otherwise suffused the *Anstalten*.

48 Ahrbeck, "Zum Prinzip der Selbsttätigkeit," 75, 77.

the boys went to artisans' workshops to watch demonstrations of various crafts.[49]

Once a week the *Paedagogium*'s classes visited the *Naturalienkabinett*, a science and technology museum located in the grounds of the orphanage complex. The *Naturalienkabinett* contained specimens of flora and fauna sent to Halle by missionaries from all over the world, as well as models (Copernican and Brahean) of the universe, instruments for scientific experiments, and models demonstrating work implements, construction processes, and work methods.[50] Many of the technological exhibits were built by the pupils themselves. Both the *Naturalienkabinett*, a listing of whose collections filled a 375-page catalogue in 1740, and the orphanage library, which included some eighteen thousand volumes by 1721, were open to pupils of the *Anstalten*, university students, and townspeople all day long every day of the week except for Sundays and religious holidays.[51]

The importance placed by Francke on the applicability of both religious and practical training was in keeping with a de-emphasis on status distinctions within the Halle *Anstalten*. The school system was arranged in accordance with the status divisions of contemporary society – an arrangement necessitated in part for financial reasons, in part by the wish to convince the public that the Pietists respected the traditional social hierarchy.[52] What mattered most to Francke, however, was the success of his reform movement, which depended in turn on his schools' producing graduates who were not only God-fearing and disciplined but also competent in the specialized forms of knowledge useful for the spiritual and material improvement of the human condition. A vital aim of Francke's

49 Dorothea Goetz, "Der Anteil des Pietismus an der Herausbildung des naturwissenschaftlichen Unterrichts im 18. Jahrhundert," *Schriftenreihe für Geschichte der Naturwissenschaften, Technik und Medizin*, 11 (1974): 96–97.

50 *Ibid.*, 99–100; Jürgen Storz, "Hauptbibliothek, Archiv und Naturalienkabinett der Frankkeschen Stiftungen," in *A. H. Francke: Das humanistische Erbe*, 105.

51 Storz, "Hauptbibliothek, Archiv und Naturalienkabinett," 96–97, 106. Such public museums, be their exhibits artistic or scientific, are typical manifestations of modern, democratic societies. Hence in the early eighteenth century such an institution as the *Naturalienkabinett* was extremely unusual. As Daniel Boorstin points out, during the premodern period collections of books, artifacts, and paintings were typically the private property of kings and aristocrats. Only after the mid-eighteenth century in England and the Revolution of 1789 on the Continent were these holdings converted into museums open to the public. See Boorstin, *The Image: A Guide to Pseudo-Events in America* (New York, 1982), 99–102.

52 Oschlies, *Die Arbeits- und Berufspädagogik*, 96. For a theoretical discussion, see Goffman, *Asylums*, 119–22.

schools, consequently, was to discover each boy's special talent and advance him in that field as quickly as possible. Talented male pupils in the German school, be they orphans or children of townspeople, were given scholarships to attend the Latin school. Level of achievement also determined the grouping of pupils for nonreligious classes in the upper schools.[53]

The merit system of the orphanage-complex schools did not, of course, apply to all the children or always benefit the Pietist movement. All the girls and a great majority of the boys attending the German school went on to work as house servants or as apprentices to tradesmen, while many graduates of the *Paedagogium* returned home to administer their family's businesses, estates, or princedoms. Even those who went on to a university did not necessarily study under a Pietist-dominated faculty. A significant percentage of pupils from the Latin school and the *Paedagogium* did, however, continue their education at the University of Halle.[54] There, the theological and medical faculties supervised the training of future leaders of Halle Pietism in a setting where religious indoctrination reached even greater levels of intensity.

THE UNIVERSITY OF HALLE AND THE TRAINING OF CADRES

The theology program

Francke's system of primary and secondary education placed an unusually heavy burden on the teacher. Teachers in the Halle *Anstalten* had to possess not only a broad range of knowledge but also exemplary moral qualities and the commitment to enforce Pietist norms inside and outside the classroom. The success of Francke's reform effort depended on a large, growing supply of such teachers. In eighteenth-century German schools the teacher was in most cases also the local pastor or else was supervised by him. Since pastors were trained at the universities, Francke's plan could not be fulfilled unless the universities regularly produced pious candidates to fill clerical and teaching positions. Francke believed, however, that

53 Oschlies, *Die Arbeits- und Berufspädagogik*, 125–28.

54 Between 1690 and 1730 more boys from Halle matriculated at the university than from any other city, including Berlin. For the complete list, see Fritz Juntke and Franz Zimmermann, eds., *Matrikel der Martin-Luther-Universität Halle-Wittenberg, 1690–1730* (Halle, 1960), 576–80.

student life at the typical German university was not conducive to spiritual rebirth and growth in faith. The endemic rowdiness, drinking, duels, debts, and disruption of the Sabbath led him to conclude that the students pursued their course work in order to "achieve as much honor, riches, and good living (*guten Tagen*) in the world as possible."[55] No wonder, then, that Francke regarded the founding of the University of Halle as an act of Providence. Since the theology faculty consisted only of Pietists – Paul Anton, J.J. Breithaupt, and Francke himself – it could train students in its own image, thereby furnishing society with teachers and pastors "whom one afterwards will be able to employ usefully" for the benefit of all.[56]

In order to produce such pastors and school teachers, the cadres for Francke's world reform, the theology faculty adopted the same pedagogical procedures used by Francke in the schools of the orphanage complex. The teaching staff in both institutions placed a higher priority on a reform of the will than on scholastic attainment. Accordingly, the first demand made on the young people in each environment was a fundamental reorientation of the will. In the case of the theology program at the university, this meant a "born-again" conversion. The theology faculty did not precisely specify how this rebirth was to be achieved, and they allowed students to continue their studies even if they did not immediately undergo a conversion experience. But the expectation that they would do so, sooner or later, was made unmistakably clear. As the unquestioned leader of the theology faculty, Francke regarded a conversion as the "foundation of study."[57] Students who had not yet experienced a "breakthrough" were expected to exhibit a repentant attitude and demonstrate that they were preparing intensively to be "born again."

Once a student had achieved this state, he was ready for what Francke called "constant growth in study," the product of a total immersion in a theological curriculum designed to reinforce the student's conversion. The core of this curriculum consisted of biblical exegesis, which necessarily entailed study of the original biblical languages. In Francke's words, "a student of theology must take as his first principle, that he make himself familiar with the New

[55] A. H. Francke, "Der grosse Aufsatz," 78.
[56] Ahrbeck-Wothge, "Über Franckes 'Lehrart,'" 18.
[57] Quoted in Erhard Peschke, "A. H. Franckes Reform des theologischen Studiums," in *A. H. Francke: Festreden und Kolloquium*, 93.

Testament text in Greek and with the Old Testament in Hebrew."[58] Students were accordingly expected in their first year to read the Greek New Testament twice and the Hebrew Old Testament once. Their exegetical labors were conducted within the framework of two ongoing *collegia publica*, attendance at which was required during the student's entire stay at the university. Thus, even though the first year was the one in which preoccupation with the biblical texts was most intense, the faculty intended their students continually to increase their familiarity with the Scriptures. Advanced students supplemented this basic course of study by working with the Septuagint Old Testament, the Apocrypha, and the works of the Church Fathers.[59] At the highest level of the program, a few of the most talented and committed students were invited to participate in the *Collegium Orientale Theologicum.* This scholarly group was not so much a colloquium as a "Bible research institute" whose members studied and taught ancient Middle Eastern languages, among them Chaldean, Syriac, Arabic, and Aramaic.[60]

In designing this curriculum, the theology faculty was governed by its conviction that the Bible was the basis for theological study. Like the pupils of the *Anstalten* schools, the theology students were obliged to know the Bible as intimately as possible because Francke regarded the Holy Scriptures as *the* guide book to spiritual development. In order to be included in the Halle curriculum, other sources for theological education had to meet the standard of "usefulness" set by the Bible.[61] Since Pietists regarded philosophy and dogma, the two bulwarks of orthodox Lutheran theological training, as deficient in this respect, they gave them relatively little emphasis in the Halle program. Philosophy was offered to advanced students only for the purpose of aiding their understanding of the Platonist terminology used by the Church Fathers. A colloquium on dogmatics was required at Halle, to be sure; but the class dealt almost exclusively with moral theology. Such "useless" subjects as scholastic philosophy and abstract theology had no place, even there. Thus

[58] Quoted in Kurt Aland, "Der hallesche Pietismus und die Bibel," in Aland, ed., *Der Pietismus im modernen Welt*, 41.

[59] Peschke, "A. H. Franckes Reform des theologischen Studiums," 97–99

[60] Aland, "Der hallesche Pietismus und die Bibel," 44; see also Otto Podczeck, "Das Collegium orientale theologicum A. H. Franckes," *Wissenschaftliche Zeitschrift Martin-Luther-Universität Halle-Wittenberg: Gesellschafts- und Sprachwissenschaftliche Reihe*, 7 (1958): 1060.

[61] Stoeffler, *German Pietism during the Eighteenth Century*, 45–46.

theology as taught at Halle was not systematic theology informed by a metaphysical perspective but an "honest, diligent ... experientially verified exposition of all lucid passages of Holy Scripture."[62]

The use of the phrase "experientially verified" in this context indicates that for Francke and his faculty colleagues absolute truth consisted of something more than expert interpretation of the Bible. The Halle theologians, especially Paul Anton in his *Commentatio theologica de analogia fidei*, were constantly holding up the ideal of a perfect unity between knowledge of the Bible and the direct experience of God. Even more interestingly, Anton and the others viewed this unity as residing in the collective faith of a "regenerated community of believers."[63] Thus despite the linguistic and exegetical skills of its theologians, Halle Pietism depended for its conception of God's Word, in theory, on the spontaneous operation of the Holy Spirit among the "children of God."

In practice, however, the unity between Word and experience, between theologians and ordinary parishioners, was the product of manipulation, rather than spontaneity. The spiritual experiences of those influenced by Halle Pietism were defined in terms of the language common to all those educated at the University of Halle. Halle theology students were expected to interpret their exegeses and their own religious development in terms of such code words as "new birth," "living faith," "growth in faith," "for the good of thy neighbor," "active Christianity," and so forth.[64] Even though the Halle Pietists repudiated Aristotelian scholasticism and metaphysics in general, they created in its place this standardized vocabulary that served to define absolute ethical imperatives. The concepts of this "sacred science" were designed to encompass the spiritual condition of the entire human race. Lifton aptly describes both Chinese thought reform and Halle Pietism when he says of the former: "The most far-reaching and complex of human problems are compressed into brief, highly reductive, definitive-sounding phrases easily memorized and easily expressed."[65]

The student was compelled to master the categories of Halle theology because he was obliged to live up to the standards of conduct enunciated through them. In Francke's view, the calling of

[62] *Ibid.*, 48.
[63] *Ibid.*, 48–49.
[64] Stoeffler makes the same observation. *Ibid.*, 49.
[65] Lifton, *Thought Reform and the Psychology of Totalism*, 429.

the theology student consisted of filling the same office (*Amt*) that Christ had carried out while on this earth. Such an exalted occupation required its practicioners to imitate Him, to justify their authority over others by adopting a completely different mien from the people they would be serving. [66] Teaching students to become moral exemplars, then, was one of the missions of the theology faculty. Although the moral standards expected of the theology students were more elevated and strict than those applied to pupils in the *Anstalten* schools, the theology faculty relied on the same basic techniques to produce compliance: namely, exhortation and coercion. The major difference from the orphanage-complex schools was that the three theology professors alone could not supervise their students' every waking moment and therefore had to rely to a great extent on the students themselves to exhort and police one another.

In regard to inculcating the values of Halle Pietism, the faculty assumed primary responsibility, though the students also participated in this process. Faculty exhorted students through close counselling and the exegetical collegia, one of whose major aims was to bring out the relevance of scriptural passages for the life of the "true Christian." In addition, every student was required to attend a weekly "paranetical lecture" given by Francke every Thursday between ten and eleven. In these lectures Francke admonished his hearers, either through biblical exegesis or direct comment, on ways in which students could improve in their studies or in their Christianity.[67] To supplement this exhortation from the faculty, students were expected to catechize themselves daily and form prayer groups. Students were also obliged to keep diaries, exercise self-control, and conduct annual self-evaluations to assess the progress they were making.[68]

Faculty and students likewise shared the burden of enforcing the institutional code of behavior. The faculty's role consisted mainly of handing out rewards and punishments. In the paranetical lectures Francke denounced, "without naming names," the behavior of individual students.[69] In the examinations given before the granting of the degree, the faculty based their evaluation of the student as much on his personal piety as on his academic attainments. Con-

66 Peschke, "A. H. Franckes Reform des theologischen Studiums," 95.

67 Aland, "Der hallesche Pietismus und die Bibel," 43.

68 Peschke, " A. H. Franckes Reform des theologischen Studiums," 101, 104.

69 *Ibid.*, 111–12.

sideration of the student's level of morality also determined to a large extent the outcome of the competition for fellowships.

Such disciplinary measures could not have been applied, however, had the faculty not received a steady stream of information about the conduct of their students. Students were urged not only to serve as behavior models for one another but also to make each other's sins known to the faculty. Indicative of the expectations placed on the students was the set of requirements Francke established for those poorer students who applied for a daily meal at the "free table" in the orphanage's refectory. In addition to indicating a "not unrepentant" heart, renouncing all worldly pleasures, and accounting for every hour of his time, the applicant also had to report on the moral weakness of his fellow students.[70] In light of the large surplus of applicants for the limited number of places at the "free table," the competition among the students to disclose secrets about each other must have been intense. This system of mutual surveillance must have worked well enough because a more formal system of spying on students, though in existence for a time, was eventually discontinued.[71]

Like the education offered in the *Anstalten* schools, theology training at the University of Halle demanded that the student break with his "old self," learn and internalize the precepts of Halle Pietism, and demonstrate a "real change" in behavior. But again, proper spiritual orientation and ascetic self-discipline had to be supplemented by preparation in the practical aspects of serving one's neighbor. The Halle theological faculty sought to train their students to apply their religious knowledge toward the improvement of others. The faculty required daily self-catechization from the students in part because they felt students should thoroughly accustom themselves to using the language of the catechism – the means by which they would best communicate with their future parishioners. In addition, the Pietist professors gave formal instruction in the principles of homiletics and encouraged their students to attend sermons by the faculty and study them as models.[72]

The bulk of the practical training available to students consisted of performing part-time jobs for the theological faculty or the orphanage complex. Opportunities for such experience appealed

70 Ahrbeck, "Zur Dialektik von Ziel und Methode," 40.
71 Peschke, "A. H. Franckes Reform des theologischen Studiums," 104.
72 *Ibid.*, 100–01.

especially to poorer students, since those who worked for the Pietists, while receiving no cash payment, were entitled to one or two meals a day at the "free table." Some of the jobs offered contributed only marginally to the students' professional expertise. Such positions entailed working in the orphanage library, answering letters from parents of pupils at the *Paedagogium*, or recording and transcribing Francke's sermons and his paranetical lectures.[73]

A much more desirable form of practical training was the opportunity to teach two hours a day in the *Anstalten* schools. To guide their efforts, student teachers could rely on printed teaching manuals, composed by Francke, which imparted not only Francke's educational philosophy but also detailed instructions on how to teach every subject in the curriculum at all levels of difficulty. The students worked within the framework of a "teachers' seminar," the *Seminarium Praeceptorum*, and were closely supervised by the inspector of the orphanage-complex schools. Every week the inspector conducted a meeting of the *Seminarium* in which the teachers shared experiences, compared notes about certain pupils, and received constructive criticism about their performances.[74] As there was no comparable teacher-training program in Germany at that time, the student teachers had no difficulty in finding jobs, particularly in Brandenburg-Prussia. And wherever they went, they took with them at least something of Francke's spirit and methods.

The medical clinic

Though obviously the centerpiece of Francke's reformed university, the program for theology students was complemented by a medical school that was also strongly Pietist in orientation. Francke's interest in medicine stemmed in part from the problem posed to the *Anstalten* by the unhealthy environment of Halle and its surroundings. Glaucha, in particular, was an unsanitary place; its populace, ignorant of elementary hygenic principles, lived amid the filth and stench of pig pens and distillery wastes. Such conditions were one of the factors behind the original decision to build the orphanage. When Francke sent his assistant Neubauer to Holland in 1697 to gather information about the construction and operation of Dutch orphanages, the questionnaire Francke drew up for him showed an

[73] Oschlies, *Die Arbeits- und Berufspädagogik*, 91–95.

[74] Francke, *Schriften über Erziehung und Unterricht*, ed. Richter, 346–67.

unusual sensitivity to the importance of sanitary practices and building design for the children's health.[75]

Francke's interest in medicine was also an outgrowth of his doctrine "for the good of thy neighbor." His commitment to bodily health did not arise from any sense of the intrinsic worth of the body. Love of the body was an aspect of the more generalized love for "this world" so strongly opposed by Francke. Francke esteemed the body, rather, as an instrument in the service of the soul. For the reborn Christian, a healthy body, in conjunction with sound vocational training and adequate financial resources, permitted the person to be more useful to God and his or her neighbor.[76]

For the task of incorporating medical research and practice into his reform movement, Francke found willing collaborators on the University of Halle medical faculty and among the students trained by them. The professor of practical medicine at Halle, Friedrich Hoffmann, was a very religious man who at first donated money to the orphanage. Hoffmann's students volunteered to care for sick orphans and school children, especially during the epidemic of 1698–99.[77] In the years after 1700 Hoffmann and his students kept a certain distance from the Halle *Anstalten*, not from any feelings of antipathy toward Francke but because of Hoffmann's professional rivalry with his polemically minded colleague at Halle, Georg Ernst Stahl, professor of theoretical medicine. Stahl found Hoffmann's mechanistic view of bodily processes and disease incompatible with his animistic concept of sickness as an effort to the soul to restore disturbed internal balances.[78] As Stahl's emphasis on the primacy of the soul accorded better with Pietist theology than did Hoffmann's Cartesianism, Stahl's students naturally tended to gravitate to the Pietist institutions, causing Hoffmann's protégés to back away.[79]

Two of Stahl's students played crucial roles in strengthening the connections between the university medical school and the Halle *Anstalten*. The first, Christian Friedrich Richter (1676–1711), twice

[75] Piechocki, "A. H. Franckes sozial- und schulhygienische An- und Einsichten," 45–47.

[76] Endre Zsindely, *Krankheit und Heilung im älteren Pietismus* (Zürich, 1962), 41.

[77] Werner Piechocki, "Die Krankenpflege und das Klinikum der Franckeschen Stiftungen," in *A. H. Francke: Das humanistische Erbe*, 52.

[78] J. Karcher, "Die animistische Theorie Georg Ernst Stahls im Aspekt der pietistischen Bewegung an der Universität Halle an der Saale im zugrundegehenden 17. und beginnenden 18. Jahrhundert," *Gesnerus*, 15 (1958): 3–8.

[79] Wolfram Kaiser, Karl-Heinz Krosch, and Werner Piechocki, "Collegium clinicum Halense," in *Collegium Jahre zweihundertfünfzig Clinicum Halense, 1717–1967: Beiträge zur Geschichte der Medizinischen Fakultät der Universität Halle* (Halle, 1967), 25–26.

served briefly as chief doctor of the orphanage in the late 1690s, after which he devoted himself chiefly to writing hymns and manufacturing medicines for the orphanage's apothecary.[80] Richter started the practice of providing informal training to medical student volunteers and occasionally offered a clinical *collegium* with the blessings of the medical faculty.[81] In 1705 Richter wrote perhaps the first widely disseminated manual of practical medicine in the German language, the *Kurzer und deutlicher Unterricht von dem Leibe und natürlichen Leben des Menschen*.[82] This synthesis of Pietist religiosity and medical knowledge encouraged Francke to convert a cattle barn on the premises of the orphanage into a small hospital. Well before 1710, moreover, he authorized the orphanage doctor to dispense free medicines to the poor in periodic "consultation hours" (*Sprechstunden*), at which student trainees assisted.[83] The availability of this hospital, plus contact with outpatients through the *Sprechstunden*, provided a framework within which opportunities for medical students to receive practical experience could be expanded still further.

Although Richter initiated a small clinic staffed largely by medical student volunteers, its importance began to rival that of the *Seminarium Praeceptorum* only when under the leadership of Johann Juncker (1679–1759). In his youth a theology student at Halle and an instructor at the *Paedagogium*, Juncker studied briefly under Stahl before leaving Halle to continue studying medicine on his own. Returning to Halle around 1717 as director of the orphanage clinic, Juncker became an exemplary Pietist doctor, for whom meeting the medical needs of the poor filled his life with meaning.[84] One of Juncker's first acts as director of the clinic was to arrange for the incorporation of the *Collegium clinicum* into the regular curriculum offered by the Halle medical faculty. The availability of a credit-bearing clinical program led to a manifold increase in the number of medical students matriculating at Halle.[85] As more student assist-

80 For a full-length study of Richter, see Eckhard Altmann, *Christian Friedrich Richter (1676–1711): Arzt, Apotheker und Liederdichter des Halleschen Pietismus* (Witten, 1972).

81 Piechocki, "Die Krankenpflege und das Klinikum," 54–55.

82 The work had gone through fourteen editions by 1747. See Piechocki, "A. H. Franckes sozial- und schulhygienische An- und Einsichten," 50.

83 Piechocki, "Die Krankenpflege und das Klinkum," 56. In 1711 Francke reported to Crown Prince Frederick William that his medical staff distributed gratis medicines with a market value of 1000T. Deppermann, *Der hallesche Pietismus und der preussische Staat*, 167.

84 Piechocki, "Die Krankenpflege und das Klinikum," 57.

85 Wolfram Kaiser and Werner Piechocki, "Berliner Ärzte des 18. Jahrhunderts als hallesche Doktoranden," *Deutsches Medizinsches Journal*, 20 (1969): 186.

ants became available, Juncker's clinic could expand its services. The reputation of the institution, commonly regarded as the third best of its kind in Europe, attracted increasing numbers of patients, so that by the 1750s over one thousand people a month were treated at the clinic. Assisted by only one other doctor, Juncker had to rely heavily on his student staff members, who therefore received a great deal of first-hand experience.[86]

The purpose of the clinic, however, went beyond providing free medical care for the poor and practical training for future physicians. Francke and his followers viewed a person's stay in the hospital as an opportunity to minister to the soul as well as the body. Francke justified intervention in the patient's spiritual life by an adaptation of Stahl's animistic theory of illness. For Francke, God inflicted disease as punishment for the unconverted or as a temptation for the converted, so that a healing of the soul was needed if the medical cure was truly to succeed.[87] To further this end, Francke formulated a precise conception of the duties of both doctor and patient. In his most important work on medicine, the "Projekt von der Verpflegung der Krancken," Francke stipulated that the patient's most important duty was to recognize sinfulness as the cause of his or her sickness and pray for recovery. The doctor was obliged to keep careful records on each patient, use the best available treatment, and realize that his effectiveness was derived from Christ.[88] Preferably, the doctor would be assisted by a medically oriented theologian, though even better care would result if, in addition to the presence of a theologian, the doctor himself had some theological training.[89]

Over several decades Juncker developed Francke's directives into an elaborate system of regulations. These procedures, scrupulously followed by his co-workers, enabled the clinic to handle efficiently thousands of patients each year. Juncker's rules also embodied an ongoing effort to "improve" the spiritual lives of the patients. To achieve this aim, Juncker not surprisingly adopted the basic control mechanisms of the Halle school system. Just as Francke sought to monitor the behavior of everyone under his pedagogical supervision,

[86] Rosemarie Ahrbeck, "Franckes Idee der Humanitas: Wirklichkeit und Vision," in Ahrbeck and Thaler, eds., *August Hermann Francke, 1663–1727*, 11. See also Piechocki, "Die Krankenpflege und das Klinikum," 58.

[87] Zsindely, *Krankheit und Heilung*, 57–58, 61–70.

[88] *Ibid.*, 74–78, 112–15. See also Piechocki, "Die Krankenpflege und das Klinikum," 56.

[89] Kaiser, Krosch, and Piechocki, "Collegium clinicum Halense," 56.

so Juncker's ideal was to keep the entire building "under constant watch." Juncker's staff, teams of theology and medical students, carried out the task of exhorting the patients and enforcing the institutional norms. The clinic director, in turn, "closely watched" these students, just as the inspector of the *Anstalten* schools constantly observed the labors of his student teachers.[90]

Francke and his colleagues sought to reform the world through pedagogical institutions, including the medical clinic, which were designed to produce conformity to the ethical precepts of Francke's theology. The discrepancy between these precepts and the more worldly norms of German society at that time necessitated, in Francke's mind, the closed controlled environment within which Pietist education took place.[91] In this sense, the Halle *Anstalten* and the university's theological and medical programs bear a family resemblance to what Erving Goffman called "total institutions." Goffman put this label on such facilities as mental hospitals, prisons, and work camps because they subject each inmate's every waking moment to tight regulation enforced by a single supervisory authority.[92] Goffman also recognized that the rationale for total institutions provides a "language of explanation" (Lifton's "sacred science") that can be brought to bear on "every crevice of action in the institution."[93] In this way, the Halle *Anstalten* embodied Francke's strenuously pursued attempt to compel at least the limited world under his control to "verify experientially" the truth of his Lüneburg conversion.

As was not the case with most of the total institutions treated by Goffman, however, one of the official aims of the Halle *Anstalten* was expansion. In the first quarter of the eighteenth century, an extraordinary growth did indeed occur. The number of orphans cared for rose from 9 at the end of 1695 to 133 in early 1722. At the time of Francke's death in 1727, enrollment in the German schools was 1725, in the Latin school 400, and in the *Paedagogium* 82, a total of over twenty-two hundred pupils supervised by a teaching staff of 167.[94] After its founding in 1692, the University of Halle quickly became the largest university in Germany, with an average student

[90] *Ibid.*, 50.

[91] For reflections on the acuteness of this discrepancy and its consequences, see Lehmann, "Pietismus und soziale Reform in Brandenburg–Preussen," 107–08.

[92] Goffman, *Asylums*, 6.

[93] *Ibid.*, 83.

[94] Welsch, "Die Franckeschen Stiftungen," 12; Oschlies, *Die Arbeits- und Berufspädagogik*, 41.

body of fifteen hundred during the 1710s and 1720s, with perhaps as many as one thousand of these studying under the theology faculty.[95] Eduard Winter estimates that the theology program produced an average of one hundred and twenty graduates a year.[96] We have already noted the somewhat belated, but equally spectacular growth in the university's medical program and in the numbers serviced by the orphanage clinic.

Part of the prosperity of Francke's enterprise must certainly be attributed to the spontaneous appeal of Halle Pietism, particularly in the first twenty years or so after Francke's arrival in Halle. In a Germany with such severe social problems and elites so preoccupied with status-seeking at princely courts, Francke's theology and pedagogical institutions attracted many intelligent, forceful individuals to his side. The Halle *Anstalten* could never have succeeded as they did without the dedication of such an able group of collaborators. Francke's movement also generated a certain amount of genuine enthusiasm at the university. Zealous student converts not only contributed to the *Anstalten* as student teachers and medical interns but also spread Francke's message wherever they went after graduating from the university. Their publicizing efforts, in turn, encouraged still more religiously oriented people to come to Halle and participate in the awakening at its source.

It would be unrealistic to ignore, however, the other sorts of considerations that played a part in Francke's ability to attract new recruits. Many students of less than wealthy backgrounds enrolled in the Halle theology program because of the meals provided at the "free table" and the concomitant vocational training they received through the *Seminarium Praeceptorum*.[97] The clinical experience offered by the medical school likewise brought into the world of Halle Pietism many students who would ordinarily have remained aloof from it. Many academically proficient boys in the orphanage received scholarships to attend the Latin school and even, in some cases, the university. The orphanage bore the costs of providing these opportunities, as well as the expenses incurred from dis-

95 Wilhelm Schrader, *Geschichte der Friedrichs Universität zu Halle*, vol. 1 (Berlin, 1894), 249–50.

96 Eduard Winter, *Halle als Ausgangspunkt der deutschen Russlandkunde im 18. Jahrhundert* (Berlin, 1953), 79.

97 For a wide-ranging discussion of the relationship between Halle Pietism and vocational opportunity in eighteenth-century Germany, see Anthony LaVopa, *Grace, Talent and Merit: Poor Students, Clerical Careers and Professional Ideology in Eighteenth-Century Germany* (Cambridge, 1988), 137–64.

tributing free medicines, furnishing free medical care, and running the German schools. How did the Halle *Anstalten* acquire the substantial financial resources needed to fund these programs? The answer to that question will provide a fuller explanation of how material and spiritual factors interacted to produce the amazingly rapid growth of the Halle *Anstalten*.

CHAPTER 8

Halle Pietism II: growth and crisis

ECONOMIC GROWTH AND WORLDWIDE MISSION

The nature of the Halle *Anstalten*'s educational program was not without implications for the character of the orphanage complex as an economic unit. The tightly controlled institutional setting not only restricted social communication with the outside world but also tended to limit economic contact. In addition to the attempted supervision of every moment of the children's time, the self-imposed isolation of the orphanage necessitated a planned, largely self-sufficient economy. As Goffman puts it, "to say that inmates of total institutions have their full day scheduled for them is to say that their essential needs will have to be planned for."[1] In order to minimize both uncertainty in the planning process and possible spiritual contamination, Francke and his associates preferred, in Francke's words, "to carry out all work processes with our own resources to the greatest possible extent."[2]

Francke's economic objectives were not limited, however, to bolstering internal control through planned self-sufficiency. The "world reform" proclaimed in the "Grosse Aufsatz" required a constantly increasing income for the *Anstalten*. Francke's attitude toward material wealth was analogous to his views on knowledge and physical health. Neither wealth nor poverty in itself conferred any spiritual advantage; how a person exploited his or her material condition made all the difference. Breaking with the medieval tradition of exalting the spiritual blessings of poverty, Francke tended to look favorably on capital accumulation, since financial

[1] Goffman, *Asylums*, 10.
[2] Quoted in Böhme, "Heinrich Julius Elers," 153. See also Goffman, *Asylums*, 40.

strength enabled the "children of God" to accomplish more for the good of their neighbors.[3]

Francke realized, of course, that the merchant's calling placed extraordinary demands on a person's ascetic self-control, especially on resistance to the temptation of valuing money for its own sake.[4] But Francke believed that God approved of commercial activity so long as it served pious purposes. The Pietists regarded the existence of opportunities to make money for the Halle *Anstalten* as evidence of God's support for their cause. Indeed it would have been morally wrong, in their eyes, not to employ every possible means to take advantage of divinely offered chances for material gain. And not a moment was to be wasted in pursuing such aims.[5]

Francke's desire to combine entrepreneurial drive with a self-contained, controlled economy posed obvious difficulties. That this tension was resolved in a highly creative way can be explained in part by some important advantages enjoyed by the orphanage complex. Most obviously, the institution's reputation for charitable deeds helped to procure for it the strong external support crucial to its initial phase of development. Privileges granted by the Brandenburg-Prussian state in 1698, 1702, and 1703 gave the *Anstalten* a strong legal basis.[6] Highly significant, too, were gifts and bequests from patrons of the orphanage. The largest donations were received as a result of capital-raising drives during periods of peak building activity, notably 1698–1701 and 1710–15. At these times the rate of giving sometimes exceeded ten thousand Taler a year, but even unexceptional years yielded a harvest of cash gifts ranging from two to eight thousand Taler.[7] During the first two decades of the Halle *Anstalten*, these contributions provided starting-up capital for business operations and facilitated the rapid growth of the school network and other services provided by the orphanage complex. It is difficult to overstate the role played by donations in these early years. As late as 1713, gifts constituted 55 percent of the total annual

[3] Bondi, "Der Beitrag des halleschen Pietismus," 28, 33. For a comprehensive treatment of the essentially identical viewpoint of the Puritans on this matter, see Todd, *Christian Humanism and the Puritan Social Order*, 152–56.

[4] For the difficulties involved, see Böhme's account of the anxieties that Elers endured as a consequence of his business activities. These problems occasionally took on such seriousness that Francke would have to admonish Elers to carry on for the sake of the movement. Böhme, "Heinrich Julius Elers," 178.

[5] *Ibid.*, 177, 186; Bondi, "Der Beitrag des halleschen Pietismus," 29.

[6] See above, pp. 131–32, 135.

[7] Welsch, "Die Franckeschen Stiftungen," 41–42, 46.

income of the orphanage. Only after that date did this percentage fall (to a low of 7 percent in 1726) as yields from giving declined slowly in absolute terms, while income from other sources rose dramatically.[8]

In the long term, the economic success of the orphanage stemmed from the Pietists' ability to use the inflow of capital from gifts to establish profitable businesses. One precondition for this success was the very low level of labor costs resulting from the effect of Pietist values on the institution. In the Halle *Anstalten*, work was performed, not for personal gain but for ideological or pedagogical reasons.[9] The orphans – specifically, those orphans not selected for scholarships to the Latin School and consequently required to attend school only four hours a day – provided unpaid labor. Nearly all the teaching and clinical staff members received just the two free meals a day as compensation. Even Francke's right-hand men were expected to subsist on very little: Neubauer's allowance for personal needs was two Taler a week; Elers lived on less than forty Taler a year.[10] In the Pietist view, higher wages would be superfluous or even burdensome because the lives of "true Christians" should consist only of prayer and work with no time permitted for sinful, costly diversions.[11] This principle of economizing on consumption applied to all aspects of operating the *Anstalten*. The staff exercised strict control over the quantity of paper consumed by each pupil, made sure that old shirts were cut up into handkerchiefs, and even put the deceased orphanage dog to use on the dissection table of an anatomy class.[12]

The dedication to Pietist values on the part of Francke's closest collaborators made possible an administrative apparatus that was not only cheap but also hard-working, efficient, and easy to coordinate. These attributes were essential to the orphanage's success,

[8] *Ibid.*, 123.

[9] In total institutions, a similarly non-market motivation for work is the rule. See Goffman, *Asylums*, 90.

[10] The only serious conflict among members of Francke's staff occurred over this question of compensation due to staff members. Because of the high profits accruing to the orphanage as a result of the pharmaceutical products he created, C. F. Richter demanded and received salaries far above those of Elers and Neubauer. These two, in turn, felt that Richter's high salary violated the Pietist code of self-sacrifice for the benefit of others. Böhme, "Heinrich Julius Elers," 137–40.

[11] Leube, *Orthodoxie und Pietismus*, 149; Bondi, "Der Beitrag des halleschen Pietismus," 36.

[12] Ahrbeck-Wothge, "Zu Fragen der Arbeitserziehung und der Allgemeinbildung bei A. H. Francke," 119.

since Francke's commitments to his pastorate and his university teaching precluded his being more than a part-time administrator of the business enterprises. Although Francke formulated overall policy and retained ultimate responsibility for its implementation, he had to rely on his trusted inner circle for the detailed planning and execution.[13] A department head, in matters affecting only his operation, frequently made decisions on his own initiative, after at most an informal consultation with Francke. Questions of broader significance were usually handled by an administrative conference of inspectors and department heads. This group likewise possessed a great deal of autonomy; after 1705 Francke did not even attend its meetings. Only when the conference did not reach a consensus or when a matter was of overriding importance did it refer the issue to Francke. In such cases, the conference secretary formulated in the minutes the various positions taken in the meeting, and Francke then made a notation in the margin to indicate his decision.[14]

Despite the availability of capital, low operating costs, and a committed staff, Francke still faced the problem of devising a strategy that would capitalize on these assets without threatening the religious and pedagogical character of the *Anstalten*. In the years during and immediately following the building of the orphanage, Francke and his closest collaborators attempted to expand the economic base of the Halle *Anstalten* through a series of manufacturing ventures. The plans emanating from Francke's circle during this period (*c.* 1698–*c.* 1706) demonstrated the great ambition typical of Halle Pietism. A memorandum written in 1698 by Neubauer detailed a scheme for exploiting a nearby iron mine donated by Baron von Canstein. Neubauer envisioned the acquisition of a fleet of ships in order to transport iron, plus iron products manufactured by the orphans, down the Saale and Elbe rivers to the great entrepot of Hamburg. The ships would carry return cargoes of colonial products and North Sea herring for resale at the Leipzig market.[15]

Although Francke went so far as to purchase a ship in 1699, Neubauer's plan failed because of opposition from a mining and

13 Welsch, "Die Franckeschen Stiftungen," 32; Böhme, "Heinrich Julius Elers," 90.

14 Welsch, "Die Franckeschen Stiftungen," 33. Welsch adds the observation that Frederick William I likewise noted his decisions in the margins of minutes from committees of his top officials.

15 *Ibid.*, 106–08. It is interesting to note the similarities between this scheme and the Great Elector's attempts to induce the merchants in his Baltic ports to ship locally produced grain directly to Amsterdam. See above, p. 57, n. 73.

shipping monopoly based in Magdeburg. Following this setback, the Pietists tried to set up first a glassworks and then a stocking-making enterprise. All these projects rested on the potential profits resulting from the combination of cheap labor supplied by the orphans with the use of up-to-date industrial technology. In his proposal for a metal-working plant, Neubauer made the still unusual recommendation that the iron be smelted with coal. The technological consultant for the glassworks project was none other than Walter von Tschirnhaus, the Saxon inventor who was the first European to replicate the Chinese method of manufacturing porcelain.[16] A final feature common to all these industrial schemes was the anticipation of savings arising from the coordination of manufacture, transport, and marketing by one organization. Neubauer, for example, noted that, during the months when ice blocked river transport, the labor of the orphans involved in the shipping operation could be redirected to fill other needs of the organization.

Despite this vision and astuteness, the basic strategy behind the manufacturing ventures possessed serious flaws. Part of the problem lay in the opposition of entrenched interest groups. More fundamental, however, was the inability of the orphanage's labor force to produce goods of sufficient quality to compete in the unprotected, international market place. The experience of the stocking works, the only one of these projects that came close to succeeding, illustrates the difficulties involved. At first, the children had serious problems mastering the complicated hand process of stocking fabrication. Typically, only those children just about old enough to leave the institution could adequately perform the necessary tasks.[17] In its early stages, then, the operation never failed to lose money. Only after expensive machinery was installed and extremely harsh work rules instituted did it seem possible to make a profit. But the longer hours and high production quotas required by the new rules led to rebelliousness among the children. The unrest became especially acute in August and December 1705.[18] Not only did the orphans' nannies support the children's protest, but Francke also had to

[16] Böhme, "Heinrich Julius Elers," 72.

[17] Oschlies, *Die Arbeits- und Berufspädagogik*, 67. This same inability to overcome the opposition of traditional corporate groups, together with the severe shortage of skilled labor, also lay behind the failure of most of the manufacturing schemes initiated by the Great Elector. See above, pp. 55–57.

[18] Welsch, "Die Franckeschen Stiftungen," 98–99.

contend with orthodox attacks denouncing the Pietists' exploitation of the children.

In 1706, with the decision to cease producing stockings for sale on the Leipzig market, Francke recognized that mass-production manufacturing for the open market was not the solution he was seeking. Although economic, pedagogical, and political factors contributed to this realization, the gradual emergence of a different method of generating income made the decision to change course an easier one. This alternative strategy evolved from the ongoing effort to make the Halle *Anstalten* as self-sufficient as possible. From the very beginning Francke had arranged the orphanage operation in such a way that in-house labor supplied many of the institution's basic necessities. Francke viewed the orphanage and school complex as a family, so that he felt justified in assigning chores to all his "children." Girls helped in the kitchen and did the laundry; poorer boys hauled water from the river, while even pupils in the *Paedagogium* sawed wood in wintertime.[19]

In addition, the orphans worked in conjunction with resident artisans to produce everyday articles of consumption. Under a typical arrangement, the *Anstalten* contracted the full-time services of a tailor, who cut all the clothes for the orphans in return for a modest annual salary of 16T, plus free room, board, and laundry. The linen for these clothes, in turn, was provided by a part-time weaver, whose thread was spun from flax by girls in the orphanage. Similarly, a bakery and a brewery on the premises filled the demands of the numerous "tables" in the orphanage refectory.[20] Run by the orphans under artisanal supervision, these operations relied on the farms owned by the Halle *Anstalten* for at least part of their raw materials.[21] This tendency toward vertical integration not only accorded with Francke's pedagogical aims but also kept down expenses and allowed the school system to take on more pupils.

The trade in books and medicines arose from the same set of motivations. The orphanage press developed from the need to publish Francke's sermons and print Bibles for use in the *Anstalten* schools.[22] The beginnings of the apothecary date from 1698–99, when an epidemic necessitated large expenditures for medicines and

19 Oschlies, *Die Arbeits- und Berufspädagogik*, 59–60.
20 Welsch, "Die Franckeschen Stiftungen," 101–04.
21 *Ibid.*, 83–85.
22 Böhme, "Heinrich Julius Elers," 26.

demonstrated the need for a cheap source of medical supplies.[23] The method of procuring labor for these enterprises was in keeping with the autarchic character of their origins. Elers managed the press with the help of apprentices recruited from boys about to leave the orphanage.[24] In the apothecary, orphan girls prepared the medicines from plants, many of which were collected by the botany class on field trips to an herb garden belonging to the orphanage. The medicines thus manufactured were supplied cheaply to the orphanage or distributed gratis to the poor during the *Sprechstunden.*[25]

Unlike other such operations designed to promote self-sufficiency, the publishing house and apothecary soon found markets for their products outside the Halle *Anstalten.* In 1699 the Saxon government granted permission for orphanage press books to be sold at the Leipzig market. The very next year sales in Leipzig brought in 4,582 Taler. Further possibilities for growth resulted from the opening of a retail outlet in Berlin in 1702 and the securing of access to the Frankfurt book fair, Germany's largest, in the same year.[26]

Although Francke had always intended the devotional works printed by his "poor people's press" (*Armenverlag*) to be sold outside Halle, the development of the trade in medicines was quite fortuitous. At first Francke anticipated little more than the modest profits from selling surplus stocks from the apothecary to local physicians. The prospect for far greater gains soon presented itself, however. Having received an alchemical recipe from an anonymous source, C. F. Richter quickly succeeded in producing the substance, a gold tincture, in his laboratory at the apothecary. Facilities for manufacturing this cure-all medication, known as the *essentia dulcis,* were completed by 1701. Almost immediately the *essentia dulcis* became a profit-making item because of its quickly acquired reputation for miraculous cures and because of the extremely low costs associated with its production.[27]

By 1704–06, just at the time when difficulties with the glassworks

23 Welsch, "Die Franckeschen Stiftungen," 49.

24 Böhme, "Heinrich Julius Elers," 41–43.

25 Welsch, "Die Franckeschen Stiftungen," 52, 54.

26 Böhme, "Heinrich Julius Elers," 37, 46, 50–52, 62.

27 Welsch, "Die Franckeschen Stiftungen," 65–66, 73. Although the Halle Pietists were strongly opposed to the "superstitions" associated with the traditional folk culture, the use in this way of the *essentia dulcis* shows how willing they were to invent or encourage myths about their own operations. The same ambiguity is also noted by Briggs with respect to the Catholic reformers in France. See his *Communities of Belief,* 378.

and stocking-making operation reached their high point, the growth potential of the publishing and pharmaceutical enterprises had become apparent to Francke. Already in the "Grosse Aufsatz" (1704), he had spoken optimistically about the prospects for trade in books and medicines.[28] From 1706 on he instructed his staff to concentrate their entrepreneurial activity in this area. The consequences of this change in policy were momentous. Exploiting the cheapness of orphan labor ceased to be the basis for plans to generate revenue for the Halle *Anstalten*. Neither of the two manufacturing processes placed heavy demands on the orphanage's supply of labor, and each concern was able to expand production considerably with only minor increases in the amount of orphan labor.[29] The economic success of the *Anstalten* now depended, rather, on the Pietists' ability to create sizeable markets for their books and medicines. Since these products did not possess any significant price advantage relative to the competition, the challenge facing Francke and his co-workers was to differentiate them in some way from comparable goods and fashion a group of distributors and retailers to market them.

The favorable solution to these problems was inherent in the products themselves and in the nature of Francke's movement. Graduates of the Pietists' schools, particularly the theology students, were expected to devote themselves to the good of their neighbors. The continual obligation of "true Christians" was to spread the Word of God among the "unconverted." Elers, for example, habitually used his business trips to book fairs and markets as occasions for missionary activity.[30] In addition to winning converts, Elers in the course of his travels also established contact with Halle alumni or with other Pietist sympathizers. Networks of Halle supporters crystallized in most North German cities and in the countryside, where a large circle of pious nobles saw in Halle a kind of "alternative court" to the princely establishments whose immorality they found so distasteful.[31] Such friends of the *Anstalten* were natural customers and salesmen for products of the orphanage. Selling an edition of Francke's sermons or a bottle of the *essentia dulcis* also gave them the

28 Francke "Der grosse Aufsatz," 147–48.

29 Expanding the output of medicines required only a modest increase in the size of the apothecary's small labor force, and it was easy enough to take on more apprentices to accommodate the increased demand for books.

30 Böhme, "Heinrich Julius Elers," 104, 107n.

31 *Ibid.*, 108–09.

satisfaction of collecting as much as a ten percent commission.[32] Even more to the point: in so far as these people were seeking to induce change in the spiritual lives of their neighbors, precisely the items they needed most to assist their proselytizing efforts were the books and medicines produced for that purpose by the Halle *Anstalten*.

The missionary activity associated with Halle Pietism, then, served both to create demand for orphanage products and to function as a mechanism for marketing them. As is well known, Francke thought in terms of a missionary effort to reform the entire world. What is generally less well appreciated is that such a conception was relatively new to the Protestant churches, which for over one hundred years after the Reformation had opposed sending out missionaries. Only in the last quarter of the seventeenth century did a small number of Protestant leaders begin to lay the groundwork for what became by the late nineteenth century an enormous, worldwide missionary campaign. Since in the years around 1700 advocates of overseas missions were still a minority within each Protestant church, these groups tended to reach across confessional divisions and cooperate with one another. Already one of the strongest of these missionary groupings, Halle Pietism was able to broaden the scope of its proselytizing and economic activity by joining forces with like-minded members of other Protestant churches.

Even though the core area of Francke's movement remained the Lutheran areas of northern and central Germany, through its international connections it acquired followers and sympathizers in other countries as well. Foremost among its contacts was Heinrich Wilhelm Ludolf, private secretary to Prince George of Denmark, the consort of Queen Anne of England.[33] Ludolf, whose uncle had served with Francke's father under Duke Ernest the Pious of Gotha, brought the Halle Pietist movement to the attention of the mission-oriented Society for Promoting Christian Knowledge (SPCK), founded in London in 1699.[34] As one of the aims of this Anglican group was to promote the establishment of "charity schools," or

32 Welsch, "Die Franckeschen Stiftungen," 73.

33 For an account of this important but unjustly obscure figure, see Winter, *Halle als Ausgangspunkt*, 32f.

34 Geoffrey F. Nuttall, "Continental Pietism and the Evangelical Movement in Britain," in van den Berg and van Booren, eds., *Pietismus und Reveil*, 215. See also Oschlies, *Die Arbeits- und Berufspädagogik*, 44–45.

schools for poorer children, the startling success of Francke's orphanage and school system aroused their curiosity.

Francke himself soon became a corresponding member of the SPCK, but the most important intermediary between Halle and the English churches was Anton Wilhelm Boehm, a former theology student at Halle, who arrived in London in 1701 and became Lutheran chaplain at the Court of St. James in 1705. Quickly becoming a leading member of the SPCK, Boehm saw his role as strengthening the charity-school movement by making available to it the story of the Halle *Anstalten*.[35] Consequently, Boehm translated into English Francke's "Segensvolle Fusstapfen" (1705) and Arndt's *True Christianity* (1709).[36]

Though both books went through several editions, it was the "Segensvolle Fusstapfen," rechristened in English as the "Pietatis Hallensis," which created the deepest impression. "The book which the Evangelical leaders all read" inspired the life work of Griffith Jones, who at his death in 1761 had founded some 3,495 charity schools in Wales, "in which children were taught to read the Bible in Welsh."[37] In general, the appeal of the "Pietatis Hallensis" in the English-speaking world lay in the description of how Francke's absolute trust in God's Providence enabled the orphanage to overcome all adversity. As George Whitefield expressed it, "Professor Franck met with unspeakably more contempt and calumny [than I] whilst he was building the Orphan-House in Germany. He began very low, and left behind him an Orphan-House which contains now, if I mistake not, 2 or 3000 Students, notwithstanding the erecting of it was attended with as many Improbabilities as this in Georgia."[38]

Besides aiding the educational labors of Anglo-American evangelicals, the connection between Halle Pietism and the Ludolf–Boehm circle in London also promoted missionary work among non-Christians overseas. Probably through the instigation of Ludolf, the Danish Lutheran church requested its counterpart in Berlin to

35 Erich Beyreuther, *A. H. Francke und die Anfänge der ökumenischen Bewegung* (Hamburg, 1957), 133.

36 Böhme, "Heinrich Julius Elers," 115. See also Ernst Benz, "Ecumenical Relations between Boston Puritanism and German Pietism: Cotton Mather and August Hermann Francke," *Harvard Theological Review*, 54 (1961): 161n. Boehm also translated Francke's *Nicodemus*, a work later abridged and published by John Wesley. Nuttall, "Continental Pietism and the Evangelical Movement," 221.

37 Nuttall, "Continental Pietism and the Evangelical Movement," 214, 221.

38 Quoted in Kuno Francke, *Cotton Mather and August Hermann Francke* (Boston, 1896), 66.

send them two candidates for a mission in the Danish colony in South India. The church in Berlin chose two Halle theology students, Bartholomäus Ziegenbalg and Heinrich Plütschau, who arrived in Tranquebar, India, in 1706. Ziegenbalg's reports back to Halle, first published by the orphanage press, were translated into English by Boehm and published by the SPCK.[39]

Boehm also served as a go-between in Francke's correspondence with Cotton Mather, who was conducting a missionary campaign of his own among the Indians in New England. In addition to supplying Mather with detailed information about Ziegenbalg's mission, Francke's letters reinforced Mather's understanding of missions "as a global task involving all Protestant churches."[40] From the materials he received about Halle Pietism, Mather perceived an identity between Francke's movement and his own. In his letters to Francke he even called New England Puritans "American pietists."[41] According to Mather, the two groups' common ground consisted of a rejection of theological dogmatism in favor of an ethically oriented "true Christianity" (Mather had read Boehm's translation of Arndt's work). Mather believed that, on subscribing to the few fundamental principles containing the "true essence" of the Christian faith, the different Christian churches could not only work together in proselytizing among the "heathen" but also begin the process of uniting themselves into a single communion in Christ.[42]

Such ecumenical hopes inspired the most important mission undertaken by Halle Pietism, that in Russia and Eastern Europe. Francke was quite sanguine about the unlimited potential for an awakening within what he regarded as the "so long moribund" Orthodox church. At first Francke believed it would be possible to penetrate that church by training Greek students at Halle, expecting these reborn few to effect a transformation of the orthodox church from within.[43] Although five Greeks did study and teach at the *Collegium Orientale Theologium* between 1703 and 1705, Francke soon realized that the mission in Russia and Southeast Europe required a more politically oriented strategy. Here again Ludolf

[39] Böhme, "Heinrich Julius Elers," 126; Oschlies, *Die Arbeits- und Berufspädagogik*, 46.
[40] Benz, "Ecumenical Relations," 162, 178–79.
[41] *Ibid.*, 171.
[42] *Ibid.*, 172–74.
[43] Francke, "Der grosse Aufsatz," 137.

provided the initial connection. An even more gifted student of languages than Francke himself, Ludolf published the first vernacular Russian grammar. Thanks to his language proficiency and diplomatic finesse, Ludolf in the early 1690s turned an official English trade mission in Russia into a personal triumph. During that visit Ludolf fashioned a network of contacts at the very top of the Russian ruling elite, and he was later able to convince these people of the advantages to be gained from working closely with the Halle Pietists.[44]

The Russian government's support for Pietism was assured by the strong endorsement of Peter the Great himself, who urged his bureaucrats and officers to employ Pietists as foreign-language tutors and who in 1719 sent a top aide to conduct a personal inspection of the Halle *Anstalten*.[45] With this kind of official patronage, missionaries from Halle found a ready response among the German communities in Moscow and Petersburg, especially among the politically powerful Baltic German nobility. By gaining influence among the Germans in the Tsar's service and assisting the native Russian elite in building a more westernized Russia, Francke expected that these high government officials would eventually call on him to help institute a Pietist-style reform in the Russian Orthodox church.[46]

In the Habsburg lands and Poland, by contrast, Halle Pietism had to contend with the active hostility of the Roman Catholic authorities. In these areas Francke knew that his only possible support in the short term would come from the Protestant minorities scattered throughout the region. Despite the difficulties posed by the Catholic governments, the Pietist mission did remarkably well in rallying Protestant groups whose faith had survived over a century of persecution. The most conspicuous Pietist success was in the Upper Silesian city of Teschen. After an agreement in 1709 between Sweden and the Habsburg empire compelled the latter to permit a Lutheran church in that city, Francke acted quickly to gain the allegiance of Teschen's forty thousand Protestants. He sent two of his best students, Wilhelm Schneider and Christian Voigt, to serve as pastors to this Lutheran community. The Habsburg authorities, alert to the implications of a strong Halle contingent in Teschen,

44 Winter, *Halle als Ausgangspunkt*, 72–73.

45 *Ibid.*, 66.

46 Hinrichs, *Preussentum und Pietismus*, 43.

quickly forced the departures of both Pietists, along with that of another Halle-trained man, Anhard Adelung.[47]

Francke's influence in Teschen remained strong, nevertheless. A successful fund-raising drive among Silesian nobles sympathetic to Halle Pietism contributed substantially to the building of a church, a rectory, and a school. In the 1720s, under the leadership of Johann Adam Steinmetz, a Pietist not quite so closely identified with Halle as Schneider or Voigt, Pietism in Teschen reached its high point. From its base in this city, Halle Pietism strengthened its position in the neighboring areas of Silesia, Galicia, Moravia, and Slovakia.[48] Adelung, after his departure from Teschen, journeyed to Hungary, seeking to combine the appeals of Pietism and Magyar resentment against the Habsburgs. A secret agent for Brandenburg-Prussia, Adelung pursued his anti-Habsburg mission while posing as a wine trader.[49] Voigt, too, left Teschen for a wandering, adventuresome life, founding a *Paedagogium* in Hermannstadt (now Cluj, Rumania), setting up a substantial book-selling business in Vienna, and finally settling down as a pastor in Slovakia.[50]

The careers of Adelung and Voigt illustrate the close relationship between the expansion of missionary activity and the economic growth of the Halle *Anstalten*. Except in areas where the political authorities were hostile to Francke's movement, Pietist teachers, pastors, and doctors could readily find jobs because of the advanced training and on-the-job experience they had received at Halle. As they exposed more people to the Pietist message through their work, they increased demand for the devotional literature and medicines produced by the orphanage's enterprises. Winning over new followers also produced additional patrons, who either collected money for the orphanage, as did Cotton Mather, or sent their sons to the Halle *Paedagogium*, as did rich English merchants and confidants of Tsar Peter.[51]

Both old and new converts, moreover, were willing to act as distributers and retailers for Halle products. As networks of such

[47] Herbert Patzelt, *Der Pietismus im Teschener Schlesien, 1709–1730* (Göttingen, 1969), 13, 24, 88–89.

[48] *Ibid.*, 166.

[49] Böhme, "Heinrich Julius Elers," 121–22; Winter, *Halle als Ausgangspunkt*, 61; Patzelt, *Der Pietismus im Teschener Schlesien*, 53–54.

[50] Böhme, "Heinrich Julius Elers," 122–23; Patzelt, *Der Pietismus im Teschener Schlesien*, 48–50.

[51] Kuno Francke, *Cotton Mather and August Hermann Francke*, 58; Böhme, "Heinrich Julius Elers," 115; Winter, *Halle als Ausgangspunkt*, 61.

traders proliferated, new possibilities for profit making presented themselves to Francke and his inner circle. In order to supply the apothecary's needs for raw materials, for example, a wholesale trading operation was begun in 1706. Within a few years, supplying the apothecary became less important than the profits made from simply trading in items of an often quite worldly character. Agents for the orphanage procured and sold such goods as sugar, tea, coffee beans, wine (from Hungary), as well as honey, talc, caviar, furs, and beeswax (from Russia).[52] These groups of merchants above all contributed to the rapid growth in sales of products made in the orphanage. By 1727 revenues of the orphanage press reached 13,000 Taler, an enormous sum for a German publishing house at the time.[53] Selling the *essentia dulcis* was an even more lucrative undertaking. After 1714 *profit* exceeded expenditures every year, and from 1719 on that profit was never less than 12,000T.[54]

As a result of the success of these enterprises, the orphanage's annual income more than doubled between 1710 and 1727 – from 14,516T to 30,023T.[55] Characteristically, Francke invested a substantial portion of these funds in improvements designed to make the *Anstalten* still more self-sufficient. Between 1715 and 1718 he hired mining engineers to build a network of underground tunnels and wooden pipes over five thousand meters long in order to secure for the orphanage its own supply of water.[56] Similarly, Francke and Elers had always wanted to free the printing operation from dependence for its paper on outside sources. In 1725 they purchased a paper mill for 6,500T and spent another 1,500T on refurbishing it with new machinery ordered from Holland.[57] The largest of all these investments in self-sufficiency consisted of a series of acquisitions of agricultural property. Between 1714 and 1727 purchases of land amounted to roughly 40,000T, about 25,000T of which was expended in 1725 and 1726 alone. The ability of the *Anstalten* to live off their own food supply correspondingly increased. During the period from 1714 to 1719 the Pietist institutions produced between 15 percent and 25 percent of what they

52 Welsch, "Die Franckeschen Stiftungen," 55–61.
53 Böhme, "Heinrich Julius Elers," 156.
54 Welsch, "Die Franckeschen Stiftungen," 71.
55 *Ibid.*, 123.
56 Piechocki, "A. H. Franckes sozial- und schulhygienische An- und Einsichten," 47–48.
57 Böhme, "Heinrich Julius Elers," 153.

consumed; this figure rose to 40 percent in 1723, 60 percent in 1726, and 66 percent in 1727.[58]

If missionary activity made possible such economic gains, the prosperity of the orphanage contributed, in turn, to a further expansion of the Pietists' pedagogical and missionary efforts. In the early years of the Halle *Anstalten*, the schools had to rent both classroom space and living quarters for boarders from residents of Glaucha. This practice raised costs, made supervision of boarding pupils more difficult, and placed limits on the number of children that could be educated.[59] In 1710 Francke judged the trade in books and medicines to be promising enough to enable him to embark on a large-scale building campaign designed to remedy his school system's lack of facilities. Between 1710 and 1716, five major buildings – housing classrooms, dormitory space, dining halls, and an auditorium – were constructed at a cost of roughly thirty-eight thousand Taler.[60] Together with the orphanage building, these structures henceforth comprised the core of the Halle *Anstalten*'s physical plant. As substantial profits from the economic enterprises began to accumulate in the late 1710s and 1720s, Francke authorized two more construction projects. In order to provide space for Juncker's expanding medical clinic, a two-story stone hospital was erected during 1721–22 for 2,447T.[61] Similarly, the growth of the book collection and the *Naturalienkabinett* necessitated the building of an attractive stone library, completed in 1728 at the cost of 4,751T.[62]

In addition to investing in training facilities, Francke and his collaborators marshalled profits as well as donated funds in order to provide their cadres with materials necessary for success in the expanding missionary effort.[63] For spreading the Word of God

58 Welsch, "Die Franckeschen Stiftungen," 87, 135.

59 *Ibid.*, 80.

60 Kaiser, Krosch, and Piechocki, "Collegium clinicum Halense," 18; Welsch, "Die Franckeschen Stiftungen," 127.

61 Piechocki, "Die Krankenpflege und das Klinikum," 58.

62 Welsch, "Die Franckeschen Stiftungen," 28; Storz, "Hauptbibliothek, Archiv und Naturalienkabinett," 97.

63 Though the discussion henceforth will focus on pastoral mission work, missionary doctors benefited from similar efforts to equip trainees going out into the field. Juncker supplied the young doctors trained at his clinic with most necessary instruments and with field apothecaries. Piechocki, "Die Krankenpflege und das Klinikum," 57. For a detailed account of this medical mission, see Wolfram Kaiser and Karl-Heinz Krosch, "Zur Geschichte der Medizinischen Fakultät der Universität Halle im 18. Jahrhundert," *Wissenschaftliche Zeitschrift der Martin-Luther-Universität Halle-Wittenberg: Math.-naturwiss. Reihe*, 13 (1964): 141–80, 363–430, 583–616, 797–836.

among all classes of society, the Halle-trained missionary's most vital need was a plentiful supply of inexpensive Bibles. Although the printing press of the *Anstalten* produced its first edition of Luther's Bible in 1702, this edition yielded only a limited number of fairly expensive copies.[64] The fundamental difficulty lay in the high costs associated with traditional printing operations, by which the type set was disassembled after each printing and the individual pieces of type were recombined for the next publishing project. Francke applied all his managerial talents to overcoming this obstacle to mass production of Bibles. Having learned of an edition of the English Bible printed in Holland on a standing type set, Francke by 1709 had raised the capital necessary for purchasing this equipment, largely through a donation made by Baron von Canstein. The Canstein Bible Institute (*Bibelanstalt*) was established in 1711, legally separate from the Halle *Anstalten* but integrally connected in its operations with the orphanage press.[65] During its first eight years, the Institute published eighty thousand complete Bibles and one hundred thousand copies of the New Testament. The latter sold for two groschen, the equivalent of less than a half a day's subsistence wages; a complete Bible cost a mere six groschen.[66]

Freed from having to print German Bibles, Elers's press could devote itself to publishing a greater variety of other texts. Already in 1712 there were almost two hundred titles in the press's catalogue; by 1717 this number had grown to over three hundred titles by some seventy authors.[67] Although some of these works, such as legal and medical compendia by faculty members of the University of Halle, were unrelated to the Pietist mission, the overwhelming majority served the Halle cause. These included school textbooks to satisfy the needs of Francke's curricula, collections of sermons (many of these were by Francke), collections of biblical verses, and commentaries intended to aid popular understanding of the Bible.

64 Böhme, "Heinrich Julius Elers," 102.

65 *Ibid.*, 100.

66 Oskar Söhngen, "Festrede," in Söhngen, ed., *Die bleibende Bedeutung des Pietismus: Zur 250-Jahrfeier der von Cansteinschen Bibelanstalt* (Witten and Berlin, 1960), 14. During the Institute's first one hundred years, sales totaled one million copies of the New Testament and almost two million complete Bibles – the latter figure being approximately ten times the quantity of Bibles sold in Germany in the ninety-two years following the printing of the complete Luther Bible in 1534. For a more complete listing of sales figures, see Beyreuther, *August Hermann Francke, 1663–1727: Zeuge des lebendigen Gottes*, 212; see also Aland, "Der hallesche Pietismus und die Bibel," 36.

67 Böhme, "Heinrich Julius Elers," 157.

The same pedagogical motivations led to the composition and publication of a "massive number of hymns."[68] Meant for both private and group worship, these hymns were written in order to touch the "inner being" (*Gemüt*) of the singers. For that reason, the Halle hymn writers employed up-to-date musical forms very similar to the arias in Baroque opera because the newer melodies were able to attract or inspire larger numbers of people.[69] The press also printed testimonies of individuals whose lives had been changed by a Pietist rebirth.[70] These autobiographies, professions of faith, and accounts of conversion provided "experiential verification" of the "sacred science" of Halle Pietism. The Pietists especially prized simple statements of piety by unlearned men and women, whose words represented proof that God's word was reaching the masses of the German people.[71]

In terms of publications and total copies printed, German-language works dominated the output of the orphanage press. But the seriousness with which Francke pursued his missionary goals in Eastern Europe is demonstrated by the material and human resources devoted to translating key texts into the Slavic languages. Arndt's *True Christianity* was translated into Polish, Czech, and Ukrainian.[72] As early as 1709, a New Testament in Czech appeared, followed by complete Bibles in Czech (1722) and Polish (1726). According to Winter, both constituted "philological achievements of the first order" that had a profound impact on the later development of national literatures in both languages.[73] Even in the short-term, the effect of these translations was by no means negligible as some 10,350 Czech full Bibles and 15,250 Czech New Testaments were sold.[74] Francke's early commitment to the Russian mission induced him in 1704 to make the orphanage press the first German printing plant equipped with Cyrillic type pieces. Even though

[68] Stoeffler, *German Pietism during the Eighteenth Century*, 56.

[69] Schmitt, "Die pietistische Kritik der 'Künste,'" 66–68.

[70] Helmut Obst, "Elemente atheistischer Anfechtung im pietistischen Bekehrungsprozess," *Pietismus und Neuzeit*, 2 (1975): 35.

[71] Schmitt, "Die pietistische Kritik der 'Künste,'" 34, 40, 47, 52. A specific example of this tendency was the attitude of Elers, who on his business trips organized conventicles of "quite simple people," subsequently editing and then publishing their spiritual pronouncements in the orphanage press. Böhme, "Heinrich Julius Elers," 107.

[72] Oschlies, *Die Arbeits- und Berufspädagogik*, 43.

[73] Eduard Winter, "August Hermann Francke und seine Beziehungen zu den slawischen Völkern," in *A. H. Francke: Festreden und Kolloquium*, 15, 17.

[74] Aland, "Der hallesche Pietismus und die Bibel," 54.

Francke's dream of a cheap Russian Bible was never realized, the "Elizabeth" Bible of 1751, the first Bible in Russian to go through several editions, was prepared by translators trained at the Halle press.[75]

This investment in devotional materials constituted the final component in a comprehensive strategy for expanding the Halle movement's economic base and proselytizing power. It is possible now to summarize this strategy, which worked by means of a simple feedback mechanism. The Pietists' pedagogical institutions produced a steady stream of graduates, whose testimony encouraged still more families to send their youngsters to Halle for their education. Halle alumni and other Pietist sympathizers raised large sums of money for constructing the educational facilities needed to accommodate the influx of recruits. Donated funds also permitted Francke and his assistants to start up highly profitable operations, such as the orphanage press and the apothecary, which catered to the demand for books and medicines created by the mission effort. The additional revenues derived from these sources, in turn, made possible further improvements in the services offered at the *Anstalten* and in the quantity and diversity of religious publications. By enabling missionary recruiters to expose new social and ethnic groups to Francke's message, the availability of these key texts in Slavic languages was intended to keep in motion the self-perpetuating process of what Francke had always intended to be a truly "world reform."

THE FATE OF FRANCKE'S "WORLD REFORM"

As the only well-organized, mission-oriented Protestant movement in Northern, Central, or Eastern Europe, Halle Pietism was not lacking in opportunities to expand its influence in those regions. In 1713 Francke established contact with a group of thousands of Swedish prisoners-of-war at Tobolsk in Siberia. To aid these victims of the Great Northern War, the Pietists in Halle sent missionaries, books, medical supplies, and cash, all of which contributed to the opening of a school in the camp.[76] At the other end of the Russian empire, in Estonia, another Pietist school took shape in 1717 around an orphanage in Alp, a small community near Reval. Here a Baltic

[75] Ahrbeck, "Franckes Idee der Humanitas," 13; Winter, *Halle als Ausgangspunkt*, 253.
[76] Böhme, "Heinrich Julius Elers," 123.

German landowner and a Pietist in Petersburg formulated plans for a "second Halle," and within a few years Peter the Great's inspectors reported that close to one hundred pupils were being taught such subjects as Greek, Arabic, and Hebrew in the style of the Halle *Paedagogium*.[77]

These two cases illustrate a side to the expansion of Halle Pietism that has not yet been sufficiently emphasized. Francke did not conceive of the Halle *Anstalten* and the University of Halle as the only such training centers for his movement. In his "Projekt zu einem Seminario universali" of 1701, Francke referred approvingly to new *Anstalten*, modelled on his own, that had already appeared in several cities in Brandenburg-Prussia, notably Stargard and Königsberg.[78] In order to advance the cause of "world reform," Francke and his disciples worked to replicate the Halle *Anstalten* in foreign lands as well. Besides Alp and the Tobolsk school, noteworthy examples of strong Pietist establishments included the *Paedagogium* founded by Voigt in Transylvania; a *Lyzeum* in Bratislava, made over in the Halle image by Francke's protégé Matthias Bel; and the Jesus school in Teschen, where enrollment reached 140 pupils in 1724.[79] Francke kept in close contact with these institutions through correspondence and through the graduates these secondary schools sent to the University of Halle.[80] Thus although the Halle complex remained the parent institution, its numerous offspring functioned as autonomous, regional centers of a movement held together by adherence to the theology of Halle Pietism.

The process of expansion through replication of the original *Anstalten* depended on the good will of the political authorities in the places where the Pietist orphanages and schools were being established. As late as the early to mid-1720s, the international situation remained conducive to the growth of Halle Pietism. In Sweden the return of the prisoners from Siberia after the peace treaty of 1721

77 Winter, *Halle als Ausgangspunkt*, 267–69.

78 Francke, "Projekt zu einem Seminario universali," 114.

79 Böhme, "Heinrich Julius Elers," 122; Jan Kocka, "Über den Einfluss A. H. Franckes auf Matthias Bel," in Ahrbeck and Thaler, eds., *August Hermann Francke, 1663–1727*, 96–98; Patzelt, *Der Pietismus im Teschener Schlesien*, 159.

80 In the *Matrikel* for the University of Halle, 1690–1730, ten or more students are listed from each of the following East European cities: Teschen, Pressburg (Bratislava), Hermannstadt, and Kronstadt. The same source also indicates that forty students came from Livonia and twenty-three from Transylvania (in addition to those from Hermannstadt and Kronstadt). See Juntke and Zimmermann, eds., *Matrikel der Martin-Luther-Universität Halle-Wittenberg*, 541, 585–86, 602, 638, 662, 673–74.

gave Francke's movement considerable influence and support in that country. In Central Europe, the Habsburgs continued their policy of limited toleration of Protestants, while in Eastern Europe Peter the Great was still endeavoring to attract Pietists to assist him in his policy of Westernization.

This favorable conjunction of circumstances, however, was short-lived. Divided leadership at the educational complex at Alp led to its folding by 1725, the year of Peter the Great's death.[81] In 1727 the Swedish government yielded to the pressure of the orthodox Lutheran party and banned Pietist conventicles, thereby ending Swedish Pietism as a public movement.[82] Most seriously of all, the Habsburg government began to crack down on Protestantism within its territories. In 1730 authorities in Teschen closed down the Jesus school and expelled the Pietist leaders. Persecution of Lutherans in Bohemia led directly to anti-imperial uprisings in 1732 and 1737. Many of these Czech Protestants eventually sought refuge in Prussia, as did the entire Lutheran community of Salzburg, whom the Archbishop of Salzburg had forced to leave their native city as early as 1732.[83]

Recovery from these setbacks would have been easier had it not been for a simultaneous crisis in the theology program at the University of Halle. Although the number of graduates continued at a high level well into the 1730s and the Pietist monopoly on the professoriate remained unbroken, such external signs of prosperity could not hide a diminution in religious enthusiasm among the students. Sometime around 1715 Francke himself noted a lack of response to his lectures, and all his efforts in the next twelve years failed to recreate the enthusiasm of the 1690s and 1700s.[84]

Historians have not yet analyzed this phenomenon in detail, but its basic causes are not difficult to discern. In accordance with the Promethean spirituality of Halle Pietism, the overwhelming emphasis in its pedagogical institutions was on ethical action carried out to fulfill a harsh, demanding ascetic regimen. Such a legalistic orientation, however, ultimately undermines the faith that is the source of any religious movement's vitality. As Merton explains:

[81] Winter, *Halle als Ausgangspunkt*, 269–75.
[82] Zsindely, *Krankheit und Heilung*, 46.
[83] Patzelt, *Der Pietismus im Teschener Schlesien*, 166.
[84] Ahrbeck, "Franckes Idee der Humanitas," 6.

The more we insist ... [that Christianity consists of] "being good" and ... doing one's duty, the more we make it difficult for men to really believe, and the more we make faith into a mental and spiritual problem, contingent on a certain ethical achievement. The only way faith continues to be humanly possible in such a situation is for it to be understood as a virtue and duty among other virtues and duties. One believes because one is *told to believe*, not because of a living and life-giving aspiration to know the living God. Faith itself becomes shot through with existential doubt which, nevertheless, one ignores out of duty, while going about one's business of avoiding evil and doing good.[85] (author's emphasis)

In his work on Chinese thought reform, Lifton has uncovered the social and psychological dynamics by which the doubt bred by the ideologically controlled environment of that system (and by that of Halle Pietism) developed and had its inevitable impact. Lifton notes that in a "reform-saturated environment" a latent hostility to the tight controls on behavior and to the narrowness of the "sacred science" exists alongside the more or less genuine enthusiasm for the movement. Though initially repressed, this hostility can surface in response to overly intensive indoctrination or to the penetration of the controlled milieu by a subversive point of view.[86] At the University of Halle the "new philosophy," that is, the Enlightenment, taught by Christian Wolff, most likely served to undermine the Pietists' authority in just this way. The vehemence of Francke's attacks on Wolff certainly support this supposition.[87]

Once such a shift from enthusiasm to ambivalence or outright hostility occurs, Lifton points out that converts to the "sacred science," even those "who outwardly seem active and involved," develop a "protective inner passivity."[88] This coping strategy induces the trainee not so much to rebel as to conform to the external demands of the program while withholding total inner commitment. In both Chinese thought reform and Halle Pietism, such a stance was difficult to sustain without incurring the supervisors' suspicions. The instructing cadres in both movements constantly forced their charges to confess their innermost convictions. In light of this psychological pressure, the ambivalence of the trainees toward the ideals they were supposed to embrace produced

85 Thomas Merton, *Conjectures of a Guilty Bystander* (Garden City, N.Y., 1968), 167.

86 Lifton, *Thought Reform and the Psychology of Totalism*, 411.

87 For a full account of the struggle between Wolff and Francke, see Hinrichs, *Preussentum und Pietismus*, 388–441.

88 Lifton, *Thought Reform and the Psychology of Totalism*, 413.

a situation that tended to "transform genuine inner experience into histrionic display."[89] It is apparent from the paranetical lectures of Francke's later years that the students' protestations of piety did not always convince the Pietist leader. Francke's awareness of their lack of complete sincerity led him to denounce the students repeatedly for passing themselves off as converted when they had not in fact undergone what he regarded as true repentance.[90]

These harangues indicate that Francke's strategy for breaking through the students' passivity consisted of using his standard pedagogical tools of exhortation and coercion in a more extreme form. In the paranetical lectures he told stories of students who had ignored the admonitions of the theology faculty and had come to a bad end. He also reminded his listeners in this same forum that, because theologians exercised such an enormous responsibility, failure in such a vocation would provoke a correspondingly greater punishment from God on Judgment Day. To complement these threatening exhortations, Francke also placed an increased reliance on coercion, especially on the more open manipulation of the selection process for places at the "free table," for teaching jobs in the *Anstalten* schools, and for scholarships.[91]

Such methods, however, succeeded merely in producing more passivity and hypocritical behavior – that is to say, more alienation – on the part of the students.[92] Even Frederick William I's expulsion of Wolff from the university in 1723 did not help. As Lifton remarks in describing the Chinese party leaders' dilemma after their thought-reform campaign had begun to lose its effectiveness: "the balance between enthusiasm and coercion . . . [since the high point of 1951–53] shifted to a decrease of the former and an increase of the latter." Hence the Communist leaders could "neither achieve their perfectionistic thought-reform goals, nor cease trying to; and every wave of thought-reform . . . [made] the next wave more necessary."[93]

The struggle to maintain religious enthusiasm at the University of Halle drained vitality from Francke's movement. The crisis was

89 *Ibid.*, 426.

90 Peschke, "A. H. Franckes Reform des theologischen Studiums," 109.

91 *Ibid.*, 113–15.

92 Friedrich de Boor, "A. H. Franckes paränetische Vorlesungen und seine Schriften zur Methode des theologischen Studiums," *Zeitschrift für Religions- und Geistesgeschichte*, 20 (1968): 320.

93 Lifton, *Thought Reform and the Psychology of Totalism*, 413.

exacerbated by the deaths, in rapid succession, of the top Pietist leaders: Baron von Canstein in 1719, Boehm in 1722, Neubauer in 1725, Francke himself in 1727, and Elers in 1728. Worse still, the best hopes from the younger generation died prematurely: Johann Daniel Herrnschmid, Francke's heir apparent, in 1723; and Johann Jakob Rambach, a dynamic lecturer in moral theology, in 1733. The weak leadership provided after Francke's death by his son, Gotthilf August, and J. A. Freylinghausen was incapable of taking the initiative in the mission field or devising new pedagogical or economic strategies.[94] Except for continued growth in sales of the *essentia dulcis*, in the clinic managed by Johann Juncker, and in the number of Bibles disseminated by the Canstein Institute, Halle Pietism by the 1730s had lost its impetus toward expansion. And within Francke's own frame of reference, once a Christian group stops its "growth in faith," backsliding is the inevitable result.

In one important sense, however, it is misleading to speak in terms of a "decline" in Halle Pietism. Just as Francke's movement succeeded Spenerian Pietism, so the mission of the Halle Pietists was carried on in a different form by the new Hohenzollern king, Frederick William I (1713–40). In terms of spirituality, Frederick William was no more a carbon copy of Francke than the latter was of Spener. Nor was it inevitable that Frederick William would assume the role of promoting Halle Pietism within his kingdom. But the course finally taken by the king had far-reaching consequences for the propagation of Pietist ethical values. By subjecting the *Anstalten* to tight regulation and acting as the chief employer of theology graduates from the University of Halle, Frederick William I effectively harnessed the still considerable energies of Halle Pietism to his own cause. Although in this process the Pietists lost some of their freedom of action, the extent to which they could influence society as a whole increased considerably.[95] Thanks to the far greater coercive powers of the state, the king could enforce "milieu

[94] Deppermann describes G. A. Francke as "spiritually dense" (*geistig borniert*). Deppermann, "Die politischen Voraussetzungen für die Etablierung des Pietismus," 52.

[95] Böhme, "Heinrich Julius Elers," 150. As both this section and the following chapter make clear, I agree with Deppermann in his opposition to the widely held view that the alliance between Halle Pietism and the Prussian state led to the decline of the former from a dynamic, world-wide missionary movement to a comparatively passive state religion. See Deppermann, "Die politischen Voraussetzungen für die Etablierung des Pietismus," 51–52.

control" over his entire country. Using pedagogical methods similar to Francke's own, Frederick William I would create from the disparate territories of Brandenburg-Prussia a political unity organized around a Pietist ethos and known to posterity as Prussia.

CHAPTER 9

Pietist–Hohenzollern collaboration

THE PIETY OF CROWN PRINCE FREDERICK WILLIAM

The impressive growth of the *Halle Anstalten* after 1700 and the sense of solidarity and self-consciousness that developed among the Pietist cadres initiated a new phase in relations between Halle Pietism and the Hohenzollern state. Thanks to its economic strength and world-wide missionary connections, Francke's movement was no longer so dependent on the Brandenburg-Prussian government. Partly because of this increase in the power of Halle Pietism and partly because of circumstantial political factors in Berlin, the nature of the relationship between the Pietists and the state underwent a series of changes between 1700 and 1713. During this period of transition, all the possibilities inherent in the situation were realized. The Pietists contemplated using the state for their own purposes; the Berlin regime took steps to cut the Pietists "down to size," and the impending ascension to the throne of an intensely religious prince offered the prospect of close collaboration between the two parties. Since this interaction between Pietists and Hohenzollerns took place at a time of acute political instability in Berlin, the final outcome was by no means predetermined. Ultimately, however, the decisive factor was the precise character of the religious convictions of the heir apparent, who in 1713 ascended the throne as Frederick William I.

As we have seen, Francke's strategy for achieving "world reform" developed in the years immediately following 1700. Within these all-encompassing plans, Francke envisioned the role of the political authorities as one of assisting in the saving work of "reborn" clergymen. The "governing estate" (*Regierstand*) should guarantee order, promote economic prosperity, and forcibly suppress any opposition to Pietism.[1] In the spring of 1704, the same year in which he wrote

[1] Peschke, *Studien zur Theologie August Hermann Franckes*, 95.

the "Grosse Aufsatz," Francke drew up a proposal in which he revealed the form he felt that the Pietist–Hohenzollern collaboration, in particular, should take. Undoubtedly, the strong position of his movement within Brandenburg-Prussia and the previous support given him by Frederick's government encouraged Francke to conceive this ambitious scheme for a joint effort of church and state to improve moral and material conditions in society.

The key element in Francke's proposal was the establishment of a general commission chaired by a member of the privy council, then the highest administrative agency in Brandenburg-Prussia. As its first order of business, the commission would supervise visitations of each province in the kingdom. The visitation committees would consist of Francke, Breithaupt, two clergymen from the province being visited, and one member of the local estates, though the latter could not be a member of the provincial government. After receiving the reports of the visitors, the commission would reconstitute itself as a *Kirchencollegium* with supervisory powers over all the provincial Lutheran churches. The agenda Francke set for the commission included increased state support for the theology program at the University of Halle, improvement in the care for orphans, elimination of begging through the founding of workhouses, and the setting up of "common schools" in order to train all the children of the country in religion and useful skills.[2]

To ensure that the commission would have sufficient means for carrying out its charge, Francke was willing to grant the state absolute power over the administration of the church. In particular Francke proposed strict limitations on the nobility's "patronage right" of appointing pastors. Instead, the king should make all such appointments, presumably on the recommendation of the *Kirchencollegium.* Francke intended, of course, that this latter body be dominated by his supporters; in the original "Projekt" of 1704 he suggested that Canstein be a permanent member of the *Collegium.*[3] Francke's plan thus consisted of organizing a centralized church and school administration in Brandenburg-Prussia under the *de facto* control of Halle Pietism. As such, it constituted an attempt to use the power of the central government to continue the expansion of Pietist

2 Deppermann, *Der hallesche Pietismus*, 148–50.
3 *Ibid.*, 148–49.

influence at the expense of the estates, particularly in the Halle-Magdeburg area.[4]

The chief difficulty with Francke's proposed *Kirchencollegium* was that the policy of Frederick I's government was one of reconciliation with the estates, not one of direct assault on their customary privileges. Even Fuchs, the minister of religious and cultural affairs who had supported Francke in the crises of 1692 and 1700, opposed the latter's desire "to reform everything all at once."[5] Frederick's policy makers sought, rather, to overcome the opposition between the reformed court and administration, on the one hand, and the Lutheran estates, on the other, by means of a negotiated union between the two Protestant faiths.

The top priority given to the quest for union during the reign of Frederick III(I) did more than place a limit on state support for Francke's domestic initiatives. It also precipitated a deterioration in relations between the Pietists and the court, which had reached a high point in 1700–03. Spener, Francke, and their followers in Brandenburg-Prussia had always been skeptical of such an external unity of confessions, believing that a spiritual rebirth of all parties must precede organizational unity. In 1703, therefore, when Frederick I announced his intention to form a *collegium* of Lutheran and Reformed clergy for the purpose of working toward the desired union, Spener refused to participate.[6]

As the court had expected the Pietists to serve as a mediating force in the negotiations, Spener's refusal to take part in them was a serious setback for the regime. Frederick's advisors were even more discomfited by the controversy following the publication later in 1703 of an anonymous pamphlet entitled the *Arcanum regium*. The treatise, which was considered to reflect the views of Halle Pietism, argued that a genuine unification could take place only through the king's appointment of Halle Pietists to clerical offices.[7] Although Francke publicly repudiated the *Arcanum regium*, its appearance provoked an anti-Pietist attack by Valentin Löscher, the leader of Lutheran orthodoxy, as well as polemical battles between Reformed and Lutheran theologians. The furor further undermined the pros-

[4] In the same memorandum, Francke also suggested "reforming" the provincial government in Magdeburg by putting in positions of power Pietist sympathizers from outside the province. See *Ibid.*, 150.

[5] Quoted in Hinrichs, *Friedrich Wilhelm I.*, 583.

[6] Deppermann, *Der hallesche Pietismus,* 155.

[7] Delius, "Berliner Unionsversuche," 41.

pects for union and aroused resentment toward Halle Pietism on the part of high-ranking Reformed officials in Frederick I's government.[8]

In the years following 1703, unfavorable developments continued to jeopardize the Pietists' position. When their staunchest patron within the government, Fuchs, died in 1704, some of his responsibilities over church and university affairs were assigned to Marquard Ludwig von Printzen, a passionate supporter of confessional union and a bitter opponent of the Pietists. Between 1704 and 1707, moreover, three more of the strongest advocates of the Pietist cause in Berlin died, including Spener himself. The resulting isolation of Canstein and General Natzmer in a court otherwise hostile to Pietism accounts for the vulnerability of the Pietists by 1709. Beginning in that year, Printzen was able to mount a strong campaign to name a Reformed theologian to the Halle theology faculty. Unchecked by Canstein's opposition, Printzen went so far as to grant the title of professor to the director of a Reformed gymnasium in Halle. Although the theology faculty refused to recognize Printzen's action, its resistance incurred the disfavor of Frederick I.[9]

The king's already negative feelings towards the Pietists were greatly intensified by the latter's misguided attempt to win over the queen, Frederick I's third wife, to their cause. Sophie Luise, a Lutheran princess from Mecklenburg, married Frederick I in 1708, but she could not adjust to the complex ceremonies and constant intrigues of the Berlin court. She responded by withdrawing into a religious world of her own. Soon she began expressing doubts as to whether her husband could be saved. In October 1709 Francke journeyed to Berlin to meet the queen, hoping to cure her spiritual malady and simultaneously gain her adherence to Halle Pietism. Although Francke's efforts at first seemed to produce improvement in her psychological condition, the net result of his ministrations was to reduce the queen to a more erratic and confused state. As her mental condition continued to deteriorate, Frederick I increasingly blamed Francke for her afflictions. This royal disapproval of Francke, shared by Crown Prince Frederick William, encouraged opponents of the Halle *Anstalten* to step up their anti-Pietist agitation.[10] By 1711 it seemed as though the existence of the orphanage

[8] *Ibid.*, 42–43.
[9] Deppermann, *Der hallesche Pietismus*, 156–57, 162.
[10] *Ibid.*, 159–64.

complex itself might be in danger, unless the Pietists could soften or reverse the antagonism of the crown prince, who had become the dominant force behind the throne following the coup against the Wittgenstein clique in December 1710.

The opposition to Pietism of young Frederick William (b. 1688) was based mainly on loyalty to his father, who in turn felt he had been wronged by Francke. Tempering this reaction to the situation of the moment was the prince's grasp of the long-term reality that Lutherans constituted the overwhelming majority of the kingdom's population and that the Pietist movement offered the best hope for bridging the gap between the Lutheran community and the Reformed monarchy. As the crown prince assumed, after 1710, ever more responsibility for handling the day-to-day affairs of state, he therefore realized that he needed to form his own independent judgment of Halle Pietism. Frederick William's decision would determine the subsequent relationship between Halle Pietism and the Hohenzollern state. As his evaluation of the Pietists ultimately rested on religious considerations, the key factor in the outcome of the investigation was the degree to which the crown prince found the Pietists' spirituality to be in accord with his own.

It is important to realize that Frederick William's personal religiosity was fully formed before his contact with the Pietists.[11] The prince's precocity in religious matters resulted from a boyhood and youth laden with intense spiritual conflicts. As a child, Frederick William displayed a fiery temper, an aversion to doing his schoolwork, and a refusal to obey anyone but his father. Only one tutor had any success in subduing him. Philippe de Rebeur, a Calvinist from the Brabant, inculcated fear of the judgment in the prince, persuading the boy that his aggressive, malicious acts were signs of his having been predestined for damnation.[12] From this point on, Frederick William felt somewhat more constrained in his behavior, but he continued to rebel against the court ceremonial and scholarly learning that his mother in particular attempted to foist upon him. As he internalized Rebeur's theology, he increasingly regarded the routine of court festivities as frivolous, immoral, and meaningless.[13]

[11] For a convincing demonstration of this point, see Karl Wolff, "Ist der Glaube Friedrich Wilhelms I. von A. H. Francke beeinflusst?" *Jahrbuch für brandenburgische Kirchengeschichte*, 33 (1938): 71–80.

[12] *Ibid.*, 75. See also Carl Hinrichs, "Friedrich Wilhelm I.: König von Preussen," in Hinrichs, *Preussen als historisches Problem*, 44.

[13] Hinrichs, "Friedrich Wilhelm I.: König von Preussen," 46.

The intense energy of his disposition found a congenial outlet in the world of the military, but even his total immersion in the soldierly way of life did not calm his anxieties, since his awareness of the sinful aspects of a soldier's existence left him acutely uneasy over his chances for ultimate salvation.

The manner in which these tensions and insecurities were resolved determined the nature of Frederick William's spirituality as an adult. The decisive event occurred in his twentieth year, shortly after the death in infancy of his first-born son. What followed that trauma was a full-blown conversion experience that initiated for Frederick William a personal relationship with God that lasted for the rest of his life.[14] The prince's direct experience of God's grace imparted to him a sense of certainty that despite his wretched sinfulness God would forgive and bless him with the grace of Christ. Frederick William's postconversion letters reveal a passionate conviction that creatures depend on God's help, that His help is undeserved, but that God nevertheless will give aid when called on through prayer.[15] Especially liberating for the future king was the realization that the grace of Christ is universal, that His sacrifice was for all humanity, and that no soul is damned from the beginning of time. Thus Frederick William's rebirth allowed him, through his new, intimate relationship with God, to overcome the doubts and despair resulting from the effects on him of Rebeur's form of predestination theology.[16]

The crown prince's postconversion life was dominated by an unbounded sense of obligation toward the God who had rescued him from what he perceived as a state of irredeemable iniquity. Viewing himself as absolutely dependent on God, Frederick William felt a continual need for the feeling of being close to God, of being in God's favor, of experiencing God's grace.[17] His devotional life was therefore a very active one of assiduous Bible reading, daily household prayers, faithful church attendance, intense interest in sermons, and frequent partaking of communion. Like Francke,

[14] Frederick William I, "Das politische Testament," in W. M. Pantenius, ed., *Erlasse und Briefe des Königs Friedrich Wilhelms I. von Preussen* (Leipzig, 1913), 82.

[15] Wolff, "Ist der Glaube Friedrich Wilhelms I. von A. H. Francke beeinflusst?" 77–80.

[16] Hinrichs, "Friedrich Wilhelm I.: König von Preussen," 44. On the important soteriological questions of grace and election, therefore, Frederick William's positions were essentially the Lutheran ones. See Wilhelm Stolze, "Friedrich Wilhelm I. und der Pietismus," *Jahrbuch für brandenburgische Kirchengeschichte*, 5 (1908): 175.

[17] Gericke, ed., *Glaubenszeugnisse und Konfessionspolitik*, 61. See also Georg Küntzel, *Die drei grossen Hohenzollern*, 84.

moreover, Frederick William's desire to feel spiritually reassured was so insatiable that his struggle to satisfy God extended to, and ultimately centered on, his vocational life, his work.[18] Frederick William conceived of his work as a means of fulfilling his almost limitless responsibility to God and as a way of combating the evil he felt to be within himself and in others. When despite his most strenuous efforts, God seemingly withheld grace or when Frederick William himself relapsed into sinful behavior, especially his recurring fits of rage and ill-temper, he would accept these occurrences as punishments from God designed to remind him of the need for still greater obedience.[19]

Since Frederick William possessed this kind of experientially based faith, it was vitally important for him to receive "rewards" from God in the form of positive tangible results from his earthly labors.[20] Throughout his postconversion life, the crown prince, later king, was generally able to regard his sustained submission to God's will and the signs of favor He bestowed on Frederick William's work as justifying his feeling of being in "good standing" with his Maker.[21] Thus despite serious health problems for the last decade of his life and the great burden of his work, the second king of Prussia pronounced himself "completely satisfied" with God and did not depart from his characteristic form of spirituality for the rest of his days.[22]

As should be quite evident, Frederick William's piety bears an overwhelming similarity to that of Halle Pietism despite his life-long allegiance to the Reformed church and the complete lack of Pietist influence on his early religious development.[23] The affinity empha-

[18] For emphatic statements of the king's work ethic, see Frederick William I, "Das politische Testament," 82, 84.

[19] Stolze, "Friedrich Wilhelm I. und der Pietismus," 178–79; Küntzel, *Die drei grossen Hohenzollern*, 84, 87. One reason historians have shied away from characterizing Frederick William I as a Pietist is that they have found it hard to square the king's inner turmoil with what they regard as the typically Pietist "stillness" or "peacefulness" – the result of the characteristically Lutheran sense of trust in God's grace. Hence Wendland's verdict that Frederick William should not be considered a "full Pietist." Walter Wendland, "Märkischer Pietismus," in *Festgabe zum deutschen Pfarrertag, Berlin 1927* (Eberswalde, 1927), 34. The flaw in such analyses rests in the fact that especially after 1690 there were several different types of "Pietism" and that one of these, Francke's spirituality, possessed the same type of inner uncertainty as that experienced by Frederick William I. See above, pp. 148–49.

[20] Wolff, "Ist der Glaube Friedrich Wilhelms I. von A. H. Francke beeinflusst?" 97.

[21] Frederick William I, "Das politische Testament," 82.

[22] Wolff, "Ist der Glaube Friedrich Wilhelms I. von A. H. Francke beeinflusst?" 94.

[23] Gericke and, to a lesser extent, Wolff dissent from this view because to them Frederick William held to a somewhat different conception of the nature of grace than did the Pietists. According to Gericke, the Pietists regarded the grace received through conversion as a permanent possession, whereas for Frederick William I grace was a promised blessing

sized by Hinrichs was the combination of the Puritan work ethic with the Lutheran doctrine of universal grace, which yielded a concept of vocation in which one's daily work constituted a sacrifice of self for the spiritual and material benefit of one's neighbor.[24] For both the Halle Pietists and Frederick William, this commitment constituted the central purpose of their postconversion lives.

At least equally significant, however, was the common psychological basis between the experiential piety of Francke and that of the Hohenzollern prince. What drove each to carry out their labors for the collective good was the need to experience over and over again the sense of obeying God's commandments and receiving His grace. Common to both, too, was the expectation of being indemnified in both this world and the next for this kind of submission to God. Compared to this emotional and personal relationship with God, abstract theological doctrines seemed as unimportant to the crown prince as to the Halle Pietists. Frederick William was convinced that a Lutheran had just as much chance of being saved as a member of the Reformed communion, and he attributed the split between the churches purely to the "bickerings of the preachers."[25] In an instruction to an ecclesiastical official written in 1726, Frederick William asserted that for those who wish to be saved "the question is not: are you Lutheran or are you Reformed? It is: have you obeyed [God's] commandments?"[26]

At first Frederick William did not fully recognize the spiritual commonality between himself and the Pietists. In July 1711 he wrote to his closest friend, Prince Leopold von Anhalt-Dessau (whom he continually sought to convert), "I am no Pietist, but God

on which one could rely. See Gericke, ed., *Glaubenszeugnisse und Konfessionspolitik*, 59–60. Yet even this fine a distinction seems untenable given Spener's position that the rebirth and its attendant grace could be lost. See Spener, *Der neue Mensch*, 92.

24 Hinrichs found this "a uniquely Pietist combination." See his "Friederich Wilhelm I.: König von Preussen," 54. In finding this position to be *uniquely* Pietist, Hinrichs was following Weber in his unawareness of the collective, communal focus of the seventeenth-century Puritans' work activity. For the latter, see Todd, *Christian Humanism and the Puritan Social Order*, 148–52. The basically false distinction between Pietist (i.e. Prusso-German) "collectivism" and Puritan (i.e. Anglo-American) "capitalism" is a prominent theme in Hinrichs's work. Hinrichs, *Preussentum und Pietismus*, 12. This same dichotomy also formed an important part of Oswald Spengler's historical vision, where it was presented in a much more rigid and much less rhetorically restrained manner. Spengler, *Preussentum und Sozialismus*, 38–46 and *passim*.

25 Frederick William I, "Das politische Testament," 91.

26 Frederick William I, "Bescheid an den (späteren) Propst Roloff," in Gericke, ed., *Glaubenszeugnisse und Konfessionspolitik*, 201–02.

above all in the world."[27] But Frederick William was not too close-minded to pass up an opportunity to walk around the perimeter of the *Anstalten* during a visit to Halle in August of that same year. Aware that the crown prince had once threatened to shut down the *Anstalten* when he became king, the Pietists realized that they had to move quickly to capitalize on the largely favorable impression Frederick William had received from his inspection. Francke immediately composed a memorandum to the crown prince, in which he enumerated the ways in which the *Anstalten* were "useful" (*nützlich*) to the state: the inflow of donations from outside Brandenburg-Prussia, the increased excise tax receipts from the orphanage's expenditures, the employment offered artisans through the construction of new buildings, higher university enrollments because of the availability of the "free table," the inculcation of the fear of God into the pupils at the *Anstalten*, and so forth.[28]

Despite the skill with which Francke appealed to the mercantilist side of Frederick William, the latter still distrusted the Pietists' motives. Perhaps he detected in Francke's efforts to win his favor a subtle form of flattery, which would only serve to harden Frederick William's suspicion.[29] Only in November 1711 were the crown prince's doubts dispelled. On the seventh of that month General Natzmer, for whose soldierly ability Frederick William had the

27 Frederick William I, "Brief an Leopold von Anhalt-Dessau, 3. Juli 1711," in Pantenius, ed., *Erlasse und Briefe*, 99. What this statement probably means is that while the crown prince was refusing to admit an identification of himself with the Pietist (or any other) party of faction, he still felt obliged to affirm to the skeptical Leopold his sense of submission to God. That Frederick William felt it necessary to deny an affiliation with the Pietist movement suggests perhaps that many people at court had noticed the affinities between his religious position and that of Halle Pietism and were wondering whether there were any personal or political connections behind those affinities.

28 Deppermann, *Der hallesche Pietismus*, 165–66.

29 Frederick William I frequently expressed his hatred of flattery and dissimulation. See, for example, the "Instruktion König Friedrich Wilhelms I. für das General-Ober-Finanz-, Kriegs-und Domänen-Direktorium. Jagdhaus Schönebeck 1722 Dezember 20," in Gustav Schmoller *et al.*, eds., *Acta Borussica: Die Behördenorganisation und die allgemeine Staatsverwaltung Preussens im 18. Jahrhundert*, vol. III, 649. This attitude of the king's extended to theater as an art form. In this respect, Frederick William's outlook was similar to Francke's as he often, at the instigation of the Pietists, issued a large number of edicts and prohibitions against theatrical performances throughout his reign. The psychological rigidity underlying this opposition was also common to both men. Thus Frederick William I once described how comedy could disrupt his strenuously achieved sense of self-regimentation: "if one [after attending a performance] wants to pray, receive communion, and hear God's word, the pranks come back to mind again and again." Quoted in Hilde Haider-Pregler, *Des sittlichen Bürgers Abendschule: Bildungsanspruch und Bildungsauftrag des Berufstheaters im 18. Jahrhundert* (Vienna and Munich, 1982), 87.

greatest respect, pleaded the Pietists' case in an audience with the crown prince. The interview began with Frederick William bringing up, one by one, accusations commonly levied against Francke's movement and Natzmer answering each of them in turn.

Natzmer soon realized that the crown prince's position toward the Pietists depended ultimately on his judgment as to whether their motivations were sincere. According to Canstein's account of the meeting, Natzmer then said to the future king that "if these people [the Pietists] sought anything but the honor of God, then he [Natzmer] would want to be the meanest rogue and never again come before the eyes of His Highness." To which the crown prince replied that since Francke "sought God's honor alone," he "therefore should be protected." Natzmer reported to Canstein that at this point in the conversation Frederick William paused and, obviously pleased, repeated the phrase "God's honor" several times.[30] A week later Canstein wrote to Francke that the crown prince was openly declaring at court that he had arrived at a "completely different conception" of Halle Pietism as a result of his exchange with Natzmer.[31] In December 1711 Frederick William informed Francke that if he could ever render him a service, he would do it "with the greatest joy."[32]

The relationship between Halle Pietism and Frederick William became even more firmly established in the spring of 1713, following the latter's ascension to the throne in February of that year. In early April Francke petitioned the new king for a favorable settlement of the controversy over adding a Reformed professor to the Halle theology faculty. Less than a week later Frederick William I replied by means of an unannounced visit to the Halle *Anstalten*. Although he gave the premises a thorough inspection during his two-hour-long stay, the king was probably most interested in testing Francke's attitude toward soldiers and the military way of life. Frederick William's greatest concern was that Francke and his staff were inculcating pacifist values, teaching pupils that "they will pick up

30 The text of Canstein's account of the meeting is available in Theodor Wotschke, "Die Gewinnung des Kronprinzen Friedrich Wilhelm für den halleschen Pietismus," *Neue kirchliche Zeitschrift*, 41 (1930): 693–96. For more information regarding Natzmer's connections with the Pietist movement, see Hugo Gerhard Bloth, "Soldat und Vermittler: Generalfeldmarschall Dubislav Gneomar von Natzmer, 1654–1735; Pommer, Pietist, Preusse," *Baltische Studien*, N.F., 70 (1984): 90–96.

31 Wotschke, "Die Gewinnung des Kronprinzen Friedrich Wilhelm," 696.

32 Quoted in Deppermann, *Der hallesche Pietismus*, 167.

the devil if they become soldiers." Francke attempted to reassure the king by pointing out that he knew many Christian soldiers and that he had more friends and patrons among the military than among the clergy.[33]

To make sure that he had laid the king's mind to rest on this point, Francke sent him a follow-up memorandum three days later in which he spelled out his position on war. In Francke's view, war offered a ruler great temptations to sin, just as did the trade in books and medicines for the orphanage complex. Neither war nor trade was in itself unjust, however, since both could be used for Christian purposes.[34] Francke's answer must have satisfied Frederick William because in early May Francke was granted a special audience with the king in Berlin. Shortly thereafter it was announced that the privileges of the orphanage were confirmed and that the dispute over a possible Reformed member of the Halle theology faculty had been resolved in the Pietists' favor.[35] The reason for these concessions to Halle Pietism was clearly the king's conviction that Francke "sought in connection with his *Anstalten* not his own honor and utility [*Nutzen*] but sincerely sought God's honor and the good [*Nutzen*] of the country."[36]

In the spirituality of Frederick William I the phrase "for the good of the country" held a place similar to the Halle Pietists' slogan "for the good of thy neighbor." The specific policies designed to promote "the good of the country" were the product of Frederick William's years as crown prince, during which he acquired an in-depth knowledge of the problems besetting the Brandenburg-Prussian state. When Frederick William was serving his apprenticeship in statecraft between 1704 and 1710, his father's regime was a member of the coalition of states fighting France in the War of Spanish Succession. As the young prince quickly realized, however, Brandenburg-Prussia was not an equal partner in the alliance, since it was receiving substantial subsidies from the English and Dutch in return for the services of its thirty-five thousand man army. Already in 1705

33 For a transcription of the actual conversation between the two men, see Kramer, *Neue Beiträge*, 151.

34 Important passages from the memorandum are printed in Deppermann's account; see Deppermann, *Der hallesche Pietismus*, 169–70. For both the Pietists and Frederick William I, engaging in vocations where temptations were great necessitated and justified the strictest forms of self-regimentation. See above, pp. 144–45.

35 Deppermann, *Der hallesche Pietismus*, 171.

36 Quoted in Kramer, *Neue Beiträge*, 151.

at age seventeen, the crown prince understood the situation well enough to propose a reform of the royal finances as a means of raising sufficient revenue to support such an army without subsidies.[37] As he gained more experience through his work on the privy council (he never missed a meeting), he became more and more aware of the limitations of his country's resources. Frederick William therefore dedicated himself to finding a new strategy that would enable Brandenburg-Prussia to compete with the major European powers despite its deficiencies in population and material wealth.

The prince's conversion experience in 1708 intensified his commitment to increasing the power of the Hohenzollern state. When Frederick William was a boy, his tutor Rebeur admonished him that God had shown special favor to the ruling family because of its Reformed faith and its exemplary moral standards.[38] Although Frederick William never rejected this formulation of Rebeur's, his Pietism determined his conception of the kingship, making the connection between his performance as king and his personal salvation much more direct and immediate. Frederick William invested new dynamism into the long-standing definition of a ruling prince as "administrator for God" (*Amtmann Gottes*) by applying to his office a Promethean understanding of vocation similar to that of Francke.[39]

Given the resulting sense of obligation to act immediately to transform the world, Frederick William as king assumed unlimited responsibility for his subjects' welfare. The totalism of his commitment led, in turn, to his practice of taking charge of even the smallest matters and of ruling autocratically, since he believed God was holding him completely accountable for every act of his government.[40] Frederick William I thus regarded the basis of his authority to be his "good standing" with God in the day-to-day execution of his office. Though in this way the king placed himself in direct dependence on a higher power, his understanding of himself as

[37] Hinrichs, "Friedrich Wilhelm I.: König von Preussen," 49.

[38] *Ibid.*, 44.

[39] See above, pp. 143–44.

[40] For a penetrating exposition of the king's conception of rulership, see Küntzel, *Die drei grossen Hohenzollern*, 84–86. In this connection, Fritz Hartung quotes Frederick William as saying that he never shied away from "sticking his nose in all the dirt" (*die Nase in jeden Dreck zu stecken*). Hartung, *Staatsbildende Kräfte der Neuzeit: Gesammelte Aufsätze* (Berlin, 1961), 132.

being God's agent in a quite literal operational sense gave him the boundless self-assurance needed to insist on absolute subordination to his authority on the part of all his subjects, whose relationship to himself he saw as analogous of his own relationship with God. The traditional phrase, "rule by the grace of God," implied for Frederick William a simple unconditional supremacy in power granted him by God in the expectation of diligent, tireless, unceasing work for the benefit of his subjects.[41]

Like the Halle Pietists, then, Frederick William I saw himself as laboring to fulfill a mandate from God to act for the good of others, which both required and justified intrusive intervention in the lives of everyone in his kingdom for the purpose of "improving" them, i.e. converting them to his own way of thinking.[42] To carry out an "educational" undertaking of this magnitude, the king needed to employ not just the churches and schools but the entire state apparatus and every socializing institution in the country.[43] In schooling the population in the basic principles of his "sacred science," Frederick William sought to inculcate as the most fundamental value the traditional feudal one of "loyalty" (*Treue*) to God, for the king believed that "whoever is not true to God, likewise cannot be true to his king."[44]

But as was often the case with Frederick William I, a commonplace idea here acquired a fresh meaning because what he meant by loyalty to God and king was not simply outward obedience to a political authority instituted by God. Frederick William demanded from his subjects, in addition, a commitment to their vocations comparable to his own dedication to the royal *Amt*. Specifically, this required people to break with "customary, nonperformance-oriented routines" (*Schlendrian*) and internalize as their mission Frederick William's own of working beyond maximum capacity for

41 Perhaps the best known of Frederick William I's assertions of his sovereign power is contained in his 1722 instruction to the General Directory, where he states, "Wir sind doch Herr und König und können thun, was Wir wollen." Schmoller *et al.*, eds., *Die Behördenorganisation*, vol. III, 649. Georges Pariset, *L'état et les églises en Prusse sous Frédéric-Guillaume I* (Paris, 1897), 61–62; Küntzel, *Die drei grossen Hohenzollern*, 88.

42 Fritz Wagner, "Friedrich Wilhelm I.: Tradition und Persönlichkeit," *Historische Zeitschrift*, 181 (1956): 90.

43 Schmoller once observed, "Prussia before 1740 may appear to us as a large educational institution" (*Schulanstalt*). See Gustav Schmoller, "Der preussische Beamtenstand unter Friedrich Wilhelm I.," *Preussische Jahrbücher*, 26 (1870): 552. No one has previously attempted a systematic analysis of Frederick William's Prussia in such terms however.

44 Quoted in Stolze, "Friedrich Wilhelm I. und der Pietismus," 189n.

the institution (supposedly) doing the most for the common good – namely, the state.[45]

The king's pedagogical campaign, to achieve its purpose, thus needed to persuade the inhabitants of the Hohenzollern lands to identify their sense of self-worth with the growth of Prussian state power, since tangible gains in state resources constituted visible signs of obedience and self-sacrifice on the part of king and subjects. Just as the Halle Pietists found confirmation of God's support for their labor through increases in school enrollment figures and endowment size, so in this "State Pietism" of Frederick William I, the king and those who believed in his vision interpreted increases in tax revenues and army size as proof of divine approval.[46]

"State Pietism" also provides the key to understanding the essence of Frederick William I's strategy for achieving his revolutionary goal of vaulting the Hohenzollern state into the ranks of the great European powers. In 1709, the year after his conversion, crown prince Frederick William was given an opportunity to impose his ethic of self-sacrificing service on those under his command. Responsible for directing part of the Brandenburg-Prussian army in the campaign against the French that culminated in the battle of Malplaquet, he instituted daily drilling of unprecedented rigor among his troops. The impressive results he quickly achieved made him realize that the qualitative superiority of well-drilled soldiers could offset the larger size of the armies fielded by the major European states.[47] As for the problem of financing the army, Frederick William's answer was to eliminate the expensive court (which, as a result of his Pietist conception of the kingship, he did not need as a means of enhancing his authority), increase state revenues by heightening worker discipline and motivation, and then channel all available funds into expanding the army.

There is one final reason why an awareness of Frederick William I's spirituality – and its corresponding psychology – is crucial to understanding the nature of his regime. As was the case with Francke, Frederick William's postconversion life was characterized by periods of despair and melancholy, times when his grandiose

[45] In his 1722 instruction to the General Directory, Frederick William I specifically equated reversion to the old "*Schlender*" with disobedience. See Schmoller *et al.*, eds., *Die Behördenorganisation*, vol. III, 649–50.

[46] Hinrichs, "Friedrich Wilhelm I.: König von Preussen," 57.

[47] *Ibid.*, 51.

self-confidence dissolved into very strong feelings of shame and worthlessness.[48] The experiential quality of his faith, with its continual need for external signs of success, left him emotionally vulnerable to setbacks in his state-building program, such as occurred in 1727 when a famine struck East Prussia and seemingly undid much of what had been accomplished in the preceding years. When the full (negative) implications for the royal treasury became apparent, Frederick William was incapacitated for three months, enraged by the "betrayal" of him by the people of East Prussia and convinced that the whole world was holding him up for mockery and abuse.[49] As fearful of betrayal as he was insistent on obedience, in his political testament the king cursed his successor if the latter dared to reduce the size of the army or prefer one of the two Protestant confessions over the other.[50] In his later years, suffering from dropsy, he was so unnerved by the prospect of his own death, that he shot off guns to reassure himself of his continuing vitality.[51]

Like Francke, Frederick William interpreted such crises as trials sent by God, for which the only response was a heightened obedience to God's commands. In the context of Frederick William's concept of his royal vocation, this meant that his characteristic response to his lack of inner equilibrium was to intensify his efforts to control his subjects, thereby increasing his dependence on external signs of "progress." Thence came the "dynamism," the desperate energy, and the radical disregard for customary constraints on princely authority that marked Frederick William I's attempt to transform his country in his own image.

[48] See Stolze, "Friedrich Wilhelm I. und der Pietismus," 177, where he notes the king's tendency toward "despairing sighs and prayers of penance," hallmarks of Pietism later ridiculed by *Aufklärung* satirists.

[49] August Skalweit, *Die ostpreussische Domänenverwaltung*, 101–02. In keeping with the centrality of tangible accomplishment for Frederick William I's sense of self-worth, it is not surprising that one of the forms his depression took during this period was that of doubting his efficacy, his usefulness: "denn ich in dieser Welt nichts nütze bin." Quoted in Ludwig Geiger, *Berlin, 1688–1840: Geschichte des geistigen Lebens der preussischen Hauptstadt*, vol. I, (Berlin, 1892), 171.

[50] This and other examples of Frederick William I's tendency to curse those who would thus "betray" him are given in Dietrich, ed., *Die politischen Testamente der Hohenzollern*, 73–74. The king's tendency to see things in terms of dichotomies of blessing/curse and faithfulness/betrayal "betrays" the Manichaeanism that is implicit in his, and Francke's, spirituality.

[51] Pariset, *L'état et les églises en Prusse*, 78–79.

THE SPREAD OF HALLE PIETISM THROUGHOUT PRUSSIA, 1713–40

The reconciliation of the Halle Pietists with Frederick William I ensured the long-term survival of the Halle *Anstalten* and the continued Pietist domination of the theology faculty of the University of Halle. In addition, the compatible religious convictions of Frederick William I seemed to offer unlimited prospects for combining state power and Pietist activism in a common endeavor to transform society in the Hohenzollern lands. A social transformation brought about by an intense Pietist pedagogical campaign did indeed occur during the reign of Frederick William I. This campaign, however, was not a single coordinated project with a consistent pattern of collaboration between the Pietist movement and state agencies. The Prussian ethos came into being, rather, as the result of a complex process characterized by a division of labor between the king and Halle Pietism. Generally speaking, the Pietists' efforts were concentrated in the churches and schools, while Frederick William worked through the army and the bureaucracy. Yet there was considerable overlap between the two sets of institutions – the military church being only the most obvious example – and each party needed the support of the other to be successful in its own special sphere of educational activity.

It would have taken a certain amount of time in any case for the intricacies of such a complex joint endeavor to be worked out by the two sides, but other factors kept the collaboration from becoming very close in the years immediately following Frederick William's accession in 1713. To be sure, in his early years on the throne, the king appointed Halle Pietists to a number of key positions. Lampertus Gedicke became provost (*Feldpropst*) of the military church; Johann Gustav Reinbeck, provost in Berlin-Cölln; and Heinrich Lysius was placed in charge of the effort to rebuild the school and church system in plague-devastated East Prussia.[52]

Despite these signs of favor on Frederick William's part, Francke and his followers still had strong reasons for distrusting the king's intentions. Most unsettling to the Pietists were the methods practiced by recruiters for the royal army, who during the rapid military build-up in the mid to late 1710s had license from the king to

52 For more information on Lysius's appointment and accomplishments during his tenure, see Terveen, *Gesamtstaat und Retablissement*, 86–92.

impress by force young men from any walk of life, including theology students at the University of Halle.[53] In addition, even though Frederick William was obviously more sympathetic to the Lutheran church than his father, he pursued for a time Frederick III(I)'s policy of trying to negotiate a union between the Lutheran and Reformed confessions. In 1716 he even forced the Lutheran clergy of Berlin, led by the Pietist provost Johann Porst, into the position of having to refuse publicly to cooperate in the negotiations.[54] A final reason for Francke's reluctance to commit himself and his movement totally to an alliance with the Hohenzollern state was his long-cherished vision of Halle Pietism as a *worldwide* missionary effort; hence his resistance when in 1718 Frederick William I ordered Philipp Michaelis, pastor in Archangel and one of the strongest Pietist leaders in Russia, to return to Prussia as army chaplain for the king's Potsdam regiment.[55]

Indicative of the distance between the two parties during this period was the lack of direct contact between Francke and Frederick William I as the king sent the Pietist leader only eight letters between 1713 and April 1722.[56] By the early to mid-1720s, however, Frederick William, who was continually exposed to, and impressed by, the sermons of Halle-trained army chaplains, had become increasingly aware of his need for the services of large numbers of Pietist cadres.[57] The rapid increase in the size of the army, especially in and around Berlin, had created serious social problems stemming from the poverty and alienation of the soldiers and their families. The king's inspections of Pomerania and East Prussia, moreover,

53 Francke made no secret of his opposition to this forced recruiting. See Hinrichs, *Preussentum und Pietismus*, 129f.

54 Delius, "Berliner Unionsversuche," 93. Additional evidence of the importance of this tension can be found in its role in the career of Lampertus Gedicke, the leader of the military church. For years Gedicke feared that the king would attempt to unite the two churches by fiat on terms dictated by the Reformed theologians. He also feared that his anti-Union activities were jeopardizing his position. For this reason he kept secret, and eventually had to cut off, his correspondence with the orthodox Lutheran superintendent of Gotha, Ernst Salomo Cyprian. See Theodor Wotschke, "Lampert Gedickes Briefe an Ernst Salomo Cyprian," *Jahrbuch für brandenburgische Kirchengeschichte*, 20 (1925): 105.

55 Hinrichs, *Preussentum und Pietismus*, 156.

56 Stolze, "Friedrich Wilhelm I. und der Pietismus," 187n.

57 What Frederick William liked about Pietist sermonizing, to the point of publicly preferring Lutheran Pietist preachers to their Reformed counterparts, was their straightforward, down-to-earth, edificatory style. See Walter Wendland, "Märkischer Pietismus," 34–35. For statements from Frederick William I portraying Francke as *the* model preacher, see Robert Stupperich, "Aus dem kirchlichen Leben der Mark in den Tagen des Soldatenkönigs," *Jahrbuch für brandenburgische Kirchengeschichte*, 32 (1937): 52–53.

had made it very clear to him that for the people of these provinces to be as efficient and productive as he wanted them to be a major effort to upgrade the local church and school systems was necessary.[58]

Political factors in these same regions also induced Frederick William to turn to the Pietists for help. Stettin and part of western Pomerania were annexed by Prussia from Sweden in 1720 as a consequence of the Great Northern War. As long as they held Stettin and its environs, the Swedes had done everything possible to cultivate an intensely orthodox Lutheran church establishment there in order to set up a cultural barrier between their part of Pomerania and the neighboring Hohenzollern territories, where the Reformed religion was actively promoted by the ruling dynasty. Consequently, when Frederick William I took over this territory and encountered civil disobedience from the Lutheran clergy, he realized he needed the Pietists to assist him in overcoming the anti-Prussian orientation of the Pomeranian Lutherans.[59] Similarly, in East Prussia the king concluded in 1727 that his efforts at reconstruction were being thwarted by the opposition of the native East Prussian elite and that the only way to create a large enough base of support for the Hohenzollern state in that province was to encourage the Pietists to establish themselves there in force.

At the same time that Frederick William I was identifying specific missions requiring large-scale Pietist participation, the Halle Pietist movement was beginning to experience both increasing difficulties in its missionary work outside Prussia and a change in leadership to a new generation.[60] Under these circumstances, the opportunities offered by the Prussian king ultimately claimed most of the energy and personnel of Halle Pietism. Already by 1720 Francke had given up his opposition to large numbers of Halle-trained Pietists' entering the Prussian service as army chaplains.[61]

58 Stolze, "Friedrich Wilhelm I. und der Pietismus," 189.

59 Hellmuth Heyden, *Kirchengeschichte von Pommern*, vol. 1 (Stettin, 1937), 174–75; Hellmuth Heyden, "Die Kirchenpolitik in Pommern von der Teilung des Landes 1648 bis zur Mitte des 19. Jahrhunderts," *Baltische Studien*, N.F., 57 (1971), 55; Hermann Waterstraat, "Die Stettiner Geistlichkeit in ihrem Verhalten gegen Gustav Adolf von Schweden (1630) und Friedrich Wilhelm I. von Preussen während des Sequesters (1713–1720)," *Forschungen zur brandenburgischen und preussischen Geschichte*, 10 (1898): 120–28.

60 See above, pp. 195–98.

61 According to Hinrichs, Francke's decision was the result of his judgment that the social problems unleashed by the rapid military build-up were so threatening to Prussian society

As the 1720s progressed signs of closer, warmer cooperation began to proliferate. From 1722 on, correspondence between Francke and the king became more frequent, especially in connection with the construction, organization, and staffing of a military orphanage in Potsdam. In 1723 Frederick William acted on Pietist accusations of atheism against Christian Wolff and ordered him to leave the country within forty-eight hours.[62] Francke spent several weeks at the Berlin court in 1725, the same year that the king finally decided to give up his effort to negotiate a union between the two Protestant churches. When Francke died in 1727, Frederick William I immediately invited his two successors to come to his estate at Wusterhausen so that he could get to know them and establish a working relationship with them. In 1729 the king decreed that all candidates for Lutheran pastorates in the Hohenzollern kingdom were required to have studied at least two years at the University of Halle. When the Pietist community in Teschen was dispersed by Habsburg persecution in 1730, Frederick William gave its leader, Adam Steinmetz, a prominent post in the Lutheran church in the Magdeburg region.[63]

Frederick William I's most significant service to the Pietist movement, however, was to appoint Pietists from the new generation to high-ranking clerical positions in Pomerania and East Prussia, from which they were ultimately able to transform the church and school life of those lands in accordance with Halle Pietist ideals. Though the Pietists had possessed a foothold in eastern Pomerania since the 1690s, especially in Stargard,[64] control of the church in Stettin, the provincial capital, was firmly in orthodox hands when the king in 1726 appointed Johann Gottfried Hornejus provincial assistant superintendent. A former army chaplain at Potsdam and a Halle Pietist sympathizer, Hornejus faced a very difficult challenge when he arrived at Stettin. His boss, L. David Bollhagen, the general superintendent, was firmly committed to the orthodox cause, and

that he had no choice but to do what he could to alleviate the worst evils of the situation. Hinrichs, *Preussentum und Pietismus*, 155.

62 A purge of Wolff's followers from the Prussian university system followed thereafter. See Lewis White Beck, *Early German Philosophy: Kant and His Predecessors* (Cambridge, Mass., 1969), 259.

63 Wendland, "Märkischer Pietismus," 36, 39; Stolze, "Friedrich Wilhelm I. und der Pietismus," 190–94.

64 Heyden, *Kirchengeschichte von Pommern*, vol. 1, 201–03. For source material on the connection between Spener and this early Pietist presence in Pomerania, see Hellmuth Heyden, "Briefe Jacob Speners nach Stargard i. P.: Ein Beitrag zur Geschichte des Pietismus in Hinterpommern," *Baltische Studien*, N.F., 56 (1970): 57f.

Hornejus described the rank and file of the west Pomeranian clergy as possessing an "irreconcilable hatred against Halle Pietists." That Hornejus was not exaggerating is confirmed by the fact that Frederick William I was forced to issue a special decree in 1727 to protect Hornejus from his colleagues.[65]

Hornejus, however, persevered and in 1730 received the support of a zealous collaborator when Johann Christoph Schinmeyer, a Francke protégé, became a pastor at Stettin. Schinmeyer's impact was felt immediately as he was able to establish a Halle-style orphanage by 1732. Like its prototype, Schinmeyer's orphanage, benefiting from royal privileges, spawned a school network and even a formal teacher-training institute, the first in the Hohenzollern lands. The Pietist position in Pomerania was further strengthened in the 1730s when, in response to Bollhagen's foot dragging in executing a royal order for a province-wide visitation, the king demoted him to the position of superintendent of eastern Pomerania and raised Hornejus to the superintendency of the Stettin-based region. Although the controversial Schinmeyer was forced to relinquish his pastorate in 1737, in the following year Hornejus became superintendent of the Lutheran church for all of Pomerania and remained the leader of that church until his death in 1757.[66]

In East Prussia, Frederick William promoted the Pietist cause even more vigorously. After local opposition brought about the downfall of the Pietist Lysius in 1721, the king temporarily gave the native East Prussians primary responsibility for reconstructing school and church life in the province.[67] In the meantime, however, at the behest of Francke, he appointed in 1725 two arch-Halle Pietists, Abraham Wolff and Georg Friedrich Rogall, to professorships on the theological faculty at the University of Königsberg.[68] After becoming so passionately disillusioned with the indigenous elite in 1727, Frederick William pursued a militantly pro-Pietist policy.[69] In 1728 Wolff and Rogall received the power to review the

65 Heyden, "Die Kirchenpolitik in Pommern," 59–60.

66 Heyden, *Kirchengeschichte von Pommern*, vol. 1, 189, 204–05. In the 1730s and 1740s, the Zinzendorfian form of Pietism, the *Herrnhuter* movement, had a significant impact, especially in western Pomerania. See *ibid.*, 208–11. By the early nineteenth century, Pomerania had become a stronghold of evangelical Protestantism in Germany. See Stolze, "Friedrich Wilhelm I. und der Pietismus," 194.

67 Terveen, *Gesamtstaat und Retablissement*, 92–94, 117–21.

68 Stolze, "Friedrich Wilhelm I. und der Pietismus," 191.

69 Hinrichs, *Preussentum und Pietismus*, 257. In a memorandum by Frederick William I, quoted here by Hinrichs, the king affirmed that especially for the sake of Pomerania and East

credentials and approve the certification of all candidates for pastorates in East Prussia. In 1730 the king confirmed that certification by the two Pietist professors was required even for positions over which the local nobility held patronage rights. The result was a period of confrontation between the Pietist theologians and the local establishment. Wolff and Rogall contributed substantially to the charged atmosphere as they not infrequently preferred to leave pastorates vacant rather than fill them with candidates who failed to meet the strictest Pietist standards. When the anti-Pietist attacks were most threatening, the two Pietist leaders appealed, through Halle, for royal support; and Frederick William invariably came to their rescue by censuring and disciplining their opponents.[70]

In the course of the early to mid-1730s, this polarized situation in East Prussia resolved itself into a constructive partnership between the Pietist leadership in Königsberg and the provincial elite. When Wolff and Rogall both died prematurely, in 1731 and 1733 respectively, the direction of the Pietist movement at the University of Königsberg and in East Prussia passed to F. A. Schultz, whose approach was much less confrontational than that of his two predecessors. Thanks to Schultz, the theology program at the university became so effective and so popular that in 1734 he reported to the king that the Königsberg theology faculty was turning out so many students that it was no longer necessary to recruit Halle graduates to fill pastorate positions in East Prussia. A year later, Frederick William acknowledged the parity of the two programs by no longer requiring students from the University of Königsberg to study at Halle as well. Schultz's moderation and political skill also enabled him by the mid-1730s to gain the support of the hitherto anti-Pietist East Prussian estates for a comprehensive program of church and school reform. In 1736 the first spontaneous Pietist "awakening" in Königsberg took place, affecting people from all social groups and demonstrating that Pietism was well on its way to becoming assimilated into East Prussian society.[71]

In the other provinces of the Prussian realm, the Pietists did not have to contend with such strong orthodox opposition and did not need such forceful royal backing. In these areas, the strength of the

Prussia it was "very essential that I support the good Halle *Anstalten* out of love and obligation constantly to my grave, so help me God!"

[70] Terveen, *Gesamtstaat und Retablissement*, 95–96, 122–26.

[71] *Ibid.*, 127–28; Hinrichs, *Preussentum und Pietismus*, 265–77, 289–90.

Halle Pietist movement and the pro-Pietist employment policy of Frederick William I resulted in a very substantial deepening of an already existing Pietist presence. Available data on the university backgrounds of Lutheran pastors appointed to pastorates in Prussia between 1713 and 1740 confirm that virtually every successful candidate studied at either Halle or Jena[72] – the latter university being a tolerated exception to the Halle-only appointment policy since the leader of the Jena theological faculty from 1715 to 1729, Johann Franz Buddeus, was a Halle graduate of a distinction comparable to that of his mentor Francke.[73]

The resulting influx of large numbers of these Halle and Jena graduates into the Prussian clerical ranks changed forever the character of the Lutheran church in northeastern Germany.[74] Particularly in the Mark Brandenburg, the influence of Pietism became so strong during Frederick William I's reign that, in the words of church historian Walter Wendland, it "penetrated the entire popular culture" and "became rooted ... in the circles of artisans and simple folk."[75] The Pietist imprint on the religious life of Brandenburg was reflected in the appeal of the edificatory literature of the Berlin provost, Johann Porst, and above all of Porst's hymnal, which first appeared in 1708 and for the next 150 years was "almost

[72] Out of Georges Pariset's sample of 95 Lutheran clergy who became pastors in Prussia during the reign of Frederick William I, 52 matriculated at Halle, 55 at Jena, 17 at Leipzig, and 2 at Wittenberg (many followed the practice of the time by studying at more than one university). If anything, this sample is weighted in favor of Jena and Leipzig because 16 of these matriculations date before 1690, i.e. before the founding of the University of Halle, and matriculations after 1730 are greatly underrepresented. See Pariset, *L'état et les églises en Prusse*, 268–69. For corroborative evidence from the Neumark, see Wendland, "Märkischer Pietismus," 36.

[73] For a brief sketch of Buddeus's life, in addition to the source cited above (p. 114, n. 38), see the *Neue deutsche Biographie*, vol. II (Berlin, 1955), 715. For a suggestive account of the Buddeus/Jena network in Brandenburg – which consisted of former students who kept in contact with Buddeus, of clergy and teachers who recommended to him candidates for admission to the Jena theology program, and of people who wrote to Buddeus for spiritual and scholarly guidance – see Stupperich, "Aus dem kirchlichen Leben der Mark," 60–63.

[74] The scope of the Pietist influence among north German Protestant clergy in the eighteenth century is a central theme of a recent study by Anthony LaVopa, who not only affirms the sheer numbers of clergy who were trained at Halle, but also in a series of intellectual biographies shows the profound impact of Pietist ideas on key eighteenth-century cultural figures. See LaVopa, *Grace, Talent, and Merit*, 139 and *passim*.

[75] Wendland also notes in this connection that "Friedrich Nicolai, leader of the *Aufklärung* party in Berlin [in the 1770s and 1780s], was of the opinion that the *Bürger* and common people of Berlin must be classified as pietistic" in their religious orientation. See Wendland, "Märkischer Pietismus," 36.

more than the Bible *the* devotional book of the Brandenburg communities."[76]

Important as this extraordinary spread of Pietism through the Prussian Lutheran church was, it was only a part of a larger process of "Prussianization." The cultural impact on the population of an ever wider exposure to Pietist spirituality through such church-sponsored activities as sermons, catechization, schools, and prayer hours was strongly reinforced in the workplace by the pedagogical efforts of the king himself. With respect to the task of inculcating his ethic of obedience and hard work for the greater good of the Prussian state, Frederick William was not content simply to turn over the church and school system to the Pietists as Francke had proposed in his "Projekt" of 1704. The king was determined from the outset to train, with Pietist help, his own cadres and deploy them, in those institutions over which he had complete power of command – namely, the army and the bureaucracy. As the following chapter will make clear, Frederick William, feeling the same need to impose his behavioral norms on those under his institutional control, used pedagogical techniques identical to those of the Halle Pietists to turn Prussian soldiers and bureaucrats into transmitters of State Pietism to the rest of the Prussian people.

[76] *Ibid.*, 36–37, 40. For more biographical information on Porst, see Walter Delius, "Aus dem Briefwechsel des Berliner Propstes Johann Porst mit A. H. Francke in Halle," *Jahrbuch für Berlin-Brandenburgische Kirchengeschichte*, 39 (1964): 89–96. In the following pages (97–113), Delius presents excerpts from Porst's correspondence with Francke, which consisted of 82 letters written between 1712 and 1727. Most of these dealt with recommendations for candidates to study at the University of Halle, to enroll in the Halle *Anstalten* schools, or teach in the *Anstalten* complex. Some of Porst's letters also inform or solicit Francke's opinion on state–church relations or ask Francke to recommend names of candidates for possible appointment to pastorates in Berlin and the surrounding area.

CHAPTER 10

The impact of Pietist pedagogy on the Prussian army and bureaucracy

THE COMMON SOLDIERS

Although Frederick William had made most of the day-to-day decisions in his father's government since the coup of December 1710, he did not have the freedom to carry out his own policies until the death of Frederick I in February 1713. When Frederick William I ascended the throne, he was already quite familiar with the inner workings of state institutions and had no doubts about the necessity of completely overhauling them. Frederick had hardly been buried, therefore, when Frederick William began to put his radical plans into effect. In order to increase the overall size of the army while simultaneously eliminating from it men of smaller physical stature, Frederick William I instituted a drastic policy of forced recruitment throughout the kingdom. Impressment gangs seized tall and strong young men from peasant households, merchants' stores, artisans' shops, and university lecture halls.[1] Through such arbitrary methods, Frederick William I increased the size of his army by nine thousand men in 1713 alone, and the pace of recruitment slackened only marginally in the next several years.[2]

Assembling this much larger army was only the first step. Frederick William knew that to compete with the still larger armies of Europe's major states his own forces had to be qualitatively superior in discipline, tactical maneuverability, and fire power. To achieve this desired capability, Frederick William sought to extend to his entire army the daily drill that he and Prince Leopold von Anhalt-

[1] Besides incurring the opposition of the Halle Pietists, the recruiters created such insecurity among the population in Prussian Pomerania that young men fled in large numbers to Mecklenburg or Swedish Pomerania to try to escape impressment. See Berthold Schulze, "Die Kantone Pommerns, 1733–1786," *Baltische Studien*, N.F., 38 (1936): 266.

[2] Carl Hinrichs, "Der Regierungsantritt Friedrich Wilhelms I.," *Jahrbuch für die Geschichte Mittel- und Ostdeutschlands*, 5 (1956): 218–21.

Dessau had instituted among a few select units during the campaign of 1709. This proved to be a difficult pedagogical task, in large part because of the hostility of the troops to the heavy demands placed on them by the drilling exercises. The troops' resistance to drill was only one indicator, however, of the type of problems facing those seeking to make these men into highly effective soldiers. For it is easy to see why the recruits were hard to motivate. The methods by which these people were recruited left most of them bitterly resentful toward the military authorities. In addition, although some common soldiers were the sons of well-off peasants and townspeople, most came from the desperately poor, culturally deprived rural population of Prussia or from streets, taverns, and prisons throughout Germany.[3]

Probably only strict rules and the toughest possible enforcement could have maintained military discipline among such men. In July 1713 Frederick William I issued the first of a series of regulatory "articles" that spelled out the required code of conduct. Common soldiers had to maintain high levels of personal cleanliness, take special care of their uniforms, behave in an upright fashion, and obey their officers unquestioningly. To enforce these standards, officers and noncoms were obliged to carry batons with them at all times, on and off duty. Beyond continual canings, the typical soldier could expect a far worse fate if he were found guilty of a major offense. The most common punishment was having to run a gauntlet of some two hundred men. And not just once. Drunkenness was punished by eight to ten runs; disobeying or talking back to an officer by up to thirty runs (spread over three days). Other punishments included consignment to hard labor on a fortress-building detail or death (for theft or repeated desertions).[4]

Necessary as such external discipline may have been, Frederick William I saw his most important task as creating a spirit of voluntary obedience among the troops. Facilitating the achievement of that goal were a variety of psychological and socioeconomic factors. As William McNeill points out, the rhythmic movements of parade-ground exercises can create bonds of social solidarity powerful enough to offset some of the stresses of military life.[5] The king's

[3] Jany, *Geschichte der Königlich Preussischen Armee*, vol. I, 711. See also Redlich, *The German Military Enterpriser*, vol. II, 180.

[4] Jany, *Geschichte der Königlich Preussischen Armee*, vol. I, 712–14.

[5] William H. McNeill, *The Pursuit of Power: Technology, Armed Force, and Society since A.D. 1000* (Chicago, 1982), 131–32.

frequent appearances on the drill fields and the delight he evinced in mingling with his uniformed "children" certainly reinforced the soldiers' group pride.[6]

Moreover, after about 1720 the rate of increase in the army's size slowed appreciably, thereby making possible the gradual appearance of a more orderly recruiting system within Prussia. Selected youngsters from each recruiting district (*Kanton*) were "enrolled" as adolescents and eventually joined the locally stationed regiment within a few years. After a two-year training period, each *Kantonist* was allowed to return to his village or town on furlough for nine months a year. Even troops recruited from abroad were eventually allowed to work as laborers or artisans for several months a year in the garrison towns where their regiments were quartered.[7] Besides their obvious economic benefits, such procedures mitigated one of the eighteenth-century soldier's most demoralizing fears: the sense that being recruited by the army meant the end of any hope for a normal life.

Frederick William I, however, demanded more from his troops than a subconscious affirmation of, or resigned acquiescence to, their fate. He wanted them to share his belief that to endure suffering in this world was the duty of the God-fearing individual. Accordingly, the king did everything he could to promote a Pietist acceptance of hard work and self-sacrifice among the common soldiers. In 1718 he reorganized the military church, separating it totally from the still largely orthodox-controlled civilian church. As director of the military church, he appointed, as already noted, Lampertus Gedicke, a former instructor at the Halle *Paedagogium*, later a chaplain at the Berlin garrison. The new provost was in charge of recruiting and supervising chaplains for the rapidly expanding army, and he aggressively used his position to make the military church a stronghold of Halle Pietism. Although regimental commanders still formally retained the authority to nominate chaplain candidates, Gedicke quickly acquired *de facto* control over the selection process and actually appointed most of the chaplains himself.[8] With Frederick William's blessing, Gedicke capitalized on his connection with Francke to fill as many of these positions as

6 Hinrichs, "Der Regierungsantritt Friedrich Wilhelms I.," 218.

7 Büsch, *Militärsystem und Sozialleben*, 18–19.

8 Hinrichs, *Preussentum und Pietismus*, 157; Langhäuser, *Das Militärkirchenwesen*, 32–33; Hartmut Rudolph, *Das evangelische Militärkirchenwesen in Preussen* (Göttingen, 1973), 22.

possible with theology graduates from Halle.[9] Thus, for example, over half of the army chaplains appointed to regiments stationed in East Prussia between 1714 and 1736 had matriculated with the theology faculty of the University of Halle.[10]

The army chaplain's job consisted of inculcating in the troops the concept of a moral order, the notion that they must accept God's purpose in putting them in their present situation. Resistance to this message from the alienated and disaffected men was often intense. When chaplain Michaelis first assumed his duties in Potsdam, he needed a bodyguard to escort him on his daily rounds.[11] The king did his best to assist the chaplains by regularly attending services at the newly built garrison churches in Berlin and Potsdam, indulging his taste for Pietist sermonizing in the process.[12] He also required officers personally to march their soldiers into church on Sundays and post sentries at the door to make sure no one left.[13] In the words of a contemporary observer, the Prussian soldiers "were conducted [to church] by their Officers, in the same Order, and with the same Silence, as if they were going to Battle."[14]

Under such circumstances the one hundred or more chaplains carried out their pastoral labors. Like Francke in his early days at Glaucha, they soon discovered that the ignorance and illiteracy of the parishioners constituted a major barrier to the success of their mission. On their own initiative many chaplains started special

9 Frederick William I explicitly instructed Gedicke to correspond with Francke regarding suitable candidates. According to Karl Weiske, Gedicke wrote at least fifty letters to Francke between 1712 and 1727, in which personnel matters were a dominant theme. Weiske, "Pietistische Stimmen aus der Mark Brandenburg," *Jahrbuch für brandenburgische Kirchengeschichte*, 24 (1929): 206.

10 This conclusion rests on a comparison between the list compiled by Friedwald Moeller of *Militärpfarrer* serving regiments garrisoned in East Prussia during the eighteenth century and the *Matrikel* of the University of Halle between 1690 and 1730. See Moeller, *Altpreussisches evangelisches Pfarrerbuch von der Reformation bis zur Vertreibung im Jahre 1945*, vol. 1 (Hamburg, 1968), 238, 240, 241; Zimmermann and Juntke, eds., *Matrikel der Martin-Luther-Universität-Halle-Wittenberg*. The drop-off in Halle appointments beginning in 1737 was almost certainly a result of the previously discussed emergence of the University of Königsberg as a center of Pietism comparable to Halle itself.

11 Hinrichs, *Preussentum und Pietismus*, 163.

12 If the king happened to take a liking to a particular preacher, the result could be rapid promotion to high position. Gedicke's rise from Berlin garrison chaplain to provost of the military church was almost certainly due to the king's positive, personal response to sermons he heard Gedicke preach in Prussian military camps during the Pomeranian campaign in 1715. See Weiske, "Pietistische Stimmen aus der Mark Brandenburg," 208.

13 Langhäuser, *Das Militärkirchenwesen*, 37, 43–44.

14 Elézar de Mauvillon, *The Life of Frederick William I, late King of Prussia: Containing many Authentick Letters and Pieces*, trans. William Phelips (London, 1750), 524.

classes to teach reading and writing to the soldiers and their wives.[15] Initial opposition to these efforts was often very great, though in one recorded instance a chaplain succeeded in motivating the men to read the Bible by appealing to their soldiers' sense of pride.[16] Catechization of the adults could also be a long and tedious process. Every soldier and soldier's wife who took communion was examined on the catechism. The chaplain carefully recorded their responses in a book listing all his communicants. Next to these entries he often added such notes as: "Promised, however, with many tears, to better himself."[17] Those who committed serious moral offenses were required to undergo "public church penance," in which they confessed their sins to the assembled congregations. As a last resort, chaplains had the power to excommunicate the "unrepentant or irreconcilable." Perhaps the most difficult duty of all for the chaplain was to counsel deserters condemned to death shortly before their execution.[18]

The mission of the military church also extended to educating the soldiers' children. There was no way for the civilian schools in the garrison towns to accommodate the large numbers of these materially and often culturally deprived youngsters.[19] The centerpiece for the military school system designed to fill this need was the military orphanage at Potsdam. Although in 1720 Francke declined Frederick William's offer to personally organize and direct the orphanage, the Pietist leader did supply the king a detailed plan of the Halle facility. On that basis, Frederick William I went ahead with the project on his own. The orphanage opened its doors in November 1724 to 179 children and four Halle-trained teachers. The youngsters in the orphanage, whose numbers reached over fourteen hundred by 1740, were not exclusively orphans; some merely had parents judged incapable of raising their children "in Christianity."[20]

Designed to educate the boys and girls "in the service of God and one's neighbor," the curriculum of the orphanage school and the

[15] Hinrichs, *Preussentum und Pietismus*, 163.
[16] Erich Schild, *Der preussische Feldprediger*, vol. 1 (Eisleben, 1888), 8.
[17] Langhäuser, *Das Militärkirchenwesen*, 38; Hinrichs, *Preussentum und Pietismus*, 164.
[18] Hinrichs, *Preussentum und Pietismus*, 164–65. For similar accounts by Gedicke and Hornejus of the trials of being a chaplain in the Prussian army, see Weiske, "Pietistische Stimmen aus der Mark Brandenburg," 202–03, 218.
[19] Friedrich Wienecke, *Das preussische Garnisonschulwesen* (Berlin, 1907), 6.
[20] Hinrichs, *Preussentum und Pietismus*, 166–67; Jany, *Geschichte der Königlich Preussischen Armee*, vol. 1, 722.

hundreds of regimental schools founded throughout the kingdom in the 1720s emphasized discipline, the catechism, and basic reading skills.[21] Many officers contributed funds to support these schools, especially to furnish them with Bibles, New Testaments, hymn books, and catechisms. The regimental chaplain supervised the schools under his jurisdiction; the teaching staff consisted mainly of discharged non-commissioned officers. In theory at least, every child of a military family was supposed to acquire literacy skills, since Frederick William I ordered chaplains not to confirm young people who could not read.[22]

How effective was this combination of precise rules, ferocious discipline, vocational opportunity, Pietist exhortation, and systematic education? It would be absurd to assert that the troops' sense of alienation or the social problems stemming from their poverty were overcome in any definitive way, especially in places such as Berlin where large numbers of army personnel were concentrated.[23] Fritz Redlich was surely right, however, when he observed that the "achievement and devotion of the Prussian common soldier in the three Silesian wars (fought between 1740 and 1763) exclude the assumption that the troops were held together only by the cane."[24] The image of a loyal soldiery is confirmed by a desertion rate of only 1 percent per year between 1727 and 1740, "a small percentage by eighteenth-century standards."[25] Despite the terrors and humiliations perpetrated by the noncoms, the Prussian soldier gradually developed a sense of pride in being one of the king's "children." By the mid-eighteenth century many furloughed *Kantonisten* in fact had such a well-developed sense of self-worth that their noble masters found them insufficiently obsequious and deferential.[26]

[21] Langhäuser, *Das Militärkirchenwesen*, 42.

[22] *Ibid.*, 41; Wienecke, *Das preussische Garnisonschulwesen*, 5–9.

[23] For the seamier sides of garrison life, see August Skalweit, "Die Eingliederung des friderizianischen Heeres in den Volks- und Wirtschaftskörper," *Jahrbücher für Nationalökonomie und Statistik*, 160 (1944): 215f.

[24] Redlich, *The German Military Enterpriser*, vol. II, 202.

[25] Willerd R. Fann, "Peacetime Attrition in the Army of Frederick William I, 1713–1740," *Central European History*, 11 (1978): 326. It would be naive, however, to underestimate the restraining effects of the system which Frederick William I set up to make desertion extremely difficult, especially in peacetime. For the elaborate regulations designed to "encourage" the civilian population to turn in deserters, see Frederick William I, "Instruktion ... für das General- ... Direktorium ... 1722," in Schmoller *et al.*, eds., *Die Behördenorganisation*, vol. III, 600–01. See also Christopher Duffy, *The Army of Frederick the Great* (London, 1974), 66–67, where Duffy compares the Prussian army on campaign under Frederick the Great to a "mobile prison."

[26] Jany, *Geschichte der Königlich Preussischen Armee*, vol. I, 711.

Another indication that the soldiers' behavior had attained a reasonably high standard of orderliness was the very viability of the garrison system instituted by Frederick William I. Under the Great Elector and Frederick III (I), no permanent method for garrisoning troops was developed, in part because during the long frequent periods of war most of the army was fighting outside the borders of the Hohenzollern lands. When during this pre-1713 period it was necessary for the dynasty's troops to live off the home territories, the units were moved quickly from place to place since their relationship to civilian society was an unregulated, essentially predatory one.[27] One of the most radical changes Frederick William I made was to garrison his much larger peacetime army in the cities and towns of the kingdom, with even very small urban communities' being compelled to host at least one company on a more or less permanent basis.[28] With barracks available only in the large cities, and even there just for troops passing through and not for the regular garrisons, soldiers had to be quartered in the homes of urban *Bürger* on a very large scale.[29]

How the adjustment to this unprecedented situation was made is an as yet untold story, though it is an important aspect of the social history of early eighteenth-century Prussia. All existing accounts affirm, however, that by the end of Frederick William I's reign a surprisingly complete integration of the civilian and military sectors of society had been achieved.[30] The positive impact of the garrison on the towns' economies was undoubtedly a factor in the communities' acceptance of the military presence, but that outcome still

27 Wilhelm Rohr, "Märkische Garnisonen im 18. Jahrhundert," *Brandenburgische Jahrbücher*, 2 (1936): 110.

28 Even a cursory glance at the data on seventeenth- and eighteenth-century Prussian garrisons compiled by Günther Gieraths would reveal how ubiquitously the presence of Frederick William I's army pervaded Prussian urban society. In heavily agrarian East Prussia, for example, no fewer than 54 towns and cities hosted garrisons for a minimum of five years during the reign of the *Soldatenkönig*. See Gieraths, *Die Kampfhandlungen der brandenburgisch-preussischen Armee, 1626–1807* (Berlin, 1964), 592–618. By the death of Frederick the Great in 1786, the militarization of Brandenburg had reached the point that there were as many troops garrisoned there then as there were in July 1914. Rohr, "Märkische Garnisonen," 110.

29 In the East Prussian community of Heiligenbeil, for example, 1,300 civilian inhabitants were obliged to quarter in their often small, primitive homes over 400 soldiers, a considerable number of whom had a wife and children with them. Walther Grosse, "Kleine ostpreussische Garnison vor 250 Jahren," *Der redliche Ostpreusse*, 17 (1966): 81.

30 As evidence for an overall good relationship between the garrisoned soldiers and the residents of small East Prussian towns, Grosse cites the "very numerous" instances of *Bürger* who served as godparents for soldiers' children. *Ibid.*, 82.

would not have occurred unless the Prussian soldiers had attained such levels of self-discipline that civilians no longer hesitated to mix with them.[31] This was indeed a "tremendous educational achievement,"[32] a product of the diligence of the cadre groups responsible for the common soldiers and the townspeople: the army chaplains, the officer corps, and the royal bureaucrats. How the latter two groups of functionaries became such effective instruments of the royal will is the subject of the final two sections of this chapter.

THE OFFICER CORPS

The state of the Prussian officer corps in 1713 reflected the methods by which the Great Elector and Frederick III(I) had built up the original power base of the Hohenzollern monarchy. Aware that the bulk of the Junker elite was content in its provincialism and opposed to any changes in its traditional way of life, the two rulers elected not to try transforming the attitudes of these aristocrats. Instead, they brought into a Lutheran country large numbers of Reformed foreigners to serve as their top aides and as army officers, bureaucrats, and entrepreneurs. Though some members of the native elite joined the ruling groups associated with the Berlin court, most of the Junker aristocrats and town patricians held aloof from a regime whose character they judged primarily in terms of its heterodox religion and its constant demands for higher taxes.[33]

Even with regard to the collection of noblemen, ambitious commoners, Huguenot refugees, and foreign adventurers that constituted the pre-1713 officer corps, the state did not attempt to change its mores, which were those generally associated with seventeenth-century European officers. The gentleman–soldier of the day belonged to an international society of privileged individuals, who in some cases possessed considerable learning and a cosmopolitan outlook. Regardless of the level of cultural attainment, however, contemporary officers tended to look on their military activities as

31 For an essay which argues that in the long run the soldiers' presence improved the discipline and morality of the civilian population, see D. Forberg, "Entwurf einer Entstehungsgeschichte der Garnison der Stadt Insterburg," *Zeitschrift der Altertumsgesellschaft Insterburg*, 18 (1925): 39.

32 Redlich, *The German Military Enterpriser*, vol. II, 206–07.

33 The lack of connection between the native nobility and the officer corps is demonstrated by the fact that in the first years of Frederick William I's reign many Junkers supported their peasants' resistance to impressment. See Büsch, *Militärsystem und Sozialleben*, 79–80.

only one part of a multi-faceted existence.[34] Eager for the glory that they could win through bravery in battle, these cavaliers cared little about the training and provisioning of the soldiers they led. Their common practice was to collect payments from their warlord for maintaining their troops and then to spend as little of that sum on their men as possible. Such commanders generally did not make long-term commitments to the service of any one lord, preferring instead to seek the best available opportunity for the riches and renown their fighting spirits could bring them.[35]

Frederick William I was determined to transform both the composition and values of the Prussian officer corps. The king intended to build his officer cadre around the native nobility in order to overcome the sense of separation between the Junkers and the state as well as use their social status to help enforce discipline in the ranks.[36] As was also the case with the common soldiers, Frederick William did not shrink from coercive measures in assembling the personnel needed to carry out his overall plan. The king ordered every royal official in the countryside to submit yearly lists of all the noble families in his district, including information on the number, ages, and current occupations of each family's sons.[37] On identifying a likely candidate for officer training, Frederick William would contact his family to urge them to have the boy join the cadet corps in Berlin. In such instances, the king argued that it lay in the young man's interest to be "instructed in Christianity and introduced to the academic skills and military exercises necessary" for a successful army career.[38] If, as frequently happened, persuasion did not achieve the desired results, the king's agents would kidnap however many Junkers' sons were needed to fill the vacancies in the Berlin corps of cadets.[39] Frederick William also kept his district commissars busy monitoring the activities of young noblemen to discourage them from entering the service of another prince.[40] Those who did

[34] Friedrich-Karl Tharau, *Die geistige Kultur des preussischen Offiziers von 1640 bis 1806* (Mainz, 1968), 60.

[35] *Ibid.*; Carl Hinrichs, "Preussen als historisches Problem: Zur heutigen Auffassung Friedrich Wilhelms I.," in Hinrichs, *Preussen als historisches Problem*, 29; see also above, pp. 57–58.

[36] Büsch, *Militärsystem und Sozialleben*, 82.

[37] Hinrichs, "Preussen als historisches Problem," 28.

[38] Tharau, *Die geistige Kultur*, 63.

[39] Jany, *Geschichte der Königlich Preussischen Armee*, vol. I, 726–27.

[40] Frederick William I, "Instruktion ... für das General- ... Direktorium ... 1722," in Schmoller *et al.*, eds., *Die Behördenorganisation*, vol. III, 592. In thus restricting foreign travel by sons of the native well-born, the king was motivated not only by the desire to prevent

were convicted of desertion *in absentia* and never allowed to return to their homeland.

Frederick William's recruitment policies used the carrot as well as the stick. The Prussian monarch took a number of steps designed to enhance the prestige and social solidarity of the officer corps. One of his first acts as king was to issue a revised order of ranks. In this new listing of the hierarchy of titles and offices by which salaries and court standing were determined, military positions dominated the upper end of the scale in an unprecedentedly lopsided fashion.[41] Frederick William further sought to elevate the status of military service by establishing a special relationship between the officer corps and the kingship.[42] To symbolize his own feelings of identity with his officers, the king never wore anything at court but the uniform of a regimental commander. All officers were required to wear that same type of uniform, not only to demonstrate their close relationship with the king but also to minimize the differences of wealth and lineage among themselves.[43] Socially and vocationally, Frederick William I did not distinguish between the wealthiest magnate of the Old Mark and the poorest country squire from Pomerania; all officers had equal, immediate access to the king.[44] The royal policy of selecting officers almost exclusively from the native Prussian nobility further stimulated a sense of cohesion within the officer elite.

Highly significant though they were, such incentives alone could not have created the new type of officer desired by Frederick William I. Not only did the king want a socially homogeneous, native Prussian office corps, but he also demanded a total commitment on the part of his officers to the ideology of State Pietism. Having raised the officer cadre to be the highest status group in

"defections" but also by the fear that those who did study or work outside the country would be spiritually "contaminated" by the "sinfulness" of alien, allegedly more worldly ways. Frederick William put forward this latter consideration as his justification for prohibiting the sons of the Reformed clergy from studying abroad, even though this had been customary since the conversion of John Sigismund in 1613. Thadden, *Die Brandenburgisch-preussischen Hofprediger*, 91–92.

41 Hinrichs, "Der Regierungsantritt Friedrich Wilhelms I.," 200.

42 It is important to remember that in European society at that time even the rank of colonel did not in itself confer any particular distinction. See Redlich, *The German Military Enterpriser*, vol. II, 165.

43 The uniform became known, significantly as the *Königs Rock*. Duffy, *The Army of Frederick the Great*, 24.

44 Jany, *Geschichte der Königlich Preussischen Armee*, vol. I, 728; Redlich, *The German Military Enterpriser*, vol. II, 122, 127, 128.

society, Frederick William simultaneously sought to discipline his officers to make them obedient instruments.[45] For the Prussian officer, the type of obedience required by the king entailed a complete break from the cavalier conception of his vocation. In keeping with his Pietist work ethic, Frederick William expected his officers to make fulfillment of their vocational duty the overriding factor in their lives.[46]

In contrast with the traditional aristocratic way of life, the Prussian officer was not only to have a narrower vocational focus but also was compelled to assume a much greater variety of responsibilities as part of his command. He had to perform with utmost seriousness the tasks of accountant, drillmaster, quartermaster, and recruiter – as well as leader in battle.[47] In the terminology of State Pietism, to discharge these obligations diligently and efficiently, in perfect obedience to royal commands, demonstrated "faithfulness in service" (*Treue im Dienst*). As such faithfulness brought honor to the King of Prussia and benefit to the country, it conferred honor (*Ehre*) on the officer.[48] In other words, faithful performance of even routine duties deserved the reward of "honor" because it contributed to the good of the state. Such a reevaluation of the concept of *Ehre* becomes comprehensible only when one considers the "almost mystical" quality that the state possessed in the value system of Frederick William I and eventually came to assume in that of the Prussian officer corps as well.[49]

45 In the 1722 "Instruktion König Friedrich Wilhelms I. für seinen Nachfolger," Frederick William I described his ideal conception of the nobility's role: "from their youth on, the entire nobility should be educated in your service and know no other sovereigns [*Herren*] than God and the King in Prussia." Quoted in Dietrich, ed., *Die politischen Testamente*, 78.

46 Tharau, *Die geistige Kultur*, 62; see also Wolfgang Roehder, *Das Staatserziehungswerk Friedrich Wilhelms I. von Preussen: Die Formung des preussischen Menschen* (Heidelberg, 1937), 42–44. The latter work, written from an unabashedly Nazi viewpoint, is indicative of how easily the cultural legacy of Prussian pedagogy could be, and was, coopted by Nazism.

47 Hinrichs, "Friedrich Wilhelm I.: König von Preussen," 60; Tharau, *Die geistige Kultur*, 61.

48 For the central significance of *Ehre* in the value system of the Prussian officer corps, see Büsch, *Militärsystem und Sozialleben*, 92.

49 Scharfenort, "Friedrich Wilhelm I. über die Erziehung der militärischen Jugend," *Jahrbuch für die deutsche Armee und Marine*, 91 (1894): 277; Redlich, *The German Military Enterpriser*, vol. II, 145. In 1718 the king dramatized the difference in ethos between the officer corps of his army and those of other princes by ordering that the standard uniform for his officers use much less cloth and be of a much plainer style than the prevalent mode in that Rococo age. To clinch his point, in the year following this *Stilbruch*, Frederick William invited the French ambassador to a troop review at Tempelhof, then a village far from the center of Berlin, where he deliberately dressed his worst troops in the uniforms then in fashion at the Versailles court and made sure that their relative ineptitude was made painfully obvious to

The internalization of this "State Pietism" supplied the motivation for the energetic obedience that became characteristic of the Prussian officer corps. The virtual absence of this set of values in either the officer corps of 1713 or in the great majority of Junker families makes its acceptance during the reign of Frederick William I explicable only in terms of an intensive educational campaign. The key to this campaign was the creation, between 1716 and 1721, of a new institution, the Berlin cadet corps (*Kadettenanstalt*) through the gradual consolidation of the existing cadet academies at Colberg, Magdeburg, and Berlin.[50] The king took this step because he wanted to impose his own form of training on the prospective officer elite. The older academies had concerned themselves primarily with providing a "general education fit for contemporary aristocrats," thereby reflecting the less vocationally specialized conception of the noble officer's way of life.[51] The type of training that would be given at the *Kadettenanstalt* reflected, however, Frederick William's desire to instill in each cadet a strict discipline (something he believed to be lacking in the academies), combined with instruction in subjects that would be of practical use in the future officer's later career.[52]

The methods employed in educating the cadets strongly resembled those used by the Pietists in the schools of the Halle *Anstalten*. Since many of the young men (their ages ranged from eleven to twenty-one) had been forcibly recruited or were disinclined for other reasons to submit to the school's regimen, the institution placed an initial emphasis on breaking the wills of its pupils. Incoming cadets were immediately confronted with a strict conduct code as well as a full, holiday-free schedule of classes, military drill, and religious observances. The cadets were under constant supervision by either staff or cadet "officers," and the discipline was brutal.

all present. Gisela Krause, *Altpreussische Uniformfertigung als Vorstufe der Bekleidungsindustrie* (Hamburg, 1965), 15–17.

50 A. Crousaz, *Geschichte des Königlichen Preussischen Kadetten-Corps nach seiner Entstehung, seinem Entwicklungsgange und seinen Resultaten* (Berlin, 1857), 48–49.

51 Redlich, *The German Military Enterpriser*, vol. II, 151.

52 Crousaz, *Geschichte des Königlichen Preussischen Kadetten-Corps*, 50, 59. Not coincidentally, the type of education received by the cadets was nearly identical with that of Crown Prince Frederick. For a description of Frederick William I's plan for his eldest son's education, see Pierre Gaxotte, *Frederick the Great*, trans. R. A. Bell (New Haven, 1942), 7–10. The fundamental affinity between the pedagogical methods of Frederick William I and Francke becomes manifest when one compares Crown Prince Frederick's education with a startlingly similar plan for the education of a prince drawn up by Francke in 1704. For the latter, see Deppermann, *Der hallesche Pietismus*, 151.

Besides caning, the stocks or detention were the customary methods of punishment, though on at least three occasions major outbreaks of violence forced the staff to sentence the guilty parties to hard labor on the fortress-building detail.[53]

As was the case with all the king's educational endeavors, the cadet corps's primary purpose was to teach subordination of the young nobleman's will to the diligent execution of orders. In inculcating this mentality, the teaching staff relied heavily on religious exhortation. At the beginning and end of each day, the resident chaplain led the cadets in half-hour prayer sessions, which also included hymn singing and Bible reading.[54] To underscore the importance of these gatherings the corps commander and all the staff officers attended the evening session. Although formal classroom instruction in religion amounted to only two hours a week, on Sundays the cadets spent most of the day learning the catechism and attending church services. It was no accident that Frederick William appointed as first commander of the cadet corps Colonel Finck von Finckenstein, one of the strongest supporters of Halle Pietism in the Prussian army.[55]

The lessons taught in the *Kadettenanstalt* were repeated over and over again once the young cadet left the corps to join a regiment as a non-commissioned officer.[56] In this capacity, he underwent a further period of apprenticeship, lasting at least three years, during which he spent most of his time drilling the common soldiers. Frederick William I prescribed a puritanical code of behavior for his future regimental commanders by issuing orders prohibiting them from going into debt, playing cards, drinking excessively, and so on.[57] Superior officers, whom the king held responsible for any

53 Crousaz, *Geschichte des Königlichen Preussischen Kadetten-Corps*, 73, 79, 83; see also Bernhard Poten, *Geschichte des Militär- Erziehungs- und Bildungswesens in Preussen* (Berlin, 1896), 55; Roehder, *Das Staatserziehungswerk*, 50.

54 Crousaz, *Geschichte des Königlichen Preussischen Kadetten-Corps*, 55–56; Scharfenort, "Friedrich Wilhelm I. über die Erziehung der militärischen Jugend," 278.

55 Hinrichs, *Preussentum und Pietismus*, 170.

56 According to Duffy, one-third of the eighteenth-century Prussian officer corps was trained at the *Kadettenanstalt*. Duffy, *The Army of Frederick the Great*, 28. Other preferred educational institutions for future officers were the *Paedagogium* at Halle and the *Paedagogium* attached to the orphanage at Züllichau in the Neumark, founded in 1719 by Siegmund Steinbart, a pious master needle maker. The Züllichau complex received royal privileges similar to its Halle model, and by 1732 a book publishing business was established there; throughout the eighteenth century, it continued to receive large gifts from officer circles. Hinrichs, *Preussentum und Pietismus*, 340–42.

57 Jany, *Geschichte der Königlich Preussischen Armee*, vol. 1, 723, 734.

subordinates' misdeeds, closely supervised the young drillmasters. Failure to live up to the conduct codes was severely punished; continual violations could mean that the noncom would never be promoted. Every year the regimental commander was required to submit reports on the vocational performance and moral conduct of every noncom and officer under his command. The king carefully read each of these reports and made them the basis of his personal examinations of individual noncoms and officers.[58] In this manner, the king himself decided on all cases of possible promotion; indeed, the system of strict rules and constant surveillance extended all the way up the military hierarchy. Regimental staff officers were continually obliged to inspect the company commanders under them, and the king conducted personal inspections of the mustered regiments as often as he could.[59]

In the never ending process of educating his officers, the king adhered to the teaching methods of the *Kadettenanstalt* and complemented enforcement of external discipline with a strong emphasis on religion. Frederick William himself served as an influential role model by means of his regular church attendance, daily Bible reading, and frequent prayer. He also distributed Bibles periodically to officers, cadets, and common soldiers.[60] The king's exhortations would have remained limited in effect, however, were it not for the reinforcement they received from Halle Pietism. The Halle-trained army chaplains preached to, and heard confession from, officers as well as common soldiers. In addition, there were many Pietist supporters among the officer corps. In Berlin alone, besides Natzmer and Finckenstein, three prominent generals – Löben, Wartensleben, and Gersdorff – exerted considerable influence on behalf of the movement.[61]

At the beginning of Frederick William's reign, Leopold von Anhalt-Dessau, whose prestige in the army was second only to the king's, acted as the center of anti-Pietist feeling in the officer corps. But Frederick William deliberately stationed Leopold's regiment in Halle so that, even though Leopold never "converted" in a Pietist sense, eventually he decided it was necessary to reach an under-

[58] Hinrichs, "Preussen als historisches Problem," 29; Tharau, *Die geistige Kultur*, 63; Jany, *Geschichte der Königlich Preussischen Armee*, vol. 1, 723.
[59] Jany, *Geschichte der Königlich Preussischen Armee*, vol. 1, 732–33.
[60] Hinrichs, *Preussentum und Pietismus*, 160.
[61] *Ibid.*, 154.

standing with Francke. In 1720 Leopold asked the Pietist leader to preach before his regiment and afterwards had the sermon printed and widely distributed among officers in Berlin. Christianity soon became *de rigueur* among the officer elite and remained "in great esteem" even during the succeeding reign of the deist Frederick.[62]

Thus during the formative period in the history of the Prussian officer corps, the Pietism of Francke and that of Frederick William I combined in shaping its characteristic ethos, based on self-sacrifice in service to God and state and on a practical, efficient, non-ceremonial approach to the business at hand. English observers of Frederick the Great's army were most struck by the humorlessness of the Prussian military elite, by their "pensive attention to duty," and by a "staid, serious appearance, exceedingly different from the grave, dissipated, *dégagé* air of British or French officers."[63] Though behind this collective persona widely diverse personal attitudes toward Christianity undoubtedly existed, the official support of religion and the existence of a significant number of officers with Pietist beliefs made it much easier for the army chaplains to perform their mission among the common soldiers. The spirit of discipline and obedience that so permeated the military also exerted an important influence over the civilian bureaucracy, which, as we shall presently see, constituted yet another Prussian institution formed by the pedagogy of Frederick William I.

THE BUREAUCRACY

The development of the Prussian bureaucracy during the reign of Frederick William I paralleled the simultaneous transformation of the officer corps. In both cases the king inherited a heterogeneous elite group whose members lacked a strong commitment to serving the state. Like their military counterparts, early eighteenth-century bureaucrats typically failed to expend much effort on their official responsibilities, devoting their energies instead to enriching them-

62 *Ibid.*, 148–51. Note, for example, Anton Büsching's remark, "Religion stood in great esteem and was loved and practiced by generals, officers, and common soldiers alike." Quoted in G. Meyer, "Der Hallenser Pietismus August Hermann Franckes in seinem Verhältnis zum brandenburgisch-preussischen Staat," *Jahrbuch der Schlesischen Friedrich Wilhelms Universität zu Breslau*, 10 (1965): 69. For a list of prominent commanders in Frederick's army "who combined the soldier's profession with 'true Christianity,'" see Duffy, *The Army of Frederick the Great*, 47.

63 Duffy, *The Army of Frederick the Great*, 52.

selves through bribe-taking and embezzlement.[64] Just as he did with the officers, Frederick William aimed to instill in his bureaucrats a spirit of obedience to his authority and diligence in the performance of duty. Since the gap between the prevailing mentality in the bureaucracy and the king's requirements was as great as in the case of the officer corps, the task of bringing the body of civil servants up to his standards presented no less a challenge to Frederick William's pedagogical skills.

In carrying out the campaign to reeducate his bureaucrats, Frederick William I used a strategy in many ways similar to that of his officer-training program. His first step was to renounce his father's method of governing through favorites and to assert a personal, military-like command over the entire bureaucracy.[65] As part of his power of command, the king assumed the right to appoint all his officials, no longer permitting cliques of high-ranking ministers or the provincial estates to hand out royal offices as rewards to their supporters.[66] Having secured control over the process of selecting officeholders, Frederick William pursued personnel policies whose priorities matched those of his officer recruitment effort. Explicitly abandoning the Great Elector's preference for foreigners, Frederick William I sought for his bureaucracy native-born Prussians of either Reformed or Lutheran religion.[67] This policy, like its military counterpart, was a key element in Frederick William's effort to induce his most socially prestigious or vocationally ambitious subjects to pursue careers in his service rather than to persist in remaining aloof from the Hohenzollern state.

In his role as commander, Frederick William I subjected the bureaucrats to the same combination of exhortation, exacting work requirements, and relentless discipline as that prevailing in the officer corps. As he did in every one of his supervisory roles, Frederick William set the necessary example of hard work and devotion to his task. Reports from subordinates never arrived quickly enough; the king continually carried out inspections, and his mastery of

64 Hinrichs, "Preussen als historisches Problem," 29.

65 In the king's own words, "Ich habe Kommando bei meiner Armee und soll nicht Kommando haben bei die tausend sakramentischen Blackisten?" Quoted in *ibid.*, 30.

66 Schmoller, "Der preussische Beamtenstand," 158.

67 A. Kamp, "Friedrich Wilhelm I. und das preussische Beamtentum," *Forschungen zur brandenburgischen und preussischen Geschichte*, 30 (1917): 34. See also Opgenoorth, *"Ausländer" in Brandenburg-Preussen*, 47.

detail was astounding.[68] Not the least intimidating aspect of his leadership was his practice of issuing detailed instructions to every class of official from top-ranking minister to the "humblest collector of the excise at the gate of every town."[69] These orders not only spelled out exactly how each official should perform his job but also contained provisions enumerating the levels of achievement and pattern of behavior expected by the king. Just as in the military, supervisors had to submit annual conduct reports indicating just how faithfully each of their subordinates was adhering to the king's instructions. Provincial officials were subject, like their military counterparts, to surprise inspections by superiors from Berlin or by the king himself. After evaluating all the information on his bureaucratic personnel, Frederick William made his decisions on promotion or dismissal based on the same familiar criteria: piety (fear of God), obedient performance of duty, and level of productivity.[70]

In applying his basic pedagogical strategy to the training of his officials, however, Frederick William I was forced to overcome obstacles that he did not have to face with respect to the officer corps. Compared to the officer cohort, the bureaucrats seemingly lacked many of the preconditions for developing into a special status group with its own peculiar ethos. Since technical knowledge of farming, trade, or the law was the king's primary criterion for accepting a person into the civil service, no single socializing institution served as the preferred route of entry into the bureaucracy.[71] Even when a person had joined the civil service, there was no equivalent of basic training, no drill, to function as a distinctive socialization experience capable of setting off those who shared it from the rest of society.

In addition, the royal bureaucrats were neither numerous nor concentrated enough to possess their own social or cultural institutions; in particular, they had no separate church. Their vocation, moreover, required bureaucrats, far more than army officers, to be in continual contact with the public whose affairs they regulated. The bureaucracy's cohesion was further tested by the intraservice

68 Schmoller, "Der preussische Beamtenstand," 258, 265.

69 *Ibid.*, 254–55; Walter Dorn, "The Prussian Bureaucracy in the Eighteenth Century," *Political Science Quarterly*, 47 (1932): 90.

70 Hinrichs, "Preussen als historisches Problem," 30; Dorn, "The Prussian Bureaucracy in the Eighteenth Century," 94.

71 For an account of the various entry routes into the royal bureaucracy, see Schmoller, "Der preussische Beamtenstand," 168–70.

rivalry between the General Finance Directory, which administered the royal domains and represented the economic interests of the agrarian community, and the General War Commissariat, which collected the excise tax and worked to promote manufacturing and commerce. Finally, service in the bureaucracy offered few of the emotional and symbolic satisfactions associated with membership in the officer corps. No common bond of nobility, no sense of a special relationship with the king existed to give the bureaucrats that feeling of honor so important in motivating the officer corps to do its duty.

Although these characteristics of the bureaucracy made it more difficult for Frederick William I to indoctrinate this cadre group, he worked hard to compensate for them. The most important factor in making his job easier was that, even though the king did everything he could to prevent educated Prussians from entering the service of another prince, he did not have to use force in recruiting candidates for civil service positions.[72] People joined voluntarily because a bureaucratic career offered an otherwise unavailable opportunity for upward mobility in a rigidly stratified society. Although during the reign of Frederick William I commoners in the army could work their way up through the ranks to earn an officer's commission and noble status, the process either took such a long time or required such unusually good fortune that only a fairly small number of non-nobles could rise higher than the rank of non-commissioned officer.[73] In the civil service, however, commoners faced no such status barriers to advancement, particularly during the reign of Frederick William I.[74] The importance that Frederick William placed on productivity and performance made him an especially strong promoter of meritocracy. Unlike later Prussian monarchs, Frederick William I made no legal or professional distinction between subalterns and higher ranking civil servants, and he con-

72 For the measures the king used to keep prospective candidates from leaving the country, see Kamp, "Friedrich Wilhelm I. und das preussische Beamtentum," 34.

73 Jany, *Geschichte der Königlich Preussischen Armee*, vol. I, 724.

74 Rosenberg notes that under Frederick William I there was a "sharply marked ascendancy of parvenus" in the Prussian bureaucracy. See Rosenberg, *Bureaucracy, Aristocracy, and Autocracy*, 67. Not all kinds of social outsiders were welcome, however. According to a report submitted to Frederick William in 1716, a considerable number of the domain administrators in East Prussia were Jews. In keeping with his hostility to Jews, the king responded by issuing a number of decrees designed to replace them with Christians. Stern, *Der preussische Staat und die Juden*, vol. II, pt. I, 162–63.

tinually affirmed the possibility for the lowliest secretary or clerk to ascend to the level of tax commissar or department head.[75]

The often strong motivations that candidates for the civil service brought to their jobs made unnecessary some of the elaborate socialization process required in the training of both officers and common soldiers. Frederick William nevertheless had to find ways to promote in his bureaucracy a sense of unity based on his ethic of service to the state. In the king's eyes, one of the obstacles he faced was the nature of the legal education that many of his officials had received at universities prior to their entering the royal service.[76] Since much of the content of this training tended to be irrelevant for most bureaucratic positions and since law faculties generally produced contentious, egoistic graduates, Frederick William resolved to introduce a more suitable alternative into the curriculum of his universities.

By a decree issued in 1727, the king created two professorships in cameralist studies, one each at the universities of Halle and Frankfurt a. d. Oder. The lectures given by the two cameralists, the first such professors in the history of German universities, covered the basic technical and legal aspects of the Prussian state's economic, finance, and police systems.[77] Thus just as he did with the curriculum of the *Kadettenanstalt*, Frederick William I instituted a program of schooling whose cognitive content focused on transmitting knowledge of immediate vocational utility.[78] To encourage enrollment in

75 Wilhelm Naudé, "Zur Geschichte des preussischen Subalternbeamtentums," *Forschungen zur brandenburgischen und preussischen Geschichte*, 18 (1905): 2; Kamp, "Friedrich Wilhelm I. und das preussische Beamtentum," 34.

76 It is important, though, not to overestimate the numbers of university-trained people in the Prussian bureaucracy in the early eighteenth century. Thus the officials charged with administering the royal domain lands (the *Pächter*), a numerous and important subgroup within the bureaucratic structure, were recruited mostly from among the better-off peasants and small-time industrial entrepreneurs – elements of the population not likely to have undergone any higher education. See Gustavo Corni, "Absolutistische Agrarpolitik und Agrargesellschaft in Preussen," *Zeitschrift für historische Forschung*, 13 (1986): 292.

77 Erhard Dittrich, *Die deutschen und österreichischen Kameralisten* (Darmstadt, 1974), 81–84.

78 The king's Francke-like emphasis on practical applied knowledge was also evident in his quest to supply his regiments and society at large with medical personnel, including midwives, trained in the latest techniques. Beginning with the institution of regular lectures in an "Anatomical Theater," Frederick William established in 1723 the College of Medicine and Surgery, which with its large faculty and up-to-date scientific curriculum served as *the* Prussian medical school until the founding of the University of Berlin in the early nineteenth century. For a good summary, see Reinhold Dorwart, "Medical Education in Prussia under the Early Hohenzollerns." *Bulletin of the History of Medicine*, 32 (1958): 337–47. For a more detailed account, see Herbert Lehmann, *Das Collegium Medico-Chirurgicum in Berlin als Lehrstätte der Botanik und der Pharmazie* (Berlin, 1936).

the cameralist program, the king immediately adopted the policy of favoring former students of cameralism in his hiring and promotion policies.[79]

Another group of job candidates especially favored by the king consisted of military personnel. The large numbers of retired or honorably discharged soldiers who became civil servants during the reign of Frederick William I strongly reinforced the king's efforts to instill in the other bureaucrats the desired spirit of loyalty and devotion to duty. Former army men permeated all levels of the bureaucracy. Ex-noncoms received automatic preference for subaltern positions, especially for jobs involving police duty, tax collection, or supervision of clerical personnel.[80] Retired officers had almost exclusive claim to jobs, particularly that of district commissar (*Landrat*), in which their high social status would benefit the state.[81]

Also eligible for high positions in the bureaucracy were former quartermasters and "auditors," the latter having served as legal advisors to regimental commanders. Both quartermasters and auditors had usually had some university or other advanced training prior to their military experience. After their switch to the civil service, they frequently became tax commissars (*Steuerräte*), the key government officials in the cities and towns.[82] To enhance still further the impact of the military presence within the civil administration, the king routinely appointed high officers still in active service to lead special investigations of officials suspected of crimes or neglect of duty.[83]

Frederick William I also worked to make the bureaucracy more like the military in terms of being segregated from society at large and more cohesive in internal structure. To help seclude the civil service from the rest of the population, the king imposed a veil of

[79] Rosenberg, *Bureaucracy, Aristocracy, and Autocracy*, 63. Despite the long-term importance of these faculty appointments for the development of cameralism as an academic discipline and as a body of knowledge, it is simply not correct to see these university programs in cameralism as having a critical influence on the emerging ethos of the Prussian bureaucracy during its formative period under Frederick William I. In assessing the impact of the cameralist faculty at Halle, Keith Tribe concludes, "It cannot be said, therefore, that this first attempt to teach Cameralism within the university met with great immediate success . . . whether we consider student numbers, consistency of teaching, quality of teaching, or the suitability of the textbooks used and produced, wherever we look the picture is one of dubious clarity and indifferent outcome." See Tribe, *Governing Economy*, 43.

[80] Jany, *Geschichte der Königlich Preussischen Armee*, vol. 1, 719.

[81] Büsch, *Militärsystem und Sozialleben*, 132.

[82] *Ibid.*, 129; Hinrichs, "Preussen als historisches Problem," 37.

[83] Büsch, *Militärsystem und Sozialleben*, 138.

secrecy on the instructions he issued to his officials and around the whole bureaucratic decision-making process.[84] Frederick William went so far as to prohibit secretaries from gossiping about the proceedings of their superiors' meetings, and he sometimes deliberately deceived the public in order to keep it ignorant of the orders he had given his officials.[85]

Behind this artificial but effective barrier, Frederick William I gradually centralized the organization of his bureaucracy. Beginning in 1711, when he already exercised considerable authority as crown prince, Frederick William strove first to unify internally the two most important agencies, the General Finance Directory and the General War Commissariat. These initial reforms not only combined previously unconnected departments and treasuries but also imposed collegial leadership on each central agency and its subordinate, provincial branches.[86] The effect of these measures was thus not only to increase the authority of each agency but also to strengthen the monarch's control over them, since the collegial principle made it extremely difficult for a single official to control as his own an office, bureau, or agency.[87] Of course, by increasing the power and efficiency of each of the bureaucracy's two major branches, the king also succeeded in making the incessant wrangling between them all the more disruptive. In order to eliminate this friction, Frederick William in the winter of 1722–23 combined the General Finance Directory and the General War Commissariat into a new, collegially organized agency.[88] This consolidation at first embraced only the top levels of each agency, but the king soon ordered that their provincial arms be unified as well.[89]

Within this structural framework and with the help of the former military personnel, Frederick William I carried out the task of educating his officials in his ethic of hard work and loyal service.

[84] At the conclusion of his 1722 "Instruktion" to the General Directory, for example, Frederick William I warned that its contents should be kept top secret on pain of severe punishment. Schmoller *et al.*, eds., *Die Behördenorganisation*, vol. III, 650.

[85] Schmoller, "Der preussische Beamtenstand," 255–56; Dorn, "The Prussian Bureaucracy in the Eighteenth Century," 91.

[86] See Reinhold Dorwart, *The Administrative Reforms of Frederick William I of Prussia* (Cambridge, Mass., 1953), 34, 39, 124–27, 144, 148, 158–60.

[87] W. Neugebauer, "Zur neueren Deutung der preussischen Verwaltung im 17. und 18. Jahrhundert: Eine Studie in vergleichender Sicht," *Jahrbuch für Geschichte Mittel- und Ostdeutschlands*, 26 (1977): 551.

[88] Originally titled the General-Supreme-Finance-War-and-Domain Directory, it is usually referred to as the General Directory.

[89] Dorwart, *The Administrative Reforms of Frederick William I*, 167.

The system of detailed instructions, conduct reports, mutual surveillance, and inspections proved to be as powerful a pedagogical tool with respect to the bureaucracy as it had been with the military. For this control system to produce the desired obedience in the military, however, it had been necessary first to break the wills of the prospective officers through drill and religious indoctrination. Since the bureaucracy lacked a counterpart to the *Kadettenanstalt* or a Pietist-dominated vocational church, Frederick William needed to find a substitute mechanism with the equivalent psychological effect.

The king worked to create the type of disciplined behavior he desired by relentlessly exhorting his bureaucrats in the basic values of State Pietism. Some of the clearest statements of Frederick William I's ideology are to be found in the instructions to his officials. Of a person filling a position in the General Directory or on the provincial war-and-domain boards, the king demanded that he "besides God prize nothing more highly than the grace of his king, serve the latter out of love and more out of honor than for monetary remuneration, and seek in all his conduct of affairs purely and simply the interest and service of his king, shunning all intrigues."[90] In other words, to become a Prussian bureaucrat one had to make obedience and loyal service to the king one's calling – a complete break with existing practice whereby the bureaucrat's relationship with his master was a contractual one, "with mutually binding, precisely determined rights and duties."[91]

The instructions were also very clear as to what constituted obedience. At all costs the official was to break with the customary laxity in carrying out royal decrees. Commands had to be followed "in all points *accurat*" and "were not to be mitigated in the slightest bit."[92] To enforce to the letter all the king's decrees required, of course, extraordinary diligence as did the concomitant royal expectation that officials should gather complete information about the places and people under their charge.[93] To ensure the necessary

90 Frederick William I, "Instruktion ... für das General- ... Direktorium ... 1722," in Schmoller *et al.*, eds., *Die Behördenorganisation*, vol. III, 647.

91 Hartung, *Staatsbildende Kräfte*, 139.

92 Frederick William I, "Instruktion ... für das General- ... Direktorium ... 1722," in Schmoller *et al.*, eds., *Die Behördenorganisation*, vol. III, 649.

93 To press home his point that total administrative control requires total knowledge, Frederick William used an analogy close to his heart. Officials should be as familiar with inhabitants under them as "an army captain knows his company, whereby the internal and

"application" on the part of his bureaucrats, Frederick William prescribed for them an hour-by-hour schedule that had to be followed or else severe punishment would result. In addition, the king was tireless in admonishing his civil servants to ever greater efforts. The instructions were saturated with commands accompanied with such phrases as "with all conceivable [*ersinnlichen*] diligence and application."[94] "Indefatigable" (*unverdrossen*) was an especially favorite word. The very Protestant ethic of the king was encapsulated by a series of phrases describing the way in which he expected the members of the General Directory to carry out his requests: "with extreme exactitude, tireless diligence, and spotless fidelity [*unbefleckter Treue*]."[95]

Powerfully reinforcing the pressure exerted by these injunctions was Frederick William I's policy of keeping his bureaucrats in a perpetual state of fear concerning the security of their jobs and persons. Frederick William so deeply distrusted his civil servants that he did not hesitate to subject them to a degree of surveillance and arbitrary punishment unknown in the military.[96] For those who did not follow his instruction "in every respect" and who thereby sought to go back to the "old lax routines" (*Schlender*), for such "disobedience," these people "should be punished ... in the Russian manner."[97]

The king's fear of "betrayal" in this sense was so intense that in addition to operating through conduct reports and inspections, he gathered information on his bureaucrats through royal agents called fiscals.[98] Responsible only to the king, these official spies were

external qualities of each of the soldiers entrusted to that captain must be completely known to him." See *ibid.*, 579–80.

94 *Ibid.*, 602.

95 *Ibid.*, 649.

96 For a list of the abusive terms Frederick William most frequently used in describing his officials, see Kamp, "Friedrich Wilhelm I. und das preussische Beamtentum," 43. For the limits of the royal control system's ability to check rule violations among the officer elite, see Büsch, *Militärsystem und Sozialleben*, 127–29.

97 Frederick William I, "Instruktion ... für das General- ... Direktorium ... 1722," in Schmoller *et al.*, eds., *Die Behördenorganisation*, vol. III, 649.

98 For the most complete account of the fiscal system, see Schmidt, *Fiskalat und Strafprozess*. In addition to the fiscals, Frederick William I also relied on unofficial spies and informers. Thus he deputized one member of the General Directory, Christoph von Katsch, to report directly to him if any of his colleagues were remiss in their duties. For the text of the letter written by the king to Katsch, see Baumgart, ed., *Erscheinungsformen des preussischen Absolutismus*, 56. Frederick William also authorized the General Directory to develop a network of informers in the provinces to ensure that the provincial war-and-domain boards were providing their superiors a complete picture of the state of affairs in their area. Frederick

charged with making sure that the king's instructions were obeyed to the letter. The fiscals "had access to all the documents of every official, they inspected the local treasuries and were admitted to all discussions and meetings."[99] Fiscals reported irregularities directly to the king, who could appoint an investigatory commission or simply dismiss the suspected official without any trial or hearing whatever.[100] Missing two meetings constituted grounds for dismissal *cum infamia*; more serious breaches of the code were punished by imprisonment in Spandau. Flagrant offenders, such as the East Prussian official who allegedly embezzled funds earmarked for settling religious refugees from Salzburg, were publicly hanged.[101]

Under constant performance pressure and constant threat of denunciation, the Prussian bureaucrat learned to subordinate his will to those of his superior and his king.[102] If he did so long enough and well enough – and avoided any stigma of disobedience – he would eventually receive the material rewards he had originally sought. But in the meantime he had become a member of what Schmoller described as a "church militant," imbued with "idealism for the state" and dedicated to leading and "educating" civilian society.[103] The bureaucracy's mission was to produce a larger revenue for the King of Prussia by improving the organization and motivation of the country's labor force. On their success or failure depended whether Frederick William's finances would be sufficiently sound to support his large, well-drilled army without the benefit of foreign subsidies. The achievement of this goal, in turn, constituted the final objective in Frederick William's plan for raising Prussia to a place among the great powers in Europe.

William I, "Instruktion . . . für das General- . . . Direktorium . . . 1722," in Schmoller *et al.*, eds., *Die Behördenorganisation*, vol. III, 611.

99 Dorn, "The Prussian Bureaucracy in the Eighteenth Century," 92.

100 *Ibid.*, 92, 94.

101 Schmoller, "Der preussische Beamtenstand," 544–45, 548; Kamp, "Friedrich Wilhelm I. und das preussische Beamtentum," 47–48.

102 Dorn, "The Prussian Bureaucracy in the Eighteenth Century," 93.

103 Schmoller, "Der preussische Beamtenstand," 551–52. Given an absence of studies on the actual attitudes individual Prussian bureaucrats had concerning their vocation, it is impossible to say how much of this "idealism for the state" was born of conviction, how much of simple fear of the king's wrath. In any case, however, it is clear from the overall performance of the bureaucracy (see the next chapter) that the professional norms enunciated and inculcated by the king were internalized by this cadre group. Indicative of the impression the king had made on his officials were the cases of "excessive zeal." On one occasion, for example, the Pomeranian war-and-domains board proposed that young people who failed to make adequate progress in learning how to spin wool and flax be denied the eucharist and even permission to marry. This was too much even for Frederick William. See Hartung, *Staatsbildende Kräfte*, 138.

CHAPTER II

Civilian mobilization and economic development during the reign of Frederick William I

In 1713 Frederick William I inherited from his father an economic system in which growth was dependent mainly on foreign subsidies for the army and the inflow of skills and capital from religious refugees. Although the Peace of Utrecht (1713) portended an extended period of international stability, the generation of war that preceded it (1688–1713) had left the Prussian state with a valuable asset – an experienced army considerably larger than one would expect from a country of Prussia's size and level of economic development. As an asset, however, this fighting force was highly specific: that is, it possessed a much higher value in its intended use than in other possible uses. With the impending end of English and Dutch subsidy payments, the collapse of the market for the thirty-five thousand man Prussian army seemed inevitable. Frederick I was prepared to accept the loss and cut back the size of his military establishment; but his death in early 1713, occurring shortly before this order would have gone into effect, gave his son the opportunity to maintain the army's size. No one expected Frederick William I to be able to accomplish even this limited aim, though, since it did not seem possible for the Prussian state's finances to pay the army's wages, let alone provide it with food, equipment, and munitions.

Yet Frederick William intended to do precisely that, to purchase the services of his own army and organize the domestic economy around supplying its needs. This "nationalization" of the army required far-reaching structural changes in the Prussian economy. Otherwise, it was difficult to see, in 1713, whence additional resources for state building would come. For Prussia, despite the efforts of the Great Elector to establish export industries and a colonial trade, still constituted a classic case of an "underdeveloped" country, exporting raw materials (grain and wool) and importing manufactured goods of all kinds. The easiest way for such an economy to earn more income was to increase its raw material exports. Unfortunately, the low price levels for grain and wool in early eighteenth-century international markets meant that additional Prussian exports would have had the effect of depressing prices still further and of not significantly raising the country's foreign exchange earnings. Yet economic growth in some form was required if state revenues were to increase, for the domestic economy's ability to absorb higher levels of taxation had already reached its limit during the reign of Frederick I.

To be sure, especially in the first few years of his kingship, Frederick William I boosted state power by intensifying the state's exploitation of the rest of society. Most egregious were the state-sanctioned impressment gangs that in their army-recruitment campaigns disrupted the households of thousands of civilian families and the economies of whole villages before their activities began to be restricted in the early 1720s.[1] Scarcely less subtle was the fiscal pressure resulting from Frederick William's demands on his officials to forward ever higher amounts of revenue to the central treasuries. Though in theory the higher sum (the *Plus*) was to be "real" (*reel*) and not "illusory" (*windig*), in East Prussia at least officials in the late 1710s tended to meet the king's requirements by extorting still more money from the already overtaxed peasantry.[2]

Nevertheless, to sustain the sort of outlays required to maintain the Prussian army of 1713 – let alone to support the much larger force that Frederick William was in the process of assembling – it was incumbent on the king to go beyond the fiscalism of his predecessors. Part of what was new in Frederick William I's policies was an austerity in expenditure that reflected his Pietist outlook. At the beginning of his reign, large sums were saved by dismantling most of his father's court establishment, reducing officials' salaries, and paring drastically all non-military expenditures. The king himself set the example in the practice of frugality, appropriating only 52,000 Taler annually for the maintenance of the royal household, an extremely small sum by contemporary standards. To dramatize

[1] See above. p. 223.

[2] For the gruesome picture that emerged from a royal investigative commission in the early 1720s, see August Skalweit, *Die ostpreussische Domänenverwaltung*, 210–16. It is no coincidence that in the "Instruction für die Kreisräte im Königreich Preussen," written shortly thereafter, Frederick William at the very beginning of that document spells out a whole series of measures designed to prevent such practices on the part of the lower levels of his bureaucracy. See Pantenius, ed., *Erlasse und Briefe*, 37.

his commitment to parsimony, the king wore nothing but his uniform or the plainest Prussian-made clothing.[3] In doing this, Frederick William sought not only to prune governmental expenditures but also to impress on the better-off parts of the population that they too could – and should – do without foreign-made luxury goods, whose purchase drained the country of precious foreign exchange.[4]

The other, ultimately decisive prerequisite for the success of Frederick William's grand strategy was simply that of raising the overall level of economic activity in the country. Perhaps the most basic prerequisites for such a result were the settling of abandoned farm lands, especially in East Prussia, and an expansion in the size of the industrial labor force. Immigrants were the most obvious source of the additional labor required, and Frederick William clearly recognized their significance.[5] Like his predecessors, Frederick William I moved quickly to attract large communities of Protestants driven from their homelands by religious persecution. His biggest coup in this respect was the resettlement of over ten thousand of the Salzburg refugees in the rural Lithuanian district of East Prussia.

Despite this continuity with previous regimes with respect to the Prussian government's immigration policies, Frederick William I introduced new strategies that made Prussia much less dependent on the repressiveness of other states. More systematically and energetically than his father or grandfather, Frederick William sought to attract prospective artisans and agrarian colonists by granting them generous incentives and immunities if they would emigrate to Prussia.[6] Immigration of an involuntary sort, the forced recruitment

[3] The king also succeeded in having the cloth content in each uniform reduced by almost 50 percent between 1714 and 1725, thereby saving money for the treasury and, more importantly, creating a garment that by its angularity and tightness symbolized the strict discipline that he was seeking to impose on society as a whole. Krause, *Altpreussische Uniformfertigung*, 17. See also Büsch, *Militärsystem und Sozialleben*, 29.

[4] Hartung, *Staatsbildende Kräfte*, 137. It should be noted, however, that the austerity drive had a highly disruptive impact on the Berlin economy, geared as it had been to Frederick's court. This was yet another sector of society whose initial response to Frederick William I's state-building policies could only have been quite negative.

[5] For a summary of Frederick William's position, see Dietrich, ed., *Die politischen Testamente*, 83.

[6] Between 1713 and 1727 some 17,000 craftsmen, many of them weavers, took advantage of the king's offer. Ergang, *The Potsdam Führer*, 181, 183. Incentives for immigrant artisans included freedom from all quartering obligations, immediate unconditional guild membership, and the right to operate as many looms and employ as many workers as they wished without regard to guild restrictions. See Alfred Stark, "Die Leinenindustrie in Preussen unter Friedrich Wilhelm I.," (Phil. Diss., U. Berlin, 1939), 44.

of foreigners for the Prussian army, occurred in even greater numbers. In the course of the eighteenth century, between three and four hundred thousand soldiers recruited from foreign lands were settled permanently in Prussia, most of these so-called *Freiwächter* being employed during periods of leave as wage laborers or artisans in the garrison towns.[7]

In addition to simply increasing the size of the labor force through immigration, Frederick William I also instituted policies designed to channel workers into places and trades where they were needed. With regard to skilled labor, artisans who hitherto lived in the countryside were compelled by royal commissars to move into urban areas.[8] Perhaps the most urgent need in the Prussian manufacturing sector was the textile industry's demand for enormous quantities of spun yarn, which required the king to mobilize on an unprecedented scale hitherto underutilized sources of labor and set them to work spinning yarn.[9] The Prussian authorities enlisted many different categories of people in this effort. In the military, especially in provincial garrison towns, captains often established spinning facilities for *Freiwächter* and their wives.[10] In Berlin, the state-run "warehouse" (*Lagerhaus*) distributed wool to soldiers of the garrison and their wives.[11] Similarly, in the countryside many peasant families were offered a chance to earn extra money by working for a putting-out operation. Many such ventures were organized by the tax commissars, who sent female spinners into the countryside to act as instructors to the peasant women and as deliverers of wool from the *Lagerhaus* or local entrepreneur.[12]

In some cases, the state used coercive measures to increase the supply of spun thread, as when it compelled women who were street peddlars to spin or knit while they were tending their stands.[13] The authorities also rounded up beggars, vagabonds, and prostitutes and placed them in workhouses. Not surprisingly, the population of

[7] Büsch, *Militärsystem und Sozialleben*, 62.

[8] Rachel, "Der Merkantilismus in Brandenburg-Preussen," 233.

[9] For a discussion of the chronic shortage of spinners throughout Central Europe during the eighteenth century, see Melton, *Absolutism and the Eighteenth-Century Origins of Compulsory Schooling*, 126–27.

[10] Redlich, *The German Military Enterpriser*, vol. II, 82–84, 86.

[11] In most cases, the necessity of supplementing the soldier's wages compelled military families to accept this employment opportunity. A. Skalweit, "Die Eingliederung des friderizianischen Heeres in den Volks- und Wirtschaftskörper," 215.

[12] Carl Hinrichs, *Die Wollindustrie in Preussen unter Friedrich Wilhelm I.* (Berlin, 1933), 311f.

[13] Rachel, "Der Merkantilismus in Brandenburg-Preussen," 231.

these *Zucht- und Arbeitshäuser* increased considerably during the reign of Frederick William I.[14] The Pietists had long taken the position that no one should receive charity without working for it, and this idea was realized with a vengeance in the tightly controlled spinning operations set up in the Prussian workhouse system.[15] This principle was extended to institutionalized orphans as well; the fourteen hundred children at the Potsdam military orphanage were required to spin several hours each day after a morning of catechization and instruction in the three "R's."[16]

Despite the significance of these efforts to increase the supply of available labor, the success of Frederick William I's economic policies depended most crucially on his ability to raise the level of productivity per worker. As was the case with the army officers and bureaucrats, Frederick William was determined to educate the common people of his lands to be willing to break with customary work routines and carry out obediently and diligently the tasks assigned them by the state. The king knew very well that the surplus-producing standards he was demanding went against the deeply rooted belief of his subjects that individuals should only work hard enough to support the standard of living to which they were accustomed.[17] In order to convince the people of Prussia to accept his Pietist work ethic, Frederick William I mobilized the exhortative powers of church and state to inculcate in them his conception of

14 In addition to the Potsdam military orphanage, eight new workhouses were established between 1713 and 1740, and the number of inmates at the Grosse Friedrichshospital in Berlin doubled to about 600 by 1728, 500 of them children. Helga Eichler, "Zucht- und Arbeitshäuser in den mittleren und östlichen Provinzen Brandenburg–Preussens; Ihr Anteil an der Vorbereitung des Kapitalismus: Eine Untersuchung für die Zeit vom Ende des 17. bis zum Ausgang des 18. Jahrhunderts," *Jahrbuch für Wirtschaftsgeschichte* (1970) Teil 1: 134, 146–47.

15 For the Pietist influence on the development of this system, see Hinrichs, *Preussentum und Pietismus*, 305–06. For the regimen imposed on the inmates, see Herbert Lieberknecht, *Das altpreussische Zuchthauswesen bis zum Ausgang des 18. Jahrhunderts, insbesondere in den Provinzen Pommern und Ostpreussen* (Göttingen, 1921), 27–28. Hellmuth Heyden notes that Frederick William I ordered a heavy emphasis on strict discipline and Christian devotion for the inmates of the *Spinn- und Zuchthäuser* in Pomerania. See Heyden, *Kirchengeschichte von Pommern*, vol. 1, 184.

16 *Geschichte des Königlichen Potsdamschen Militärwaisenhauses, von seiner Entstehung bis auf die jetzige Zeit* (Berlin, 1824), 393f.

17 One does not have to accept the post-Pietist, eighteenth-century German bureaucratic view of the bulk of the population as lazy, shiftless, etc. to acknowledge that the traditionalistic peoples of East Central Europe did not share the Puritan/Pietist exaltation of work as an end in itself. For a critique of the stereotypes reflected in the contemporary bureaucratic literature, see Melton, *Absolutism and the Eighteenth-Century Origins of Compulsory Schooling*, 127–31.

work as a divinely – and royally – required duty. Frederick William thus wanted his subjects to internalize the principle that the best indicator of their fear of god was the singlemindedness with which they devoted themselves to their occupational labors. The corollary of this notion was that the neglect of one's daily work demonstrated a lack of faithfulness (*Untreue*) to the common effort of ruler and subject to work together "for the good of the country."[18]

As much as possible, the king attempted to educate the people himself in his direct, personal way. Whether inspecting remote provinces or roaming the streets of Berlin or Potsdam, Frederick William visited the homes and workplaces of his humblest subjects, urging them on in their work or caning them if he caught them slacking off.[19] With respect to changing the attitudes of the population toward their work, however, the king realized that the most fundamental form of exhortation had to be religious in nature. For it was not simply out of piety that Frederick William said in the midst of the struggle to reconstruct East Prussia: "If I rebuild and improve the land and make no one a Christian, then all my effort helps me not a bit."[20]

In this context, of course, to "make one a Christian" meant to transform that person into an "active" Christian of the Pietist sort, presumably through indoctrination in the churches and schools. As has already been described, Frederick William I used his position as *summus episcopus* to staff the civilian church with Pietist pastors and superintendents, many of them former army chaplains. The energy and independent initiative of those pastors was particularly crucial for the realization of the king's plans because, constitutionally, the latter's direct administrative control over the personnel of local church and school networks was not nearly comparable to that which he could exert over the members of the war-and-domain

18 Hinrichs, "Preussen als historisches Problem," 30.

19 Ergang, *The Potsdam Führer*, 167; Hinrichs, "Der Regierungsantritt Friedrich Wilhelms I.," 216. In the cities and towns the tax commissars, as royal surrogates, presumably assumed this same role, though this aspect of their duties has never been investigated to my knowledge.

20 Quoted in Meyer, "Der Hallenser Pietismus August Hermann Franckes," 68. This quotation is usually cited as evidence of Frederick William's personal commitment to Christianity and its propagation; but in light of his Promethean spirituality, this sentiment of his should also be read as anticipating later cameralists and heads of state, who viewed the spread and deepening of an ethically oriented, do-your-duty-now-and-go-to-heaven type of Christianity as a means to the end of increasing state power.

boards.[21] Through experience, Frederick William found that the only clergy on which he could rely to pursue his pedagogical goals energetically at the grassroots level were the Pietists.[22]

Besides preaching from the pulpit their characteristic attitude toward work, that is "faithfulness in even the smallest details" (*Treusinn im geringste*), the Pietist clergy also sought to use the primary school network to put this message across to the younger generation.[23] The customary arrangement whereby the pastor supervised the local schoolmaster(s) was not only maintained during the reign of Frederick William I but also given new vigor by the infusion of Pietist personnel into this system. In East Prussia, the ordinance of 1734, drafted by the Pietist Schultz, actually required pastors to participate in teaching, especially in catechization.[24] Many of the East Prussian deacons, moreover, who did the bulk of the classroom work, were theology students from the University of Königsberg, future Pietist pastors who were receiving on-the-job training in the best tradition of the Halle *Anstalten*.[25] In most cities and towns throughout the kingdom, the highest ranking cleric also

[21] As Hannelore Juhr demonstrates, as late as 1737, even after several stages in the process by which the king increasingly shifted responsibilities from the provincial *ständisch* administrative system to the bureaucratic organs of the centralized state, a "dualistic" form of administration in East Prussia still prevailed with respect to school, church, hospital, and judicial matters. Juhr, *Die Verwaltung des Hauptamtes Brandenburg/Ostpreussen*, 106, 126–31.

[22] In East Prussia, for example, the king repeatedly tried to enlist the support of reform-minded orthodox people in the Lutheran church, such as superintendent Quandt, but he could only rarely secure from them the sort of "unconditional commitment" to his goals that he could get from the Pietists, who therefore "almost inevitably ... became the chief bearers of his reform work." Terveen, *Gesamtstaat und Retablissement*, 130.

[23] This doctrine was essentially the same as that taught the officer corps: diligent performance of routine duties, to the letter of the royal command, was a proof of one's loyalty to God and king. As such, this Pietist attitude was identical with that Puritan mentality which compelled individuals to scrutinize their most minor actions and thoughts in order to get a "reading" of their chances for salvation. One of the Puritan divines even acknowledged that what Preus calls the "Puritan obsession with trivia" was comparable with the Pharisees' emphasis on the smallest points of the Law. See Preus, "Secularizing Divination," forthcoming.

[24] Terveen, *Gesamtstaat und Retablissement*, 138.

[25] Skalweit, *Die ostpreussische Domänenverwaltung*, 241. While Melton is correct in maintaining that those who received teacher training in eighteenth-century Prussia usually became pastors, the implication that they – and their precious experience – were therefore lost to the school system underestimates the importance of the pastors' supervisory role. See Melton, *Absolutism and the Eighteenth-Century Origins of Compulsory Schooling*, 49–50. What Walter Wendland says about the time of the *Aufklärung* applies equally to the time of Frederick William I: "The entire Prussian primary school system during the *Aufklärung* still lay in the hands of the pastors." Wendland, "Die praktische Wirksamkeit Berliner Geistlicher im Zeitalter der Aufklärung, 1740–1806," *Jahrbuch für brandenburgische Kirchengeschichte*, 11/12 (1914): 233.

supervised the private schools, which tended to cater to children from better-off families. According to the 1738 ordinance regulating the private schools of Berlin, presented to the king by the magistracy, to gain employment teachers had to possess a *Testimonium* of "true and unfeigned *Gottseligkeit*" from the local church authorities. As for the stated goals of primary education and the curriculum prescribed for achieving them, this ordinance could have been written by Francke himself.[26]

In so far as he was able, the king sought to extend this system to the entire population of his kingdom. This aim underlay the well-known decree of 1717, among the first in the German lands to mandate universal, compulsory primary education.[27] Although historians have long recognized that in itself this ordinance did little to increase the rate of school attendance,[28] Frederick William I did help lay the groundwork for the long-term achievement of the goals of this legislation by carrying out a school-building program of unprecedented scope. In this area the king's attention was particularly focused on the East Prussian countryside, where even before the disaster of 1708–10 the settlement pattern of small, widely scattered villages made it extremely difficult to provide schooling for most of the population. Almost from the beginning of his reign Frederick William had attempted to work with the provincial government and the East Prussian Lutheran church in order to make primary education available to the people there. Only in the mid-1730s, however, when the conflict between the Pietists and the provincial elites was resolved through Schultz's leadership, could a large-scale coordinated effort get underway.[29]

Aided by an endowment of 50,000 Taler provided by Frederick William I (the so-called *Mons pietatis*), the school-building campaign proceeded very rapidly. By 1739 some nine hundred new schools

[26] "Ordnung für die deutschen Privatschulen in Berlin, 1738," in Reinhold Vormbaum, ed., *Evangelische Schulordnungen*, vol. III (Gütersloh, 1864), 440–45.

[27] For the provisions of this edict, see Gloria, *Der Pietismus als Förderer der Volksbildung*, 46–47.

[28] See Ferdinand Vollmer, *Friedrich Wilhelm I. und die Volksschule* (Göttingen, 1909); Wolfgang Neugebauer, "Bemerkungen zum preussischen Schuledikt von 1717," *Jahrbuch für die Geschichte Mittel- und Ostdeutschlands*, 31 (1982): 155–76.

[29] The necessity of local involvement for any program of school reform to be effective, as demonstrated by the East Prussian case, illustrates the inability of even Frederick William I simply to impose his will in the area of primary education and the crucial importance of the Pietist clergy for the carrying out of the king's pedagogical agenda. See Wolfgang Neugebauer, *Absolutistischer Staat und Schulwirklichkeit in Brandenburg-Preussen* (Berlin, 1985), 625–34.

had been built in East Prussia, nearly all of them in the towns and on the royal domains.[30] But on his last visit to East Prussia in that same year, the king declared himself still unsatisfied and initiated a new round of building, vehemently admonishing Schultz and the local elites that if they neglected this task he, Frederick William, would accuse them before God on Judgment Day.[31] When the campaign finally ended in 1742, the report of a royal commission indicated that over 1,100 new schools had been built and a total of 1,660 schools had been either built or repaired.[32]

The campaign to use the church and school network to admonish the Prussian people to ever greater diligence was not the only dimension to Frederick William I's effort to increase the levels of motivation and productivity of his work force. As has been emphasized, a key element of Frederick William's own piety was the psychological importance of receiving tangible benefits in this life as signs of God's providential favor; and, as was his habit, Frederick William projected this need upon his subjects. Thus an important assumption behind the king's domestic policies was that individual peasants or artisans would work harder for the good of the state if their own material circumstances improved in the process.[33]

In the 1722 instruction to the General Directory, the king accordingly warned that his subjects through "badly organized economic structures and far too heavy burdens [were so] enervated that they could not in whole or in part meet the customary obligations due their sovereign." Therefore Frederick William charged his commissars to direct their efforts "with great diligence and application" to the "conservation" of his subjects, meaning not only that they be spared excessive exactions by the state but also that they be preserved in a state of "prosperity" (*gutem Flor und Wohl-*

30 The opposition of the nobility in the countryside to the program hindered the construction of schools on their lands. Erich Reicke, *Die Schulreorganisation Friedrich Wilhelms I. in den samländischen Hauptämtern Fischhausen und Schaaken* (Königsberg, 1910), 105. August Skalweit claims that this deficiency was made up by Frederick the Great, who was able to compel the nobility by exhortion to fulfil their duty to build and maintain schools. See Skalweit, *Die ostpreussische Domänenverwaltung*, 243.

31 Skalweit, *Die ostpreussische Domänenverwaltung*, 243.

32 Gloria, *Der Pietismus als Förderer der Volksbildung*, 50.

33 In 1721, after a conference devoted to the problems of the East Prussian peasantry, the king declared that to help the peasant acquire the self-motivation needed to "better his as yet miserable situation and way of life" it was necessary to enact reforms that would put the peasant in a realistic position to acquire "a certain prosperity." Quoted in Skalweit, *Die ostpreussische Domänenverwaltung*, 218.

stand).[34] The king's concept of "conservation" even extended to the physical well-being of his workers; hence came his extensive efforts, directly analogous to those of Halle Pietism, to improve basic sanitation practices, raise the level of education among medical personnel, and distribute cheap medicines on a wide scale.[35]

Frederick William I's recognition that a full treasury depended upon the health and material well-being of his people was certainly not new, but in keeping with the radical dynamism of his rule he intervened aggressively in the economic life of his kingdom in order to modify existing organizational structures that had served to limit productivity. In the countryside, one of the policy changes the king made in the management of the royal domains was to reduce systematically forced labor quotas for state serfs. Particularly in East Prussia, he sought to lessen the predominance of unfree labor by settling colonists in villages on domain lands and giving them the status of legally free small landholders.[36] In Pomerania, he took the first steps to protect the non-domain peasantry from unfair expropriation of their land by the nobility, a policy that under Frederick II was expanded and became known as "protection of the peasantry" (*Bauernschutz*).[37]

The same goal of enhancing the productivity of small producers also motivated Frederick William I's policy toward the guilds, the institutional bodies that regulated the urban labor force. From the king's point of view, there were many important features of the guild system that restricted his options for restructuring the country's manufacturing sector. The guilds' costly ceremonial, chronic contentiousness, and high legal expenses acted as a drain on the time and financial resources of the more industrious craftsmen. In addition, the rigid conservatism of the guilds prevented the introduction of new, more productive technology and work rules; their sense of

[34] Schmoller *et al.* eds., *Die Behördenorganisation*, vol. III, 589–90. I even resist using the term "paternalism" to describe these policies because the intent behind them was so utterly lacking in any real spirit of generosity and was so obviously one of calculated state interest.

[35] For a summary of Frederick William's initiatives in the medical area, see Günter Birtsch, "Friedrich Wilhelm I. und die Anfänge der Aufklärung in Brandenburg-Preussen," in Hauser, ed., *Preussen, Europa und das Reich*, 93–94.

[36] For a detailed account of these changes and their consequences, see Skalweit, *Die ostpreussische Domänenverwaltung*, 179–87.

[37] Heyden speculates that these measures, by giving the peasantry hope for a better life, provided the social and psychological basis for the subsequent spread of Pietism among the villages of rural Pomerania. Heyden, "Die Kirchenpolitik in Pommern," 60. For critical analyses of Frederician *Bauernschutz*, see Büsch, *Militärsystem und Sozialleben*, 56–58; and Corni, "Absolutistische Agrarpolitik und Agrargesellschaft," 305–08.

exclusivity and "honor" led them to refuse to admit orphans and soldiers' children, oppose the settling of immigrants in the towns, and limit access to mastership to sons of existing masters.[38] Opportunities for ambitious journeymen were further limited by differences in the nature of the "privileges" that governed the guilds of the various localities, thereby hindering the migration of journeymen from community to community.[39] The result was not only an inefficient economic system but also a widespread condition of poverty and alienation among the journeymen, a discontent that not infrequently found violent and destructive expression.[40]

The first step in eliminating these negative effects of the guilds was the reorganization of the central bureaucracy that culminated in the creation of the General Directory in 1722. Until the reign of Frederick William I, the magistrates of the cities and towns had been subject to only occasional interference by commissars with respect to the quartering of soldiers and the collecting of excise taxes. After 1722, however, the tax commissars (*Steuerräte*) for the first time possessed decisive judicial and economic control over the urban areas in their charge, though remnants of the old "dualistic" administration persisted long afterward.[41] The king immediately took advantage of the inspection and enforcement capability of the *Steuerräte* and beginning in 1724 decreed a whole series of detailed regulations pertaining to the cut, material, and price of army uniforms, as well as the material content and method of fabrication of the accessories.[42] Though the standardization of the army uniform was one aim of this legislation, another was to wrest important areas of economic regulation away from the textile guilds, which had to conform to these state-mandated requirements because the Prussian army had become their most important customer.

Yet even these measures did not enable the Prussian state to alter the time-honored practices that governed the internal workings of

38 In an incident described in an earlier chapter that typified this attitude, the guilds in Halle successfully opposed Francke's desire to admit orphans without birth certificates into apprentice associations. See above, p. 132.

39 Moritz Meyer, *Geschichte der preussischen Handwerkerpolitik nach ämtlichen Quellen*, vol. II (Minden, 1888), 17–24. See also Hinrichs, *Preussentum und Pietismus*, 335.

40 Krause, *Altpreussische Uniformfertigung*, 27.

41 Juhr, *Die Verwaltung des Hauptamtes Brandenburg/Ostpreussen*, 118–26.

42 For more information on these regulations, see Krause, *Altpreussische Uniformfertigung*, 14. For their impact on the linen industry, see Stark, "Die Leinenindustrie in Preussen," 46–47.

the guilds, for without imperial legislation it could not revoke the privileges granted to the guilds in earlier times.[43] Therefore from the early 1720s on the Prussian delegation at the imperial diet lobbied for appropriate changes in the laws of the Empire, and in 1731 the Prussian government got what it wanted when the diet issued a decree forcing all guilds in the Holy Roman Empire to acquire new privileges from their territorial masters and setting forth the guidelines to which those privileges had to conform. The new Prussian privileges, decreed for sixty-one different trades between 1734 and 1736, greatly liberalized admission requirements both to the guild itself and to the acquisition of master status, set minimum educational requirements for apprentices, forebade drinking in guild assemblies, prohibited expensive ceremonies, and placed the guilds under direct authority and supervision of the royal tax commissars.[44] The economic independence and initiative of individual guildsmen in the textile industry were directly encouraged, moreover, by the provision that master weavers who produced for more than just the local market could employ as many journeymen and operate as many looms as they wished.[45]

While the Prussian state thereby sought to rescue peasants and artisans from institutional forces that served to perpetuate the old *Schlendrian*, this does not mean that Frederick William I intended to unleash the productive energies of his subjects through the creation of a freer, more market-dominated economy. On the contrary, the king was determined to create an economic system designed to prevent craftsmen from becoming subject to unregulated market forces. Thus the state-managed Berlin *Lagerhaus*, a textile manufactory as well as a magazine for storing wool, guaranteed work to all prospective spinners and weavers who requested it, paid wages twenty-five percent above the going rate, and provided supplies of wool at a consistent and low price.[46] In the provincial cities, artisans were similarly shielded from exploitation from speculators and entrepreneurs through the establishment of a dense network of wool

43 On the ineffectiveness of Frederick William I's guild reform before the 1730s, see Meyer, *Geschichte der preussischen Handwerkerpolitik nach ämtlichen Quellen*, vol. II, 22f.

44 *Ibid.*, 90–94. Ergang, *The Potsdam Führer*, 169–71.

45 Hinrichs, *Preussentum und Pietismus*, 337.

46 *Ibid.*, 308. The tax commissars' offices constantly monitored the quality of the cloths produced and provided the artisans with technical training if they needed it. Henri Brunschwig, *Enlightenment and Romanticism in Eighteenth-Century Prussia*, trans. Frank Jellinek (Chicago, 1974), 43.

magazines and through the 1725 regulation that required purchasers of uniforms, i.e. company commanders, to deal directly with the tailors rather than with merchants or wholesale distributors.[47] This principle of economically linking small-scale textile manufacturers with the local garrison became such a significant feature of Frederick William's social policy that two promising state-sponsored textile manufactories in East Prussia were allowed to go bankrupt because their centralized, province-wide operations threatened to undermine the livelihoods of artisans in the towns outside of Königsberg.[48]

This type of "conservation" policy, however, reflected more than just the king's commitment to the material welfare of his subjects by providing them with steady, secure employment opportunities. Just as was the case with the Halle *Anstalten*, so with the Prussian state of Frederick William I, the totalistic ideology motivating the entire operation demanded the complete subordination of the individual to the goals of the institution – and this relationship extended to the economic sphere as well. In restructuring the Prussian economy, Frederick William sought not only to stimulate economic growth and encourage the development of industries needed to supply the army with essential commodities but also to subject the economic sector to the Prussian state's system of ideological and administrative control.

In light of this latter priority, the regime's attitude toward entrepreneurs – large-scale entrepreneurs especially – was ambivalent, if not downright hostile. The reason, of course, was the tendency of those engaged in that vocation to seek independence from state interference and to pursue their own interests irrespective of the "good of the country." In the view of Carl Franz Reinhardt, chief economic adviser to Frederick William I and drafter of much key legislation of the 1720s and 1730s, merchant–manufacturers were "poor patriots" because they paid low wages during prosperous times, laid off workers during recessions, and then took their

47 Hinrichs, *Preussentum und Pietismus*, 317. For the spread of the wool magazine system in East Prussia, see Hinrichs, *Die Wollindustrie*, 279–82.

48 The histories of the two firms, the wool textile partnership of Sarry and Kessler and a linen textile manufactory founded by Pinet and Boltz, parallel each other neatly, both being organized around 1722–23, flourishing briefly, then experiencing intense opposition from the Königsberg merchants, and finally expiring by 1728 because garrison commanders persuaded the king that it was in his best interest to let them go under. For the former, see Hinrichs, *Die Wollindustrie*, 268–75; for the latter, see Stark, "Die Leinenindustrie in Preussen," 48–51.

enhanced supply of capital out of the country without even indemnifying the state for having to take care of unemployed ex-workers reduced to beggary.[49]

Though the state could not completely dispense with entrepreneurs, it used them only selectively and subjected them to extensive regulation. Thus they were allowed to perform such functions as the marketing of textile exports abroad and the supplying of wholesale cloth to regimental commanders.[50] The private firm that enjoyed the best relationship between Frederick William was the partnership of Splitgerber & Daun, to whom the king leased the entire Prussian armaments industry on generous terms. The unique success of Splitgerber & Daun in this regard was precisely because of Splitgerber's ability to convince Frederick William I of his willingness to accept state direction and to undertake on behalf of the state whatever tasks the king desired.[51]

Much more adversarial were the dealings between Frederick William and J. A. Krautt, the original owner of the *Lagerhaus*, whose fortune the king had "persuaded" him to invest in this enterprise.[52] Probably with good reason, Frederick William I greatly distrusted Krautt and kept the entire *Lagerhaus* operation under his close personal scrutiny.[53] After Krautt's death in 1723, the king brought forth accusations of capital crimes against him and within two years had succeeded in "nationalizing" the largest firm in his kingdom.

A similar fate ultimately overtook the second largest complex of private businesses in the Hohenzollern lands, the enterprises of

49 Reinhardt's views, so contrary to the mainstream of earlier mercantilist thought in Central Europe, are most clearly set forth in his "Denkschrift über Staat, Unternehmer und Arbeiter," in the *Aktenanhang* of Hinrichs, *Die Wollindustrie*, esp. 407–09.

50 Hinrichs, *Die Wollindustrie*, 278; Krause, *Altpreussische Uniformfertigung*, 18.

51 Wilhelm Treue, "David Splitgerber: Ein Unternehmer im preussischen Merkantilstaat, 1683–1764," *Vierteljahrschrift für Sozial- und Wirtschaftsgeschichte*, 41 (1954): 255–56. Besides the fairly brief treatment in Treue's work, the most informative article on the armaments industry, including information on the period 1713–40, is by Paul Rehfeld, "Die preussische Rüstungsindustrie unter Friedrich dem Grossen," *Forschungen zur brandenburgischen und preussischen Geschichte*, 55 (1944): 1–31.

52 For more information on Krautt's background and the founding of the *Lagerhaus*, see Hinrichs, *Preussentum und Pietismus*, 302–09.

53 Harald Reissig argues that Krautt was under such tight control that even as head of the *Lagerhaus* he was able to take hardly any personal initiatives in its management. The "state commission" that directed the business after Krautt's death was ironically able to act more "entrepreneurially" because the king trusted them more. See Reissig, "Das Berliner Lagerhaus, 1713–1816: Zum Einfluss von Regierung und Wirtschaft auf die Entwicklung einer altpreussischen Staatsmanufaktur," *Jahrbuch für die Geschichte Mittel- und Ostdeutschlands*, 29 (1980): 73–74.

Severin Schindler, which featured an export-oriented gold-and-silver thread factory, the one major luxury-goods operation to survive the accession to power of Frederick William I. Continual badgering by the king induced Schindler to turn over to the state both this factory and a lucrative alum mine before his death in 1737. These concerns were then managed by the same bureaucratic state commission that had been overseeing the *Lagerhaus* since Krautt's death. In keeping with Frederick William's Pietist social agenda, the considerable profits from all these state-run enterprises were used to support the Potsdam military orphanage.[54]

In addition to expropriating existing businesses, Frederick William I also minimized the role of pure entrepreneurship in the Prussian economy by assigning substantial entrepreneurial responsibilities to his functionaries. One such group of state-supervised entrepreneurs were the company (and regimental) commanders in the army, who annually received from the king a carefully budgeted sum for recruiting and paying soldiers and for buying the necessary supplies and equipment. Since the commanders could keep for themselves whatever they did not have to spend in order to maintain their companies sufficiently well to pass the annual inspections, they had every incentive to buy uniforms from the most efficient artisan and every reason to avoid paying excess wages by furloughing native soldiers and finding employment for their *Freiwächter*.[55]

Another such hybrid type of official/entrepreneur were the leasees of royal domain lands, the *Pächter*. Since the royal bureaucracy had scrupulously assessed the potential productivity of their leased lands and set their rents accordingly high, the *Pächter* were obliged to cooperate with royal efforts to raise productivity by settling colonists, compelling the labor force to accept new techniques and work routines, and establishing mills and breweries on domain lands.[56]

In an economy thus permeated by monopoly and direct bureaucratic administration, it was necessary for Frederick William I to

[54] Hinrichs, *Preussentum und Pietismus*, 311–13, 328–29, 339, 341.

[55] Büsch, *Militärsystem und Sozialleben*, 113–16.

[56] Skalweit, *Die ostpreussische Domänenverwaltung*, 161, 183–87, 193–97. According to Corni, the *Pächter* were often quite innovative and entrepreneurial, but this very tendency led them to seek to exploit the peasantry and thus undermine the regime's goal of "conserving" its peasant subjects. The weakness of the royal judicial administration – combined with the individual *Pächter*'s own considerable powers as a state official – meant that in practice abuses of authority by the *Pächter* could be checked only by the (often inadequate) oversight given by the provincial war-and-domain board. Corni, "Absolutistische Agrarpolitik und Agrargesellschaft," 287–91.

devise policies and administrative procedures to regulate the economy as a whole in such a way that the needs of the various interest groups could all be more or less satisfied simultaneously. Thus almost immediately after the *Lagerhaus* set up shop, Krautt complained to the king that his business's demand for wool was driving up its price, since the *Lagerhaus* had to compete with Saxon and Silesian concerns for the raw wool produced in Brandenburg. To enable the *Lagerhaus* to make a profit and to subject the economy to tighter state control, Frederick William responded to Krautt's pleas by gradually restricting wool exports before finally prohibiting them in 1719.

For essentially the same reason – to enable favored producers in the domestic economy at least to break even – the king was also compelled to practice vigorous state intervention to guarantee them adequate markets. Under an officially negotiated deal with the Russian government, between 1725 and 1738 the fledgling Prussian textile industry was given the monopoly of supplying the Tsar's army with uniforms.[57] Export premiums paid by the state also permitted other branches of the textile industry, such as Pomeranian linens, to secure a place in foreign markets.[58]

The most significant legislation of this type, however, affected the structuring of the domestic market. The rapidly expanding army, for example, was intended to serve as the most important buyer of Prussian-made goods. Already in 1713 Frederick William ordered his company commanders to buy uniforms from domestic producers. To increase this institutional demand still further, the king decreed in 1724 that the army would have to purchase new uniforms every year.[59] To make sure that this and other key markets remained protected ones for Prussian industry, the king systematically sought to eliminate foreign competition. Thus, by 1718 duties on imported metal goods, such as nails, scythes, and axes, reached seventy-five or even one hundred percent of the value of these goods; by 1719 the king had banned all imports of foreign cloth, and by 1724 all imports of armaments were likewise forbidden.

For similar reasons, the king increasingly accorded the agri-

[57] Organizing the deliveries of cloth to Russia was one of the tasks that Splitgerber & Daun performed for the king. See Treue, "David Splitgerber," 259–60. For the most complete history of this "Russian Company," see Gustav Schmoller, "Die russische Kompagnie in Berlin, 1724–1738," *Zeitschrift für preussische Geschichte und Landeskunde*, 20 (1883): 1–116.

[58] Stark, "Die Leinenindustrie in Preussen," 64.

[59] Hinrichs, *Preussentum und Pietismus*, 317.

cultural sector this same kind of protection. Since it became increasingly clear that the *Pächter* could not consistently meet their (high) rent obligations to the state in the face of competition from cheaper, higher quality Polish grain, the king prohibited the importation of the latter in 1722. In order to accommodate further the needs of the *Pächter*, the king also began to expand the network of grain magazines in the 1720s. Originally intended to serve as a reserve for feeding the army in time of war, the magazines also played the role of stabilizing domestic grain prices, both to keep the price up for the *Pächter* in years of abundance and to prevent it from going too high for the common people, especially the soldiers, during years of dearth.[60] Naturally, too, these same agrarian policies benefited the Junker estate owners in the identical manner.

The scope and intensity of the Prussian state's role in directly administering and coordinating the economic life of the population was perhaps greater than that played by any other European state up to that time. One-third of all the country's arable land was part of the royal domain, and Frederick William I not only succeeded in taking away from the provincial estates the administration of those domain lands but also spent five million Taler to increase substantially the size of the state's holdings.[61] The state also either controlled or else very tightly regulated the two largest branches of the Prussian industrial sector – armaments and textiles. Additional sources of labor, be they immigrants or hitherto underutilized domestic workers, were channeled exclusively into the state-dominated sectors. Extremely strict protectionist policies enforced by a committed bureaucracy with the power to inflict draconian penalties shielded the state's economic complex from international market competition.[62] Though at first it was only in the core area of

[60] Rachel, "Der Merkantilismus in Brandenburg-Preussen," 233–34; Ergang, *The Potsdam Führer*, 180, 182; Wilhelm Treue, "David Splitgerber," 259; Skalweit, *Die ostpreussische Domänenverwaltung*, 166–70. Corni questions this standard view by arguing that the military purpose of the magazines remained primary and that the regime used them to regulate the market price of grain only in exceptional circumstances. Corni, "Absolutistische Agrarpolitik und Agrargesellschaft," 299.

[61] Juhr, *Die Verwaltung des Hauptamtes Brandenburg/Ostpreussen*, 96–106; Büsch, *Militärsystem und Sozialleben*, 101–02.

[62] For a statement of Frederick William I's commitment to the principle of what we would today call "import substitution," which he found to be "an extremely useful end goal," see his "Instruktion . . . für das General- . . . Direktorium . . . 1722," in Schmoller *et al.*, eds., *Die Behördenorganisation*, vol. III, 595. For those caught exporting wool, the punishment was hanging, see *ibid*, 596. The surveillance network of the bureaucracy was also brought to bear on enforcing the protectionist system. When the prohibitions on importing foreign

Brandenburg that the regulations defining this system could be fully applied, by 1740 all the East Elbian territories of the monarchy, including, most impressively East Prussia, functioned as a unified economic entity – in many crucial respects as a single, enormous firm.[63]

As was the case with the Halle *Anstalten*, the Prussian state/economy under Frederick William I was able to combine this kind of ideological control and ever greater self-sufficiency with growth in the material resources available to the institutional complex. As early as 1716, the domestic cloth industry produced sufficient quantities of uniforms to meet the army's needs. Wool used for manufacturing in Berlin increased from 34,969 stones in 1720 to 81,955 in 1735.[64] Besides fulfilling the requirements for uniforms from both the Prussian and Russian armies, this rapidly developing textile industry was able to satisfy domestic demand as well, including the need for higher quality clothing products.[65] By 1730 the arms factories in Spandau and Potsdam were exporting weapons to Denmark, Poland, Russia, and the Habsburg empire.[66]

In addition, the military build-up and corresponding expansion of local industry resulted in demographic growth in urban centers throughout the kingdom, which in turn created a considerable demand for new housing.[67] During the reign of Frederick William I,

textiles were extended to East Prussia in 1732, the state showed its determination to enforce these rules by slapping heavy fines on violators, one-quarter of which went to the informer. Hinrichs, *Die Wollindustrie*, 277. For the difficulty foreign merchants had in penetrating the shield around the eighteenth-century Prussian economy, see Helen Liebel, "Laissez-faire vs. Mercantilism: The Rise of Hamburg and the Hamburg Bourgeoisie vs. Frederick the Great in the Crisis of 1763," *Vierteljahrschrift für Sozial- und Wirtschaftsgeschichte*, 52 (1965): 207–38.

63 For the initially difficult but ultimately successful integration of the Pomeranian port of Stettin into the Prussian economic system, see Wilhelm Braun, "Zur Stettiner Seehandelsgeschichte, 1572–1813," *Baltische Studien*, N.F., 52 (1966): 65–75. The economic life of the Prussian territories in western Germany could not, however, be so completely integrated into this state-directed economy. Thus the highly developed linen textile industry centered in Bielefeld remained so underutilized by the Prussian state that military units in wool-rich but linen-poor Brandenburg ultimately imported linen from Austrian Silesia rather than from "Prussian" Bielefeld. Stark, "Die Leinenindustrie in Preussen," 77–78.

64 Ergang, *The Potsdam Führer*, 168.

65 According to Reissig, this kind of production for the private sector became an increasingly important priority for the *Lagerhaus*, especially after 1723. By 1733 private, non-military sales exceeded deliveries to the army. See Reissig, "Das Berliner Lagerhaus, 1713–1816," 73–74.

66 Treue, "David Splitgerber," 259.

67 The prosperity of provincial cities and towns, not just of Berlin, constituted a major distinguishing factor between the economic system established by Frederick William I and that of his immediate predecessors. For the example of Stettin, where the population

the urban population in the Mark Brandenburg doubled in size, so that the construction industry in Berlin alone was building an average of 90 houses a year, reaching a peak of 152 new homes a year in 1733.[68] The requirements for wood and metal products on the part of a flourishing construction industry, not to mention the textile and armaments manufacturers, encouraged the founding of new woodworking and metalworking concerns to handle the spin-off business generated by the major industries. To facilitate the exchange of the increased volume of goods being produced, the king issued new comprehensive regulations intended to overturn customary limits on market activity and to increase enormously the number of wool, cloth, cattle, and general retail markets.[69]

Since these dynamic sectors were the ones most intimately linked with the state, their prosperity was reflected in the flourishing nature of the state's finances. Despite rising expenditures for an army that came to number 83,000 by 1740, revenues grew even more rapidly. Income from administering the royal domains, for example, increased from 1.8 million Taler in 1713 to 3.3 million Taler in 1740. Agriculture in general benefited from increased demand from the cities, the exclusion of Polish grain, and the state's policy of stockpiling grain.[70] As a result of these favorable conditions, the state was able to collect increasingly higher rents from the leaseholders of its domain lands, and its yield from the *Kontribution* tax on private landholdings also rose. The other major source of state revenues, the excise tax, was an obvious beneficiary of the increase in urban populations and the corresponding growth of internal trade. Together with receipts from the land tax, revenues from the excise reached 3.6 million Taler in 1740, 1.1 million more than in 1713. In short, total state revenues increased from 4.8 million Taler in 1713, one-half million of which consisted of foreign

doubled and the construction industry boomed, see Braun, "Zur Stettiner Seehandelsgeschichte," 74.

68 Ergang, *The Potsdam Führer*, 181; Karlheinz Böhme, *Untersuchungen über die Charité Patienten*, 5. The aesthetic standards of this often hastily constructed residential building reflected the king's puritanical and militaristic values, with all the houses lacking any ornamentation whatever and all looking very much alike. In the parts of the city dominated by the new building, the impression made on observers was that "the whole city seemed like a single, gigantic barracks" (*Kaserne*). Geiger, *Berlin, 1688–1840*, vol. 1, 185.

69 Rachel, "Der Merkantilismus in Brandenburg-Preussen," 235.

70 As Büsch points out, state controls over the level of the price of grain limited opportunities for large speculative gains, but the system did guarantee a market year in year out not only for the *Pächter* but also for the Junkers. Büsch, *Militärsystem und Sozialleben*, 111–12.

subsidy payments, to 7 million in 1740. Moreover, since the royal accounts regularly produced surpluses, the king left his successor a hoard of 9.3 million Taler, a reserve fund (*Tresor*) designed to compensate the state for the loss of tax revenues resulting from keeping the entire army mobilized during time of war.[71]

How can one explain, analytically, this extraordinary increase in Prussian state revenues? Historians have customarily labelled Frederick William I's economic policies as "mercantilist." Rudolf Vierhaus, for example, views this sort of "statist economic policy" as operating throughout the German lands but "most effective[ly] in Brandenburg-Prussia, where economic development could be placed in the service of state expansion, militarism, and the social disciplining of the population."[72] In seeking to determine more precisely how these state-sponsored goals actually produced economic growth in eighteenth-century Prussia, it would be perhaps more fruitful to conceptualize the Prussian economy not so much in terms of such a general concept as "mercantilism," but rather as an early example of a modern "command economy," i.e. an economic system in which at least the most important processes of resource allocation are determined not by market forces but by the administrative decisions of a central political authority.

Since by far the most intensely studied example of a growth-oriented command economy has been the "Soviet-type" system of the present century, findings from works analyzing that system should be able to provide a theoretical basis for identifying causal factors contributing to the periods of rapid growth sometimes enjoyed by such economies. It was true in the Soviet case and, with appropriate qualifications, in eighteenth-century Prussia that the command economy worked best when it was the case of a less developed economy "with a smaller number of commodities and enterprises and a more stark set of priorities to guide the adjustments the balancers [Frederick William I, in the Prussian case] had to make.'[73] When such conditions prevail, the centrally administered economy can, in its first decades, grow rapidly and accumulate large amounts of capital (*e.g.* the *Tresor*) by "constraining consumption

[71] Klein, *Geschichte der öffentlichen Finanzen*, 49–52.

[72] Rudolf Vierhaus, *Germany in the Age of Absolutism*, trans. Jonathan B. Knudsen (Cambridge, 1988), 30.

[73] Robert W. Campbell, *The Soviet-type Economies: Performance and Evaluation* (Boston, 1974), 38–39.

... [and] transferring people from sectors in which their labor was underutilized to those where it could be fully utilized, increasing participation rates in the labor force, and devoting large resources to training and education to build up a stock of modern skills in the population."[74]

In addition to these factors common to both systems, Frederick William I fashioned the Prussian economy in such a way that even in its most intensively regulated sectors there were built-in incentives for entrepreneurial behavior and technological innovation. Besides the already discussed examples of the company commanders and the domain *Pächter*, an important illustration of the Prussian blend of central control and individual initiative was the subgroup within the tailors' guild who prepared army uniforms for the troops of the local garrison. On one level, the state relieved these tailors of some entrepreneurial tasks by providing the cloth and trimmings and, to a certain extent, guaranteeing the market, though the company chiefs could contract with any tailor they wanted. To win contracts for supplying the army's needs on a regular basis, masters had to meet production deadlines, use efficiently the stringently limited amount of allocated material, and pay their workers out of the relatively low price they received. In response to the discipline imposed by these parameters, the master tailors developed new production techniques that, far more than those still prevalent in the private sector, anticipated the fundamental characteristics of the mass-production clothing industry of the nineteenth century. These tailors prospered to such an extent that they acquired the highest status within their guild and contributed to a "transformation in spirit within the guild."[75]

Despite the importance of such economic factors, in command economies dedicated to mobilization of a country's resources for the benefit of the state, the lynch-pin of the entire system is ultimately

[74] *Ibid.*, 142.

[75] Krause, *Altpreussische Uniformfertigung*, 46–49, 51, 54. It should be pointed out, however, that such efforts by Frederick William I to restructure entire sectors of the Prussian economy were not always exempt from the characteristic failings of modern command economies. In attempting to raise agricultural productivity in East Prussia, for example, the king sought to impose on that province's domain lands the cultivation methods characteristic of the Magdeburg region of central Germany, despite substantial differences between the two regions in soil-moisture levels and growing-season length. As a result, the royal interventions were in many cases completely counterproductive, and much wasted effort and capital resulted from Frederick William's rigidity and stubbornness in this campaign. Skalweit, *Die ostpreussische Domänenverwaltung*, 193–95.

the acceptance of the official ideology on the part of the population.[76] The campaign to inculcate that ideology in the population has to succeed at least to some extent because "there must be ... some internalization of the goals of the organization that will ease the conflict between what is good for the organization and the personal interest of the participants."[77] Otherwise an attempt to impose through administrative means a much more specialized division of labor on the economy would incur unacceptably high costs from having to overcome the people's inertial resistance to the radical disruption of everyday life accompanying such changes.

The substantial expansion in the productive capacity of the Prussian economy after 1713 thus provides additional confirmation that Frederick William I had successfully imposed his value system of State Pietism on his country, particularly on the cadre groups.[78] Over time, of course, the educational efforts initiated by Frederick William I and the Pietists would create nothing less than a new collective mentality, so that in the words of Walter Dorn, the Prussians became "the most highly disciplined people of modern Europe."[79] Some sense of just how deeply rooted this mentality became and how tenaciously it persisted can be gleaned from this account by the Austrian writer Stefan Zweig of his visit to Berlin around the year 1900:

Thanks to the old Prussian thrift, there was no suggestion of general elegance. Women went to the theater in unattractive home-made dresses, and everywhere one missed the light, deft, and lavish hand which in

[76] For a theoretical model of the "mobilization system" as a political means for fostering "development" in post-colonial African countries, see David E. Apter, *The Politics of Modernization* (Chicago, 1965), 357–90, where the role of "political religion" is given a heavy emphasis.

[77] Campbell, *The Soviet-type Economies*, 29. For an in-depth analysis of the centrality of "Soviet ethics" in the functioning of the Soviet system, see Herbert Marcuse, *Soviet Marxism* (New York, 1961), 179–252. On page 250, Marcuse characterizes this "Communist morality" as "political Puritanism," an "ethics of work and discipline, of competitive patriotism in love and toil."

[78] According to Duffy, contemporary observers of the eighteenth-century Prussian army, such as the British general John Burgoyne, concluded that the unusual effectiveness of the Prussian army resulted from "the technical proficiency of the lieutenants and NCOs and their principle of unthinking obedience." Duffy, *The Army of Frederick the Great*, 52. Skalweit calls the creation of a competent and loyal cadre of *Pächter* in East Prussia a "product of royal education," a feat especially impressive because most of them were natives of that province and were by implication presumably more resistant to obeying orders from Berlin, particularly in the fashion demanded by Frederick William I. Skalweit, *Die ostpreussische Domänenverwaltung*, 91.

[79] Walter Dorn, *Competition for Empire, 1740–1763* (New York, 1940), 58.

Vienna, as in Paris, could create an enchanting abundance out of very little. In every detail one felt the closefistedness of Frederician husbandry. The coffee was thin and bad because every bean was counted ... Cleanliness and rigid and accurate order reigned everywhere instead of our musical rhythm of life. Nothing seemed more characteristic to me than the contrast between my landladies in Vienna and Berlin. The Viennese was a cheerful, chatty woman who did not keep things too clean, and easily forgot this or that, but was enthusiastically eager to be of service. The one in Berlin was correct and kept everything in perfect order; but in my first monthly account I found every service that she had given me down in neat, vertical writing: three pfennigs for sewing a trouser button, twenty for removing an inkspot from the tabletop, until at the end, under a broad stroke of the pen, all of her troubles amounted to the neat little sum of 67 pfennigs. At first I laughed at this; but it was characteristic that after a very few days I too succumbed to this Prussian sense of orderliness and for the first, and last, time in my life I kept an accurate account of my expenses."[80]

[80] Stefan Zweig, *The World of Yesterday: An Autobiography* (New York, 1943), 112–13.

Conclusion

Through the process of mobilization just described, the Prussian state between 1713 and 1740 broke through the limits that had prevented any German territorial princedom from acquiring sufficient military and financial strength to challenge the post-1648 supremacy of the Habsburgs within the Empire. By the end of Frederick William I's reign, the Prussian army numbered 83,000 troops in peacetime, approximately double the peak size of the Hohenzollern force that had fought during the War of Spanish Succession with half of its budget funded by foreign subsidies. Frederick William I also left his son meticulously maintained fortresses, well-stocked grain magazines, and a war chest of nearly ten million Taler, which obviated the need for outside assistance for at least the early stages of any prospective war.

This remarkable increase in state power was the result of the establishment by Frederick William I of what a contemporary observer called "a form of government, which was probably 'till then without example, and perhaps had not existed 'till then."[1] What was revolutionary about the Prussian state in the context of the early eighteenth century was, of course, the sudden replacement of the customary system of princely rule through the court by a recognizably modern bureaucratic structure. In the words of Gianfranco Poggi: "Frederick William I and his successor ruled through, [and] at the center of, a much larger, more elaborately constructed and regulated body of public organs engaged in administrative activities that were more continuous, systematic, pervasive, visible, and effective than anything Louis XIV [or any of his German imitators] had ever contemplated."[2]

1 Mauvillon, *The Life of Frederick William I*, 79.

2 Gianfranco Poggi, *The Development of the Modern State: A Sociological Introduction* (London, 1978), 74. For a similar verdict, see Eberhard Weis, "Absolute Monarchie und Reform in

Such a revolutionary change could ultimately have been the product only of a multitude of factors operating both in Europe as a whole and in the Hohenzollern realm. Yet it is possible to identify, at least in the particular case of Prussia, the catalyst that induced all the contributing elements to react with one another in such a powerful way. In this study I have shown that Frederick William I possessed a new vision of the nature of the state, based on a concept of ethical action that derived in turn from the puritanical piety that emerged in late seventeenth- and early eighteenth-century German Protestantism. Animating Frederick William's state-building efforts was his conviction that his obligations to God with respect to his monarchical office required not only unceasing labor on his part but also his subjects' unquestioning obedience to his commands. Recognizing no differentiation between his own duty and the best interests of the inhabitants of his state, this self-centered, autocratic king justified the demands he placed on them on the grounds that to serve the Prussian state was to further God's work in the world.[3]

Since most of the Prussian people were not spontaneously attracted to the Spartan regimen that Frederick William I sought to impose on them, the new relationship – or "covenant," if you will – between ruler and subjects developed as a result of the intensive "reeducation" campaign organized by the king. Pedagogical methods that in the rest of Europe were used only in workhouses and comparable institutions were applied to Prussian society as a whole. As we have seen, the most important goal of this training, from the perspective of both the Halle *Anstalten* and the Prussian state, was the initial one of "breaking the will" of the trainees, to make them internalize a sense of obedience and subordination to the authority of the institution. As was the case with the Pietist conversion experience, moreover, initiation into the Prussian state service was merely the prelude to a lifetime of zealous striving to conform to the precepts of morality and performance by which one was to measure one's degree of fidelity to God and country. Just as Francke did with his "rules for living" and his meticulously detailed school ordinances, so Frederick William I spelled out complete, very specific

Deutschland des späten 18. und des frühen 19. Jahrhunderts," in Franklin Kopitzsch, ed., *Aufklärung, Absolutismus und Bürgertum in Deutschland* (Munich, 1976), 193–94.

3 This rationale was, of course, analogous in every way to Francke's claim with respect to the providential mission of the Halle *Anstalten*, which similarly demanded conformity to strict standards of behavior and total dedication to the cause of the institution.

codes of conduct for members of every category of state servant – common soldiers, officers, bureaucrats, guild members, domain managers, toll-gate keepers, etc. These codes included not only ethical exhortations but also precise, binding instructions as to how to carry out the entrusted duties. The tremendous quantity of this kind of legislation produced by Frederick William I effectively encompassed the entire state apparatus, giving these codes, taken all together, the character of a consistent, comprehensive body of administrative law.[4]

The *Soldatenkönig*, finally, like Francke, built into his administration a very extensive capability for surveilling and evaluating every state servant's faithfulness in adhering to these rules. The success achieved in conditioning Prussian soldiers and bureaucrats to obey commands given in the same standardized language contained in the conduct codes made possible the efficient, concerted quality of performance characteristic of the eighteenth-century Prussian bureaucracy.[5]

The isomorphic relationship between the Halle *Anstalten* and the Prussian state, as artificial societies whose unity was constructed upon a similar set of spiritual and normative bases, extended to their economic structures as well. Most revealing of this profound affinity are the analogies between the feedback mechanism responsible for the growth of the Prussian economy under Frederick William I and that which enabled the Halle enterprises to expand so dramatically. Both systems operated by continuously recruiting new members – agrarian colonists and impressed soldiers in the case of the Prussian state. As the Halle *Anstalten* and the Prussian army expanded with the influx of personnel, each institutional complex in effect created a demand that its economic enterprises were reorganized to supply, though in the case of the Prussian economy the state had to impose a very strict protectionism in order to minimize foreign competition. Lastly, both the Halle *Anstalten* and the Prussian state exerted tight disciplinary controls over both producers and consumers to prevent "dissipation" of resources that did not advance the ideological goals of these institutions.

[4] For the novelty and significance of this Prussian administrative law, see Poggi, *The Development of the Modern State*, 75–76.

[5] For the importance of a standardized language grounded in a consistent normative outlook, see Fulbrook, *Piety and Politics*, 172–73. For the role of this kind of "code" in Halle Pietism, see above, p. 166.

With respect to the original germination of the Prussian political culture and the eighteenth-century Prussian state system, then, the Protestant Prometheanism of Frederick William I and Halle Pietism played a decisive, energizing role. In light of the fact, however, that the collaboration between the two lasted only about twenty-five years, it remains to be explained how the legacy from that comparatively brief period could have endured for so many generations to come. Part of the answer lay in the way trends in the European economy helped ensure the longevity of the *dirigiste* economic structure created by Frederick William I. Rapid population growth had already resumed throughout Europe in the 1720s or 1730s; and since the Hohenzollern lands were sparsely settled, it was not difficult for the Prussian state to attract colonists and recruit soldiers for the rest of the eighteenth century. With a continuous supply of new labor inputs – the most important economic factor in the growth of a command economy – the Prussian economy was able to grow, at least in scale if not in rate of productivity, for several more decades.[6] The continued viability of this system was enhanced, moreover, by the revival of the international grain trade after 1750, which supplemented the profits the Junkers were able to make either as army commanders or as suppliers of grain to the internal market.[7] Thus even though the majority of the Prussian nobility were neither army officers nor civilian bureaucrats, the Junkers as a class were tied to the economic order established by Frederick William I and benefited from it.[8]

Even more vital to the perpetuation of the Prussian polity and ethos, however, was the role played by Frederick the Great, who ascended to the throne after the death of his father in 1740. As the survival of the still barely consolidated Prussian system depended on Frederick's ability and willingness to work tirelessly as its autocratic head, his upbringing served, not surprisingly, as a paradigmatic

6 Besides the rigidities inherent in any command economy, once its form is set, the weaknesses of the late eighteenth-century Prussian economy can be attributed to the fiscally motivated failure of the state to allow the nominal incomes of soldiers and laborers to keep up with inflation. The resulting softness in domestic demand contributed, along with a desire not to dismantle some of the existing control apparatus, to a deficiency in "proto-industrial" enterprise in the East Elbian territories, Silesia excepted. See Corni, "Absolutistische Agrarpolitik und Agrargesellschaft," 300.

7 For the opportunities for profit available to the officer/estate-owning Junker elite, especially during the reign of Frederick II, see Büsch, *Militärsystem und Sozialleben*, 113–32.

8 This addresses a point raised by Hagen, "Seventeenth-Century Crisis in Brandenburg," 335.

example of the coercion and brutality by which the "educational" system set up by Frederick William I drilled the state-service ideology into the Prussian people.[9] The strong will of the eighteen-year-old prince was finally harnessed for the great labor of state service only in the course of the horrible desertion incident, as a result of which Frederick in return for clemency from his father agreed to make service to the army and the state the central activity of his life.[10] Emerging from this ordeal psychologically scarred and devoid of religious faith, Frederick underwent a thorough apprenticeship in the areas of regimental and domain administration and remained a faithful steward of the system for the rest of his life.

Frederick's most distinguished service to the state, however, was in the field in which his father was least adept: international politics. Whereas Frederick William I retained a stubborn loyalty to the Emperor and was reluctant in any case to risk losing his precious soldiers, his son, within six months of ascending the throne, seizing a favorable opportunity, attacked and conquered the Habsburg province of Silesia. In the generation of war that followed, Frederick proved himself to be a gifted general, war leader, and diplomat, able not only to retain Silesia but later to help initiate the process of partitioning Poland, which added yet more territory to the Hohenzollern realm. Internally, despite the trials of the Silesian wars, Frederick preserved intact the basic military–bureaucratic–economic structure of the Prussian system. Even though it became increasingly difficult to exert autocratic control over the bureaucracy, Frederick's reign can certainly be characterized as the routinization, enlargement, and culmination of the Prussian state created by his father and the Lutheran Pietists.[11]

From the perspective of this study, however, it would seem as

[9] For a sense of the sadistic brutality of Frederick William I, unleashed by Frederick's thorough-going defiance of his father's pedagogical efforts, see the telling account by Gaxotte, *Frederick the Great*, 33, 44, 47, 49. The king's rationalization for his actions is also captured well by Gaxotte. Since according to Frederick William "even the Crown Prince had no right to have a personality at variance with the nature of his kingdom," by seeking to "satisfy his personal wishes ... he had revolted against the needs of the Prussian state." *Ibid.*, 76.

[10] There was, of course, a "spiritual" dimension to this father–son conflict. In the immediate aftermath of Katte's execution, while Frederick was still profoundly grieving, he was presented with the king's first demand by the Halle-trained court chaplain, Müller. It was to renounce his earlier belief in predestination and thereby to replicate in a completely contrived way his father's 1708 conversion. *Ibid.*, 74–81.

[11] For the limits on Frederick's ability to control his officials, see Hubert C. Johnson, *Frederick the Great and His Officials* (New Haven, 1975), *passim.*

though the transition in rulership from Frederick William I to Frederick the Great should not have been so smooth and successful. If the Prussian political system before 1740 had been so dependent on Pietism for ideological support, one can wonder why Frederick's personal hostility to Pietism and his adherence to the Enlightenment (*Aufklärung*) did not undermine the foundations of his father's edifice. It is true that the sophisticated Frederick, like many of the leading cameralists of his day, recognized the utility of religion in buttressing monarchical authority and therefore refrained from disturbing the workings of Prussia's ecclesiastical institutions. But unless the gap between Pietism and the Enlightenment was not so great as some contemporaries and many historians have assumed, it is hard to see how a serious crisis for the Prussian state could have been avoided.

One development that eased the transition was that a division in the Pietist movement in the 1730s foreshadowed and helped prepare the way for the coming ascendancy of the Enlightenment as the official ideology of the Prussian state. The precipitating factor here was that in the last years of his reign Frederick William I launched a characteristically iconoclast initiative to suppress the remaining "Catholic" ceremonial in the Lutheran service.[12] The Pietist leadership in Halle opposed adamantly what they regarded as a back-door attempt to unify the Lutheran and Reformed churches by making them liturgically indistinguishable.[13] Since this attitude was naturally shared by more orthodox Lutherans, Halle's fight to preserve the old liturgy united them with the leadership of the church and helped bring about a reconciliation of the bitter feud that had divided Lutheranism since the Leipzig "days" of 1689–90.[14]

Not all members of the younger Pietist generation, however, went along with Halle's lead. Hornejus in Pomerania zealously enforced the king's orders, and Schultz in East Prussia actually drafted in 1734 the *Verordnung* that served as the model for the anti-ceremonial legislation decreed for the kingdom as a whole in 1736.[15] Those

[12] For more information about this campaign to restrict the old ceremonies, see Wotschke, "Lampert Gedickes Briefe," 108–12; for documents relating to the implementation of this legislation, see Wilhelm Stolze, "Aktenstücke zur evangelischen Kirchenpolitik Friedrich Wilhelms I.," *Jahrbuch für brandenburgische Kirchengeschichte*, 1 (1904): 273–88.

[13] Stolze, "Friedrich Wilhelm I. und der Pietismus," 199.

[14] Pariset, *L'état et les églises en Prusse*, 623–24.

[15] Heyden, *Die Kirchengeschichte von Pommern*, vol. 1, 177, 189; Hinrichs, *Preussentum und Pietismus*, 273.

Pietist leaders who supported Frederick William I on this issue tended to be, like Schultz and the Berlin provost Gustav Reinbeck, open to or at least tolerant of Enlightenment ideas. Even Frederick William himself toward the end of his life began to be influenced by the ideas of Christian Wolff to the point of offering to reinstate him in his former professorship at the University of Halle.[16]

Most importantly, the *Aufklärung* ideology so assiduously promoted by Frederick was very heavily indebted to its Pietist predecessor. Not at all anti-clerical or politically subversive like the *philosophes* in France, some of the *Aufklärer* even taught theology or held positions in the Lutheran or Reformed churches; all of them inherited from Halle Pietism a strong social conscience and a commitment to reforming society without changing its hierarchical order.[17] The spiritual and material improvement desired by both Pietism and *Aufklärung* was deemed achievable, moreover, by the same instrument – education.[18] And it was basically the same type of education! The "Enlightened" showed no qualms about advocating or employing manipulative pedagogical techniques to break the wills of their charges in order to instill in them "Christian" values and render them malleable for social engineering.[19] The curricula designed by the pedagogues of the *Aufklärung* also continued, even intensified, Francke's practice of teaching practical knowledge as a means of increasing each pupil's future contribution to the common good. Like the Pietists, too, the theologians of the *Aufklärung* embraced the Puritan work ethic, regarding the acquisition of

16 Stolze, "Friedrich Wilhelm I. und der Pietismus," 202–03. See also Birtsch, "Friedrich Wilhelm I. und die Anfänge der Aufklärung," 88.

17 For a revealing account of how one individual, Johann Salomo Semler, made the transition from Pietism to *Aufklärung*, see Fulbrook, *Piety and Politics*, 170–72. For a perceptive analysis of the psychological process underlying the transition from the highly moralistic forms of seventeenth-century Christianity to the less fideistic moralism of the eighteenth century, see Briggs, *Communities of Belief*, 375. On the social conservatism of the German Enlightenment, see Joachim Whaley, "The Protestant Enlightenment in Germany," in Roy Porter and Mikulas Teich, eds., *The Enlightenment in National Context* (Cambridge, 1981), 108, 111–12.

18 Alexandra Schlingensiepen-Pogge, *Das Sozialethos der lutherischen Aufklärungstheologie am Vorabend der industriellen Revolution* (Göttingen, 1967), 166–67.

19 For the tactics advocated, for example, by J. B. Basedow, see the excerpts from his writings quoted in Alice Miller, *For Your Good: Hidden Cruelty in Child-Rearing and the Roots of Violence* (New York, 1983), 24–25, 34–36. Perhaps the deepest element of continuity between the two movements is revealed here in the common desire to impose pedagogical control. In this sense, the emergence of the fundamentally more secular mentality of the *Aufklärung* constituted the development of a world view more consistent with this aim than was that of Lutheran Pietism. For in the words of Huston Smith, *Beyond the Post-Modern Mind*, 200, "an epistemology that aims relentlessly at control rules out [in principle] the possibility of transcendence [i.e. that which is "beyond control"]."

wealth as signifying God's approval of a person's morality and diligence.[20]

To be sure, the two movements were not identical. Theologically, the *Aufklärer* rejected the Augustinian anthropology of the Pietists in favor of an optimistic view of human nature and a Pelagian view of the salvation process.[21] Despite the significance of this change, especially with respect to the difference in emotional charge between the two spiritualities, both positions in practice excluded no one from the prospective ranks of the saved and concentrated most of their energies on how Christians could achieve a moralistic kind of inner-worldly perfection.[22] Politically, this common emphasis on external behavior and the concomitant de-emphasis on doctrine made both groups equally useful to Frederick William I and his son, each of whom sought to minimize the consequences of doctrinal disagreements between Lutheran and Reformed faiths by placing the state on a non-confessional ideological basis.[23] The cultural basis for political unity in Prussia was thus to be concord of action rather than concord of belief – a standpoint that helped bridge the gap between Pietism and *Aufklärung* as well as the differences between the confessions.

The nature of the ideological continuity between the two reigns is clearly revealed in the way each king expressed the relationship between the Prussian state and its subjects. In this respect, Frederick's well-known social contract theory was simply a secularization of his father's ideas. For in both conceptions, the state is the supreme institution in society whose claim to embody the highest ethical ideals justifies unconditional obedience on the part of its subjects; as part of its ethical nature the state seeks in return to improve the welfare of its people once the needs of the military are met.[24] In light

20 Schlingensiepen-Pogge, *Das Sozialethos*, 192–93.

21 Dickey, *Hegel*, 12–32.

22 For a list of parallels between the two movements, see Klaus Scholder, "Grundzüge der theologischen Aufklärung in Deutschland," in Kopitzsch, ed., *Aufklärung, Absolutismus und Bürgertum*, 313.

23 For a clear statement of Frederick William I's antipathy toward confessional polemics, see his "Bescheid an den (späteren) Propst Roloff," in Gericke, ed., *Glaubenszeugnisse und Konfessionspolitik*, 201–02.

24 For a clear statement of Frederick William I's conception of the mission of the state, see his "Instruktion für die Kreisräte im Königreich Preussen," in Pantenius, ed., *Erlasse und Briefe*, 37. For a summary of Frederick's views, see Behrens, *Society, Government and the Enlightenment*, 35–39, 176–77. As is well known, the theories of Thomasius and Wolff served as the most important contemporary justifications for the Frederician state. I would argue, though, that, however influential they may have been in the perpetuation and further

of this contractual, utilitarian basis for legitimacy, it is not surprising that Frederick's regime, like his father's, repudiated all supernatural, mystical attributes associated with the cult of the person of the king and that Frederick maintained as modest and frugal a court establishment.[25] As for how each king felt about his role as ruler, the similarity in content, if not in form of expression, between Frederick William's being "finance minister and commander-in-chief to the King of Prussia" and Frederick's being "first servant of the state" is self-evident.[26]

As Frederick the Great's reign thus saw the continuation and partial secularization of the Protestant political culture brought into being by Frederick William I, Frederick's victories in the Silesian wars meant more than just the end of Habsburg political hegemony within the Empire. It also signified the eclipse of the strand of elite culture that had dominated seventeenth-century Central Europe.[27] Centered at the imperial court in Vienna, this culture was Baroque, aristocratic, and predominantly Catholic in character and until 1740 served to attract princes and magnates throughout the Empire to the Habsburg cause. The wartime demonstrations of Prussia's superior efficiency and staying power, however, inspired other rulers in the German lands to imitate particular features of the Prussian system.[28] In order to do this successfully, something of the Prussian spirit and mentality had to be absorbed as well, so that by the 1760s

development of the Prussian bureaucratic ethos after 1740, they played only a marginal role in its creation. Empirical studies on this point, unfortunately, are lacking.

25 For the anti-mystical basis of Frederick William's concept of kingship, see Küntzel, *Die drei grossen Hohenzollern*, 84. This repudiation of the Baroque/Rococo court culture, initiated by Frederick William I, became a common characteristic of the Enlightened rulers. Joseph II was especially fanatical in practicing frugality in court expenditures. See John G. Gagliardo, *Enlightened Despotism* (New York, 1967), 96.

26 Although Frederick William I did not describe himself frequently in such terms, the fact that he could do so shows that he anticipated the Enlightenment's typical distinction between the monarchy and the state. On that distinction, see Gagliardo, *Enlightened Despotism*, 94.

27 For an evocative analysis of why Frederick's conquest of Silesia meant the end of an era, see Evans, *The Making of the Habsburg Monarchy*, 304.

28 It was this juncture, after about 1760 according to Tribe, that cameralism, aided by the existence of the Prussian model, became a well-organized academic discipline, endowed with canonical works by Justi and Sonnenfels and capable of exerting significant impact through the reform measures of "enlightened" regimes throughout the German lands. See Tribe, *Governing Economy*, chapter 5, esp. 91. For the extent to which mid to late eighteenth-century Hessian cameralism had absorbed elements of the "Prussian spirit," such as its disregard for the "freedom of individual Hessians" and its "penchant for efficiency, organization, and uniformity," see Charles W. Ingrao, *The Hessian Mercenary State: Ideas, Institutions, and Reform under Frederick II, 1760–1785* (Cambridge, 1987), 205–06.

the *Aufklärung*, spreading from its original strongholds in the Protestant north, had penetrated the Catholic south, where the Bavarian and Austrian governments officially sponsored this cultural movement.[29] In its de-confessionalized, "enlightened" form, this fundamentally north German, Protestant, bourgeois culture asserted its primacy at all the important courts of the Empire in the second half of the century. Even territories ruled by Catholic ecclesiastical princes were not able to resist its inroads.[30]

In all these ways, then, the essential features of the Prussian system not just survived the decline of Halle Pietism and the death of Frederick William I but even became more widespread and solidly entrenched as the eighteenth century progressed. This element of continuity was crucial; for despite the charismatic leadership of the "drill-sergeant king" and the intensive pedagogical process carried out through the various state institutions during his reign, the "cultural revolution" that helped create the new bureaucratic state needed more than one generation to establish permanent ascendancy.[31] It was entirely to be expected, in retrospect, that when Frederick II ascended the throne in 1740 the East Prussian estates presented him with a list of grievances that, even though it showed acceptance of some aspects of Frederick William I's state, was mainly an expression both of hitherto repressed anger against the changes made and of hope that the new sovereign would reverse them.[32]

[29] T. C. W. Blanning, "The Enlightenment in Catholic Germany," in Porter and Teich, eds., *The Enlightenment in National Context*, 122. An important sign of this trend was the reorganization of school systems in nearly every important territory in the Empire, Catholic as well as Protestant, through the issuing of new, comprehensive school ordinances modelled on those devised by Francke for the schools of the Halle *Anstalten*. For a summary account, see Gawthrop and Strauss, "Protestantism and Literacy," 50–52.

[30] François, *Koblenz im 18. Jahrhundert*, 199–201.

[31] Making a state-sponsored morality, such as State Pietism, "genuinely collective is always an accomplishment, a struggle ... against other ways of seeing, other moralities, which express the historical experiences of the dominated." Corrigan and Sayre, *The Great Arch*, 6.

[32] For a detailed commentary on the 1740 *Gravamina*, with extensive paraphrasing of the text, see Edith Spiro, "Die Gravamina der ostpreussischen Stände auf die Huldigungstagen des 18. Jahrhunderts" (Phil. Diss., University of Breslau, 1929), 34–52. For a general discussion of the estates' discontents in 1740, see Götz von Selle, "Zur Kritik Friedrich Wilhelms I.," *Forschungen zur brandenburgischen und preussischen Geschichte*, 38 (1926): 56–76. For the determination of the Pomeranian and Old Mark estates to resist the complete political, and by extension cultural, hegemony of the central government, see Gerd Heinrich, "Ständische Korporationen und absolutistische Landesherrschaft in Preussen-Hinterpommern und Schwedisch-Vorpommern, 1637–1816," in Baumgart, ed., *Ständetum und Staatsbildung*, 162–63, and Wolfgang Neugebauer, "Die Stände in Magdeburg, Halberstadt und Minden im 17. und 18. Jahrhundert," in *ibid.*, 180–87.

In the long run, the Prussian ethos secured its place as the official cultural norm not only because of consistent pedagogical pressure but also because of the ability of the state to demonstrate, to the Junker elite in particular, that it could deliver tangible rewards for loyal service. As Max Weber observed, for a charismatic leader to sustain his following, "his divine mission must 'prove' itself in that those who faithfully surrender to him must fare well."[33] With respect to the Prussian elites, I have already noted the long-term economic gains experienced by the Junker landowners. Perhaps even more important from a cultural standpoint, however, were the military victories won by Frederick II and the honor gained by those noble officers associated with them. As a result of all these factors, by the time of Frederick's death in 1786 the main elements of State Pietism had come to form the basis of a political culture broadly enough accepted and deeply enough held to survive the dissolution between 1807 and 1819 of much of the eighteenth-century Prussian institutional structure.[34]

Assessing the impact of this political culture beyond the eighteenth century is a difficult problem, one that needs far more attention than it has received. On the one hand, a major cause of confusion has been the persistent characterization of the Prussian cultural legacy as "feudal" or "premodern," whose perpetuation into the nineteenth century has been viewed as an anachronism that prevented the full "emancipation" of Germany from its "preindustrial" past. Yet if Elvin is right when he defines the essence of modernity as "the ability to create power," including the power over human beings required to "change the structure of [social] systems," then it is necessary to reevaluate the perception of a one-sidedly reactionary *Preussentum*.[35] For one of the purposes of this study has been to show just how "modern," in this sense, the Halle Pietists and Frederick William I really were. One need only recall their profound affinities with Puritanism, their Promethean quests

[33] Weber, *From Max Weber*, 249. This was, of course, the very psychology that, as we have seen, permeated Halle Pietism and motivated the consistent desire on the part of Frederick William I to experience immediate, positive results from his state-building labors.

[34] In a sign of this change in attitude, the 1787 *Gravamina* presented by the East Prussian estates to Frederick II's successor expressed the elites' acceptance by that time of the absolutist state. Spiro, "Die Gravamina der ostpreussischen Stände," 53–79. An additional factor in this change, noted by Spiro and many others, was the favoritism Frederick showed toward the nobility, especially compared to his father's often aggressive hostility.

[35] Mark Elvin, "A Working Definition of 'Modernity'?" *Past & Present*, no. 113 (1986): 210, 211.

to transform the social environment, their keen interest in up-to-date practical knowledge, and their obsession with economic growth as a means of solving social problems. All of these aspirations, and the actions that flowed from them, had the result of laying some of the most important parts of the foundation for the cultural, technological, and economic "progress"" of nineteenth- and twentieth-century Germany.[36]

On the other hand, there has been a tendency of late to question the long-range effectiveness of Pietist and Enlightened pedagogy in creating a disciplined, obedient population. Thus James van Horn Melton points to Joseph II's need to use a secret police and to the revolutions of 1848 as evidence of the failure of eighteenth-century Austrian and Prussian pedagogical methods to produce subjects who would internalize the commands of the state to the point that political authority could be reconstituted "on a less coercive basis."[37] Similarly, Richard J. Evans, while demonstrating the perpetuation in nineteenth-century Germany of coercive, authoritarian efforts designed to mold the everyday behavior of the German people, likewise finds an abundance of evidence to suggest that the actual conduct of the latter fell short of the desired docility.[38]

Here, too, a fresh look at the eighteenth-century origins of "Prussian discipline" may help clarify some ambiguities in interpretation. With respect to Melton's point, one conclusion to be drawn from examining the pedagogy of indoctrination practiced both by the Halle Pietists and Frederick William I is that, although coercion and exhortation can achieve "internalization" of institutional expectations, the continued application of coercion is always necessary.[39] Indeed, the later history of Halle Pietism suggests that as

[36] In addressing the difficult question of the "modernity" of eighteenth-century Prussia, it is important to distinguish between the cultural qualities generated by the system and its specific institutional structures. The latter, especially during the reign of Frederick II, ultimately came to work against further "development" by striving to preserve unchanged the status and social roles of the nobility and the bourgeoisie. For a critique of the "social conservatism" of Frederician Prussia, see Corni, "Absolutistische Agrarpolitik und Agrargesellschaft," 311–13. Corni speaks here of a regime opposed to a "social dynamic ... directed toward the transition to capitalism." One must ask, however, where did this "dynamic" come from? Was there any sign of it in the Brandenburg-Prussia of 1710?

[37] Melton, *Absolutism and the Origins of Compulsory Schooling*, 239.

[38] I am referring in particular to the essay entitled "In Pursuit of the *Untertanengeist*," which is a chapter in Evans, *Rethinking German History*, 156–84.

[39] See especially the formulation by Lifton quoted on p. 158, n. 26, above. This is perhaps the appropriate perspective from which to interpret the spontaneous reassertion of their own cultural and political identity on the part of the East Prussian estates in 1740, when it

time goes on, as the enthusiasm associated with the initial crystallization of such a "movement" wanes, ever greater quantities of pedagogical pressure are required to maintain institutional momentum. Eventually, however, the psychological dynamics of such a situation result in a diminution of the cadres' ability to sustain that pressure, especially as the rigid policies of the institution prove less and less well adapted to the changing external environment.[40] At that point, the entrenched ideological movement tends to be superseded by a "revival" inspired by an updated, often even more Promethean version of the same basic vision.[41] This new movement, in turn, will unleash a new wave of manipulative pedagogy on its followers, or, if it controls a state, on the population at large.

Yet the question remains as to what *were* the effects of this kind of pedagogy. Does the undoubted failure of the Prussian (and, later, the German) people to live up to the letter of the expectations set forth by their moralistic pedagogues mean that those expectations were relatively insignificant in their historical impact? By setting forth the nature of its spiritual and psychological underpinnings, I have shown that the Prussian cult of discipline and obedience was based on a religiosity that sought to overcome existential doubt by an effort to procure divine power through sustained, to-the-letter obedience to "God's commands." Such an action-oriented piety could find its fulfillment only in the achievements of institutions established to carry out the divine plan.[42] As we have seen, these bodies, in turn, could flourish only by enlisting ever greater numbers of supporters by inculcating in them, by whatever means necessary, this same basic "spirituality."

In this evangelizing/mobilizing process, however, the central ethical teaching of Christianity itself, the doctrine of charity, was fatally corrupted. The biblical conception of love clearly entails on

appeared as though the coercive pressure that had been exerted on them was about to be lifted.

40 See above, pp. 195–98.

41 I am thinking here of the supersession of Halle Pietism by the State Pietism/*Aufklärung* of Frederick William I/Frederick II and of the latter by German nationalism. The very process of modernization, by dissolving traditional communal and corporate structures has tended to require periodic strengthenings of those artificial, non-local institutions that attempt to provide coherence and meaning for modern societies.

42 In the words of Friedrich Schleiermacher, written at the time (1814) when German nationalism was being born, it is "the state [which] joins the individual to the universal good and the divine order." Quoted in James J. Sheehan, *German Liberalism in the Nineteenth Century* (Chicago, 1978), 41.

the part of believers an identification and fellowship with their neighbors, whose dignity and humanity were at the same time to be given absolute respect.[43] It was precisely that sort of respect, however, that was absent from the ministries of the Halle Pietists and from the State Pietism of Frederick William I. The cadre groups of both movements developed the arrogance of those who regard their personal ascetic regimens as, in effect, embodying divinely inspired laws. Those whom these individuals "served" were coerced into conforming to precepts intended, supposedly, "for their own good." But as Merton points out, the pedagogy employed to carry out such a "charitable" mission can only work by awakening "guilt in the other, [and then] absolv[ing] the guilt when sufficient gestures of submission have been extorted from him by force or manipulation."[44]

The results of such "education" could hardly have been anything but profoundly ambivalent. Since the demands of the Pietist pedagogues rarely corresponded in any real way to the spiritual needs of the individual, they could be "internalized" only at the cost of alienation, suppressed anger, and longings for a genuine sense of community, for genuine love.[45] To be sure, submission to an institution or a state promoting this kind of "education" could largely be achieved – a finding consistent with Evans's conclusion that the *Untertanengeist* in modern Germany was "first and foremost a political animal."[46] Yet the submission thus extracted could not serve as a means of integrating people's lives in a healthy, meaningful way; hence Evans also discerns a difference between "collective, public attitudes to authority" and "private, individual ones."

What, then, was the historical impact on Germany of the presumably widespread incidence of this kind of psychological fragmentation? Evans believes that the incomplete nature of the internalization process negates the causal significance of long-inculcated "mental attitudes or social norms."[47] But the very dichotomy he

43 Perhaps the most challenging biblical precept enjoining respect for the integrity of others is the commandment to "judge not, lest ye be judged" (Matthew 7:1–5). *The* model of a non-coercive evangelism is found in Luke 10:1–12.

44 Merton, *Love and Living*, 214.

45 Although the intellectuals of the Prussian *Aufklärung* were generally supportive of Frederick II and his regime, there was among them a widespread complaint about people being treated merely as "cogs in the state machine." See Behrens, *Society, Government and the Enlightenment*, 181.

46 Evans, *Rethinking German History*, 182.

47 *Ibid.*

demonstrates could very well have been the basis for potentially explosive emotional conflict within large numbers of modern Germans between "doing their duty" (*Pflichterfüllung*), on the one hand, and personal doubts and aspirations more or less well controlled, on the other. And one of the possible outcomes of "the tension generated by this struggle ... [is to seek] a natural release in crusades and in the persecution of heretics, in order that we may prove ourselves 'good' and 'right' by judging and condemning evil and error in those who [we wish to believe] are unlike ourselves."[48]

In light of the demonstrated connections and affinities between Lutheran Pietism and Anglo-American Puritanism, it should be evident that these psychocultural tensions, which have haunted modern German history in perhaps an archetypal way, are endemic in the very nature of modernity itself. Although the Prusso-German path toward modernization was characterized by an unusual degree of primacy given the collective, state power, its deeper significance will elude us if we fail to focus on the Promethean lust for material power that serves as the deepest common drive behind all modern Western cultures. Thus when we look upon figures such as August Hermann Francke and Frederick William I, we should not simply dismiss them as embodying something alien but rather see them as possible reflections of ourselves.

[48] Merton, *Conjectures of a Guilty Bystander*, 167.

Bibliography

ANNOTATED BIBLIOGRAPHY OF PRIMARY SOURCES

Acta Borussica. Denkmäler der preussischen Staatsverwaltung im 18. Jahrhundert, ed. Preussische Akademie der Wissenschaften:

Die Behördenorganisation und die allgemeine Staatsverwaltung Preussens im 18. Jahrhundert. Vols. I–V, ed. Gustav Schmoller *et al*. Berlin, 1894–1910. The documents from the first volume cover, in a selective way, the period 1700–14. Volumes II–V constitute an enormous collection of chronologically arranged primary material on the administrative activity of Frederick William I.

Die Getreidehandelspolitik und Kriegsmagazinverwaltung Brandenburg-Preussens. Vol. II, ed. Wilhelm Naudé and Gustav Schmoller. Berlin, 1901. An expository introduction, written by Naudé, describes the state's grain policy and the grain trade from 1640 to 1740; the extensive collection of documents covers mostly the reign of Frederick William I.

Die Handels-, Zoll- und Akzisepolitik Preussens. Vols. I–II, ed. Hugo Rachel. Berlin, 1911–22. Volume I provides a comprehensive account of economic policy up to 1713 with a relatively small collection of documents; volume II does the same for the period 1713–40, except that it contains a second part consisting of a substantial set of primary sources.

Das preussische Münzwesen in 18 Jahrhundert. Vol. I, ed. Friedrich von Schrötter and Gustav Schmoller. Berlin, 1904. The indispensable starting point for investigation of an almost completely neglected subject: the monetary dimension of the economic policies pursued between 1640 and 1740. About half of this volume is a concise summary of the period by Schrötter; the other half consists of documents.

Arndt, Johann. *True Christianity*, trans. and ed. Peter Erb. New York, 1979. This is a recent, accessible, but abridged English translation of the author's classic *Vier Bücher vom wahren Christentum*, first published in 1605–09.

Baumgart, Peter, ed. *Erscheinungsformen des preussischen Absolutismus: Verfass-*

ung und Verwaltung. Germering, 1966. A useful, but short volume containing thirteen documents from 1653 to 1792, including an abridged version of Frederick William I's 1722 instruction to the General Directory.

Canstein, Carl Hildebrand, Freiherr von. *Die Briefwechsel Carl Hildebrand von Cansteins mit August Hermann Francke*, ed. Peter Schicketanz. Berlin and New York, 1972. This work contains over nine hundred pages of letters to Francke from Baron Canstein, the chief representative of the Pietists' interests at the Berlin court, written between 1692 and 1719. Historians have not really begun to exploit this source for the yet to be done work of chronicling the relationship between Halle Pietism and the Prussian state, especially after 1713.

Delius, Walter. "Aus dem Briefwechsel des Berliner Propstes Johann Porst mit A. H. Francke in Halle." *Jahrbuch für Berlin-Brandenburgische Kirchengeschichte*, 39 (1964).

Dietrich, Richard, ed. *Politische Testamente der Hohenzollern*. Cologne and Vienna, 1986. A recent, exemplary edition of a key category of source materials that provide clues to the character, beliefs, and intentions of the Hohenzollern princes.

Forster, Friedrich Christoph. *Friedrich Wilhelm I: König von Preussen*. 3 vols. Potsdam, 1834–35. In addition to the biography, these volumes contain some important primary material, especially, in volume III, Frederick William's letters to the imperial representative, Count Seckendorff.

Francke, August Hermann. "August Hermann Franckes Schrift über eine Reform des Erziehungs- und Bildungswesens als Ausgangspunkt einer geistlichen und sozialen Neuordnung der Evangelischen Kirche des 18. Jahrhunderts 'Der grosse Aufsatz.'" *Abhandlungen der sächsischen Akademie der Wissenschaften: Philosophische-historische Reihe*, 53, Heft 3, ed. Otto Podczeck. Berlin, 1962. The lengthiest and most wide-ranging of Francke's programmatic writings.

Franckes Instruktion für die Präzeptoren, was sie bei der Disziplin wohl zu beachten, ed. Julius Romeiks. Breslau, 1894. Published separately from the rest of Francke's pedagogical writings, this work went through five editions between 1894 and 1913.

Lebens-Regeln, ed. Georg Helbig. Berlin, 1938. This work makes manifest the character of Francke's asceticism.

Lectiones Paraeneticae, oder öffentliche Ansprachen an die Studiosi Theologiae auf die Universität zu Halle in dem so genannten Collegio Paraenetico. 7 vols. Halle, 1726–36. Available on film, these volumes present transcriptions of Francke's weekly admonitions to the assembled theology students at the University of Halle.

Nicodemus, or, A treatise on the fear of man, abridged by John Wesley. Dublin, 1749. This work is a powerful rationale for the boldness that often characterized Francke's attitude toward the worldly authorities.

Wesley's participation in this edition is indicative of the important influence of Lutheran Pietism on eighteenth-century Anglo-American evangelicalism.

Predigten I, II, ed. Erhard Peschke. Berlin and New York, 1987–89. Both are excellent editions of important sermons hitherto not readily available.

Der rechte gebrauch der zeit, so fern dieselbe gut, und so fern sie böse ist. Halle, 1713. A work in which Francke discusses a vital aspect of his ascetic regimen but one not published in any nineteenth- or twentieth-century collection of his writings.

Schriften über Erziehung und Unterricht, ed. Karl Richter. Leipzig, 1880. One of many such compilations, which tend to include much the same material – a combination of essays by Francke on pedagogical method and the ordinances that spelled out the curricula of all the schools of the *Anstalten*.

Werke in Auswahl, ed. Erhard Peschke. An extremely useful collection featuring Francke's "Lebenslauf," a selection of pedagogical and programmatic writings, and a group of sermons that reveal the essence of his spirituality.

Frederick William I. *Die Briefe König Friedrich Wilhelms I. an den Fürsten Leopold zu Anhalt-Dessau*, ed. Otto Krauske. Berlin, 1905. This most important source for any prospective biographer of Frederick William I consists of over eight hundred pages of letters from Frederick William to his closest friend. It was published as part of the *Acta Borussica*.

Erlasse und Briefe des Königs Friedrich Wilhelms I. von Preussen, ed. W. M. Pantenius. Leipzig, 1913. The best existing anthology of writings by Frederick William I. Considering this volume's length (only 118 pages) and date of publication, this fact says a lot about the level of scholarly interest in this king over recent decades.

In tormentis pinxit: Briefe und Bilder des Soldatenkönigs, ed. Jochen Klepper. Stuttgart, 1938. This volume contains plates of Frederick William's paintings, which he did as a way of distracting himself from the pain he experienced in his later years. A selection of letters from the *Soldatenkönig* to fifteen different correspondents further documents the king's emotional response to his poor health.

Gericke, Wolfgang, ed. *Glaubenszeugnisse und Konfessionspolitik der brandenburgischen Herrscher bis zur Preussischen Union, 1540 bis 1815*. Bielefeld, 1977. An extremely valuable collection of confessional documents, ecclesiological decrees, instructions for the spiritual education of Hohenzollern children, and statements of personal belief.

Grossgebauer, Theophil. *Wächterstimme aus dem verwüsteten Zion*. Frankfurt/Main, 1661. The *magnum opus* of the most important forerunner of Spener.

Hinrichs, Carl. *Die Wollindustrie in Preussen unter Friedrich Wilhelm I*. Berlin,

1933. Published under the *Acta Borussica* imprimatur, this work is essentially an overview of Frederick William I's economic policies with special emphasis on the wool textile industry; but it also contains an appendix of selected documents, some of them quite revealing of the social philosophy underlying those policies.

Hinrichs, Carl, ed. *Der Kronprinzenprozess: Friedrich und Katte*. Hamburg, 1936. An extensive compilation of depositions, hearings, court-martial proceedings, reports of the royal chaplain who visited Frederick in prison, and other documents pertaining to the conflict between Frederick William I and his son precipitated by Frederick and Katte's attempted escape from the royal court.

Hubatsch, Walther, ed. *Geschichte der Evangelischen Kirche Ostpreussens*. Vol. III. Göttingen, 1968. Though ranging from medieval times to the twentieth century, this volume of documents contains several texts critical to the church and school reconstruction in East Prussia carried out during the reign of Frederick William I.

Klepper, Jochen, ed. *Der Soldatenkönig und die Stillen im Lande: Begegnungen Friedrich Wilhelms I. mit A. H. Francke et al.* Witten, 1956. Contained in this collection are the accounts written by the two heirs to the leadership of the Halle *Anstalten* about their week-long meetings with Frederick William I held at the king's estate in Wusterhausen in 1727, shortly after the death of A. H. Francke.

Kramer, Gustav, ed. *Beiträge zur Geschichte August Hermann Franckes enthaltend den Briefwechsel Franckes und Speners*. Halle, 1861. This collection contains important primary materials on Francke's career up to 1692 as well as the Spener–Francke correspondence.

Neue Beiträge zur Geschichte August Hermann Franckes. Halle, 1875. This book is a mixture of biography and original sources, including the essays written by Francke in 1711 and 1712 to demonstrate to the then Crown Prince Frederick William the usefulness of the orphanage complex to the Hohenzollern state.

Mylius, Christian Otto, ed. *Corpus Constitutionum Marchicarum*. 8 vols. Berlin and Halle, 1737. A very extensive contemporary compilation of decrees and ordinances issued by the Hohenzollern state. The documents themselves are thematically grouped in six "sections" (*Teile*) that cover ecclesiastical, military, economic, fiscal, "police," and constitutional/judicial "matters" (*Sachen*). In each section, the documents are arranged in a chronological order going well back into the Middle Ages, though most of the documents are from the post-1640 period. The reign of Frederick William I is very well covered. Subsequent editions, especially that of 1751, furnish additional documents that date from the last years of Frederick William's kingship.

Porst, Johann, ed. *Kurzer Auszug aus den vornehmsten Königl. preuss. Edikten und Verordnungen der Kurmark Brandenburg, die etwa einem Inspectori, Prediger, Candidaten und andern zu wissen nöthig seyn möchten*. 2nd edn. Berlin, 1727.

This is a one-volume selective collection, which contains such items as penitential ordinances, edicts concerning begging, school and university legislation, clerical conduct regulations, rules for Sabbath observance, etc.

Schade, Johann Caspar. "Lebenslauf." In Gottfried Arnold, ed. *Das Leben der Gläubigen, oder Beschreibung solcher Gottseligen Personen, welche in denen letzten 200. Jahren sonderlich bekannt worden*. Halle, 1701. An autobiographical conversion account in the highly lyrical style that gave Schade, the preacher, the ability to move his hearers so profoundly.

Geistreicher und erbaulicher Schriften. 5 vols. Leipzig, 1734. A collection of writings by and about Schade, including, in volume IV, Spener's address at his funeral.

Spener, Philipp Jakob. *Der neue Mensch*, ed. Hans-Georg Feller. Stuttgart, 1966. Selections in modernized German from Spener's *Der hochwichtig Artikel von der Wiedergeburt*. This book is one of a series of such distillations from Spener's writings that were edited by Feller and published in the 1960s.

Pia Desideria, ed. Kurt Aland. 3rd edn. Berlin, 1964. The most recent English translation was made by Theodore G. Tappert and published in Philadelphia in 1964. References in the text are to that edition.

Schriften, ed. Erich Beyreuther *et al.* Vols. I–IVf. Hildesheim and New York, 1979–. A large undertaking that intends to reissue the bulk of Spener's published works in reprint form. At least sixteen volumes are planned.

Stadelmann, Rudolph. *Friedrich Wilhelm I. in seiner Tätigkeit für die Landescultur Preussens*. Neudruck der Ausgabe 1878. Osnabrück, 1965. This work features an appendix of 175 pages of documents on Frederick William I's agrarian policy, especially in connection with the reconstruction process in East Prussia.

Stern, Selma. *Der preussische Staat und die Juden*. 2 vols. Tübingen, 1962. The first volume, covering 1640–1713, and the second volume, covering 1713–40, each contain very large documentary supplements (537 and 800 pages, respectively) which detail the Hohenzollern state's activities with respect to its Jewish subjects.

Stolze, Wilhelm. "Aktenstücke zur evangelischen Kirchenpolitik Friedrich Wilhelms I." *Jahrbuch für brandenburgische Kirchengeschichte*, 1 (1904). These documents pertain to Frederick William's effort in the 1730s to limit the ceremonial element in the Lutheran liturgy.

Wotschke, Theodor, ed. "Lampert Gedickes Briefe an Ernst Salomo Cyprian." *Jahrbuch für brandenburgische Kirchengeschichte*, 20 (1925). These letters show how the issue of confessional union tended to create a certain mistrust between the Pietists and Frederick William I.

Zimmermann, Franz, and Juntke, Fritz, eds. *Matrikel der Martin-Luther-Universität Halle-Wittenberg, 1690–1730*. Halle, 1960. This is an invaluable resource, as it lists all the students in alphabetical order, gives each student's home town, and indicates when, and in which faculty, they matriculated.

SELECT BIBLIOGRAPHY OF SECONDARY SOURCES

A. H. Francke: Festreden und Kolloquium aus Anlass der 300. Wiederkehr seines Geburtstages 22. März 1963. Halle, 1964.

Ahrbeck, Rosemarie. "Franckes Idee der humanitas: Wirklichkeit und Vision." In Ahrbeck and Thaler, eds., *August Hermann Francke, 1663–1727*.

"Zum Prinzip der Selbsttätigkeit und seiner gesellschaftlichen Funktion in A. H. Franckes Pädagogik: Ein Beitrag zur Standortbestimmung A. H. Franckes in der Geschichte des didaktischen Denkens." *Jahrbuch für Erziehungs- und Schulgeschichte*, 17 (1977).

"Zur Dialektik von Ziel und Methode in Franckes Pädagogik." In Ahrbeck and Thaler, eds., *August Hermann Francke, 1663–1727*.

Ahrbeck, Rosemarie, and Thaler, Burchard, eds., *August Hermann Francke, 1663–1727*. Halle, 1977.

Ahrbeck-Wothge, Rosemarie. "Über Franckes 'Lehrart.'" *Jahrbuch für Erziehungs- und Schulgeschichte*, 3 (1963).

"Zu Fragen der Arbeitserziehung und der Allgemeinbildung bei A. H. Francke." In *A. H. Francke: Festreden und Kolloquium.*

Aland, Kurt, *Spener-Studien*. Berlin, 1943.

Aland, Kurt, ed. *Pietismus und moderne Welt*. Witten, 1974.

Anderson, Benedict. *Imagined Communities: Reflections on the Origin and Spread of Nationalism*. London, 1983.

Anderson, Perry. *Lineages of the Absolutist State*. London, 1974.

August Hermann Francke: Das humanistische Erbe des grossen Erziehers. Halle, 1965.

Barnes, Robin Bruce. *Apocalypticism in the Wake of the Lutheran Reformation: Prophecy and Gnosis*. Stanford, 1988.

Baumgart, Peter, ed. *Ständetum und Staatsbildung in Brandenburg-Preussen*. Berlin, 1983.

Behrens, C. B. A. *Society, Government and the Enlightenment: The Experiences of Eighteenth-Century France and Prussia*. New York, 1985.

Benz, Ernst. "Ecumenical Relations between Boston Puritanism and German Pietism: Cotton Mather and August Hermann Francke." *Harvard Theological Review*, 54 (1961).

Berg, J. van den, and Dooren, J. P. van, eds. *Pietismus und Reveil: Referate der internationalen Tagung, "Der Pietismus in den Niederlanden und seine internationalen Beziehungen." Zeist, 18.-22. Juni 1974*. Leiden, 1978.

Berry, Wendell. *A Continuous Harmony: Essays Cultural and Agricultural*. New York, 1970.

Beyreuther, Erich. *August Hermann Francke, 1663–1727: Zeuge des lebendigen Gottes*. Marburg, 1956.

Birtsch, Günter. "Friedrich Wilhelm I. und die Anfänge der Aufklärung in Brandenburg-Preussen." In Oswald Hauser, ed., *Preussen, Europa und das Reich*. Cologne and Vienna, 1987.

Blaufuss, Dietrich. *Reichsstadt und Pietismus: Philipp Jakob Spener und Gottlieb Spizel aus Augsburg*. Neustadt, 1977.

Böhme, Joachim. "Heinrich Julius Elers, ein Freund und Mitarbeiter A. H. Franckes." Phil. Diss., F. U. Berlin, 1956.

Bondi, G. "Der Beitrag des halleschen Pietismus zur Entwicklung des ökonomischen Denkens in Deutschland." *Jahrbuch für Wirtschaftsgeschichte*, 1964.

Boor, Friedrich de. "A. H. Franckes Beitrag zu einer umfassenden Interpretation der Römerbriefvorrede Luthers." *Theologische Literaturzeitung*, 107 (1982).

"A. H. Franckes paränetische Vorlesungen und seine Schriften zur Methode des theologischen Studiums." *Zeitschrift für Religions- und Geistesgeschichte*, 20 (1968).

Bornkamm, Heinrich *et al.*, eds. *Der Pietismus in Gestalten und Wirkungen: Martin Schmidt zum 65. Geburtstag*. Bielefeld, 1975.

Bossy, John. *Christianity in the West, 1400–1700*. New York, 1985.

Brady, Thomas A., Jr. "Luther and the State: The Reformer's Teaching in Its Social Setting." In James D. Tracy, ed., *Luther and the Modern State*. Kirksville, Mo., 1986.

Braubach, Max. *Die Bedeutung der Subsidien für die Politik im spanischen Erbfolgekrieg*. Bonn and Leipzig, 1923.

Brecht, Martin. *Kirchenordnung und Kirchenzucht in Württemberg vom 16. bis zum 18. Jahrhundert*. Stuttgart, 1967.

"Philipp Jakob Spener und das wahre Christentum." *Pietismus und Neuzeit*, 4 (1977/78).

Briggs, Robin. *Communities of Belief: Cultural and Social Tension in Early Modern France*. Oxford, 1989.

Büsch, Otto. *Militärsystem und Sozialleben im Alten Preussen, 1713–1807: Die Anfänge der sozialen Militärisierung der preussischen-deutschen Gesellschaft*. Berlin and New York, 1962.

Büsch, Otto, ed. *Das Preussenbild in der Geschichte: Protokoll eines Symposiums*. Berlin and New York, 1981.

Büsch, Otto, and Neugebauer, Wolfgang, eds. *Moderne preussische Geschichte, 1648–1947: Eine Anthologie*. 3 vols. Berlin and New York, 1981.

Campbell, Robert W. *The Soviet-Type Economies: Performance and Evaluation*. Boston, 1974.

Carsten, F. L. *The Origins of Prussia*. Oxford, 1954.

Princes and Parliaments in Germany: From the Fifteenth to the Eighteenth Century. Oxford, 1959.

Cohen, Charles L. *God's Caress: The Psychology of Puritan Religious Experience*. New York, 1986.

"The Saints Zealous in Love and Labor: The Puritan Psychology of Work." *Harvard Theological Review*, 76 (1983).

Coleman, D. C., ed. *Revisions in Mercantilism*. London, 1969.

Collegium Jahre zweihundertfünfzig Clinicum Halense, 1717–1967: Beiträge zur Geschichte der Medizinischen Fakultät der Universität Halle. Halle, 1967.

Corni, Gustavo. "Absolutistische Agrarpolitik und Agrargesellschaft in Preussen." *Zeitschrift für historische Forschung*, 13 (1986).

Corrigan, Philip, and Sayer, Derek. *The Great Arch: English State Formation as Cultural Revolution*. Oxford, 1985.

Crousaz, A. von. *Geschichte des Königlichen Preussischen Kadetten-Corps nach seiner Entstehung, seinem Entwicklungsgange und seinen Resultaten*. Berlin, 1857.

Delius, Walter. "Berliner Unionsversuche im 17. und 18. Jahrhundert." *Jahrbuch für Berlin-Brandenburgische Kirchengeschichte*, 45 (1970).

Deppermann, Klaus. *Der hallesche Pietismus und der preussische Staat unter Friedrich III.(I.)*. Göttingen, 1961.

"Die Kirchenpolitik des Grossen Kurfürsten." *Pietismus und Neuzeit*, 6 (1980).

"Pietismus und moderner Staat." In Aland, ed. *Pietismus und moderne Welt*.

"Die politischen Voraussetzungen für die Etablierung des Pietismus in Brandenburg-Preussen." *Pietismus und Neuzeit*, 12 (1986).

"Der preussische Absolutismus und der Adel: Eine Auseinandersetzung mit der marxistischen Absolutismustheorie." *Geschichte und Gesellschaft*, 8 (1982).

Dickey, Laurence. *Hegel: Religion, Economics, and the Politics of Spirit, 1770–1807*. Cambridge, 1987.

Dorn, Walter. "The Prussian Bureaucracy in the Eighteenth Century." *Political Science Quarterly*, 46 (1931) and 47 (1932).

Dorwart, Reinhold. *The Administrative Reforms of Frederick William I of Prussia*. Cambridge, Mass., 1953.

The Prussian Welfare State before 1740. Cambridge, Mass., 1971.

Droz, Jacques. "In Search of Prussia." *Journal of Modern History*, 55 (1983).

Duffy, Christopher. *The Army of Frederick the Great*. London, 1974.

Eichler, Helga. "Zucht- und Arbeitshäuser in den mittleren und östlichen Provinzen Brandenburg-Preussens; Ihr Anteil an der Vorbereitung des Kapitalismus: Eine Untersuchung für die Zeit vom Ende des 17. bis zum Ausgang des 18. Jahrhunderts." *Jahrbuch für Wirtschaftsgeschichte*, 1970.

Ergang, Robert. *The Potsdam Führer: Frederick William I, Father of Prussian Militarism*. New York, 1941.

Evans, R. J. W. *The Making of the Habsburg Monarchy, 1550–1700: An Interpretation*. Oxford, 1979.

Evans, Richard J. *Rethinking German History: Nineteenth-Century Germany and the Origins of the Third Reich*. London, 1987.

Fann, Willerd R. "Peacetime Attrition in the Army of Frederick William I, 1713–1740." *Central European History*, 11 (1978).
Francke, Kuno. *Cotton Mather and August Hermann Francke*. Boston, 1896.
Frey, Linda and Frey, Marsha. *Frederick I: The Man and His Times*. Boulder and New York, 1984.
Fulbrook, Mary. *Piety and Politics: Religion and the Rise of Absolutism in England, Württemberg and Prussia*. Cambridge, 1983.
Gawthrop, Richard L. "Literacy Drives in Preindustrial Germany 1500–1800." In Robert F. Arnove and Harvey J. Graff, eds., *National Literacy Campaigns in Historical and Comparative Perspective*. New York, 1987.
"Lutheran Pietism and the Weber Thesis." *German Studies Review*, 12 (1989).
"The Social Role of the Seventeenth-Century German Territorial State." In Andrew C. Fix and Susan C. Karant-Nunn, eds., *Germania Illustrata: Essays on Early Modern Germany Presented to Gerald Strauss*. Kirksville, Mo., 1992.
Gawthrop, Richard, and Strauss, Gerald. "Protestanism and Literacy in Early Modern Germany." *Past & Present*, 104 (1984).
Gaxotte, Pierre, *Frederick the Great*. Trans. R. A. Bell, New Haven, 1942.
Geiger, Ludwig. *Berlin, 1688–1840: Geschichte des geistigen Lebens der preussischen Hauptstadt*. Vol. 1. Berlin, 1892.
Geschichte des Königlichen Potsdamschen Militärwaisenhauses, von seiner Entstehung bis auf die jetzige Zeit. Berlin, 1824.
Giddens, Anthony. *The Nation State and Violence: Volume Two of a Contemporary Critique of Historical Materialism*. Berkeley and Los Angeles, 1987.
Gieraths, Günther. *Die Kampfhandlungen der brandenburgisch-preussischen Armee, 1626–1807*. Berlin, 1964.
Gloria, Elisabeth. *Der Pietismus als Förderer der Volksbildung und sein Einfluss auf die preussische Volksschule*. Halle, 1933.
Goffman, Erving. *Asylums: Essays on the Social Situations of Mental Patients and Other Inmates* (Garden City, N. Y., 1961).
Greschat, Martin. "Christliche Gemeinschaft und Sozialgestaltung bei Philipp Jakob Spener." *Pietismus und Neuzeit*, 4 (1977/78).
Greschat, Martin, ed. *Orthodoxie und Pietismus*. Stuttgart, 1982.
Zur neueren Pietismusforschung. Darmstadt, 1977.
Grün, Willi. *Speners soziale Leistungen und Gedanken: Ein Beitrag zur Geschichte des Armenwesens und des kirchlichen Pietismus in Frankfurt a.M. und in Brandenburg-Preussen*. Würzburg, 1934.
Gundlach, Wilhelm. *Friedrich Wilhelm I. und die Bestallung der städtischen Beamten: Ein Beitrag zur Geschichte der preussischen Verwaltung*. Jena, 1906.
Hagen, William, W. "Seventeenth-Century Crisis in Brandenburg: The Thirty Years' War, the Destabilization of Serfdom, and the Rise of Absolutism." *American Historical Review*, 94 (1989).
Hartung, Fritz. *Staatsbildende Kräfte der Neuzeit: Gesammelte Aufsätze*. Berlin, 1961.

Heckel, Martin. *Deutschland im konfessionellen Zeitalter*. Göttingen, 1983.

Heinrich, Gerd. *Geschichte Preussens: Staat und Dynastie*. Frankfurt/Main, 1981.

Heyden, Hellmuth. *Kirchengeschichte von Pommern*. Vol. 1. Stettin, 1937.

"Die Kirchenpolitik in Pommern von der Teilung des Landes 1648 bis zur Mitte des 19. Jahrhunderts." *Baltische Studien*, N.F., 57 (1971).

Hinrichs, Carl. *Friedrich Wilhelm I., König in Preussen: Eine Biographie*. Vol. 1. Hamburg, 1941.

Preussen als historisches Problem: Gesammelte Abhandlungen. Ed. Gerhard Oestreich. Berlin and New York, 1964.

Preussentum und Pietismus: Der Pietismus in Brandenburg-Preussen als religiös-soziale Reformbewegung. Göttingen, 1971.

"Der Regierungsantritt Friedrich Wilhelms I." *Jahrbuch für die Geschichte Mittel- und Ostdeutschlands*, 5 (1956).

Die Wollindustrie in Preussen unter Friedrich Wilhelm I. Berlin, 1933

Hintze, Otto. "Calvinism and 'Raison d'Etat' in Early Seventeenth-Century Brandenburg." In *The Historical Essays of Otto Hintze*. Ed. Felix Gilbert. New York, 1975.

"Einleitende Darstellung der Behördenorganisation und der allgemeine Verwaltung in Preussen beim Regierungsantritt Friedrichs II." In *Acta Borussica. Die Behördenorganisation und die allgemeine Staatsverwaltung Preussens im 18. Jahrhundert*. Vol. VI, pt. 1. Berlin, 1901.

"Die Epochen des evangelische Kirchenregiments in Preussen." In *Regierung und Verwaltung*.

"Staat und Gesellschaft unter dem ersten König." In *Regierung und Verwaltung*.

Regierung und Verwaltung: Gesammelte Abhandlungen zur Staats-, Rechts- und Sozialgeschichte Preussens. Ed. Gerhard Oestreich. Göttingen, 1967.

Hinze, Kurt. *Die Arbeiterfrage zu Beginn des modernen Kapitalismus in Brandenburg-Preussen*. 2nd edn. Berlin, 1963.

Hülle, Werner. *Das Auditoriat in Brandenburg-Preussen*. Göttingen, 1971.

Jany, Curt. *Geschichte der Königlich Preussischen Armee bis zum Jahre 1807*. Vol. 1. Berlin, 1928.

Jersch-Wenzel, Stefi. *Juden und "Franzosen" in der Wirtschaft des Raumes Berlin/Brandenburg zur Zeit des Merkantilismus*. Berlin, 1978.

Juhr, Hannelore. *Die Verwaltung des Hauptamtes Brandenburg/Ostpreussen von 1713 bis 1751*. Berlin, 1967.

Kamp, A. "Friedrich Wilhelm I. und das preussische Beamtentum." *Forschungen zur brandenburgischen und preussischen Geschichte*, 30 (1917).

Klein, Ernst. *Geschichte der öffentlichen Finanzen in Deutschland, 1500–1870*. Wiesbaden, 1974.

Krause, Gisela. *Altpreussische Uniformfertigung als Vorstufe der Bekleidungsindustrie*. Hamburg, 1965.

Krauske, Otto. "Vom Hofe Friedrich Wilhelms I." *Hohenzollern-Jahrbuch*, 5 (1901).

Kriedte, Peter. *Peasants, Landlords and Merchant Capitalists: Europe and the World Economy, 1500–1800.* Trans. V. R. Berghahn. Cambridge, 1983.

Kruse, Martin. "Preussen und der frühe Pietismus." *Jahrbuch für Berlin-Brandenburgische Kirchengeschichte*, 53 (1981).

Speners Kritik am landesherrlichen Kirchenregiment und ihre Vorgeschichte. Witten, 1971.

Küntzel, Georg. *Die drei grossen Hohenzollern und der Aufstieg Preussens im 17. und 18. Jahrhundert.* Stuttgart and Berlin, 1922.

Lackner, Martin. *Die Kirchenpolitik des Grossen Kurfürsten.* Witten, 1973.

Landwehr, Hugo. "Die kirchlichen Zustände der Mark unter dem Grossen Kurfürst." *Forschungen zur brandenburgischen und preussischen Geschichte*, 1 (1888).

Langhäuser, J. *Das Militärkirchenwesen im kurbrandenburgischen und Königl. Preussischen Heer: Seine Entwicklung und derzeitige Gestalt.* Metz, 1912.

LaVopa, Anthony J. *Grace, Talent, and Merit: Poor Students, Clerical Careers, and Professional Ideology in Eighteenth-Century Germany.* Cambridge, 1988.

Lehmann, Hartmut. "'Absonderung' und 'Gemeinschaft' im frühen Pietismus: Allegemein-historische und sozialpsychologische Überlegungen zur Entstehung und Entwicklung des Pietismus." *Pietismus und Neuzeit*, 4 (1977/78).

"Der Pietismus im Alten Reich." *Historische Zeitschrift*, 214 (1972).

"Pietismus und soziale Reform in Brandenburg-Preussen." In Oswald Hauser, ed., *Preussen, Europa und das Reich.* Cologne and Vienna, 1987.

Pietismus und weltliche Ordnung in Württemberg von 17. bis zum 20. Jahrhundert. Stuttgart, 1969.

Leube, Hans. *Orthodoxie und Pietismus: Gesammelte Studien.* Ed. Dietrich Blaufuss. Bielefeld, 1975.

Die Reformideen in der deutschen lutherischen Kirche zur Zeit der Orthodoxie. Leipzig, 1924.

Lieberknecht, Herbert. *Das altpreussische Zuchthauswesen bis zum Ausgang des 18. Jahrhunderts, insbesondere in den Provinzen Pommern und Ostpreussen.* Göttingen, 1921.

Lifton, Robert Jay. *Thought Reform and the Psychology of Totalism.* New York, 1963.

Mauvillon, Eléazar de. *The Life of Frederick William I, late King of Prussia: Containing many Authentick Letters and Pieces.* Trans. William Phelips. London, 1750.

Melton, James Van Horn. *Absolutism and the Eighteenth-Century Origins of Compulsory Schooling in Prussia and Austria.* Cambridge, 1988.

"From Image to Word: Cultural Reform and the Rise of Literate Culture in Eighteenth-Century Austria." *Journal of Modern History*, 58 (1986).

Merton, Thomas. *The New Man.* New York, 1978.

Meyer, Moritz. *Geschichte der preussischen Handwerkerpolitik nach ämtlichen Quellen.* Vol. II. Minden, 1888.

Michaelis, W. "Die Staatskrise Preussens in den Jahren 1709–10: Der Ruin des Landes, seine Ursachen und der Reformbeginn." *Geschichte in Wissenschaft und Unterricht*, 24 (1973).

Neugebauer, Wolfgang. *Absolutistischer Staat und Schulwirklichkeit in Brandenburg-Preussen*. Berlin, 1985.

Nischan, Bodo. "The Schools of Brandenburg and the 'Second Reformation': Centers of Calvinist Learning and Propaganda." In Robert V. Schnucker, ed., *Calviniana: Ideas and Influence of Jean Calvin*. Kirksville, Mo., 1988.

Obst, Helmut. *Der Berliner Beichtstuhlstreit: Die Kritik des Pietismus an der Beichtpraxis der lutherischen Orthodoxie*. Witten, 1972.

"Elemente atheistischer Anfechtung im pietistischen Bekehrungsprozess." *Pietismus und Neuzeit*, 2 (1975).

Oestreich, Gerhard. *Friedrich Wilhelm: Der Grosse Kurfürst*. Göttingen, 1971.

Friedrich Wilhelm I.: Preussischer Absolutismus, Merkantilismus, Militarismus. Göttingen, 1977.

"Fundamente preussischer Geistesgeschichte: Religion und Weltanschauung in Brandenburg im 17. Jahrhundert." *Jahrbuch Preussischer Kulturbesitz*, 1969.

Neostoicism and the Early Modern State. Trans. David McLintock. Cambridge, 1982.

Opgenoorth, Ernst. *"Ausländer" in Brandenburg-Preussen als leitende Beamte und Offiziere, 1604–1871*. Würzburg, 1967.

Friedrich Wilhelm: Der Grosse Kurfürst von Brandenburg. 2 vols. Göttingen, 1971–78.

Oschlies, Wolf. *Die Arbeits- und Berufspädagogik August Hermann Franckes: Schule und Leben im Menschenbild des Hauptvertreter des halleschen Pietismus*. Witten, 1969.

Pariset, Georges. *L'état et les églises en Prusse*. Paris, 1897.

Patzelt, Herbert. *Der Pietismus im Teschener Schlesien, 1709–1730*. Göttingen, 1969.

Peschke, Erhard. "A. H. Franckes Reform des theologischen Studiums." In *A. H. Francke: Festreden und Kolloquium*.

"Die Bedeutung der Mystik für die Bekehrung August Hermann Franckes." *Theologische Literaturzeitung*, 91 (1966).

Bekehrung und Reform: Ansätze und Wurzeln der Theologie A. H. Franckes. Bielefeld, 1977.

"Kirche und Welt in der Theologie A. H. Franckes." *Theologische Literaturzeitung*, 88 (1963).

Studien zur Theologie August Hermann Franckes. Berlin, 1964.

Piechocki, Werner. "A. H. Franckes sozial- und schulhygienische An- und Einsichten." In *August Hermann Francke: Das humanistische Erbe*.

"Die Krankenpflege und das Klinikum der Franckeschen Stiftungen." In *August Hermann Francke: Das humanistische Erbe*.

Podczeck, Otto. "Das Collegium orientale theologicum A. H. Franckes."

Wissenschaftliche Zeitschrift Martin-Luther-Universität Halle-Wittenberg: Gesellschafts- und Sprachwissenschaftliche Reihe, 7 (1958).

Preus, J. Samuel. "The Reified Heart in Seventeenth-Century Religion." In Michel Despland and G. Vallée, eds., *Religion in History: The Word, the Idea, and Reality*. Waterloo, Ont., 1992.

"Secularizing Divination: Spiritual Biography and the Invention of the Novel." *Journal of the American Academy of Religion*, 59 (1992).

Puhle, Hans-Jürgen, and Wehler, Hans-Ulrich, eds. *Preussen im Rückblick*. Göttingen, 1980.

Rachel, Hugo. "Der Merkantilismus in Brandenburg-Preussen." *Forschungen zur brandenburgischen und preussischen Geschichte*, 40 (1928).

Raeff, Marc. *The Well-Ordered Police State: Social and Institutional Change through Law in the Germanies and Russia, 1600–1800*. New Haven, 1983.

Redlich, Fritz. *The German Military Enterpriser and His Work Force: A Study in European Economic and Social History*. Vol. II. Wiesbaden, 1965.

Regge, Jürgen. *Kabinettsjustiz in Brandenburg-Preussen: Eine Studie zur Geschichte des landesherrlichen Bestätigungsrechts in der Strafrechtspflege des 17. und 18. Jahrhunderts*. Munich and Berlin, 1977.

Reissig, Harald. "Das Berliner Lagerhaus, 1713–1816: Zum Einfluss von Regierung und Wirtschaft auf die Entwicklung einer altpreussischen Staatsmanufaktur." *Jahrbuch zur Geschichte Mittel- und Ostdeutschlands*, 29 (1980).

Robisheaux, Thomas Willard. *Rural Society and the Search for Order in Early Modern Germany*. Cambridge, 1988.

Rohr, Wilhelm. "Märkische Garnisonen im 18. Jahrhundert." *Brandenburgische Jahrbücher*, 2 (1936).

Rosenberg, Hans. *Bureaucracy, Aristocracy, and Autocracy: The Prussian Experience, 1660–1815*. Boston, 1958.

"The Rise of the Junkers in Brandenburg-Prussia, 1410–1653." *American Historical Review*, 49 (1943/44).

Rudolph, Hartmut. *Das evangelische Militärkirchenwesen in Preussen*. Göttingen, 1973.

Rüttgardt, Jan Olaf. *Heiliges Leben in der Welt: Grundzüge christlicher Sittlichkeit nach Philipp Jakob Spener*. Bielefeld, 1978.

Schaller, Klaus. "Pietismus und moderne Pädagogik." In Aland, ed., *Pietismus und moderne Welt*.

Schevill, Ferdinand. *The Great Elector*. Chicago, 1947.

Schicketanz, Peter. *Carl Hildebrand von Cansteins Beziehungen zu Philipp Jakob Spener*. Witten, 1967.

Schild, Erich. *Der preussische Feldprediger*. Vol. I. Eisleben, 1888.

Schilling, Heinz. "Die 'Zweite Reformation' als Kategorie der Geschichtswissenschaft." In Schilling, ed., *Die reformierte Konfessionalisierung in Deutschland*.

Schilling, Heinz, ed. *Die reformierte Konfessionalisierung in Deutschland: Das Problem der "Zweiten Reformation."* Gütersloh, 1986.

Schlingensiepen-Pogge, Alexandra. *Das Sozialethos der lutherischen Aufklärungstheologie am Vorabend der industriellen Revolution.* Göttingen, 1967.

Schlögl, Rudolf. *Bauern, Krieg und Staat: Oberbayerische Bauernwirtschaft und frühmoderner Staat im 17. Jahrhundert.* Göttingen, 1988.

Schmidt, Eberhard. *Fiskalat und Strafprozess.* Berlin and Munich, 1921.

Schmidt, Martin. *Pietismus.* Stuttgart, 1972.

Wiedergeburt und neuer Mensch: Gesammelte Studien zur Geschichte des Pietismus. Witten, 1969.

Schmitt, Wolfgang. "Die pietistische Kritik der 'Künste.'" Phil. Diss., U. Köln, 1958.

Schmoller, Gustav. "Der preussische Beamtenstand unter Friedrich Wilhelm I." *Preussische Jahrbücher*, 26 (1870).

"Das Städtewesen unter Friedrich Wilhelm I." In Schmoller, *Deutsches Städtewesen in älterer Zeit.* Bonn, 1922.

Umrisse und Untersuchungen zur Verfassungs-, Verwaltungs- und Wirtschaftsgeschichte besonders des preussischen Staates im 17. und 18. Jahrhundert. Leipzig, 1898.

"Die Verwaltung Ostpreussens unter Friedrich Wilhelm I." *Historische Zeitschrift*, 30 (1873).

Schneiders, Werner, ed. *Christian Thomasius, 1655–1728: Interpretationen zu Werk und Wirkung.* Hamburg, 1989.

Schrader, Wilhelm. *Geschichte der Friedrichs Universität zu Halle.* Vol. 1. Berlin, 1894.

Schrötter, Friedrich von. "Das preussische Offizierskorps unter dem ersten Könige von Preussen." *Forschungen zur brandenburgischen und preussischen Geschichte*, 26 (1913) and 27 (1914).

Selle, Götz von. "Zur Kritik Friedrich Wilhelms I." *Forschungen zur brandenburgischen und preussischen Geschichte*, 38 (1926).

Sellin, Volker. *Die Finanzpolitik Karl Ludwigs von der Pfalz: Staatswirtschaft im Wiederaufbau nach dem Dreissigjährigen Krieg.* Stuttgart, 1978.

Simon, Georg. "Der Berliner Beichtstuhlstreit, 1697–98." *Jahrbuch für Berlin-Brandenburgische Kirchengeschichte*, 39 (1964).

Skalweit, August. "Die Eingliederung des friderizianischen Heeres in dem Volks- und Wirtschaftskörper." *Jahrbücher für Nationalökonomie und Statistik*, 160 (1944).

Die ostpreussische Domänenverwaltung unter Friedrich Wilhelm I. und das Retablissement Litauens. Leipzig, 1906.

Skalweit, Stephan. "Friedrich Wilhelm I. und die preussische Historie." *Jahrbuch für die Geschichte Mittel- und Ostdeutschlands*, 6 (1957).

Smith, Huston. *Beyond the Post-Modern Mind.* 1st edn. New York, 1982.

Spengler, Oswald. *Preussentum und Sozialismus.* Munich, 1920.

Spiro, Edith. "Die Gravamina der ostpreussischen Stände auf die Huldigungstagen des 18. Jahrhunderts." Phil. Diss., U. Breslau, 1929.

Stadelmann, Rudolph. *Friedrich Wilhelm I. in seiner Tätigkeit für die Landescultur Preussens.* Neudruck der Ausgabe 1878. Osnabrück, 1965.

Stark, Alfred. "Die Leinenindustrie in Preussen unter Friedrich Wilhelm I." Phil. Diss., U. Berlin, 1939.

Steensgaard, Niels. "The Seventeenth-Century Crisis." In Geoffrey Parker and Lesley M. Smith, eds., *The General Crisis of the Seventeenth Century*. London, 1978.

Stein, K. James. *Philipp Jakob Spener: Pietist Patriarch*. Chicago, 1986.

Stern, Selma. *Der preussische Staat und die Juden*. 2 vols. Tübingen, 1962.

Stoeffler, F. Ernest. *German Pietism during the Eighteenth Century*. Leiden, 1973.

The Rise of Evangelical Pietism. Leiden, 1965.

Stolze, Wilhelm. "Ein Beitrag zur Unionspolitik Friedrich Wilhelms I." *Jahrbuch für brandenburgische Kirchengeschichte*, 6 (1909).

"Friedrich Wilhelm I. und der Pietismus." *Jahrbuch für brandenburgische Kirchengeschichte*, 5 (1908).

Storz, Jürgen. "Hauptbibliothek, Archiv und Naturalienkabinett der Franckeschen Stiftungen." In *August Hermann Francke: Das humanistische Erbe*.

Sträter, Udo. *Sonthom, Bayly, Dyke und Hall: Studien zur Rezeption der englischen Erbauungsliteratur in Deutschland im 17. Jahrhundert*. Tübingen, 1987.

Strauss, Gerald. *Law, Resistance, and the State in Sixteenth-Century Germany*. Princeton, 1986.

Luther's House of Learning: Indoctrination of the Young in the German Reformation. Baltimore, 1978.

Stupperich, Robert. "Aus dem kirchlichen Leben der Mark in den Tagen des Soldatenkönigs." *Jahrbuch für brandenburgische Kirchengeschichte*, 32 (1937).

Terveen, Fritz. *Gesamtstaat und Retablissement: Der Wiederaufbau des nördlichen Ostpreussens unter Friedrich Wilhelm I*. Göttingen, 1954.

Thadden, Rudolf von. *Die brandenburgisch-preussischen Hofprediger im 17. und 18. Jahrhundert: Ein Beitrag zur Geschichte der absolutistischen Staatsgesellschaft in Brandenburg-Preussen*. Berlin, 1959.

Tharau, Friedrich-Karl. *Die geistige Kultur des preussischen Offiziers von 1640 bis 1806*. Mainz, 1968.

Thompson, W. D. J. Cargill. *Studies in the Reformation*. London, 1980.

Todd, Margo. *Christian Humanism and the Puritan Social Order*. Cambridge, 1987.

Treue, Wilhelm. "David Splitgerber: Ein Unternehmer im preussischen Merkantilstaat, 1683–1764." *Vierteljahrschrift für Sozial- und Wirtschaftsgeschichte*, 41 (1954).

Tribe, Keith. *Governing Economy: The Reformation of German Economic Discourse, 1750–1840*. Cambridge, 1988.

Vann, James A. "New Directions for Study of the Old *Reich*." *Journal of Modern History*, 58, suppl. (December 1986).

Vann, James A., and Rowan, Steven, eds. *The Old Reich: Essays on German Political Institutions, 1495–1806*. Brussels, 1974.

Vierhaus, Rudolf. *Germany in the Age of Absolutism*. Trans. Jonathan B. Knudsen. Cambridge, 1988.

Vollmer, Ferdinand. *Friedrich Wilhelm I. und die Volksschule*. Göttingen, 1909.

Wagner, Fritz. "Friedrich Wilhelm I.: Tradition und Persönlichkeit." *Historische Zeitschrift*, 181 (1956).

Wallmann, Johannes. "Geistliche Erneuerung der Kirche nach Philipp Jakob Spener." *Pietismus und Neuzeit*, 12 (1986).

Kirchengeschichte Deutschlands seit der Reformation. 3rd edn. Tübingen, 1988.

"Philipp Jakob Spener in Berlin, 1691–1705." *Zeitschrift für Theologie und Kirche*, 84 (1987).

Philipp Jakob Spener und die Anfänge des Pietismus. 1st edn. Tübingen, 1970.

"Zwischen Reformation und Humanismus: Eigenart und Wirkungen Helmstedter Theologie unter besonderer Berücksichtigung Georg Calixts." *Zeitschrift für Theologie und Kirche*, 74 (1977).

"Zwischen Reformation und Pietismus: Reich Gottes und Chiliasmus in der lutherischen Orthodoxie." In Eberhard von Jüngel *et al.*, eds., *Verifikationen: Festschrift für Gerhard Ebeling zum 70. Geburtstag*. Tübingen, 1982.

Weber, Max. *From Max Weber: Essays in Sociology*. Eds. H. H. Gerth and C. Wright Mills. New York, 1958.

The Protestant Ethic and the Spirit of Capitalism. Trans. Talcott Parsons. New York, 1930.

Wechssler, Eduard. "Preussengeist und calvinisch-stoicische Erziehung." *Zeitschrift für Geschichte der Erziehung und des Unterrichts*, 23 (1933).

Weiske, Karl. "Pietistische Stimmen aus der Mark Brandenburg." *Jahrbuch für brandenburgische Kirchengeschichte*, 24 (1929).

Welsch, Heinz. "Die Franckeschen Stiftungen als wirtschaftliches Grossunternehmen: Untersucht auf Grund der Rechnungsbücher der Franckeschen Stiftungen." Phil. Diss., U. Halle, 1956.

Wendland, Walter. "Märkischer Pietismus." In *Festgabe zum deutschen Pfarrertag, Berlin 1927*. Eberswalde, 1927.

"Die pietistische Bekehrung." *Zeitschrift für Kirchengeschichte*, 2nd ser., 1 (1920).

"Studien zum kirchlichen Leben in Berlin um 1700." *Jahrbuch für brandenburgische Kirchengeschichte*, 21 (1926).

Wienecke, Friedrich. "Die Begründung der evangelischen Volksschule in der Kurmark und ihre Entwicklung bis zum Tode Friedrichs I., 1540–1713." *Zeitschrift für Geschichte der Erziehung und des Unterrichts*, 3 (1913).

Das preussische Garnisonschulwesen. Berlin, 1907.

Winter, Eduard. *Halle als Ausgangspunkt der deutschen Russlandkunde im 18. Jahrhundert*. Berlin, 1953.

Wolff, Karl. "Ist der Glaube Friedrich Wilhelms I. von A. H. Francke beeinflusst?" *Jahrbuch für brandenburgische Kirchengeschichte*, 33 (1938).

Wotschke, Theodor. "Die Gewinnung des Kronprinzen Friedrich Wilhelm für dem halleschen Pietismus." *Neue kirchliche Zeitschrift*, 41 (1930).

Zsindely, Endre. *Krankheit und Heilung im älteren Pietismus*. Zürich, 1962.

Index